From BINGHAMTON *to the* BATTLEFIELD

The Civil War Letters of
ROLLIN B. TRUESDELL

AMY J. TRUESDELL

**EXCELSIOR
EDITIONS**

Published by
STATE UNIVERSITY OF NEW YORK PRESS, ALBANY

© 2023 State University of New York

All rights reserved

Printed in the United States of America

Excelsior Editions is an imprint of State University of New York Press

For information, contact State University of New York Press, Albany, NY
www.sunypress.edu

Library of Congress Cataloging-in-Publication Data

Names: Truesdell, Rollin B., correspondent. | Truesdell, Amy, annotator, editor.
Title: From Binghamton to the battlefield : the Civil War letters of Rollin B. Truesdell / Amy J. Truesdell.
Description: Albany : State University of New York Press, [2023] | Includes bibliographical references and index.
Identifiers: LCCN 2022014122 | ISBN 9781438491257 (hardcover) | ISBN 9781438491264 (paperback) | ISBN 9781438491271 (ebook)
Subjects: LCSH: Truesdell, Rollin B.—Correspondence. | United States. Army. New York Infantry Regiment, 27th (1861–1863) | Soldiers—Pennsylvania—Liberty—Correspondence. | United States—History—Civil War, 1861–1865—Personal narratives. | New York (State)—History—Civil War, 1861–1865 Regimental histories. | United States—History—Civil War, 1861–1865—Regimental histories.
Classification: LCC E523.5 27th .T78 2023 | DDC 973.7/410922—dc23/eng/20220909
LC record available at https://lccn.loc.gov/2022014122

10 9 8 7 6 5 4 3 2 1

In loving memory of my father,
James S. Truesdell

CONTENTS

CONTENTS

ILLUSTRATIONS

ACKNOWLEDGMENTS

Appropriately, the wind was howling and there was a chill in the air as I began my search through the old graveyard that late November morning. I was in Lawsville Center, a village within Liberty, Pennsylvania, looking for the headstones of my ancestors—the parents and grandparents of Rollin B. Truesdell. On that final morning of a research trip to New York and Pennsylvania to consult with local historians for this book, I thought about how saturated I was with the week's discoveries, and how powerful it was to be learning so much about my family history. The research project had transitioned from academic to personal.

Persuaded by my father to stop back in Lawsville en route home, I found myself wandering through the cemetery. Soon, a woman and her amiable labrador retriever came jogging along the dirt road that abuts the property. She greeted me with a hearty, "beautiful morning, isn't it?" I agreed, though not truthfully, and then asked if she had lived in the area long. She said she had lived there all her life and was familiar with the Truesdell family name. She would help me look for the family plot. Though the cemetery is not large, and we separated to search for it, the Truesdell grave site eluded us. As she turned to leave, she told me her full name was Meg Laws—as in Lawsville. When I thanked her, she merely shrugged and matter-of-factly stated, "It's important to know where you come from." And I turned around to directly face the little hill of Truesdell family headstones. When I embarked on this project, I hadn't bargained for the feeling that somehow I had found a part of me that I didn't even know was lost. I hope that this book may inspire others to learn more about where they came from too.

The toiling to bring together the material for this book began long before I picked up the baton. The 27th New York Volunteers' regimental history and William Westervelt's book on his Civil War experiences are detail-rich and a delight to read. Westervelt was Rollin's tentmate and dear friend. These books were invaluable resources in understanding the backdrop for Rollin's story. In

1916, my great-grandfather, Arthur Truesdell, transcribed all of Rollin's letters. In 2001, my father, James S. Truesdell, retyped the letters to create digital files and initiated research around the battles in which Rollin fought. In 2019, when I began to ponder the feasibility of this book, my father offered his enthusiastic and unwavering support, as well as his editorial acumen.

Many people helped to propel me in my quest to illuminate Rollin's family life and point of view during the Civil War. Julina Albert graciously invited me into her home, the brick farmhouse in Liberty that my great-great-great-great-grandfather built, when I knocked on her door and explained who I was. Erica Johnson, the previous owner of the house whose family also hailed from Liberty, sent me a painting and brown-and-white photos of what was Rollin's home, along with inspiration. Rachel Dworkin, archivist at the Chemung County Historical Society in Elmira, New York; Broome County, New York Historian Roger Luther and Patricia Chubbuck of the Broome County Local History and Genealogy Center; and Curator Betty Smith, Assistant Curator Lisa Forba, and Research Assistant Bonnie Yuscavage of the Susquehanna County Historical Society in Montrose, Pennsylvania, all shared treasure troves of local history linked to the Civil War and Rollin.

I am enormously indebted to John Hennessy and Dr. Thomas (Tom) Clemens. John, Chief Historian at the Fredericksburg and Spotsylvania National Military Park (ret.), opened up his extensive personal files on the 27th NY Volunteers Regiment to me and offered candid advice for writing and publishing this book. He introduced me to Tom, the Antietam and South Mountain expert, who shared his encyclopedic knowledge of these battles as we stood on the land Rollin and his comrades crossed when entering battle 157 years earlier. Jim Gandy and Christopher Morton from the New York State Military Museum guided me when I initiated this project and led me toward innumerable fruitful research paths. Don Troiani confirmed that Rollin's uniform had been in his collection and was to be included in the National Museum of the U.S. Army at Fort Belvoir, Virginia, under the careful curation of Cornelius (Neil) Abelsma. I will forever be grateful for Neil's herculean efforts facilitating my visit to see Rollin's uniform in the museum's care. Lindsey Davis and Paul Miller patiently and expertly led me through a remarkable morning at the museum warehouse for that purpose. Author and historian Noah Andre Trudeau provided invaluable recommendations for unlocking information sources and approaching the myriad steps leading to publication. Michael Gray, professor of history at East Stroudsburg at the University of Pennsylvania, advised me on the manuscript and encouraged me to pursue publication at a critical time.

I am grateful to Richard Carlin at SUNY Press for bringing Rollin's story to print.

Finally, I want to thank friends and family for their enthusiastic and generous support. They bore with me throughout the research and writing as I found connections to Rollin and this book no matter what topic of conversation they introduced. My fervent wish to hand a copy of this book to my father was not to be. This book is for him.

INTRODUCTION

He signed his first letter, *Yours for the Union, Rollin B. Truesdell.* He was twenty-one, optimistic, and determined to volunteer for service when our country faced its most fearsome foe—ourselves. My great-great-grandfather enlisted three weeks after the rebel attack on Fort Sumter in South Carolina on April 12, 1861 and served in the 27th New York Volunteers, Infantry. The blistering dispute between the North and the South had formally transitioned to war. Without hesitation, Rollin traveled north from his home in Liberty, Pennsylvania, to be among the first volunteers for the Union. He would not be a bystander watching as the Union and the Constitution teetered toward collapse. He began his service without previous military experience but eager to learn. Demonstrating the kind of leadership and resolve that got noticed, Rollin was promoted twice during his enlistment and mustered out as sergeant.

Like many other soldiers who desperately missed family and friends as the war ground on, and the shock of gory battle became emblazoned on his soul, Rollin tethered himself homeward by devotedly writing letters to loved ones in Susquehanna County, Pennsylvania. These letters, over one hundred of which were preserved by the Truesdell family, tell the story of Rollin's awakening to the costs of war even as he solidified his conviction that this war, and winning it, was imperative. Sacrificing our country was not an option.

The first of his letters brimmed with enthusiasm as Rollin settled into the reality of his decision. ("I love a soldier's life and the excitement connected with it." August 22, 1861.) By the time his service drew to a close, Rollin was war-weary and frustrated at the lack of federal progress in ending the war. ("I am anxious to have this terrible drama close." March 26, 1863.) Nonetheless, Rollin remained resolute in his commitment to the cause. ("I would willingly stand my chances for life or death in another seven days fight, another Antietam, . . . if I could feel sure that by another New Year's Day we could conquer and dictate terms of peace which would be lasting and ensure prosperity and happiness to the nation." March 26, 1863.)

The 27th NY Volunteers received accolades from commanding generals within the Army of the Potomac because of their reputation for steadfastness and quality leadership. They could be depended on to follow orders and to fight. They thus suffered the fifth highest loss of life among the thirty-eight two-year regiments from New York State; 146 of their total enrollment of 1,155 men died.[1] Only 566 soldiers in the regiment had weathered the vicious storm and mustered out in May 1863.

Major General Henry W. Slocum was the 27th NY's first colonel. Brevet Major General Joseph J. (J. J.) Bartlett was the regiment's major. In his letters, Rollin wrote frequently and affectionately of Slocum and Bartlett as sterling examples of soldiers, and as decent men. Their bravery, selflessness, and clarity of mission stood in stark contrast to other federal political and military leaders, in Rollin's estimation.

Soldiers and witnesses to the war wrote contemporaneously and reflectively of their insights and experiences in newspaper articles, speeches, and books. Rollin's peers from his regiment published *The History of the 27th Regiment N.Y. Vols* in 1888, and tentmate William Westervelt penned *Lights and Shadows of Army Life, as Seen by a Private Soldier* in 1886. Through Rollin's own words and additional supporting context, this book complements and builds on his comrades' recollections. The rolling narrative traces events from the day Rollin swore his oath to the stars and stripes on May 8, 1861, until his return home to Liberty, Pennsylvania, on June 5, 1863, permitting readers to walk alongside Rollin as he steers his path through the chaos and heartbreak of war. Rollin transforms from an earnest young man to a battle-hardened veteran—though no less driven by the values and standards instilled in him as a youth.

His trek is rife with the brutalities and truths of war but also the camaraderie that stems from a shared struggle. As we will learn in his letters, Rollin was afflicted with the measles soon after enlisting; elevated to company clerk; selected for recruitment duty; dazed by hunger and thirst during the Seven Days Battles to the point of dreaming achingly of drinking from the cold spring at the family homestead; and marched alongside his comrades while barely conscious. He carried a soldier from another New York regiment for a half mile on his back from the battlefield at Gaines' Mill to safety. He learned the euphoria of victory in battle. He slept alongside corpses of friends killed in battle. He narrowly missed losing his own life when a shell exploded next to him, leaving him badly concussed during the final campaign fought by the 27th NY Volunteers—Chancellorsville. (The chapter on this campaign reflects

Rollin's incapacitation, and the words of his comrades in the regiment fill in the narrative when Rollin was unable to write home.)

Rollin was a clear, largely unemotional, reporter of what he saw on such bloody battlefields as Crampton's Gap, Antietam, and Fredericksburg, but also in the camps where soldiers endured the slow passage of time between engagements with the rebel forces. Rollin vividly described his day-to-day life as a soldier. He wrote of the improvised Thanksgiving meal he and Westervelt cooked in November 1862, of the infamous dreaded "Mud March" of January 1863, and of the first time he shot a man. His letters allowed him an outlet for the shocks of the war, a means to chronicle events, a vehicle to form arguments and test theories about the war effort, and a reassurance of home and the life he would return to after the war. He relished the letters he received from loved ones and insisted that family write him back "immediately."

The youngest of six children, Rollin had three brothers and two sisters. Elder brothers John Calvin and Martin Luther no longer lived near the family homestead in Liberty when the war broke out and were not in regular correspondence with Rollin. Due to a broken hip, John used a cane for years and was unable to enlist, but he did organize a company called the "Truesdell Rangers" for a Wisconsin Regiment. Martin was in the Signal Service and lived to regale his family with such war stories as when his station was shot out from under him, forcing him to slide down a rope—instruments and dispatches in tow—to escape. Of his brothers, Rollin was closest to his brother Albert, who wanted to enlist but was thwarted due to having asthma. Albert corresponded with Rollin and visited him in the field. Julia, the eldest, was sometimes the target of Rollin's good-natured cajoling to write him more often— ("ask sister Julia if she has run out of paper." March 9, 1863.) Clarissa (Clara) was the sibling closest to Rollin in age. The affection they felt for each other is clear within the banter in the many letters Rollin wrote to her.

Rollin appreciated correspondence from all his family and friends but yearned the most for letters from his father and mother, Samuel W. and Lucy Truesdell. ("Write me as often as you can for I prize letters from my parents above all others." September 27, 1862.) He, in turn, wrote conscientiously to them; most of the preserved letters were addressed to his parents. These letters reflect Rollin's desire to appear confident and healthy to assuage his mother's concerns; they also provide a window into Rollin's bond with his father, his confidante.

Though over 150 years have passed since the conclusion of the American Civil War, the reverberations from this epoch are still felt. This war was by far the most personal of all the wars in which the United States has engaged, imperiling the very existence of the country. Approximately 10 percent of the American population entered service from 1861 to 1865, and as a modest estimate, some 620,000 died—a sobering toll.[2] Today, the United States again weathers rancorous times, and it is commonplace to hear that "our country is tearing itself apart." My great-great-grandfather volunteered to put himself on the front line of battle to safeguard the Union during the most direct threat to its perpetuity—the Civil War.

Chapter 1

HAD TO BE

GROWING UP IN LIBERTY

Peering down from his perch in the family tree, Rollin observed familial examples of pluck and altruism to inspire him as he was growing up. He would have been regaled by the stories of his pioneer grandparents, who were among the first settlers in Liberty, Pennsylvania. Emily C. Blackman wrote in her *History of Susquehanna County, Pennsylvania*, "the early settlers [of Liberty] appear to have been men of great physical endurance and firmness of mind . . . They were generally persons of very limited means, and were obliged to sustain themselves by their own energy and industry."[1] Rollin's grandparents, Samuel and Lucretia Truesdell, arrived in 1811 from Connecticut and laid claim to a vast tract of land for farming that was eventually bequeathed to Rollin's father, who was also Liberty's justice of the peace for twenty years.[2] During his time away from home, as he anxiously counted down the days until the end of his enlistment, Rollin spent considerable time weighing whether he would follow in his father's footsteps as a farmer.

Rollin grew up in the two-story brick farmhouse that his grandfather built, and which still stands today. Nestled on a hill overlooking the countryside, this house drew generations of Truesdells through its front door as they worked to build up the community, even as they toiled to make the farm successful. In the year before the Civil War broke out, Rollin's maternal grandmother, who recalled detailed stories from the Revolutionary War, passed away in the farmhouse at the age of ninety-three.[3] His grandmother Truesdell would have coaxed the household to join her in worship at the Union Congregational Church she helped found in 1813. And Rollin's mother surely reminisced with the family about being the first school mistress at the nearby brick schoolhouse. Rollin dreamed of the "red brick house" as he lay under the rain-spattered canvas of his leaky tent as a soldier and felt so far away from Liberty. (See figure 1.1.)

Rollin's opinions and values were shaped not only by the immediate community in which he lived but also by public discourse in the surrounding environs of Susquehanna County and his neighbors just over the state line in New York. Given its location in the far north of the county, hugging the border with New York (then the most populous state), the closest population center to Liberty was Binghamton, New York, with some 8,000 residents in 1860. Newspapers published in Binghamton such as the *Binghamton Daily Republican* and the *Broome Republican* were important sources of news for the Truesdell family in the lead-up to and during the war.

Susquehanna County itself was sparsely populated, accounting for 36,267 of the 2,906,215 people tallied in Pennsylvania's 1860 census.[4] Be it Susquehanna County or Binghamton, in 1860, the debate ringing loudest in Rollin's ears was whether the country would stave off a civil war. Could a bridge be built between the increasingly divergent paths of the northern and southern states?

The fissure between the industrializing North and the agrarian, enslaved-labor dependent South, gaped wider and wider in the decades leading up to 1860. By that year in Pennsylvania, over 50 percent of the land area was devoted to farming, but cash crops were neither labor intensive nor hitched to slave labor for profitability.[5] In New York, the state's one million or so immigrants had fueled the state's brisk trade with the western and southern states and overseas to make it a national leader in finance, industry, and commerce. Indeed, at this time, northern dominance in the economy ranged from firearm production (97 percent of US total) to boots and shoes (90 percent of US total), all of which was transported to markets via rail and canal networks that were the envy of the South.[6]

Assimilating the vast number of immigrants arriving across America into the economy was not seamless, however. Many living in the northern states saw the newcomers as threats to their jobs and positions in society, and in the 1850s even created the short-lived political party the "Native American Party," also called the "Know Nothings," to clamp down on immigration. The two main political parties at the time, the Democrats and Whigs, tussled with the continued viability of slavery and how it might doom opportunities for Whites, particularly as they cast their eyes westward to the new territories.

FIGURE 1.1 Truesdell Farmhouse in Liberty, Pennsylvania.

The Kansas-Nebraska Act of 1854, which allowed settlers to decide whether to accept slavery within their territories, served as a kind of dress rehearsal for the Civil War. Northern Whigs strongly opposed the Act, while a number of northern Democrats joined southerners in supporting it. Each side flooded into Kansas to tip the scale in their direction. The result was disastrous, with violent conflict between the sides over several years earning the state the moniker "Bleeding Kansas." The Republican Party emerged from the disintegrated Whig Party, filled with outrage over "Bleeding Kansas" and the expansion of slavery.

Of course, the chasm splitting America was about more than the economics of slavery. The immorality of slavery ignited a determined, though initially minority, movement in the North that focused first on local action and then on nationwide abolition. Pennsylvania and New York reformers were among the loudest and earliest in the nation to take a stand.

In Pennsylvania, the Society of Friends (Quakers) had denounced slavery since 1688, and by the mid-1700s began calling for a statewide ban. They inspired the creation of the Pennsylvania Abolition Society in 1775, the first such society in colonial America. This society was instrumental in passage of the 1780 law that called for gradual abolition. In 1826, Pennsylvanians took a step further by outlawing slavecatchers from forcibly transferring Black Pennsylvanians out of state. Agitation toward abolition grew even stronger with the founding of the American Anti-Slavery Society (AAS) in Philadelphia in 1833, which sought the unconditional and immediate end to slavery while it sheltered fugitive enslaved people. Black members assumed positions of authority within the organization and some, such as Frederick Douglass, took on extensive speaking tours to sway the public and to petition the government to abolish slavery.

Rollin's home county of Susquehanna was active in the anti-slavery movement and known to be a safe haven for runaway enslaved people. As early as 1792, former Connecticut slave Printz Perkins founded a small Black settlement for fugitive slaves. Four decades later, reformer Robert Hutchinson Rose further expanded the Black population by establishing a community for Black farmers. And in 1836, residents formed the Susquehanna County Anti-Slavery and Free Discussion Society, which supported the immediate abolition of slavery through, "moral suasion and debate."[7] Living in a community fraught by the slavery question, the Truesdells would have regularly discussed abolition at the dinner table. In a meditative letter dated May 19, 1903, Rollin's sister Clara wrote to Rollin's son, Arthur (my great-grandfather), about her recollections of the war. She remembered: "My father was a lifelong friend of the slave, but never a violent Abolitionist. My mother signed the first set of resolutions ever adopted at an Abolition meeting in Susquehanna County, a marvelous thing for a woman to do at that time." These would be strong bearings on Rollin's moral compass.

The vote to end slavery in Pennsylvania came in 1847. New Yorkers had made slavery unlawful in the state from July 4, 1827, having voted for gradual abolition in 1799. Though these laws inspired similar laws in the North, legal momentum toward abolition was put to an abrupt halt with the Fugitive Slave Act of 1850. Slaveholders and their sympathizers successfully advocated for passage of this law, which gave the federal government powers to hunt and return alleged fugitive enslaved people in every state. The Act effectively made slavery legal across the country.

The Fugitive Slave Act drove some in the abolition movement toward more drastic, sometimes violent, measures. In 1852, the Philadelphia Vigilant Committee reorganized to help fugitive enslaved people escape through the North to Canada—beyond the reach of federal slave catchers—via the Underground Railroad. Rollin's sister Clara noted: "Montrose [Susquehanna's county seat] was without doubt a station on the Underground Railroad which helped so many slaves over the border. It was and is still a matter of pride that no fugitive slave was ever taken from Montrose."[8]

New Yorker John Brown is likely the person most closely associated with the radicalized component of the abolitionist movement. Angered and impatient by the passage of the Fugitive Slave Act and the US Supreme Court Dred Scott decision of 1857 denying Black people a route to citizenship, Brown plotted to overtake the national arsenal in Harpers Ferry, Virginia. His goal was to spur an armed revolt of enslaved people in the Southern states using the seized weapons. Brown led his band of eighteen co-conspirators, including his three sons and five Black men, on the failed raid on October 16–18, 1859. A company of US Marines led by First Lieutenant Israel Greene, and under the overall command of Colonel Robert E. Lee, defeated the raiders. John Brown, found guilty of treason, was hanged on December 2, 1859, and later buried in his hometown of North Elba, New York. The animosity between Northern abolitionists and Southern slaveholders was not buried with him, however. Politicians from the South became more vocal about the advantages of leaving the Union, which they saw as a state right.

It is hard to imagine a country more polarized than the United States when the presidential election was held in 1860. Abraham Lincoln, the nascent Republican Party candidate, beat three other contenders by sweeping the northern states and winning California and Oregon. New York, with thirty-five electoral votes, and Pennsylvania, with twenty-seven, were the biggest prizes in the contest and pivotal for Lincoln's win. Lincoln's closest rival was John C. Breckenridge, the Southern Democratic candidate who carried the vote in the South to uphold states' rights and leave the system of slavery unchanged. John Bell, representing the Constitutional Union Party—formed from the remnants of the Whigs and the Know Nothings—sought to avoid secession by sidestepping the topic of slavery. He won Tennessee, Kentucky, and Virginia. Stephen A. Douglas, the Northern Democratic candidate, holding the position that each territory should decide whether to allow slavery, won only Missouri.

The Republican Party was clear about its stance on slavery: even as no moves would be made to eradicate it in the states, slavery would be prohibited in the territories. The Party called for a strong central government and an industry-based economy. It staked the country's future on a silver-tongued moderate from Illinois.

THE SUSPENSE ENDS

Much of the North held its collective breath once Lincoln was elected president, and prayed that war was not a foregone conclusion. The reaction in the South to Lincoln's election was almost immediate. Not trusting that the new government would stop at the territories in making slavery illegal, South Carolina was the first state to announce it would secede from the Union. It wasted no time in convening a state convention to vote on secession. On December 20, 1860, the ordinance passed 169 to 0.

In the dead of night on December 26, 1860, the commander of Fort Moultrie in South Carolina acted on instinct. Major Robert Anderson, a Kentuckian who was foremost loyal to the flag, proactively abandoned the easily overrun fort. Understanding their vulnerability, Anderson led his eighty or so men a mile across the bay to the more defensible island position of Fort Sumter, which guarded the entrance to Charleston Harbor, and waited.

An editorial in *The Independent*, a New York newspaper, captured the Northern sense of incredulity that the country could be facing this crisis given the careful construction of the US Constitution. Charles L. Brace noted that in all the debates and writings accompanying the Constitution, little had been said of secession. He pondered what the reaction would have been if the Pinckneys and Madisons had said, "Gentlemen, you need not be troubled at this provision of the Constitution. Whenever it becomes burdensome or disagreeable to you, you have only to fall back on your prerogative as sovereign states, and refuse to obey, and dissolve the compact!"[9]

As Frederick Phisterer wrote in his history, *New York in the War of the Rebellion*, pacification in sentiment and preparation in act were the order of the day.[10] New York Governor Edwin D. Morgan typified this stance in his annual address to the legislature on January 1, 1861, when he firmly disavowed any moves toward secession by the Southern states, while also offering to reconcile estrangements. Just eight days later, New Yorkers were jolted into a new reckoning. On January 9, the New York–based swift merchant steamer *Star of the West*, filled with relief supplies and reinforcements, was fired upon by South Carolina militia in Charleston harbor as it attempted to reach Fort Sumter. The vessel was forced to return home without delivering the urgently needed cargo to Anderson and his men.

Pennsylvania Governor Andrew G. Curtin, undoubtedly stirred by the audacity of the attack on the *Star of the West*, forcefully rebutted the Southern states' right to secession in his inaugural address on January 15, 1861. He declared: "No part of the people, no State nor combination of States, can voluntarily secede from the Union, nor absolve themselves from their obligations to it . . . It is the first duty of the National authorities to stay the progress of anarchy and enforce the laws, and Pennsylvania with a united people, will give them an honest, faithful and active support."[11]

Before Lincoln had even given his inaugural speech, six more states followed South Carolina with their own declarations of secession: Mississippi (January 9), Florida (January 10), Alabama (January 11), Georgia (January 19), Louisiana (January 26), and Texas (February 1). As the Southern states voted to secede, they also helped themselves to federal assets such as forts and arsenals within their states, including Fort Moultrie in South Carolina.

At a convention in Montgomery, Alabama, on February 4, 1861, delegates from the seceding states met to make their secessions official.[12] They voted to create the Confederate States of America—popularly known as the Confederacy—and elected Democratic Senator Jefferson Davis of Mississippi as provisional president until elections could be held. Delegates borrowed from the US Constitution when drafting their Confederate Constitution but emphasized the primacy of state autonomy. This unrecognized republic moved swiftly to begin creating a Confederate Army, knowing the provocative act of secession would not go unanswered. On March 6, 1861, the Confederate Congress voted to establish an army of 100,000 volunteers for one year's service. Units were immediately organized from existing militias.

Abraham Lincoln gave his much-anticipated inaugural address on March 4, 1861. Primarily directed toward citizens of the South, his tone was conciliatory but firm. The *Binghamton Standard* editorialized that Lincoln "with characteristic frankness and directness comes right to the point. He shows that the Republican Party has not and will not interfere with the rights of the South . . . and that they must fulfill their Constitutional obligations . . . The right of secession does not exist."[13] President Lincoln matter-of-factly stated that the government would hold, occupy, and possess federal property, and collect taxes, but stopped short of suggesting that action to remedy the seizures in the South was imminent. On the contrary, in closing his address, Lincoln said, "In your hands, my dissatisfied fellow-countrymen, and not in mine, is the momentous issue of civil war. The Government will not assail you. You can have no conflict without being yourselves the aggressors. Though passion may have strained, it must not break our bonds of affection."[14]

Six weeks later, the suspense ended. On April 11, responding to a communique from President Lincoln that he was sending an unarmed vessel to resupply Fort Sumter, Brigadier General Pierre Gustave Toutant (P.G.T.) Beauregard bolstered and organized his fighting force in Charleston and demanded that Major Anderson surrender the fort. Anderson pleasantly replied that he was unable to comply. Goaded into action, South Carolina militia batteries at Fort Moultrie and Cummings Point opened fire on Fort Sumter at 4:30 a.m.

on April 12, 1861. Major Anderson and his men, within days of being starved out due to depleted provisions, shot back until much of the fort was up in flames. Anderson surrendered after a thirty-three-hour bombardment with no relief from the federal government forthcoming. He and his men evacuated the fort on April 14.

On April 15, President Lincoln called for 75,000 volunteers to crush the rebellion.

BECOMING A SOLDIER

It seemed a thing incredible and not to be believed, even after the final call for troops. It was all so strange and hard to comprehend, a mild excitement, in fact, to what came afterward.

—Clara Truesdell[1]

Rollin's sister Clara, conjuring up memories of the dawn of the Civil War, captured the mood of the nation in April 1861 in a letter to Rollin's son written decades after the cataclysmic event. The unthinkable had happened. On April 15, 1861, President Abraham Lincoln called up 75,000 volunteers to bear arms in battle against fellow Americans. Staring into the inescapable morass that had befallen his ward, his country, Lincoln implored: "I appeal to all loyal citizens to favor, facilitate, and aid this effort to maintain the honor, the integrity, and the existence of our National Union, and the perpetuity of popular government, and redress wrongs already long enough endured."[2] With the urgent remit of protecting the nation's capital and reclaiming federal properties seized by secessionists, the volunteers were to be plucked from loyal state militias for a commitment of three months. In the same proclamation, the President called for both Houses of Congress to convene at noon on the 4th of July, 1861, to consider what further measures may be necessary.

One could speculate that Lincoln's proclamation on April 15 reflected confidence that the rebellious South could be dealt with in quick order, and that he need not overreach by requesting more than three months of service from the Northern militias. However, the proclamation reflects the limited tools the President had to quickly form a loyal fighting force to counter rebel belligerence. The newly minted president was intent not to hypocritically break US Constitutional requirements to deal with Southerners who were themselves in breach of the Constitution. Because the Constitution stipulated that only Congress had the power to raise armies and call them forth to protect against invasions and suppress insurgencies, Lincoln needed to get creative. He based his demand for volunteers on the Militia Act of 1795, which gave the President the authority to call out the militias of any portion of the states in the case of an emergency. But there were stipulations that included: (1) no militiaman could be compelled to serve more than three months after his arrival at the place of rendezvous in any one year, and (2) the militia so called forth may be continued, if necessary, until the expiration of thirty days after the commencement of the next session of Congress.

Lincoln timed the special session of Congress well. By July 4, an army would already exist. The sanctity of the Union would be no less in peril. Therefore, the supposition would go, Congress must feel compelled to support the preparations for war. Certainly, the South was doing so. By the time President Lincoln issued the order for 75,000 troops, the South was already kluging together 60,000 or so men in disparate militias to form the budding Confederate Army.

Lincoln was rather quickly reassured that, generally, Northern sentiment was behind him. News of the attack and subsequent surrender of Fort Sumter spread as quickly as did Northern indignation. States in the North did not wait until Lincoln issued his proclamation to begin preparing for the inevitable. Though state militias were mostly paper organizations in 1861, Lincoln had ensured that his request was in keeping with the language of the Militia Act.[3] Unfussed by the legal necessaries, the loyal states quickly began recruitment to fulfill their quotas of the 75,000 troops requested—from local militias or not.

Pennsylvania Governor Curtin, a loyal supporter of President Lincoln, acted before shots were even fired in South Carolina. Anticipating their call-up, Curtin pushed for, and the Pennsylvania legislature passed (on April 11) an Act to improve the organization of the state militia along with the associated $500,000 appropriation to fund it.[4] By the time Lincoln issued his proclamation, Pennsylvania was ready.

In New York, Governor Morgan met with the Speaker of the Assembly, members of the military and finance committees in both houses, and other state officers on the afternoon of April 14 to plan legislation for raising and paying for troops.[5] On April 16, Governor Morgan signed a bill that went beyond the President's request; it authorized the enrollment of 30,000 volunteers for a two-year commitment and appropriated $3 million to meet that expense. Two days later, the governor issued a proclamation requesting volunteers to meet New York's initial quota of seventeen regiments; they would rendezvous at War Department–designated locations in Elmira, New York City, and Albany. On April 25, Morgan issued another order to form twenty-one additional regiments to reach the goal of 30,000 volunteers. These thirty-eight regiments would be the only ones from New York to serve two-year terms of service.

In the two weeks that elapsed from the issuance of Lincoln's proclamation, the governors of the Northern states left no doubt of their support for the President's call to service, and their intention to have more than their share of troops ready. State legislatures quickly passed bills to organize, equip, transport, and fund the volunteers in response to the President's proclamation. The Commonwealth of Virginia only added to the sense of urgency by seceding from the Union on April 17, 1861.

By the end of April, President Lincoln had dropped the pretense; the signal from the Northern states was clear. Gambling that Congress would ignore his technically impeachable action, President Lincoln cited his constitutional power as Commander-in-Chief and issued a proclamation on May 3 calling for 42,000 three-year volunteers, 23,000 additional men for the regular army, and 18,000 seamen to enforce a blockade of the southern coastline instituted from April 19. Though the War Department no longer sought three-month troops, the lengthened mandatory commitment did not squelch enlistment enthusiasm, which continued to rage. And during the extraordinary session of Congress that President Lincoln called on the 4th of July, 1861, Congress ratified what had been done and authorized the army to be increased by an additional 500,000 volunteers and supported by a $500,000,000 budget.[6] The demand to play a part in the history of the United States, to sew up the fraying fabric of the Union, was overwhelming.

AND THEY CAME RUSHING IN

Panic. That is the word Washington correspondent D. W. Bartlett used to describe the reaction within the nation's capital to the attack on Fort Sumter in his April 15, 1861, column in the New York newspaper, the *Independent*. Prophesizing Virginia's imminent declaration of secession, Bartlett wrote: "From the moment that she quits the Union, her soil becomes the camping ground of the entire Confederate army. Washington will then be the grand object of their desires . . . Washington can easily be shelled and destroyed. Twenty thousand troops from the free states are needed in Washington this very hour."[7] In the midst of terrified families fleeing the city, public buildings under twenty-four-hour guard, and mounted soldiers clattering through the streets, this journalist laid bare what was at stake.

Writing one week later, on April 22, Bartlett fairly pleaded for troops and provisions to avert a catastrophe in Washington: "In a word, the Capitol is in danger! Unless troops arrive there soon, it will be in the hands of the rebels before the people of the free states can hold communication with their Government."[8] By that time, telegraph wires and mail into and out of Washington had been cut. Private individuals scrambling out of Washington became the only sources of information (and rumors) for Northerners frantic for news. Rail links between Washington and Baltimore were severely restricted after secessionist violence erupted in Maryland. Market supplies were severed from Maryland and Virginia into Washington, exacerbating fears of famine. Bartlett reported that Commanding General Winfield Scott warned that day that "he could hold the city for ten days longer if he could rely upon the District troops [2,000 regular and Northern troops then in the city]."[9] With lines of communication broken, Scott would not have had confirmation that a tidal wave of insistent volunteers was close on the heels of those who had already propelled themselves to Washington with unimaginable speed to protect the capital.

The first to arrive in Washington had been three-month infantry regiments from Pennsylvania and Massachusetts. With no military barracks yet constructed to house these determined volunteers, they initially quartered in the US Capitol Building. Five companies from the 25th Pennsylvania, dubbed the "First Defenders," later joined by five additional companies, were the first off the mark. These men had been active in various militia units across the state and assembled in Harrisburg on April 17. On the morning of April 18, they took the military oath. By that evening, they arrived in Washington. The following day, the 6th Massachusetts Militia hobbled into Washington, bloodied by the mobs of Southern sympathizers who descended upon them as they transited Baltimore. Four soldiers died in the imbroglio. News of their abuse further fueled the flames of anger and disbelief in the North, and intensified the drumbeat for more troops in Washington.

The 7th NY Militia was the first to mobilize in New York. Also committing to three months, this elite unit, answering a special call from President Lincoln, departed from its home base in New York City amidst great fanfare on April 19. Choosing a route that would avoid direct conflict with Southern sympathizers and deliver them to their first objective, they chartered a steamer from Philadelphia, Pennsylvania, to Annapolis Junction, Maryland. They arrived on April 24 and occupied the state capital; they reached Washington on April 25. From April 21 to 30, nine additional regiments of the New York militia left for Washington. The remaining New York militia regiments, poised to depart when called, were held in place due to the May 3 order that abruptly halted soldiers entering service for three-month tours of duty.

We, a Committee of the citizens of Binghamton . . .

Even as state militia scrambled in haste to organize and deploy to Washington, eager volunteers simultaneously answered the call to enlist in droves. From cities to villages, the race was on to build, company by company, the volunteer force that Lincoln had requested. In New York alone, eighty-two companies were organized by April 22, just one week after Lincoln's order.[10] Public meetings, posters, and newspapers all proclaimed the same message: time is of the essence—enlist now!

While the enlistment fever raged around him, Rollin would have been pulled northward to most expeditiously answer the call to volunteer. (The War Department had named the downstate hubs of Harrisburg and Philadelphia as Pennsylvania rendezvous; Elmira in New York was geographically much closer.) Binghamton, in Broome County, New York, the closest sizable rallying point to Rollin's hometown of Liberty, Pennsylvania, was a magnet for Rollin.[11] A committee of citizen leaders in Binghamton formed immediately after Lincoln's proclamation, channeling the community's anger and fear into action. A poster signed by the committee boomed, "PATRIOTS OF BROOME! Are you ready to do your part for the defense and honor of your Country? We solemnly and earnestly call upon you to form, immediately, in your several Towns, as many Volunteer Companies as you can, and report yourselves to this Village."[12] Displayed in public gathering places, this poster also reflected the zeal to redress the assault on the 6th Massachusetts in Baltimore that had occurred four days earlier: "Our countrymen . . . have been attacked and murdered. Their blood cries to us from the ground."[13] To Northerners, this incident likely begged the question, could such violence migrate to my hometown? (See figure 2.1.)

Colonel Jacob C. Robie, previously commander of the 21st NY Militia, was the enrolling officer who received the volunteers motivated by the exhortations of Binghamton's citizen committee.[14] Three companies of some eighty men each were quickly organized. On May 2, companies formed by Captain J. J. Bartlett and Captain Hiram C. Rogers were accepted into service. Rollin proudly announced to his friends in his first letter home that he had enrolled in the third company to take the military oath, that of Captain Peter Jay. This company, known as "C" in Binghamton was accepted on May 8, 1861.

PATRIOTS OF BROOME!

A CIVIL WAR, commenced by a combination of Traitors and Conspirators, now threatens the existence of our Government, and all that we hold most dear and sacred. Your Country calls for your services. The Capital of the Nation, bearing the name of WASHINGTON, the Father of his Country, is in danger. Our countrymen, on their peaceful way to defend it, in passing through the borders of a neighboring State, have been attacked and murdered. Their blood cries to us from the ground. The time for action has arrived. Every hour is precious. Are you ready to do your part for the defense and honor of your Country? Will you see the glorious Flag of our Republic, baptised in the blood of the Revolution, and bequeathed to us as a sacred inheritance, insulted and dishonored?

"'Tis the Star-Spangled Banner, oh! long may it wave,
O'er the land of the free and the home of the brave!"

We, a Committee of the citizens of Binghamton, solemnly and earnestly call upon you to form, immediately, in your several Towns, as many Volunteer Companies as you can, and report yourselves at this Village. Each Company will comprise one Captain, one Lieutenant, one Ensign, four Sergeants, four Corporals, two Musicians, and sixty-four Privates---seventy-seven in all. No Company can have less than thirty-two persons.

☞ **The requisite clothing, arms, and accoutrements,** will be furnished at the expense of the State, or the United States, to the non-commissioned Officers, Musicians and Privates.

☞ **Ample provisions will be made for the comfortable** support and protection of the families of those who shall volunteer and enlist in the several Towns. Each Town is requested to provide for the families of its own Volunteers.

☞ **The Officers and Men will receive, while in service,** the same pay and rations as the Officers and Men of the same rank and arm of the service in the Army of the United States.

We know you will rush to the rescue of your Country, in this, the hour of her peril. She calls upon you, if need be, to---

"Strike till the last armed foe expires!"

FIGURE 2.1   Patriots of Broome Recruitment Poster.
Courtesy of the Broome County Historical Society.

Binghamton May 9th 1861

Dear Friends

I am feeling quite easy, having just enrolled my name in the C. Company and took the oath of allegiance to the Stars & Stripes, amid the cheers and hurrahs of the company and bystanders. The company is much like the company at Gt. Bend, having for its members very good men, good men, middling, poor and very poor.[15] There are several that I am acquainted with. Mr. Andrus, of Kirkwood, is one, a very good man. Captain Jay is a very pleasant man. I just had a talk with him and find him a better man than I expected.

I met Ephraim Smith Jr. this morning who informed me of the death of "Aunt" Lucy Buck. She died at Uncle Lyman's and is to be buried in Franklin today.

It is the supposition of the officers of this company that we shall remain in Elmira six weeks at least and perhaps three months so I am not going quite out of the World this move.

I leave this place at 3 o'clock P.M. today. I have no more time to write this time but will write again as soon as I get to "Camp." Remember me to all the Gt. Bend Volunteers, "especially to those who presented the flag to the Company."

Yours for the Union,
R. B. Truesdell

To all the friends I've got.

Within days after his arrival, Rollin and his new comrades exited Binghamton to take their next steps toward becoming soldiers. They traveled to the Elmira military depot on May 11, 1861. Sleeping in storerooms and practicing weapon handling with borrowed guns, these volunteers began their transition from civilian to soldier here.[16] Rollin excitedly reported the details of his new circumstances in his second letter home.

Elmira May 12th 1861

Dear Friends

Knowing your anxiety to know how I am faring, I take this first opportunity to write to you since I became a soldier in reality, that is, put on soldier's fare. We left Binghamton at 3 o'clock yesterday, arriving here at two o'clock, and marched immediately to quarters, which is on the corner of Lake and Mt. Zoar Streets.

In 40 minutes after our arrival, we were summoned to supper. The dining-room is a wood house open on one side, consequently easy of access. The tables are set without cloths, and each of us provided with a tin plate, pint cup, and pewter spoon. The provisions are good, not served out by rations, but every man eats all he wants. For supper we had boiled ham, dried beef, good bread, good butter, and good coffee. Mr. Wells, the proprietor, contracts to furnish two companies with eatables at 42 cents per day.

After supper, I enquired where we should lodge and was pointed to a barn a few rods distant. I walked to the premises with Capt Jay to see the conveniences of the institution. The barn was a poor one, and in the loft were spread 80 straw beds for our convenience. It looked very hard, but I concluded that I could stand anything the rest could. Capt Jay looked at the place very cooly and said, "Boys, you don't sleep in any such place as this. Stay here and be quiet, and I will see if I cannot get a better place for you." He soon found better quarters for us to sleep. It was a dry goods store. We took out the counters, laid down our ticks of straw, and laid down to pleasant dreams. I found but one fault with the beds, they were too short for me to lay myself on by two feet, but through the kindness of Capt and the necessity of the case, I was allowed an extra bed, which gave me a very good berth. Each of us was given a blanket, which, with my two beds and overcoat, I had a good night's rest.

This morning we had for breakfast, potatoes, fish, ham, bread, butter, and coffee. If I fare no worse than I have thus far, I will not complain. We are to receive our equipments this week.

There are about six thousand troops in this place.

I enquired for a church this morning, thinking to go, but was told every church in this place was occupied by soldiers.

I will write again in a day or two.

Yours for the Union
Rollin B

P.S. Ans immediately.

FORMING THE 27TH NY VOLUNTEERS

The train carrying the Binghamton recruits to the depot in Elmira was met by crowds of cheering townspeople, happy to welcome the volunteer soldiers to their hometown, which was quickly transforming into a military hub. Elmira, a town of no more than 14,000 at the time, was bursting at the seams with the avalanche of new recruits. A young man living in Elmira described the scene to his parents in a letter: "Sometimes 2,000 to 3,000 (soldiers) pass under our windows at once and their bands play on the street every night. Every other man you meet is a soldier."[17] In May and June of 1861 alone, 9,500 Union troops came in and out of Elmira, no longer a quiet rural village.[18] Feeling a bit lost in the sea of soldiers and missing the regular rhythm of Sundays at home, Rollin wrote another letter home on May 13 to converse with loved ones.

Elmira Monday 13th May 1861

Dear Friends

I wrote to you yesterday and mailed the letter this morning, but as you will not get it 'til Tuesday, I sent a dispatch this morning that you might not get too impatient. I should have telegraphed on Saturday eve, but it was a mile from the camp to the office, and I so tired I thought you could stand it 'til today better than I could walk to the telegraph office. I shall not write after today 'til Wednesday, in the time hoping to receive a letter from home.

Yesterday was a lonesome day to me, not being acquainted with any of the men, and there being no service at any of the Churches, but today I have heard directly from home. I saw Rev Mr Abbey this morning and had a long talk with him. He promised to stop this afternoon and see you if he had time. If not, he would see Mr McCrarie at the installation of Mr Dramot, and have him inform you more particularly of our situation. Ed Watson is here. I saw him this morning. For ought I know, he is the only man in the whole six thousand that I was ever intimately acquainted with.

It has been a very rainy day here, consequently we have not been out on drill.

I have just purchased me an oilcloth blanket (1½ yds wide and 2½ long) to protect me from the weather, etc.

I do not want my trunk sent immediately 'til I see more clearly what our prospects are.

The general health of the troops is good. I went up to the hospital this morning to see how things looked. There are only about 30 there, and those are regular rum-suckers.

What information has been received from the boys that went
with the Susqua Company?

I may come home in two weeks, and I may not. I cannot tell.

Remember me to all my associates, friends, etc

Yours for the Union,
R. B. Truesdell

Though it would be three years before Elmira was incorporated as a city
in 1864, it was on a path toward expansion before the Civil War began. Elmira
had an enviable combination of railway and waterway connections that Governor Morgan sought for a military depot. The Erie rail line ran east and west,
the Elmira and Williamsport rail line north and south, and the twenty-three-
mile Chemung Canal linked the Chemung River through a series of connections to the Erie Canal. These links to a wider market were lucrative for farms
and factories alike. As Rollin walked through Elmira, he would have seen such
successful enterprises as the Elmira Rolling Mill Company, which produced
iron rails; the Erie Railway Car Shops; and the Elmira Woolen Manufacturing
Company, which later won a contract for Union blue wool uniforms. Some
businesses directly supported the first surge of volunteers by offering makeshift
housing until barracks were constructed. Two barrel factories, a warehouse,
three churches, a concert hall, a judge's storage loft, the Elmira Heights Hotel,
and even a saloon served as temporary accommodation for the first volunteers
who landed in Elmira.[19]

As luck would have it, Rollin's time bunking in the dry goods store was
brief. Within days of entering the vast scrum of volunteers crowding into Elmira, he was diagnosed with the measles. The case was so severe that Rollin
was sent back to Liberty for a month to recuperate and did not return to Elmira until mid-June.[20] Upon his return to Elmira, Rollin penned a note home
to soothe concerns.

Elmira, June 20th 1861

Dear Friends,

I arrived at this place Monday evening and was met at the Depot by a member of "my" company and conducted to Capt Jay's
headquarters which is now on the south side of the river having
changed since my departure. The Capt said he thought I would not
be very strong yet and he would have me come and stay with him

for a few days, and as I might go directly to the Barracks from the Depot he sent a man after me consequently your fears of my being sick again are not realized.

I should have written yesterday but was engaged all day in making out reports and other documents for the Capt. I found the things that I left here all safe being well cared for by the Sergeant.

There is some prospect of our leaving this place in about two weeks but nothing certain.

Ed M Watson is sick in the hospital with typhoid fever. The health of our own company is good measles and mumps having ceased to rage.

I cannot write a very long letter this time as I have some more writing to do for the Capt.

Remember me to all my friends and particularly to Gallen.

Truly
R. B. Truesdell

Clara, Tell Mattie and Abby I did not have time to call and bid them goodbye. Will deputize you.

Rollin

To: "Friends"
Great Bend, PA

P.S. Dear Father, The Captain says he wrote to you immediately on the receipt of your letter and that that as well as many other letters by the same mail has never been heard from.

Yours truly
R. B. Truesdell

By the time Rollin returned, the three companies from Binghamton had joined with seven others from other parts of the state to become the "Union Regiment." They were "united" of their own will. In this new union, Rollin's unit under Captain Jay became Company "F." And the regiment had been assigned to quarter at the fourth camp established at Elmira: Robinson Barracks. Located below the Chemung River in Southport, this camp's use was relatively short-lived; the Army demolished it in 1863. (See figure 2.2.)

On June 25, Rollin wrote a letter to his brother Albert about resettling back into the army life—and of his plum assignment working in the regimental staff office.

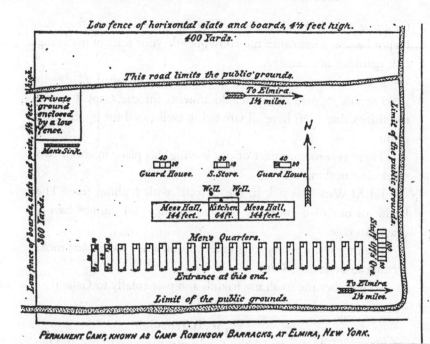

FIGURE 2.2   Drawing of Camp Robinson Barracks at Elmira,
New York by Capt. M. Lazelle, Michigan 8th Infantry. Courtesy
of the Chemung County Historical Society, Elmira, NY.

ELMIRA RENDEZVOUS
Barracks No 4,
June 25th 1861

Dear Bro,

There is nothing of special interest in military matters here,
only that our Regt received their pay & uniforms yesterday. I have
not drilled any since my return, though my health is good, excepting a slight "bit" of rheumatism in my ankle.

I am engaged a part of the time in the Col's office. I stand some
chance of a permanent appointment in the office and should a
better if it were not for a young man by the name of Button from
Edmeston. He is a better penman than I, but of rather loose habits.
The commissioned officers of my Co are figuring for me and his
officers for him so the officers that are the smartest will have their
"say" and get their man promoted. Button is well acquainted with
Mart & all Pete Hook people.

The Col has appointed Rev Mr. Buck chaplain to our Regiment. He preached to us on Sunday last, and in his style and language is a good counterpart to E. B. Tenny. "Judge for yourself" of our Chaplain.

There were four deserters from Dan'l E. Sickles' Brigade joined our Co yesterday. They tell some tough stories of Hon. "Dan'l E."[21]

Remember me to my Liberty friends, etc., etc.

Yours truly

R. B. Truesdell

U.S. Army

To: A. Truesdell

Great Bend, Pa

Robert Bruce Van Valkenburgh, commander of the Elmira depot, formally organized the Union regiment after the company officers elected the field officers. He then requested the State Military Board to confirm the officer selection and accept the regiment. They did so on May 21, 1861, and numbered the regiment "27." Regulations provided that the governors of the states furnishing volunteers commission the requisite field, staff, and even company officers (though selections at that level were rare). In practice, the man responsible for recruiting a company was elected by his men to be captain. Because military experience was not a prerequisite for the rank of captain, it was judicious to place more seasoned men in positions of higher rank within the regiment.

The men of the 27th NY Volunteers were wise in their choice for commanding colonel. They sought a coveted West Point graduate with field experience, Henry W. Slocum. He agreed to come to Elmira and was elected unanimously as Colonel of the 27th NY Volunteers.[22] The men elected Joseph J. Chambers, who had recruited the first company of the regiment, to be Lieutenant Colonel, and J. J. Bartlett of Binghamton to be Major. Slocum and Bartlett would prove to be pillars of this regiment, and of the Union Army. (See figures 2.3 and 2.4.)

Though likely frustrating to Slocum, who was adamant his men not be bystanders in the fight to end the rebellion, red tape prevented the 27th NY Volunteers from being mustered into US service until July 5, 1861.[23] Contrary to President Lincoln's May 3 call for additional volunteers to serve three year terms of service, Rollin and his comrades in the 27th NY Volunteers had enlisted under the terms of the April 16, 1861, New York state law requiring two-year commitments. Until the discrepancy between the State Military Board and the War

FIGURE 2.3   First Col. of 27th NY Vols, Henry W. Slocum.
Civil War photographs, 1861–1865, Library of Congress,
Prints and Photographs Division.

FIGURE 2.4   First Maj. of 27th NY Vols, J. J. Bartlett. Civil
War photographs, 1861–1865, Library of Congress, Prints
and Photographs Division.

Department could be rectified, the volunteers would remain in Elmira to train
for battle. Finally, on June 12, 1861, Secretary of War Simon Cameron ordered all
waiting state-enrolled regiments be mustered into United States service.[24] The
27th NY Volunteers simply had to wait their turn to mobilize.

Over the course of the many weeks spent in Elmira, the 27th NY Volunteers, like other regiments, dedicated themselves to army education, from drilling to dress parades. Rollin and his comrades were excited to receive their first pay as soldiers on June 25: $8.60 for service from May 21. A few days later, they received their uniforms of fine blue wool (overcoat, jacket, trousers) and shirts, stockings, fatigue cap, flannel drawers, shoes, blanket, canteen, knapsack,

FIGURE 2.5
Rollin B. Truesdell's
Uniform (forage cap).
Courtesy of the US Army
Museum Enterprise.

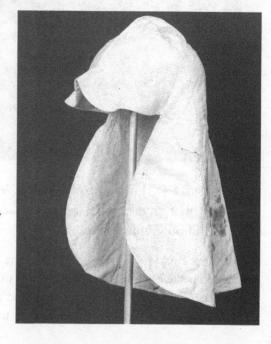

FIGURE 2.6
Rollin B. Truesdell's
Uniform (havelock).
Courtesy of the US Army
Museum Enterprise.

and haversack, along with their muskets. (See figures 2.5–2.10. Note the uniform shown is Rollin's at the end of his service. The stripes on the pant legs and chevrons were sewn on when he was promoted to sergeant.)

As time ticked closer to departure, Rollin wrote a letter home—perhaps to bolster his confidence as much as to inform loved ones he would soon be departing Elmira.

FIGURE 2.7 Rollin B. Truesdell's Uniform (haversack). Courtesy of the US Army Museum Enterprise.

FIGURE 2.8   Rollin B. Truesdell's Uniform (jacket).
Courtesy of the US Army Museum Enterprise.

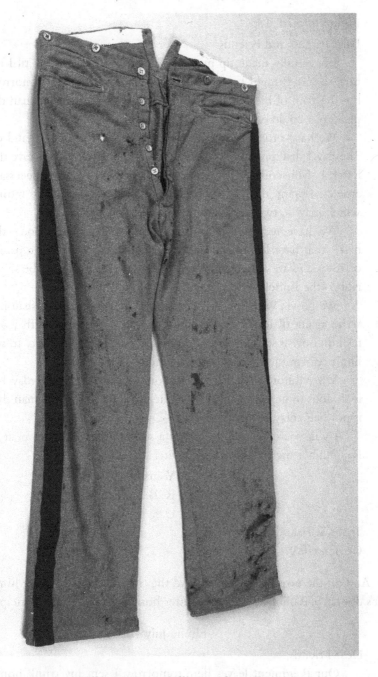

FIGURE 2.9   Rollin B. Truesdell's Uniform (trousers).
Courtesy of the US Army Museum Enterprise.

Elmira July 7th 1861

Dear Parents and Friends

I have fully made up my mind not to visit you again 'til I return to stay. I might have come yesterday and stayed 'til tomorrow, but the pain of bidding you all farewell would be greater than the pleasure I could enjoy in so short a time.

We have orders to march southward to the promised land on Tuesday. I shall probably be on my way by the time you receive this letter. I shall send my trunk home tomorrow, and all unnecessary articles. I want all my clothing carefully put away 'til my return, which may be two months and may be two years.

We have received all our equipments. They are good—the best—that have left this place. The guns are muskets of the patent of 1849, and are a superior article of infantry arms, said to be superior to the Enfield rifle.

We go via Williamsport, Harrisburg, and Baltimore. I shall not write again 'til I arrive at Washington. I am glad to hear that our friend Grow is speaker and hope I shall have an opportunity to see him performing the duties of his office.[25]

S. S. Mulford's Regt leaves tomorrow. I saw him yesterday. He is anxious to get away, and as to anxiety I don't know of a man that is not half crazy, to smell powder.

I will write as soon as I reach a stopping place wherever it is. Remember me to all my friends, etc.

> Yours aff
> R. B. Truesdell
> U.S. Army

To: S. W. Truesdell
Gt Bend, PA

And on the eve of climbing aboard the train that would bring him to the war's doorstep, Rollin wrote a final letter home, crackling with anticipation.

Elmira July 9th 1861

Dear Friends,

Our Regiment leaves here tomorrow. I sent my trunk home today and many articles that I had thought of taking with me 'til I got my knapsack.

I will write as soon as I'm at Washington.

I saw Dr. Patrick Sunday, which was as refreshing as a May shower. He was Dr. Pat as usual, "well pickled."

I am well, and in good spirits.

In haste, yours truly
R. B. Truesdell

My trunk comes by freight.

Rollin

The morning of July 10, the 27th NY Volunteers were told what they had waited weeks to hear. It was time to go.

BULL RUN SHATTERS
PERCEPTIONS

FROM ELMIRA TO WASHINGTON

Patriotic spirit overflowed. When the 27th NY Volunteers finally received word that they were to depart their training camp in Elmira on July 10, 1861, the local community enveloped them in the fanfare of the historic moment. The rhetoric soared. One local newspaper reported: "With unflinching nerve they went forth to battle . . . for the preservation of those sacred, inviolable rights, guaranteed by the Constitution—the grandest document that ever emanated from the brain of man. This was the motive that impelled them to action."[1] Though most Unionists subscribed to the popular belief that military action to halt the reckless and ill-conceived assault on the integrity of the United States would be brief and conclusive, a good many of the young men who volunteered to fight had never traveled far from their home communities, and they were green in the art of soldiering. Excitement would necessarily be tempered by these unknowns.

Friends and relatives honored the regiment with a parade before saying their goodbyes at the train depot in Elmira, "amidst loud hurrahs, waving handkerchiefs by fair hands, and the stirring roll of drums."[2] Carrying their stuffed haversacks, the men climbed aboard cars on the Northern Central Railway (NCR) destined for Baltimore, a much-traveled route during the Civil War. The journey south took over a day with several stops along the way. In Williamsport, Pennsylvania, the "patriotic ladies were out in force to give the boys one last good meal, and bid them a hearty God-speed," during a late-night banquet in a town square near the depot.[3] With eyes wide open, Rollin and his comrades from farming backgrounds would have made note of the variances in the crops as they chugged their way through Harrisburg and York en route to Baltimore.

To the men of the 27th NY Volunteers, Baltimore likely seemed quite a contrast to Williamsport. It was a city divided between Union and Southern sympathizers, and many of the latter were not ambiguous about their views. Shortly after President Lincoln called for 75,000 troops to protect the nation's capital after the attack on Fort Sumter, soldiers began arriving, using Baltimore as a transit point. Conflict between locals and the incoming troops, notoriously the 6th Massachusetts Militia, soon erupted. Amidst the chaos, Maryland Governor Thomas Hicks, in consultation with Baltimore Mayor George W. Brown and Baltimore City Police Marshal George Kane, passed an order to destroy railroad bridges to prevent Union troops from entering the city.[4] Saboteurs were successful in burning some of the overpasses on the NCR. Taking no further chances after these attacks, the federal government posted soldiers at every rail bridge crossing into Maryland; the 12th Pennsylvania Regiment guarded the tracks extending into Baltimore. The damaged bridges were repaired a month or so after the subterfuge and able to accommodate rail travel by the time the 27th NY Volunteers transited.

The regiment had no trouble during their short time in Baltimore. In fact, many of the young men may have viewed the visit as rather intriguing. In a brief note to his father upon arrival in Washington, Rollin artistically wrote that the streets were thronged with "dead rabbits," the notorious Irish American street gang from New York City that was accused of starting a riot in 1857. An officer from the regiment reported: "The men were astonished at such a state of society, the majority of them having been brought up far away from the evil influences of a city life. They had read the 'Mysteries and Miseries of New York,' by their own quiet firesides; now they were witnessing the realities in the streets of Baltimore."[5] Already, there would be much to report home.

The men of the 27th NY Volunteers continued their journey to Washington, DC, via the only railroad that entered the city from the north, the Baltimore and Ohio (B&O). This stretch of track represented a lifeline to the nation's capital for both supplies and troops and was protected as such. On May 5, 1861, Brigadier General Benjamin Butler, commanding the 6th Massachusetts, 8th New York, and Cook's Boston Artillery Battery, ordered the takeover of the Thomas Viaduct (the nation's largest multiple-arched stone rail bridge built on a curve) and the Relay train station to prevent Confederate sabotage along this critical route. Relay, then known for being the first town created by a US railroad, became the occupying Union Army headquarters for a time.[6] The 6th Massachusetts and Cook's Boston Artillery Battery were still encamped on both sides of the Patapsco River in the area around the Relay House hotel when Rollin and the other men in the 27th NY Volunteers stopped long enough to enjoy a lemonade while the train was searched for Confederate contraband.[7]

Their train arrived in Washington around 8 p.m. on July 11, and the 27th NY Volunteers marched to their quarters at Camp Anderson on Franklin Square near the White House, undoubtedly famished and filled with anticipation. Unfortunately, they would go to bed hungry that first night. Even years later, the seething of the starved men that night shines through in the regimental history account: "Before leaving Elmira, Col. Slocum had taken the precaution to send Lieut.-Col. Chambers on to Washington to provide rations for the men when we should arrive. But alas! We found nothing except two barrels of salt pork: so we had to go to bed supperless, filled with disgust at the officer who had given too much attention to refreshing his own inner man, to the neglect of his weary men."[8] In a lengthier letter home to update family and friends since arriving in Washington dated July 13, Rollin more charitably viewed the inedible fare problem as temporary.

Washington, D. C., July 13, 1861

Dear Friends,

I wrote you a line yesterday under the supposition that we were to march immediately to Arlington Heights, but a few hours later that order was countermanded and we are still quartered in Franklin Square.

There is a rumor here that a severe battle was fought last night at some point about 18 miles up the Potomac, but nothing definite can be learned until the N.Y. papers come.[9] But this much I do know, that there was fighting done somewhere, for I could distinctly hear the roar of cannon from 9 o'clock last evening 'til 4 this morning. Gen'l Scott has issued orders to all the troops in this city to turn out under arms at the signal of three guns from Arlington and the tolling of the bells, without further orders. There is a good deal of excitement in town today, and at this moment there is a balloon three hundred feet high reconnoitering the enemy's camp.[10]

I have been so fatigued since our arrival here that I have not been outside the Square, but I intend to take a peep at the "elephant" tomorrow.

Nicholas DuBois, like a good Samaritan, came to see me yesterday and invited me to take dinner with him today, but I shall defer it until tomorrow. His family are well.

Our fare since we came here inclines a little toward tough, the regular rations thus far being Navy crackers and bacon. The crackers as hard as a shingle, the bacon as fat as lard. I have not got hungry enough yet to partake of either. I boarded myself yesterday on crackers and cheese and bologna sausage at an expense of twenty cents. We shall have better fare as soon as our quartermaster can get the machine in motion and regulated.

The heat here I feel no greater than I did at home, though the crops here look entirely different from those at the north. At Elmira the farmers had not commenced their haying or harvest, but as we advanced southward, I could see a gradual change in the growth and ripening of crops. At Harrisburg, the farmers were in the midst of harvest, and at York, York Co., Pa., harvest was over, and the fields resembled the fields in Susq. Co. in September.

The railroad from Baltimore to this place is guarded night and day. I saw the charred remains of several trains of cars and a number of bridges.

We stopped at the Relay House half an hour. It is a little village about the size of Summersville. The hotel is a three story building, quite large, and shows evident signs that its occupants belong to the "southern aristocracy." As it is quite a noted place at present, I patronized it by drinking a glass of lemonade for the name of it— expense: one "levie" = 12½ cents.

A battery with three stern eyes looks the town boldly in the face, and "gently coaxes" the inhabitants to submit to the federal laws.

My love to all

Yours aff.
R. B. Truesdell

To: S. W. Truesdell
Gt Bend, Pa

POISED TO ENGAGE

Confident the rebellion would be extinguished with a couple of successful engagements, Colonel Slocum, with Major Bartlett, urgently sought an interview at the War Department when the regiment arrived in Washington. They pled to be immediately assigned to the field with a position in the column that would bring them directly into battle with the Rebels; Slocum was anxious that the regiment should not return home without some distinguished mark of honor.[11] Their request was granted. After a couple of false starts, the regiment would join the line of march southward on July 16, 1861.

In anticipation of their imminent departure from Washington and the battle to come, the men of the 27th NY Volunteers exercised what would be for many their first opportunity to discover the many novelties of the nation's capital. They perused the awe-inspiring exhibits at the Smithsonian Institute, took in the grandeur of the US Capitol and White House, and observed the societal extravaganza drawn to Washington. An officer of the regiment, lightly acknowledging such field trips from the barracks, said, "This liberty will not always be allowed them, for they are in a net, the meshes of which will continue to tighten around them in proportion as they become inured to the service, and are called upon to perform important military duties."[12]

Over these few days in July before departing Washington, the men of the 27th did also work to sharpen their skills as soldiers, albeit perhaps less rigorously than some officers would find ideal. They drilled, conducted a dress parade, and practiced target shooting all day on July 15. They were armed with smooth-bore, muzzle-loading 58-caliber Harpers Ferry muskets that used a paper cartridge the men tore open (usually with their teeth) before loading.[13] The gun had an enormous kick and was difficult to handle. According to the *27th Regimental History*, that day was the first and only for target practice with the weapons before the regiment entered battle; some uniformless newcomers joining several companies in the regiment after it arrived in Washington did not even have that one day.[14]

Brevet Lieutenant General Winfield Scott did not agree with the plan to confront the Confederate forces near Manassas Junction that summer, but he was overruled. Scott, seventy-four years old and infirm at the outbreak of the Civil War, had held the position of commanding general of the United States Army since 1841, having fought with distinction in the War of 1812 and the Mexican-American War, among other conflicts. Affectionately known as "Old Fuss and Feathers" for his insistence on military discipline and proper appearance, Scott was highly regarded for transforming soldiers into formidable fighters. Winfield Scott was a household name at the time.

Scott did not believe the Union forces were ready to challenge the Confederate Army, and particularly not against known military talents such as Joseph E. Johnston, P.G.T. Beauregard, and Robert E. Lee, all of whom had fought under his command in the Mexican-American War. President Lincoln cast aside Scott's proposal at the outset of the war to build up the regular army. Lincoln instead favored quickly infusing volunteers into the conflict. Scott was also unsuccessful in winning support for his strategy of blockading southern ports and seizing control of the Mississippi River to encircle and cut off access to the Confederate states to force surrender. Later deridingly known as the Anaconda Plan, it was designed to minimize loss of life on both sides but would necessarily take time to implement. The plan was leaked, and aching for a dramatic confrontation with the secessionists, many Northern newspapers panned the strategy. (See figure 3.1.)

General Scott continued to push for cool-headed decision making as the federal government designed its warfighting strategy, but his advice conflicted with the sentiments of the day. Scott sought to train the newly raised volunteer army in accordance with his standards of preparedness for an autumn campaign while state militia units would be detailed to defend Washington. Instead, the

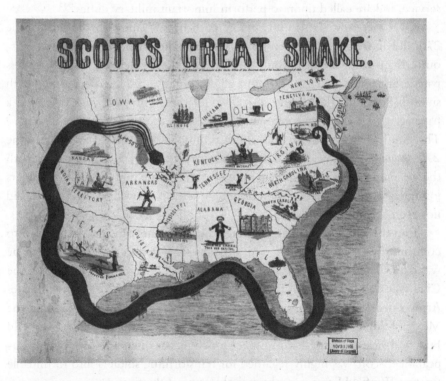

FIGURE 3.1   Cartoon Map of General-in-Chief Winfield Scott's Plan to Crush the Confederacy. Library of Congress, Geography and Map Division.

cries for immediate confrontation against the Rebel forces proved irresistable after Confederate President Jefferson Davis authorized his military adviser, Robert E. Lee, to form two armies operating in Virginia—one in Harpers Ferry under Brigadier General Joseph E. Johnston (Army of the Shenandoah), and the other in Manassas Junction under Brigadier General P.G.T. Beauregard (Army of the Potomac [Confederate]).[15]

With the three-month-commitment clock ticking for the state militias, President Lincoln heeded the popular cry, "On to Richmond!," and ordered an offensive against the new Confederate capital. No longer able to conduct field operations, Scott remained in Washington, which placed the spotlight on the field commander of Union forces south of the Potomac, Brigadier General Irvin McDowell, to neatly wrap up the rebellion. McDowell proposed driving Beauregard's force of 20,000 behind the Rappahannock River, provided that Major General Robert Patterson kept Johnston's soldiers occupied and out of the fight. McDowell requested 30,000 men for the assault.

ON TO RICHMOND!

On July 16, before starting southward, the 27th NY Volunteers were assigned to the 1st Brigade, commanded by Colonel Andrew Porter, within the 2nd Division, commanded by Colonel David Hunter, in McDowell's Department of Northeastern Virginia. Porter's brigade was comprised of a US Marine battalion, a US Infantry battalion, a US Cavalry battalion, Battery D of the 5th US Artillery, the 8th NY Militia, the 14th NY Militia, and the 27th NY Volunteers.

With envy and regret, Rollin would have watched as his new friends in the regiment hastily packed their gear upon hearing their orders. Departing around 3 p.m., the 27th NY Volunteers soon crossed the Long Bridge into Virginia, the land of the enemy. As the men marched toward an encounter they believed would lead to glorious victory—a life-changing event for each soldier, as well as the country—Rollin remained at Camp Anderson. He and fifty-seven others from the regiment were sidelined with illness, keeping them out of the fight. Rollin, barely recovered from the measles, now had mumps, a contagious disease that many from rural areas were not exposed to as children but that thrived in the close quarters of military camps during the Civil War. He was assigned to clerk the regimental headquarters while the rest were in the field. This duty would offer Rollin the opportunity to measure the pulse of the regiment as information flowed through the headquarters, and later to forge relationships with commanding officers Colonel Slocum and Major Bartlett. A couple of days after his regiment departed, Rollin wrote a brief letter to his mother explaining his predicament.

Camp Anderson D. C.
July 18th 1861

My Very Dear Mother

I am enjoying myself well, tho' in an enemy's country. Our regiment moved into Virginia day before yesterday, but it is my bad luck to be left behind on account of my having the mumps. There are fifty-eight men left behind, in the charge of Mr. Buck, the Chaplain. I am acting as his clerk, occupying headquarters and am having a good time generally.

I frequently visit our friend, Nicholas DuBois, who is a good Samaritan to me, and sends his love to you, also his wife. I have visited the Smithsonian Institute, Patent Office, White House, and Capitol, and been several miles on to the sacred soil of Virginia before our Regt left here.

There was a battle at Fairfax Court House last night; our troops now occupy it. An advance is to be made on Richmond immediately. I trust the "wars" will soon be over.

I saw Mr. Chase yesterday, who will tell you more about me than I can write.

Remember me to all our numerous family and remember me as

Your aff son,
Rollin B. Truesdell
27th Regt Co F
N.Y.S.V.

P.S.
Direct all letters to me in care of Col. Slocum
Co. F 27th Regt
N.Y.S.V.
Washington, D.C.

When Rollin's comrades reached the Virginia side of Long Bridge on July 16, they marched past the fortifications of Arlington Heights, earthworks supporting artillery that commanded the Potomac River and the surrounding four miles, and took their assigned place in the column. The men would march along the Little River Turnpike until stopping for a dinner of bread and salt pork at Bailey's Crossroads. Hearing picket firing in the front of the column, the regiment was ordered to load their muskets (each man carried forty rounds of ammunition) before continuing the march to Annandale. The march was a jumpy one for the new soldiers. Reaching camp around 10 p.m. on July 16, undoubtedly exhausted from the physical and emotional demands of the day, the men slept for the first time under the stars with only blankets to protect them from the cold. An officer from the regiment said, "in such haste had this force been collected, that the Government was unable to supply the demand for tents, and . . . temporary houses of brush was an unsuccessful experiment, proving of little avail against chilling winds and incessant rains."[16]

The bugle sounded at sunrise on July 17, and the 27th NY Volunteers were soon on the march toward Fairfax Station. They continued for several hours before dividing into platoons and quick-marching to close the gap with the rest of the column. When shots suddenly rang out and the cavalry and mounted rifles were called to the front, the men of the 27th supposed their wait was over and the fight was about to begin. Instead, the Confederate forces opted to quickly pull back rather than engage and left burning fires as evidence of their presence. Like a spring sharply uncoiling, Union troops wasted little time in scouring the town for food and other stores, but also wantonly vandalizing private property. Rollin's chum William Westervelt and others from the regiment later recalled the shameful destruction of property. Pinning the blame on two other regiments, a private in the 27th NY Volunteers reported that, "ex-Senator Thomas' house was gutted through revenge. McDowell ordered the arrest of the ringleaders and issued an order threatening to punish anyone meddling with private property."[17] Discipline would be on the minds of the men of the 27th NY Volunteers in the coming days.

The regiment was again called into line early the next morning. The men waited several hours in the blazing sun before marching from Fairfax Station approximately five miles toward Centreville, where they camped for the next two days. Though new to soldiering, the men of the 27th NY seemed determined to withstand anything the other units could, and to remain as loyal to their commanding colonel as he was to them. One private remarked in a letter dated July 19, "I cannot help but notice the difference in powers of endurance between our Regiment and the U.S. Marines with their West Point officers. In marching here yesterday with their company of 340 men, 28 fell out of ranks from the effects of the heat, while in our company of nearly 1,000, not one gave out, although half were troubled with black diarrhea."[18]

On the morning of the 19th, Rollin's comrades witnessed a frightening spectacle within the regular army battalion camped next to the 27th NY Volunteers that reportedly would be the last case of such punishment in Union forces. According to Westervelt and the *History of the 27th Regiment N.Y. Vols*, the regular army unit was called to form a square around two men who were then whipped thirty times each on their bare backs and branded on the hip with the letter D (for deserter).[19] The afternoon brought its own fascination when skirmishers escorted in as prisoners the first Rebels the men in the 27th had seen. Rollin's mates were likely still debating what should be done with the prisoners when they were sent out on picket duty that night.

In the early morning hours of July 21, the 27th NY Volunteers received the order to continue south. The day had finally come.

The shocking news came quickly. The unspeakable had happened. Instead of returning to Washington as triumphant victors, Rollin's comrades would limp back, raw after the viciousness of the battle, physically and emotionally dented. After the battle, a member of the regiment wrote home: "Our troops fought like tigers, but who could hope for success?"[20] Though the initial casualty reports from the Bull Run battlefield proved to be more alarming than the reality, the 27th NY Volunteers incurred their most significant single day of loss on July 21, 1861. Indeed, the carnage at Bull Run rattled the very foundation of the Union forces. On July 22, Rollin wrote to his father of the grim surprise.

Washington, D. C.
July 22nd 1861

Dear Father

Our troops have been defeated at Bulls Run with a very heavy loss. Our Regt are nearly one half killed including Capt. Jay and Lieut. Asa Park. Many have been taken prisoner and we cannot yet tell the exact loss, but it is very great. Capt. Jay had his head shot off by a cannon ball. Lieut. Park received two balls, one in head and one in the heart.

The wounded are on their way to this place, where they will receive proper medical attendance.

I am hearty and sound, doing the best I can for my comrades.

I will write again as soon as I hear more of the particulars.

In haste,

Yours aff
R. B. Truesdell

To: S. W. Truesdell
Gt Bend Pa
Col Slocum received a bad wound in the thigh and is considered dangerous.

For the 27th NY Volunteers, such an outcome had been inconceivable when they began their march in the predawn hours of July 21. Nor did the politicians, journalists, and other interested spectators who traveled to witness the battle that would put a halt to the southern insurrection imagine the day could end otherwise. Before sunrise, the regiment reached Centreville, crossed Cub Run, and then turned slightly north before arching southward into a thick oak forest with an opening on a distant hillside. The sounds of battle in front of them reverberated and presaged the bloodbath they would enter. Union Commanding General McDowell had rested on his laurels from morning battlefield successes a little too long. By the time the 27th NY Volunteers arrived, the momentum had shifted with the influx of Rebel reinforcements. Emerging from the woods onto an open field, Rollin's comrades recalled one of Porter's aides meeting them and ordering Colonel Slocum to move forward by waving his hand and exclaiming: "You will find the enemy down there somewhere!"[21]

With that bit of inspiration, Colonel Slocum directed his men, by then reeling from the heat and lack of water and food, onward. Confederate Brigadier General Beauregard's forces were arranged on a ridge in front of them with a valley and Young's Branch, a tributary of the Bull Run Stream, separating the two. After marching for eight hours and over fourteen miles, the men of the 27th NY Volunteers, adrenalin pumping, ran headfirst to meet their enemy. Shot and shell whistled past them, and the first man from the regiment was wounded. Westervelt and others from the regiment noted that, en route, they passed members of the 8th NY Militia in their gray uniforms tending to wounded comrades.[22] Provisions and any other encumbrances being jettisoned along the way, the regiment reached the crest of a hill. A battery of Confederate guns stared at them a short distance away.

Slocum called his men into line and immediately ordered them forward to attack the enemy. Flinging themselves down the hill, the 27th NY Volunteers charged the Rebel battery and its supporting infantry, ensconced in and around the "Stone House."[23] Leaving their dead and wounded behind, the musket-wielding Rebels fled to a location behind their battery and then hastily withdrew to a masked position to the front and left of the 27th NY. Like magnets, Rollin's mates quickly became easy targets for the Confederate artillery and musketry as they moved to the left near the Stone House to reassemble and form a line of battle. The battery unloaded canister shot on the 27th with murderous effect. Captain Peter Jay reported in a letter to hometown newspaper, the *Broome Republican*: "The rebels fired volley after volley . . .

We lost a good many in the fight and the men broke ranks, but all were willing and anxious to avenge the death of their comrades. (Cowards were off the field by this time.)"[24]

With no Union forces coming to their aid, to regain order, Colonel Slocum directed his fractured regiment to an area still further to their left. Then, in an audacious move, two regiments dressed in uniforms akin to the 8th NY Militia came out of the woods and popped up over the crest of a hill to their left and rear—directions the 27th did not expect to encounter Rebel forces.[25] In the midst of the confusion over whether the soldiers were friend or foe, whether the men of the 27th should fire into them or not, the two Confederate regiments moved to the front. Soon, a straggling member of their group approached Colonel Slocum, announcing that one of the regiments wanted to surrender. Skeptical, Slocum ordered his Adjutant to ride over with a white flag at the point of his sword to discuss the proposition. In answer to Adjutant Jenkins's enquiries, called out as he approached their commanding officer, the imposters unfurled a Confederate flag and blasted away into the ranks of the 27th NY Volunteers. One of Rollin's comrades shuddered: "our boys fell like grass before the scythe—but rallied and returned fire."[26]

Surrounded, Slocum sent Lieutenant Colonel Chambers, his jacket shred by musket balls, galloping back to the command field office to seek reinforcements.[27] Meanwhile, with guns blazing, the 27th NY Volunteers sought cover over the crest of Buck Hill, as they were also raked with fire from Confederate infantrymen waiting in a ravine to the right of them. During this movement, Colonel Slocum was shot through the thigh and evacuated to the rear where surgeons could render aid. Beloved by his men, two soldiers in the regiment later reported, that "a braver man never lived," and "our Colonel nearly wept when he could not lead us further . . . we had already had our share of the fight."[28] Lucky for the men of the 27th NY Volunteers, Major Bartlett then assumed command. As one of Rollin's comrades later opined: "there are a good many officers in the army who have seen more service than Major Bartlett that today were not so fit to lead men into battle."[29]

Bartlett led the regiment to the woods at the rear just as two regiments arrived to relieve them. The men replenished their exhausted supply of ammunition, rested a short while, and then were ordered back into battle. Rollin's comrades saw the fight raging around them as they exited the woods. Entering the chaos, Bartlett directed his men to the banks of the nearby stream, which provided valuable protection. A private in the regiment remarked, "It was almost instant death to lose cover."[30] Norman S. Barnes, the regiment's surgeon, wrote to his wife that "cannon, grape, canister, and musket balls flew thick and fast about us; men and horses killed all around me; one horse was killed under me. I lost all my instruments and medicines, and amputated 25 limbs, but the poor fellows were shot, bayonetted, or had their throats cut [by overtaking Confederate forces]."[31]

Over the course of the afternoon, Porter ordered the 27th NY Volunteers to reposition themselves several times to support the general assault on the Rebels. Union forces succeeded three times in driving the Confederates from their batteries. Each time, the Confederates roared back and retook what was theirs. As private Burrows explained in a letter to his brother and sister, "They [Confederates] had three masked batteries, one behind another, and an army two times as big as ours. They would retreat from one [battery] to have our men come and take it, then they'd open on us with another and infantry; then their cavalry would cut us down."[32] One soldier from Rollin's regiment derided Union coordination, saying, "on our side there was no order whatever; each Colonel attacked or withdrew from the field when he pleased and that is the way the fight was carried on."[33]

Major Bartlett, in his after-action report, agreed with that assessment. He pointed to the undisciplined mayhem the Union forces had inflicted upon themselves: "Small detachments engaged the enemy, and not in the order in which the attack was commanded to be made, and then were repulsed and driven back in disorder."[34] Bartlett had determined he and his men would not be drawn in similarly; he pulled the remnants of his men back into line on top of the heights overlooking the stream facing the Confederate forces in a bid to attract dissembled sister units and create a core of order in the fight. His gambit was unsuccessful.

Rollin's comrades could be excused if optimism was at a premium as the day wore on. But when they saw a heavy column of troops come onto the field late in the afternoon, the exhausted men of the 27th NY Volunteers felt relief that Major General Patterson's force based in the Shenandoah Valley had come to their rescue. But they were wrong. Instead, they would witness the steady disgorging of yet more of Confederate Brigadier General Johnston's 12,000 or so reserve troops onto the battlefield. Patterson appeared paralyzed; he failed to block Johnston and left McDowell to slug it out with the Confederate Army by himself. Any remaining hopes of Union victory that day died.

The 27th NY Volunteers remained in position while thousands of Union troops hurled themselves toward the rear. In a last-gasp effort, Bartlett marched his men toward the direction of the retreat and formed a line of battle, another attempt to attract other regiments in accordance with McDowell's command. But to no avail. Enlisted and officers alike jostled toward the rear. A mate from Rollin's regiment wryly stated, "Some of our officers showed the bottom of their feet to the enemy."[35] Bartlett led the 27th NY Volunteers off the field with colors flying and took up position in the rear guard of the retreating army.

Complete panic soon took over. With smoke and dust and the shrieking of the wounded heavy in the air, some members of the Union cavalry bolted their way through the ranks of the 27th NY Volunteers, and anyone else in front of them, to flee. That was that. The regiment's ranks were broken, and Rollin's comrades were cast into a stampede. When they reached the main road, the regiment found abandoned cannon and caissons; horses had been detached for the artillerymen's escape.

The bridge leading the gutted force of the Union to the safety of the north had the attention of Confederate batteries. Forced to ford the stream in the tumult, a number of Union soldiers drowned. The frenzy of civilians and members of Congress who had ridden from Washington to witness the battle added to the mayhem as they pushed for a spot in the retreating mass. The Honorable Alfred Ely of Rochester, New York, a spectator on the battlefield, was among those captured by Confederate forces. Private Brown from Rollin's regiment remarked that such spectators' "rashness may have cost them their lives."[36] (See figure 3.2.)

The men of the 27th NY Volunteers plodded their way back to Centreville, arriving near midnight at the camp they had left just under twenty-four hours before—then buoyant, now numb. Fortunate for this unfortunate army, Colonel Louis Blenker (1st Brigade, 5th Division) had been ordered to form a line south of Centreville that served as a net to pull the terrified retreating force to safety. There, Bartlett received orders from brigade command to march the men to Fairfax, and then back to Washington.

Barely able to walk, Rollin's mates trudged onward, awash with images of what they had just endured. They knew that the wounded and exhausted men left behind would likely be taken prisoner. One comrade remembered: "As you pass along, you see one gasping for breath, another crying for water, another begging you to blow his brains out and put him out of misery."[37] Another recalled: "The whole division was so tired out that not a man made any effort to keep along with his particular regiment; and as for making a stand anywhere along the route, probably more than half would rather have been taken prisoners than to have fought half an hour with the certainty of success."[38] These volunteer soldiers marched some sixty miles in two days without food or sleep, drank dirty water from puddles they would normally not wash

FIGURE 3.2   Ruins of Stone Bridge at Bull Run. Library
of Congress, Prints & Photographs Division, Civil War
Photographs.

their hands in, and fought their first battle as a cohesive unit under scorching fire in the name of the Union. When the men of the 27th arrived back at
Camp Anderson on Franklin Square the morning of July 22, Rollin was there
to greet them.

Four days later, the dust had settled somewhat and allowed for more clarity about the Union debacle at Bull Run. Rollin wrote a letter to his sister
with updated information about the bruising and the impact on the families
of those battered in the battle, and a letter to his brother Martin's wife Hellen
with appreciation for her uplifting words amidst the shock of the battle.

Camp Anderson, Washington DC
July 26th 1861

Dear Sister Clara
    Your letter of the 24th and two Republicans I received yesterday,
the first news I have had from home since my arrival in this place,
except via Mr Chase. They were welcome missives, I assure you.

You ask me to write more particularly about myself. I ask what would you know or could wish to know other than I am well and in good spirits. This I think is as good news as you could wish to know.

The excitement attending the great battle at Bulls Run is gradually decreasing. Our Regt not being so badly cut up as was at first supposed. Our loss is now supposed to be about one hundred and twenty. The first report I received from the battlefield was that Capt. Jay was killed, and afterward that he was taken prisoner, which proved to be true, but he afterward made his escape, and came into camp late Monday night. Lieut Asa Park was instantly killed and his body left on the battlefield. About fifty of our men were wounded, and are now in the hospital, well cared for. The loss of the Federal troops, all told, will not exceed fifteen hundred, and but one division of our troops were actually engaged in the fight.

By the by, I saw a member of the Wisconsin 2nd Regt this morning, who said he supposed Charlie Trowbridge was killed, he not having yet come into camp, but do not inform his parents 'til all hope is gone. I received a telegram from Dan'l Brewster of Montrose the 23rd inst inquiring if the body of Park could not be recovered and sent home. I sent back the reply that it was impossible, and from what I can learn, I suppose that many of our dead are now lying on the field unburied. 'Tis awful, but true.

It will probably be two months before our Col will be able to take the field again. What will be our destination in this time, I am unable to say, but one thing is sure, our men will fight under no other Col than Slocum. Not a man but thinks as much of him as they do of their parents.

Eddie Porter McCrarie left here on Thursday for home. He can tell you much about the life of a soldier, having been in service three months. I saw Dick DuBois day before yesterday; he is in the Penna. sixth, Col. "Rickett's." His health is good. He likes soldiering first rate, he says.

We fare much better now than we did when I last wrote. Indeed, it is quite endurable now but at first, it was pretty tough, I tell you. I think I can fully appreciate the luxuries of home life if I ever live to return. But do not worry about me. I can take care of myself, and live where a thousand other men can. I think if I cannot, I will "draw to my bed."

I saw a gentleman this morning from Berlin Wisconsin who is well acquainted with brother Calvin. He says he is completely absorbed in business all the time and is doing well, first rate, all of which I am glad to hear.

I wish you all to write to me often. My love to all.

> Yours aff
> R. B. Truesdell

Dear Sister Hellen,

I often regret that I did not remain at home in June till your arrival, but regrets avail nothing and as penance for not staying I will come to Edmeston soon after I return home and make you a long visit. I think if all the soldiers could receive such encouraging letters as you wrote to me they would seldom get downhearted and discouraged, and seldom give themselves up to the temptations and vices incident to camp life the causes of which are in most instances being away from friends and the social intercourse of society. I sincerely hope I shall return as good as I left home if no better. This much I do know, I am learning much every day in the lessons of human life and nature and much that I hope will be of service to me in after years.

Remember me to Brother "Luther." I must write to him soon.

> Yours very truly
> Rollin B. Truesdell

AFTERMATH

The days following the embarrassing defeat at Bull Run were ugly. Northerners grappled with how this engagement was bungled so badly, and once enthusiastic loved ones mourned the unexpected loss of their kin in a battle that was supposed to end the conflict. The Union lost over 2,700 men and the Confederacy nearly 2,000 in the battle. Over 1,300 men were listed as missing, most captured as prisoners of war. The 27th NY Volunteers suffered dearly: one officer and twenty-six enlisted men killed; two officers (including Colonel Slocum) and forty-two enlisted wounded; and sixty men, including three members of the color guard, missing.[39] The missing were likely to have been wounded and taken prisoner.

On July 31, 1861, Rollin wrote a letter to his father as more information was available about casualties, and as accusations of fault became more vivid.

Washington
July 31st 1861

Dear Father

Your letter of the 27th came to hand yesterday. Our Regt is again quartered in Franklin Square recruiting and getting ready to give the rebels another pull.

Our loss is not as great as at first supposed in consequence of some of our men getting cut off from the main body and resting in the quarters of other regiments till they were more able to march into camp. When all stragglers get into camp, I think our loss will not be much over one hundred. It is now thought here the aggregate loss of the federal troops will not be over fifteen hundred, while the rebels give their own loss at three thousand. I honestly suppose that many of our killed are unburied to this day.

One hundred and fifty Rebel prisoners were brought in here this morning who were captured near the chain bridge eight miles above here. In all probability, there will not be another attack on Bulls Run for some time, but when we do, woe be to them.

In the last attack, there was but one division engaged, probably from fifteen to twenty thousand men, and those badly managed. Some are confident that we should have routed them, but for the unsoldierlike conduct of the 14th Brooklyn Regt who broke ranks and fled in disorder on the first fire, and when a body of soldiers begins to move in confusion, they are completely unmanageable.

I yesterday visited the House of Representatives and saw our mud sills Grow and Wilmot.[40] I met Mr. Grow at the National Hotel the other day, and could not resist the good natured phiz, but introduced myself to the Hon. M. C. not thinking to say more to him than the passing compliments of the day. But to my surprise, he sat down and talked with me an hour, and when I left, invited me to call again, which fully convinced me that our M. C. is still a man though holding the office of Speaker.

I am sorry to learn that Mother has been sick; hope she will fully recover soon.

My love to all

Your aff.
R. B. Truesdell

Anxious about his mother's health, Rollin wrote a letter to her a few days later—likely to cheer each of them up.

Washington D.C.
August 6th 1861

Very Dear Mother

I this morning received letters from Father and Clara, and in answering their letters, I will write one to you. I am getting along as well as could be expected in every sense of the word. Our fare, tho' hard when we first arrived here, is now quite endurable indeed. I may safely say "good," better than many have at home. My health was never better than it is today, and as long as I enjoy those blessings, I trust that you will not borrow trouble about me.

The weather here is extremely hot, but perhaps no more so than at Gt. Bend. I stand it first rate, considering that our uniforms are woolen and better adapted to cooler weather than this.

Our Regt was paid off the 2nd inst. The amount I received was fifteen dollars, four cents which together with what I received from the Col office for labor down there, keeps me quite comfortably.

Our Regt has been badly off since their tramp to Bulls Run. Probably one-third of our members that returned have diseases of the lungs, from which they will never recover. I think I was quite fortunate in being left behind. It is quite uncertain when we shall again be ordered to march, but not very soon, I conclude. Col Slocum is improving slowly. He is to be promoted to a Brigadier General.

There is no war news of particular interest. The excitement occasioned by the late battle having entirely subsided. There is great activity in the war department, especially the department furnishing supplies of provisions to the many thousand troops quartered in and around Washington. It is nothing unusual to see a baggage train of one hundred and fifty wagons, loaded with provisions for those troops stationed at Arlington, Georgetown, and other adjacent camps.

The 6th Pa Regt is quartered about four miles out of town. Dick DuBois and several other Gt. Bend boys are members of this regiment. I saw Dick yesterday. He is well and getting along first rate. I saw Dr. Mulford a day or two since. I find more Susq Co friends here than I expected, which helps to keep my spirits up and make my soldier life more pleasant than it would be if I were entirely among strangers.

Love to Mart and Hellen and all other relatives.

Your affectionate son
R. B. Truesdell

Rollin was indeed fortunate not to suffer the afflictions that his comrades endured after their return from Bull Run. Unsurprisingly, considering the water they drank, most of the regiment suffered from debilitating diarrhea as well as respiratory afflictions for several weeks after returning to camp. However, it may have been what one of Rollin's comrades called "powder sickness" that caused the most consternation in camp: "two or three cowardly officers tendered their resignation yesterday [July 27], but I don't know if they were accepted."[41] In contrast, Rollin and his comrades drew strength from the example of Colonel Slocum, who visited their camp on August 13—the first time since he had been wounded and was appointed Brigadier General. Slocum received a rowdy reception from his loyal men.

No, the men of the 27th NY Volunteers aimed higher up when affixing blame for the rout at Bull Run. As Private Copeland told his father, "Our Colonel is loved by all the regiment, but the general movement of the army was in unskilled hands."[42] The coordination, equipment, and timing failed. One soldier charitably suggested that "by some mistake, McDowell began one day too soon."[43] (In actuality, McDowell lamented the obstacles—e.g., regiments not arriving in time and then being haphazardly thrust together in brigades, delayed arrival of ammunition, and foot-weary soldiers unaccustomed to marching—to commencing the movements earlier, as he had planned, and cited those as contributing to his failure.[44]) An officer from the regiment was having none of it. One could imagine clenched teeth when he wrote: "This disgraceful defeat of our arms was the direct result of impatience and over-eagerness to meet a well-disciplined foe, whose formation dated far back of the Federal organization; the syren [sic] song emanating from restless politicians . . . and a shameful attack and retreat was the effect that followed the policy of these pompous croakers."[45]

Though General-in-Chief Scott had warned President Lincoln against a premature assault on the Confederacy, he did not fully escape the fallout from the failure at Bull Run. The President swiftly removed McDowell and tapped George B. McClellan, the commander glowing with success in western

Virginia, to take command of the army in the eastern theater. Increasingly boxed out of meetings between the President and McClellan, Scott ultimately resigned in October 1861 rather than accept the implied diminution of status. It was now up to McClellan to turn the tide for the North.

DEFENDING THE CAPITAL

THE WHEAT FROM THE CHAFF

The Battle of Bull Run was like looking through a magnifying glass. It brought into sharp relief the flaws but also the strengths of the Union Army. President Lincoln knew he must quickly acknowledge and remove the defects while bolstering the assets or he would risk handing the momentum to the secessionist Southerners. Lincoln could not leave Northern supporters incredulous at the loss, nor leave the Union Army demoralized.

Action was swift. With the shroud lifted, the President had no choice. Victory would require more men who could be groomed into fighting as a unified force. Despite the passion of the Northern recruits, day-counting three-month militiamen would not be a dependable pillar in the construction of a Union Army facing the determination, officer experience, and pluck of its secessionist enemy. On July 22, 1861, President Lincoln signed the bill authorizing the enlistment of 500,000 three-year men and subsequently called for 300,000 more volunteers. Meanwhile, Congress quickly remedied the paucity of leadership within Union officer ranks. During a busy day in Washington on the day after the drubbing at Bull Run, Congress authorized the establishment of military boards to separate the wheat from the chaff among Union officers. In the following months, hundreds of officers either resigned or were discharged as unqualified for duty.

Commanding General McDowell of the Department of Northeastern Virginia, for one, had to go. Within a week of Bull Run, McDowell was out, and Major General George B. McClellan was in. McClellan hustled to Washington from operations in western Virginia (later to be West Virginia) to breathe fresh air into the Union Army. On July 26, President Lincoln appointed him commander of the new Union Army defending the capital. Quickly consolidating several military units in Virginia, McClellan created and then assumed the title of the first Commander of the Army of the Potomac on August 20, 1861. McDowell was appointed a division commander within this new army.

As a fellow Pennsylvanian, McClellan may have been known to Rollin for reasons other than military. McClellan was born into a prominent Philadelphia family, with social and political connections that the family was not shy about leveraging, including asking President John Tyler in 1842 to intervene in favor of young George's application to West Point.[1] Self-confident and driven, McClellan's promise shined at the military academy despite entering as a cadet a full year younger than the minimum age of sixteen. As an engineering officer, McClellan served in the Mexican–American War as well as other peacetime assignments before resigning his commission in 1857 with the rank of captain. In civilian life, McClellan translated his military experience conducting land surveys for the planned transcontinental railroad into lucrative positions with the Illinois Central Railroad (chief engineer and vice president) and the Ohio and Mississippi Railroad (president).

It is hardly surprising given his achievements and family status that McClellan was courted by several governors to lead their state militias at the outbreak of the Civil War. Selecting Ohio over Pennsylvania and New York, McClellan was commissioned a Major General of the volunteers and took command of the Ohio militia on April 23, 1861. Less than two weeks later, McClellan was appointed Commander of the Department of the Ohio, which would encompass Ohio, Illinois, Indiana, Missouri, western Pennsylvania, and western Virginia. Catapulting ever higher, on May 14, 1861, at the age of thirty-four, George B. McClellan was commissioned as a major general in the regular army, leaving only Winfield Scott as his superior in rank. (See figure 4.1.)

Success breeds success. Or so must President Lincoln have hoped when he selected McClellan to replace McDowell. At the Battle of Philippi on June 3, 1861, and on July 11 in the two-hour Battle of Rich Mountain, and again two days later in the fight at Corrick's Ford, McClellan's forces had successfully challenged Confederate soldiers in areas of western Virginia that sought to remain in the Union. Though more like skirmishes than battles, reporters heralded these wins as the mark of a great leader—exactly what Northerners craved in the aftermath of Bull Run. The tide of public opinion helped wash this young, cocksure Pennsylvanian to Washington to put the Union war effort back on firm footing.

GEORGE B. Mc CLELLAN.

FIGURE 4.1   George B. McClellan. Library of Congress,
Prints & Photographs Division, Civil War Photographs.

The men of the 27th NY Volunteers looked no farther than their own
regiment for leaders they would gladly follow in the tender time after Bull
Run. Brigade Commander Colonel Andrew Porter (who assumed the role of
division commander after Colonel David Hunter was wounded) wrote in his
official report of the battle: "Among those who deserve special attention are
Col. H.W. Slocum, who was wounded while leading his gallant Twenty-Sev-
enth New York to the charge; and Maj. J.J. Bartlett, who subsequently commanded it, and by his enthusiasm and valor kept it in action and out of panic."[2]
When Slocum hobbled into camp on crutches on August 13, still recuperating

from the bullet wound to his thigh from Bull Run, it must have been bitter-
sweet to have been so joyfully reunited with his men while knowing his promotion would necessarily remove him from their immediate command. On
August 9, 1861, Slocum had been appointed brigadier general of volunteers in
William B. Franklin's division of the Army of the Potomac.

For Joseph Chambers, the Battle of Bull Run proved to be the end of any
aspirations he may have had in military service. Derided by his men and largely
absent during the battle, his performance as lieutenant colonel of the 27th NY
Volunteers left him little choice but to resign. The day that Slocum visited the
regiment, he presented quite a contrast to his departing second in command.
An Albany newspaper caustically reported at the time: "Joseph J. Chambers . . .
is now tired of war's alarms and resigns his commission. So they go!"[3] In a
letter to his father on August 6, 1861, Rollin did not spare his disdain for the
resigning elite as he mused about the drawbacks to promotion for himself.

August 6, 1861

Dear Father
    The advice and caution I received in your letter this morning
is thankfully received and will be strictly adhered to. You notice in
the lines I have written to Mother the amount I rec'd is $15.04, ten
of which I shall send to you for safekeeping, etc. I find considerable
employment in Col's office, which is a great help to me, both as regards the pay I receive and many privileges which the other soldiers
do not enjoy. As regards promotion, I have come to the conclusion
that I am more pleasantly situated as I am than to hold some petty
Co office and like all other officers receive more or less curses from
the Co which is invariably the case.
    You speak of George Crandall's patriotism not being the sound-
est kind. I am well persuaded that one half the officers and men
enlisted in the volunteer force never expected to see active service,
and to substantiate this opinion I would say that seven commissioned officers in the 27th Regt resigned immediately after their
return from Bulls Run, including Lieut Col Chambers, who, by the
way, has proved himself to be a curse to the ground he treads, and
the most unpopular man in the Regt.
    As to the duties I have to perform as a regular soldier, they are
not very great. I believe I have been out to drill once since we came

to Washington, and at the gait I now swing, if I do not get lazy before my time is up, it will be one of the seven wonders.

Isaac L. Post is in town, probably looking after an office of
some kind.[4]

George Grey sends his respects to you.

Yours affectionately

R. B. Truesdell

To: Saml W. Truesdell

Great Bend

Susquehanna Co, Pa

Waiting patiently in the wings, the man who had taken up the reins from
the incapacitated leader of the 27th NY Volunteers amidst absolute anarchy
was ready to assume command. Rollin cheered when Binghamton native J. J.
Bartlett leapfrogged from major to colonel and was elected by the regiment
to serve as its new commanding colonel on September 5, 1861. That same day,
Rollin and his comrades elected Alexander D. Adams as their lieutenant colonel. Bartlett was commissioned on September 21, 1861.

FIRST THINGS FIRST

The placement of worthy men in leadership positions—from the regimental
level to the very top—was an indispensable tonic to ward off morale issues
in the Union Army after the failure at Bull Run. In the days that followed,
Northerners had twin concerns: (1) Is Washington adequately protected from
Confederate attack? If there are vulnerabilities, where are they and how quickly
can we plug them? (2) How soon can we hit back and take control of this war
to preserve our Union?

In a letter to his father written on August 12, 1861, Rollin's tone is light
yet somewhat tenuous, reflective of the weight of uncertainty about how and
by whom the Union Army would be led.

Washington, D. C.

Aug 12th 1861

Dear Father

Your letter of the 10th I received yesterday. You say you think
of paying me a visit next month. Nothing would suit me better
than to have you spend a few days with me, but whether it would

be policy for you to come next month is a matter of doubt in my mind, in consequence of the great heat which is upon us now, and which will continue, probably, 'til October. The sun's rays here are as penetrating as a lance, and from 9 A.M. 'til dusk it is impossible to do anything. I think you would enjoy yourself far better to wait 'til the weather is cooler.

Nicholas DuBois will leave here for Gt Bend tomorrow. I send by him $10, and my watch. I begin to think that less valuables I have about me the better. If you can, I want you to send me by Mr. Dubois a box of apples, a few dried berries, and any other kinds of fruit that you can. The retail price of eating apples here is four cents apiece and other kinds of fruit in proportion.

I have sent a gun (captured from a secessionist at the late battle) to you by a Mr. Dawson of Binghamton and ordered it left at Mays Hotel where you can get it in a few days, provided it is not taken as U.S. property by some government officer. It has letters A. L. Co H 1st Reg Ala cut with a knife on the stock. If it gets home safe, I would not take any money for it. It cost me five dollars here.

There is no particular war news to write. A large army is being concentrated on the Va side of the river, and probably when Gen Scott gets good [and] ready he will blow Bulls Run, Manassas gap, and Richmond into a warmer climate. I saw a mortar going over the river night before last which looked to me like a big 12 foot hollow butted pine log. It took seven horses to draw it.

My love to all

Yours aff
R. B. Truesdell

To: S. W. Truesdell
Gt. Bend, Pa

Eight days after Rollin wrote that letter, George McClellan ascended to the position of commander of the Army of the Potomac. Presumably, he would be the best man to answer the twin security questions burning on Northerners' minds—but McClellan wasn't doing much talking.

George McClellan's reputation for keeping best counsel with himself was on display from his first days in Washington. As a member of the 27th NY Volunteers wrote in a letter home about McClellan: "I was talking with a reporter downtown and asked about movements of troops, but he said he didn't know and couldn't find out . . . If he succeeds in keeping [Confederate General] Beauregard as ignorant of his program as he does us about Washington, he will do more than any General who has preceded him."[5] Later to be judged as superciliousness by President Lincoln and other military leaders, McClellan's penchant for secrecy and not divulging his strategic plans (even to his superiors) kept the rumor mill in full operation while also buying time to organize his forces.

McClellan sought to create order and discipline in this hybrid army of regular and volunteer soldiers. Continued training would be imperative, and would take some time. He hoped to resolve other faults through tighter restrictions on the men's privileges. Within days of his appointment in July, McClellan ordered both officers and soldiers to remain in their camps (unless they had a pass) as a check against drunkenness. Reports of drunken officers had ricocheted through the newspapers, and McClellan was determined to put a stop to them. The New York newspaper *The Independent* sermonized on July 29, 1861: "We rejoice that, at length, public attention begins to be aroused to the importance of lessening the temptations to intemperance which have threatened to demoralize our armies, and which were doubtless a chief cause of our disasters."[6] The editorial added that sixty regiments had been supplied with 1,000 temperance tracts for soldiers to study. Sobriety, in all senses of the word, was in demand.

The men of the 27th NY Volunteers had little time to contemplate such literature before they received the order to march. On August 14, 1861, they were assigned to Brigadier General Samuel P. Heintzelman's brigade and recrossed the Long Bridge from Washington into Alexandria, Virginia. Once there, the men were issued their first tents and exchanged their muskets for US Springfield rifles, which they carried for the rest of their term of service.[7] They were fortunate; the Springfields were not widely distributed within the Union forces at that point in the war.[8] The regiment now possessed the accoutrements for the long haul.

Rollin, held back from departing Washington with the rest of the 27th NY due to an unrelenting cold, spent a few days in the posh care of the DeFrees family in Washington to recuperate. John D. Defrees was appointed by President Lincoln to be "Superintendent" of Public Printing in 1860 and maintained a rather luxuriant lifestyle—particularly in comparison to camp. In a pair of letters dated August 14 and August 18, 1861, Rollin updated his father and sister Clara of his whereabouts, detailing the indulgences of this interlude in soldiering for Clara.

Washington D.C.
Aug 14th 1861

Dear Father

Our Reg received orders last night to march to Alexandria to-day, and by this time (eleven o'clock A.M.) I suppose they are well on their way there, as they left here at eight.

We have had several showers of rain here since Sunday, some very heavy ones, and today the air is cool, and things begin to look like life again as regards the temperature of the atmosphere and Scott's boa constrictor. It is evident that another forward movement will be made soon as our forces are concentrating at different points on the Va side of the river and will all move together toward the gap and cut off the rebels supplies. When this is effected, "we've got 'em."

Reuben S. Ives called to see me yesterday. He lives fifteen miles below here on the Maryland side of the river. Himself and family are well. None of the Ives's have heard from Uncle Reuben since the Bulls Run battle.

I am well convinced in my own mind, though I could not tell it for a fact, that Charlie Trowbridge is a prisoner in Richmond. I saw McCauley of Susq. Depot here on Sunday. His son is a prisoner.

I suppose you would naturally enquire why I did not go with my Reg, a question I will answer. The sudden change in the weather on Sunday from oppressive heat to cool and damp rather took me off my pins. I took a very severe cold and have been quite under the weather for two days, but I feel quite well today and shall go down to Alexandria by boat tomorrow and join the Reg.

Soldiers are now the most popular people in town. I am stop-ping with the Hon. Mr Defrees, Government printer. True it is much better and more comfortable than camp fare, but about a me-dium between the two would suit me better. You will continue to direct your letters as before our Reg moved. There is no post route farther southward than this place. The mails are carried to each Reg daily by a messenger from this post.

My love to all.

Yours truly
R. B. Truesdell

To: S. W. Truesdell
Gt. Bend, Pa

Washington Aug 18th 1861

Dear Sister

I have not received any tidings from home since last Sunday, but suppose I have one or more letters down at the encampment which I shall receive sometime, but perhaps not in two or three days.

When I last wrote, I intended to go down to Alexandria the next day, but my cold clung to me with such brotherly love, mine hostess positively forbade my going into camp until I was perfectly well. Indeed "Sis," I have a duck of a place to stay, just like home as far as kindness, care, and attention are concerned, but their style of living is entirely different. The family consists of Mr. Defrees and wife, five children—the eldest about fifteen, the youngest three. And a nephew aged twenty-two and a niece aged twenty. The house is large and furnished "a la Paris," and three servants to keep it in order. We breakfast in the morning at eight o'clock on meat of some kind, and hot shortcake or pancakes, and coffee. Lunch at twelve: cake and fruit. Dinner at four: beef steak and potatoes boiled, green corn, beans, tomatoes, beets, etc., with pie, pudding, ice cream, custard, and watermelon for dessert. Lunch at eight: tea, bread and butter, sauce, and cake. "Who wouldn't be a Soldier?"

Troops are coming into Washington in immense numbers. Such an army was never gathered together in America. I think the newspaper reporters have got quietus put upon them by the war department, and it is now quite a common occurrence to see a thousand or two troops march into Va without reading about it the next day in half a dozen New York papers. We understand by rebel prisoners just brought in that their leaders are put to their wits end to find out any information in regard to our forces, plans, etc.

Tell Mother I am happy as a clam in high water, and am coming home in a couple of years, when my time is out, if I live, but I don't expect to see the end of this war before that time. More anon.

My love to all.

Your aff brother,
R. B. Truesdell

To: "Clara"

After only a few days at Camp Vernon near Alexandria, the 27th NY Volunteers moved camp west to an area near Fort Ellsworth.[9] Perched on an elevated position overlooking the southern approaches to Alexandria, the Orange and Alexandria rail lines, and the Little River Turnpike, the fort was one of six quickly erected to defend Washington prior to the battle of Bull Run. Rollin rejoined his comrades here, clearly exuberant to be back in the fold. His letters to his father and sister of August 22, and mother on August 24, brim with confidence and enthusiasm and impatience. How long must he wait for the next battle to commence?

Camp Slocum below Alexandria
Aug 22nd 1861

Dear Father

I received a letter from you this morning which I will answer immediately to appease your anxiety for my welfare, etc. Everything is quiet in camp today, but we know not the moment we might be called out. We are in close quarters with the rebels, the pickets often exchanging shots. Our Co will be on picket guard on Sunday next. I hope to see some fun with "secesh."

The gun I sent home is returned to me, Mr. Dawson not daring to run the gauntlet of US officers. I mean to get it home some time, if possible.

I think Charles Trowbridge is a prisoner in Richmond, a man by that name being reported in the list of prisoners. I am not positive, but hope it is him. Van Valkenburg was either killed or taken prisoner at the battle.

We have a capital camping ground. It is situated on a little mound, and in fair view of the Potomac, off from which a cool breeze is constantly blowing. There is but little shipping on the river, a few sailing craft and occasionally a small steamer.

We are having the best time now that we have had since I enlisted. Just excitement enough to keep the camp wide awake. The Co from our Reg on picket guard yesterday brought in a contraband negro, a bright mulatto boy, who was servant to a rebel Capt. When brought in, he was the happiest piece of flesh I ever saw. He says the rebel soldiers are very discontented and fare tough enough.

Col. Slocum has gone to Syracuse to recruit. He will not have command of us anymore, I suppose.

Ed Watson and Burrows are both well.

You need not send me anything as it is doubtful if I could get them.

My love to all

Yours aff
R. B. Truesdell

Camp Slocum below Alexandria
Aug 22—1861

Dear Sister Clara

I received your letter this morning enclosed in one from Father and since I have received it have thought more about home than I have before in some time. Your reminding me of the Liberty folks takes me among them in imagination and I can see the faces of many of them, especially the wry ones of R. Kenyon Jr. & Co. I imagine there is some indignation felt in that tribe. I would like to see many of the Liberty people and hope I may live to walk the golden Sts of "Sicklag" once more. But just at present I am engaged in more profitable business. I love a soldier's life. I love the excitement connected with it.

Fort Ellsworth lays on a hill to the north of us with its "squint eyes" looking smilingly toward the enemy. I hope to see the lips of those monster guns open upon the traitors at an early day. I feel confident of success next time and impatiently await the order to march.

Give my love to all.

In haste
Your aff Bro
R. B. Truesdell

Camp Slocum
Aug 24th 1861

Dear Mother

Having a little leisure time this morning, I thought I could not better improve it than by writing to you, though I have written home once since I received any letter from you, but knowing your anxiety, I will write as often as I have an opportunity.

I have now had about a week's experience in camping out on the ground. I must say, I stood it first-rate, much better than I expected. We are provided with good tents, each six feet square, which accommodates five persons, so you see we do not have a great deal of sea room, yet they are proof against the weather, and make us comfortable. Everything in the shape of a table is necessarily dispensed with. I do my writing on the bottom of my tin plate, resting it on my knee. My bed is made by laying my rubber blanket on the ground and doubling the one I brought from home making it answer for an "underlid," as well as a coverlid. In this bed I sleep as soundly as I ever did on feathers.

Our food is good, and though we have not a great variety, meat, bread, and coffee being the extent, it relishes first-rate, and I can eat a piece of dry bread and drink a cup of coffee without milk just as easy as I could eat the whole of a good pie at home. I never find any fault with food that makes me as healthy and strong as I am now.

The weather is now cool and pleasant, and we have a good breeze off from the water from nine o'clock A.M. 'til evening.

We expected to be attacked by the rebels two or three days ago, but they failed to come to "time," and when we shall have a combat time only will decide. It may be today and it may be weeks. We are ready for them and wait impatiently for a reconnoitre with them.

I can write no more this time. Give my love to all my friends, and remember me as

Your aff son

R. B. Truesdell

To: Mrs. Lucy Truesdell
Gt Bend, Pa

The day after Rollin penned this letter to his mother, Commanding General McClellan visited Rollin and his comrades in the camps surrounding Washington. Equal parts brigade review and fortification assessment, field visits enabled McClellan to demonstrably encourage his troops, as well as to check the progress of the enhanced bulwarks encircling the capital. McClellan had wasted little time in diagnosing and seeking to correct the deficiencies in Washington's defenses and was gratified to rely on fellow engineer John Gross Barnard to design the network of protection. Over the course of the war, Chief Engineer of the Army of the Potomac Barnard oversaw the construction of sixty-eight forts (linked by twenty miles of trenches) in which ninety-three mounted artillery batteries projected the strength of 807 cannon and ninety-eight mortars in a thirty-seven-mile ring around the city.[10] Constructing this mammoth engineering feat necessarily required extensive manpower. Units in the vicinity, including the 27th NY Volunteers, were inducted to help.

On August 26th, each company in the 27th NY Volunteers was directed to send a detail to cut the woods and clear the ground for the construction of Fort Lyon (so named for Brigadier General Nathaniel Lyon, killed on August 10, 1861, at the Battle of Wilson's Creek in Missouri). Rollin and his comrades did not begin to move camp closer to the site, just south of Fort Ellsworth across Hunting Creek, until September 12, after having been reassigned to a new brigade. The men were reunited with their former commander when they were detached from Heintzelman's brigade and attached to Brigadier General Slocum's, along with the 16th and 26th NY Volunteers and the 5th Maine Volunteers, on September 5, 1861.

Rollin wrote to his eldest sister Julia on September 12, careful to include some good-natured brotherly ribbing even as he answered her request for details about his day-to-day as he settled into a soldier's life in the field.

Camp Vernon Alexandria Va
Sept. 12th 1861

Dear Sister Julia

Your letter of twelve lines and ten questions I received two days ago together with letters from Father, Mother, and Clara. Although it was very short, it was thankfully received, and longer ones written often will not come amiss.

You want to know all about myself, etc. I can tell you in a few words the duties I have to perform. The "Co" is drummed up at five o'clock A.M. for roll call, after which every man sees that his gun is in order and prepares himself for breakfast. This meal we eat at half past six and consists of coffee (one pint), and a piece of pork or beef. For dinner, we have meat but no coffee, and for supper boiled beans, rice, or hominy, with coffee. Every morning we draw a loaf of good bread and three ounces of sugar. These rations are of sufficient quantity and of good quality to keep hunger away. In pleasant weather, we drill from 9½ o'clock A.M. 'til 11 o'clock, and from 4 'til 5½ P.M. The rest of the time is occupied as each man is disposed.

There have been some important changes in this Reg since the battle of July 21st. Col. Slocum is promoted to Brigadier General, and having recovered from the wound he received, is now in command of this brigade and Jos. J. Bartlett is promoted from Major to Col.

This brigade is now building a fort two miles below here to be called fort Slocum.[11] This Reg worked on the trenches yesterday and will probably work each alternate day 'til the fort is completed. We are getting things in readiness today and are going to move our camp down to the new fort tomorrow so as to be near our work.

You say you are afraid I will get lazy and lousy. I think I am a little lazy, but lice and I don't agree at all. I am not troubled with them. I take great pains to keep myself clean and I entertain no fears of getting sick or lousy.

The weather here is now cool and pleasant. I enjoy myself first-rate.

I am writing on a board (a borrowed one) laid across my knees. It is an uncomfortable position, and I can write no more this time.

My love to all.

Your aff brother
R. B. Truesdell

Address care Capt Jay,
Co F. 27th Reg
N.Y.V.
Washington D.C.

Writing to his father the next day, Rollin mentioned his appreciation of Commanding General McClellan's oversight of the grand fortification construction project—and indeed of McClellan himself. Likening himself to famed Scottish diplomat and abolitionist David Turnbull, who revealed the continued trade of enslaved people in Cuba and Puerto Rico in 1840, and McClellan to former Pennsylvania Governor Joseph Ritner (1835–1839), who was an anti-slavery advocate, subject of an abolitionist poem by John Greenleaf Whittier, and delegate to the first Republican National Convention in 1856, Rollin allegorically gave his stamp of approval.

Fort Slocum, Old Virginia
Sept 13th 1861

Dear Father

We moved our camp yesterday from Alexandria two miles south onto the top of a hill where we are building a new fort. It is a good position for defense. We have a good view of Washington which is nine miles to the north of us. I can plainly see the stars and stripes flying from the Capitol.

I am now taking my nooning, having been out to work in the trenches of the fort this forenoon. There are four Reg's to work in the trenches, viz the 16th, 26th, 27th N.Y. and 5th Maine. Although we do not work hard, we accomplish a great deal of work in a day.

We are now encamped within three miles of a Rebel force estimated to be three thousand strong, which is about the strength of our Brigade. Greene's Battery of 12 pieces of field artillery is in an ambuscade in our rear, ready to support us in case we are attacked. General McClellan has an eye to all the fortifications, inspecting them frequently. I have had the Hon. of seeing him several times, and from his looks, think same by him as old Turnbull did by Gov. Wretner [sic].

The health of the army is good, no malignant or particular disease prevailing.

I must stop for the present.

Yours truly
R. B. Truesdell

To: Saml W. Truesdell
Gt. Bend, Pa

Over the course of the next month, the regiment labored to transform the clearing with a view of the Potomac River, Washington, Alexandria, and the green valley of Hunting Creek into Fort Lyon. The fort covered nine acres with a 937-yard perimeter. As Rollin's friend William Westervelt later wrote: "We put aside our drilling and exchanged our guns for the pick and shovel; we looked and acted more like railroad laborers than soldiers."[12] (See figure 4.2.)

As the novelty of the trench digging for the new fort subsided, Rollin's thoughts were of his mother and home.

Fort Slocum
Sept. 17th 1861

Dear Mother

Your letter was most thankfully received with others from home, and but one thing did I regret in regard to it, viz it was altogether too short. But I am extremely thankful for small favors in the way of letters from you, and larger ones in proportion.

I am so busy nowadays that I cannot write home quite so often as I have done, but as soon as the fort is completed, I will write oftener.

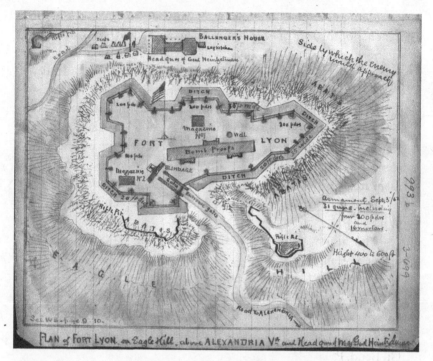

FIGURE 4.2   Plan of Fort Lyon on Eagle Hill above
Alexandria, Virginia, Robert Knox Sneden. Library of
Congress, Geography and Map Division.

My health is good. I am in good spirits, and indeed, I do not
feel uncomfortable in any respect. I enjoy a good rainstorm at night
very much. The pattering on my tent sounds just as it used to when
I slept close up under the roof of the old red house when I was a
child.

Write me a few lines occasionally. It is getting dark, so good
night and God bless you.

Yours aff

R. B. Truesdell

The work to build the fort was tedious and only occasionally broken by
picket duty. The days separated from camp, pushed toward the enemy, were a
welcome break from digging drudgery—and fodder for subsequent storytelling. In Rollin's jovial letter to his father of September 23, 1861, he described
his most recent picket duty and informed him of the steps he had taken to help
his father into a recruiting agent position.

Fort Slocum
Sept 23rd 1861

Dear Father

Your favors of a late date were duly received and answered in a letter to sister Julia, but I have a little leisure time this afternoon, so I will write again.

I have just returned from a picketing excursion on our outposts on the Fairfax road, distant from here about five miles, and from Fairfax, nine. The regular picket posts of the contending armies on this road are within one mile of each other and scouts from either party are constantly creeping out to hit his adversary a sly poke in the short ribs. We occasionally take a prisoner, which makes fun for the boys in camp when he is brought in, but if we kill one, it is talked of lightly and counted hardly worth noticing. Myself in company with three others crept up toward their outpost yesterday and tried to get a peep at them, but in vain. As we went creeping along through the scrub pine woods, I could think of nothing but hunting partridges on burndt hill. But we saw nothing, heard nothing.

We are now armed with new Springfield rifles, "a tiptop article," and from the trial I have made with mine, I have come to the conclusion that a rebel would stand "no fag at all at forty rods."

In your last letter, you expressed the wish that you had the power to enlist men and forward them to a place of rendezvous, etc. I immediately laid the matter before Col Bartlett who made out an application to the war department to have you appointed a regular recruiting agent, and General Slocum and himself signed it, and it is forwarded to the department at Washington. But under the present press of business, it may be thirty days before your application is reached. I think there is no doubt but what you will receive the order to recruit and the necessary instructions, etc.

I received a letter from Bro Albert today.

Write often. My love to all

Yours aff.
R. B. Truesdell
US Army

Another picket duty a week or so later left a particular impression on Rollin and his comrades. On October 3, Rollin's company (F) and companies from the 5th Maine and 26th New York were sent out after dark under the command of Colonel William H. Christian of the 26th NY. The men marched south all night, passed through the village of Occoquan until meeting Rebel outposts near Pohick Church around dawn, and then were ordered back rather than to try and capture enemy pickets. Westervelt sputtered: "Our doughty Colonel called us back . . . after examining the church and pew that General Washington and his family used to occupy, we started to return, reaching camp about 4pm, having marched some 30 miles on the round trip on about as useless an errand as a body of tired men were ever sent upon."[13] There would be much time to retell this story over the long winter months ahead.

CAMP LIFE

With Fort Lyon almost complete, the 27th NY Volunteers and the rest of General Slocum's brigade transitioned to their winter quarters approximately four miles north of Fort Lyon on October 14, 1861. Joining the brigades of Generals Philip Kearny and John Newton, the three comprised Pennsylvanian Brigadier General William B. Franklin's division within the Army of the Potomac. Drilling resumed until the mud was so persistent that movement was virtually impossible in mid-winter.

On November 20, 1861 (six days before the 96th Pennsylvania replaced the 26th New York in Slocum's brigade), President Lincoln and General McClellan conducted an inspection of the Army of the Potomac at Bailey's Crossroads. Accompanied by Secretary of War Simon Cameron, Secretary of State William H. Seward, and other cabinet members, Lincoln and McClellan reviewed almost 100,000 soldiers—a massive show of force. The regimental history noted: "The 27th received special praise for the splendid division lines maintained, in spite of the muddy and slippery condition of the ground over which they passed. This review was one of extraordinary grandeur, and it seemed as if there were troops enough to move through the Confederacy without a repulse."[14] And Rollin reported in a letter home on December 7 that New York Governor Morgan, simultaneously serving as Major General of Volunteers for the Department of New York, followed this with his own appraisal of New York Volunteers in Franklin's division on December 6, 1861.

As autumn slid into winter, the routine of camp life slowly took hold. For Rollin, idle time invariably ushered in thoughts of home. News came by way of regular newspaper deliveries, as well as cherished letters from family and friends. Rollin enjoyed reading the *Independent Republican* (published in Susquehanna County, Pennsylvania), which arrived at camp on a weekly basis.

Undoubtedly missing attending Sunday church services with his family, he wrote a letter to his mother on October 20, connecting with her the only way he could—via letter.

Camp Franklin Va
Sunday Oct 20th 1861

My Dear Mother,

I have written several letters home since I have received any, but I suppose writing so often to me is getting to be an old story, but I am quite different. I like to receive as many as I write, but if I don't, it will make no odds to me. I will try to keep you well informed in regard to my situation, condition, etc.

I have just come in from inspection of arms, an operation we have to go through with every Sunday. I say inspection of arms, but that is too limited a term for those not versed in military affairs to understand. It is an inspection of everything a soldier has and being inspected is regarded by a soldier in the same light as civilians regard going to church. The soldiers all take a great deal of pains to appear well and look well on Sunday.

Our Chaplain is on a visit to his home, consequently we have no religious service on the grounds today, something which has not occurred before in a long time.

We are taking things very cool at present, and quite likely shall until we are ordered into the field. When this will be you know as well as I do, but soon, I hope. I am more anxious than ever to have an attack made upon the menacing rebels in our front than I ever was before.

I received a copy of the Republican today. It is a welcome visitor, I assure you.

I hope the next missive I receive from home may contain a few lines from you. Give my love to all "inquiring" friends and remember me as

Your aff son,
Rollin B. Truesdell

And after Sunday worship on October 27, Rollin again found himself writing to his parents. This time, his longings for the comforts of home met his entrepreneurial spirit. A fifty-pound tub of butter sure would be delicious—and lucrative—in the midst of the gauging sutlers at camp!

Camp Franklin
Sunday, Oct. 27th 1861

My Dear Parents

As I sat dreamily in my tent this afternoon, weary from the morning inspection and the religious worship which soon followed, and an hour's reading, I could not resist picking up my portfolio and spending the sunset hour in writing to you, though I have written twice since I have received any letters from you.

I must acknowledge receipt of the Independent Republican, which I received this morning, a welcome visitor that I now receive regularly every Sunday morning. It is truly refreshing to read the letters from Susq Co volunteers, especially those from Liberty. I was quite amused while reading one from Wallace Southworth who tells quite a "tough" story, yet true.

It reminded me of your oft told stories of the first settlement of Susq Co when you could see the stars through the roof from your cot when waking in the night. I too can see them every night through my tent door which is so shrunk that it will not quite close. I think I can match some of those yarns, if I live to see home, which I hope I may.

The weather here is what I would call "variable," but as I have not seen an almanac in some months, I can't say what "Becket" calls it. We have warm days and cool nights, and almost every third day it rains, which makes it anything but agreeable soldiering, but we are getting used to it and "like it" for the reason we can't help ourselves.

There is no war news of importance. Things remaining the same as when I last wrote, but the "wise" predict an engagement at no distant day, a prediction which I fully indorse from my observation of the moving elements of war. Yet so often are we disappointed that it is useless to predict anything, for no one but those high in office know anything about anything of importance.

Our camp is besieged daily by a swarm of hucksters, who sell their trash at an exorbitant price. Butter sells readily at thirty cents per pound. If butter is not worth more than fifteen cents at Great Bend, if you are a mind to send me a tub of fifty pounds, I think I can "eat some" and sell the rest for enough to pay all expenses. I think there would be no risk in sending it, as many of the boys are receiving boxes and bundles from home that come all right. If you send it, put on the same address as on a letter, only send to Alexandria instead of Washington, and send by express freight.

I have no more time to write tonight, so good-bye. My love to all.

Yours Aff

R. B. Truesdell

U.S.A.

To: Saml W. Truesdell

Gt. Bend Pa

For Rollin, his duties as company clerk would help to occupy time through the fall and winter. Company clerks were either noncommissioned officers or privates known to have good penmanship and a capacity for keeping good reports and records; they represented the heart of cost control for the army during the Civil War.[15] Announcing his appointment in a letter to his father and sister, Clara, in November 1861, Rollin took pride in being selected to a post that, done correctly, was critical for maintaining morale in his unit. As such, top on the list of Rollin's duties was payroll as he wrote to his father on December 21—but that was only one of nine separate regular clerical tasks for which he was responsible.

Camp Franklin Va.

Nov 12th 1861

Dear Father & Sister

Your favors of Nov. 6th, I received last night. I had been looking for them some days and should have written to you this morning if I had not received them.

Camp life is getting pretty dull. The same routine of duty has to be gone through with every day, and when spiced with no fighting, goes long to me. But I am making the best of it that I can by a good hickory fire in my tent, a luxury that many of my fellow soldiers do not enjoy. But it is my luck to be "lucky" since I commenced military life.

I am now tenting with my Capt, and probably shall all winter. Since I enlisted, I have done no fighting, but little drilling, and a few day's work on Fort Lyon. I am now appointed "Co" clerk and excused from all military duty excepting general parades and inspections. Although the pay is no more than that of a private, it is the best berth on the "job." My time is but partially occupied with the business of the Co, consequently at our next pay day, I shall provide myself with the necessary books, and go to studying something that will be of future use to me. I enlisted to fight, but if I cannot do that, I will do something that will benefit myself, as far as lays in my power.

As to the future movements of the Army of the Potomac, I think the signs indicate no forward movement this winter. We have expected to move so many times and been disappointed that I have given up the idea.

The weather here is very fine. We have warm days and cool nights.

Genl Slocum is about, organizing a "Soldiers Land Co" on the principle of joint stocks. His Regt had such a Co in the Mexican war and at its close they had money enough in the bank to purchase seventeen thousand acres of land. I shall not invest.

I receive the Republican regularly every Saturday.

Please write often and write all items of news that you think will interest me.

My love to all.

Your aff son
R. B. Truesdell

To: Saml W. Truesdell

Camp Franklin Va
Dec 21, 1861

My Dear Father,

I have neglected writing longer than usual this time, but my reason is a good one, viz, I have been under the weather a little for the last few days, but today I pronounce myself sound and make it my business to write home. I received a letter from Bro Albert this morning and one from Sister Clara a day or two since. I always make it a point to answer one from you and one from Clara at the same time, but yours I have yet to receive.

I have been occupied all day in making out our payroll, which is no small job I assure you. The amount of writing on each sheet is about three thousand words, and upon the four, twelve thousand words. Do you wonder that I am fatigued? It is absolutely necessary that those pay sheets should be made out by tomorrow morning, but I think it exactly as necessary that I should write home immediately, that you may not be concerned about me.

The Steamer Pensacola went down the river from Alexandria this morning, and this afternoon we have heard heavy firing in the direction of Alyan Creek and Free Stone Point. I hope that it is a skirmish which will ultimately bring on a general engagement. But the cause of the firing, if of any consequence, you will learn by the papers before this missive reaches you.

Of late, there has been a great deal of sickness in camp. Yesterday, we sent the remains of Jesse P. Coon to his parents who live in or very near Brackneyville. We purchased a coffin worth fifty dollars, and the other expenses amounting in all to eighty dollars. This amount was readily and cheerfully given by the members of this "Co."

I have nearly concluded to board myself the remainder of this winter, thinking that in a case and place like this, it may not be policy to be too sparing of money and expose my health. What do you think of balancing money with health?

I am _tired_, _tired_, _tired_, so good night, and long life to you and all my friends at home.

Yours aff

R. B. Truesdell

To: Father

The men of the 27th NY Volunteers made Camp Clara, so named in honor of General Slocum's wife, as habitable as possible. As the regimental history recalled, many of the officers, having fixed up their quarters into comfortable shape, sent for their wives, and the camp, in some respects, seemed like a country village.[16] To withstand the cold, the men constructed log foundations for their tents, and fireplaces within. In a letter to his sister Clara, Rollin wrote of the first snowfall of the year on November 25, 1861, and the industriousness of the warmth-seeking soldiers.

Camp Franklin Va

Nov 25th 1861

My Dear Sister

I rec'd your letter and a sample of my dear old Mother's gown a day or two since. I also rec'd one from Mother "individually" a few days ago, and I assure you it does me more good to receive one letter from her than to receive two from anyone else.

This morning the hills and plains of the sunny south were draped in white, the first of the season, but before nine o'clock no vestige of the snowy drapery was to be seen, it being transformed into a coat of dirty mud. The chill winds of winter and those frosty nights reminds one very forcibly of the comforts of a home fireside. Comforts that it will be impossible for us to enjoy this winter but will put all of us in a way to appreciate those blessings if we live to see home again. The boys are building fireplaces in their tents which answer a very good purpose and keep them quite as comfortable as could be expected.

I received a letter from Bro Albert yesterday. He says he intended to make me a visit, but he did not know how strict the orders were in regard to crossing the Potomac. I wrote to him that I would like to see him but it was impossible for him to come nearer than Washington.

I want you to write often and write all the news. Tell "Ma" I thank her for the mittens and to keep them 'til I return for I am well provided with both mittens and socks.

My love to all

Your aff. Bro
R. B. Truesdell
U. S. A.

To: Clara

Persistent, Albert did not give up the idea of visiting his little brother easily. Rollin responded in a letter dated December 5, 1861, using humor to lead his brother away from his heartfelt, but unfeasible, request to come across the Potomac to call on him. Embedded within his letter to Albert, Rollin inserted an "Irish letter" dated November 30, 1861, that poked fun at the mythical author John Kelly to lighten the discourse with his brother.

Camp Franklin Va
Dec 5th 1861

Dear Bro'

I have just received two letters from you, both of which was thankfully placed to your credit on the "day book." I am sorry to hear of so much sickness and death in your vicinity, but those that die will cease to trouble and be troubled with accursed rebel secessionists and their unholy war against the government.

While meditating this afternoon in the sunshine in front of my tent, I was brought to my senses by a good sound slap upon my shoulder from the hand of the "millwright and particular framer" of Lawsville Centre, Lorenzo Vance who came about four miles to see me, and as he said, "religiously" keep a promise made to Father to hunt me up. He is a Sergeant in the sixty first NY Regt. I was glad to see him and entertained him as well as the luxuries of camp would afford. His health is good and he likes the service well. Turner Southworth will visit me soon.

In reply to your question "why" an order was issued prohibiting civilians to cross the Potomac, I must say that I have not had an opportunity to ask Genl McClellan. But such an order was issued and published in the papers, and is in force, but come on to Washington and I will try to get you over here some way.

I have just had a hearty laugh over an "Irish" letter and it is so rich I can afford to send you a copy.

Whitneys Point
Nov 30th 1861

Dear Brother

I take the opportunity of writing these few lines hoping to find you in health as this leaves me. I wish to inform you of the death of your Mother which is expected every moment. It is now ten o'clock. She will die about noon. I can write no more at present but will after the funeral which will probably take place on Tuesday.

No more at present from your John Kelly.

If this is not a good specimen, I'll give up.
Give my love to Frank and write often.

Yours truly
R. B. Truesdell

To: Albert Truesdell
Liberty Pa

Two days later, Rollin penned a letter to his parents. If the difficulties of crossing the Potomac weren't enough to dissuade his brother from visiting, perhaps the realities of his camp life would be! Home-cooked meals would never be far from the minds of the men as they contended with inadequately cooked rations by impatient cooks in the blustery cold. (See figures 4.3 and 4.4.)

Camp Franklin Va
Dec 7th 1861

My Dear Parents

I have not received any letter from you in some days, and I begin to think it time for me to write, or you will think me negligent and forgetting home. But I'll keep my promise good, "write, whether you do or not."

We begin to feel winter in real earnest, though as yet we have had but little snow, cold rains answering as a substitute. We can keep quite comfortable in our tents, the storms only affecting our cooking apparatus and compelling us to either eat our rations half-cooked or go without. The former is usually done, and the consequence is sickness. Generally, camp dysentery takes hold of the "biped" who is so uncareful as to eat half-cooked food to satisfy the demands of hunger. I have yet been free from that disease, but for the last two days I have been suffering severely with the toothache. It is the one I had broken off last spring, and I cannot have it extracted, or I would not have suffered what I have.

Lorenzo Vance made me a visit last week. He is well, also Turner, who is in the "Co" with him. They are encamped about four miles from here.

Major Genl Morgan reviewed the York State Volunteers in this Division yesterday.

There is no particular war news to write.

My love to all.

Yours aff
R. B. Truesdell
U. S. A.

To: S. W. Truesdell,
Great Bend, Pa.

A few days after writing to his parents, the weight of military life reached a new level when Rollin experienced a gruesome episode. On December 13, Rollin and the entirety of Franklin's division were made to bear witness to the execution of a soldier from the 1st NY Cavalry who attempted to

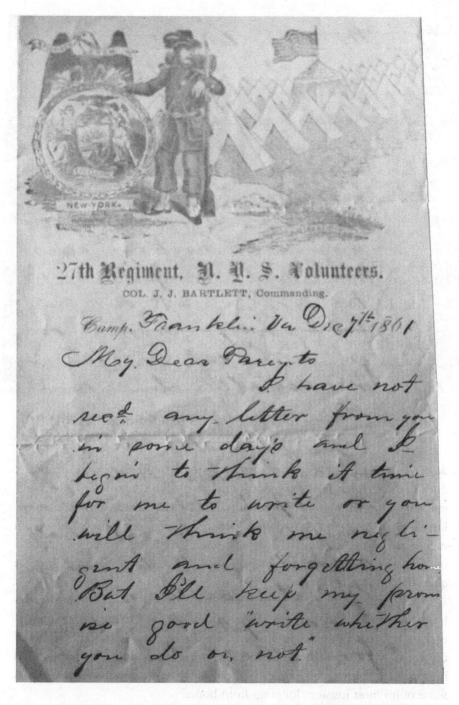

FIGURE 4.3   Letter to Rollin's Parents on December 7, 1861.

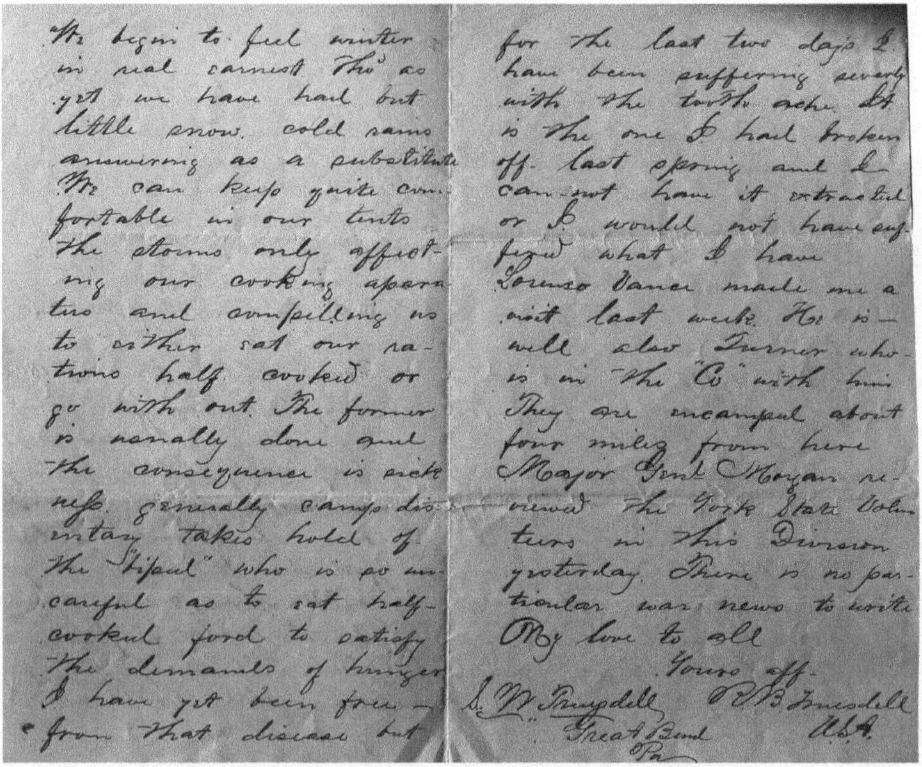

We begin to feel winter in real earnest. Tho' as yet we have had but little snow. cold rains answering as a substitute We can keep quite comfortable in our tents The storms only affecting our cooking apparatus and compelling us to either eat our rations half cooked or go with out. The former is usually done and the consequence is sickness. generally camp dis-entary takes hold of the "tipul" who is so un-careful as to eat half-cooked food to satisfy the demands of hunger I have yet been free— from that disease but for the last two days I have been suffering severly with the tooth ache. It is the one I had broken off last spring and I can-not have it extracted or I would not have suffered what I have Lorenzo Vance made me a visit last week. He is well also Turner who is in the "Co" with him They are encamped about four miles from here Major Genl Morgan re-viewed the York State Volun-teers in this Division yesterday. There is no par-ticular war news to write My love to all

Yours aff.
R. B. Truesdell
U.S.A.

S. W. Truesdell
Great Bend
Pa

FIGURE 4.4 Letter to Rollin's Parents on December 7, 1861.

desert and sacrifice his company to the enemy while they were on picket duty. The court martial delivered its sentence quickly; the soldier had mistakenly given himself up to a Union scout. The division watched as the deserter, kneeling on his coffin, was blindfolded and then shot in the chest by ten members of his company.[17] This tragic scene would be indelibly imprinted in Rollin's mind as he marched past the body and back to camp about a quarter mile away.

As if trying to blot the grim appointment later that afternoon from his head, Rollin wrote a letter to his sister earlier that day. He mentioned the execution but didn't dwell on it. Instead, he redirected himself and his family to the details of a special request he had of them. He had an idea for what would be helpful to him in his company clerk duties—and simultaneously soften some of his most insistent longings from home.

Camp Franklin Va
Friday Dec 13th 1861

My Dear Sister

Your favor of half a dozen dates I received yesterday, and I will answer it immediately, for I begin to think paper is getting scarce up north as of late my letters from home have been rather scattering.

We are having freezing weather now in the sunny south. It freezes nights and thaws days, making it muddy under foot when it does not rain, and when it does, "doubly so."

It is a kind of melancholy day in camp. No drill or military exercise of any kind. Why? A poor fellow that deserted and went over to the rebels is to be shot by order of a General Court Martial. The execution will take place about sixty rods from our camp this afternoon at three o'clock.

You ask how I kept Thanksgiving. I did not give thanks 'til Dec. 2nd, when we received a box of turkeys from Binghamton, which made me and all the rest of the soldiers from Broome Co a good dinner.

You spoke of sending me a box of <u>the good things of this world</u>. Well, send one, and put in the following articles: 1st, one loaf of good rye bread, and two of wheat; 2nd, three good long cotton shirts with bosoms and collar sewed on (the army ones are too short for winter use, but will make good wrappers); 3rd, I want Henry to make a box to send them in of the following dimensions, to answer for a bookcase to keep Co books and papers in. It must be 11 inches long and 11 deep, and of proportionate width, and partitioned off into pigeonholes so as to look something like this [small rough diagram]. The outside to be of inch board put together with screws, and the partitions to be of thin stuff, slipped in grooves so that they can be taken out and put in the bottom. The top to be on hinges with lock and key. When you send it, put the key inside, and fasten the top with screws. What spare room there is after putting in the articles I have mentioned, you may fill with eatables. Send the very best, for I get the <u>inferior</u> kinds here, and what I get from home, I want to taste <u>old fashioned</u>. Send it by express to Alexandria Va care of Capt Jay, and I'll get it sure. "Oh, put in a bottle of cider," do. Direct the same as a letter, only to Alexandria.

I never felt so well in my life as I do now. I am going to send you my photograph one of these days just to let you see how "fat" I am. I weigh 195 pounds. Astonishing, is it not?

Tell "Pa" and "Ma" to write often. Give my love to all the tribe and remember me as

Your aff Bro

Rollin B. Truesdell

To: my Sister Clara

P.S. Tell Julia to answer my letter immediately.

"Sis" I did not see that this sheet of paper was blotted 'til after I had wrote the first side.

Roll

Maintaining morale could be difficult during the restless winter as men dwelled on missed holidays with family and had few soldierly duties to fulfill. One afternoon, Colonel Bartlett provided a clever antidote. A comrade from Company B wrote affectionately of a Bartlett-instigated snowball battle: "Col. Bartlett thought the boys were aching for a fight, and ordered the Regiment to fall in without arms. The snow was about three inches deep and just soft enough to pack well. The Regiment was divided into five Companies on a side, and soon the snowballs were flying like grape and canister. The bugle would sound to retreat and rally. After about two hours snowballing, the Companies retired to their tents with sore heads and bloody noses."[18]

For Rollin, anticipating his custom-designed box filled with items that would remind him of the simple pleasures of life likely helped him endure his absence from family gatherings during Christmas. And then, like manna from heaven, his wait was rewarded. Rollin shared his joy in a letter thanking his loved ones for the gifts received on January 4, 1862. In his exuberance, Rollin contemplated drawing his father to camp for a visit.

Camp Clara Va

Jany 4th 1862

My Dear Parents, <u>Brothers</u>, Sisters, Nephews, and Nieces,

A happier "sojir" boy does not breathe than I am today. The box you sent me, a letter from Father, and one from Bro Albert I have just received. I have given a good share of the cakes to my companions, reserving only the chicken, bread, and butter for myself and Lieut. Yes I saved out the sausage and cheese. Words cannot express my thanks to you my dear friends for those articles and may The God of Heaven preserve you to a good old age is my prayer.

And as I stop to fold over this sheet my eyes fall on the one fingered mittens. May as many years be added unto the knitter's age as was added unto Hezekiah's.[19] And the old Jubilee, I was glad to see it.[20] My eyes were moist as they fell on the familiar tunes that I had so often sung in the old Church in Liberty.

That box and its contents makes home and friends more dear to me than ever. I trust I may live to see you face to face and thank you by the word of mouth. The bookcase too is just the thing I needed. If thanks would make you rich, I would make you all independent.

If you can, Father, I wish you would come and see me. The weather here is mild to what it is at Gt. Bend, though we think it cold enough in these tents.

I cannot write anything but thanks; especially I thank Frank for the chicken. Thanks, thanks to all and a hope that I may live to see you all.

Yours truly
R. B. Truesdell

To: My Dear friends at home

Only slightly less buoyant, Rollin wrote to his mother individually on January 8, 1862. Knowing that she was responsible for much of the contents of the care package, he wanted to thank her and let her know he was doing some bragging on her behalf.

Camp Clara Virginia
Jany 8th 1862

My Dear Mother

I have just lunched on a good piece of rye bread and butter and feel refreshed.

I spent an hour last Sunday with Genl Slocum. My affections are stronger for that man every time I meet him. I presented him with one of the rolls of butter which you sent me. He enquired if my Mother made it. I told him that she did. Well said he, give my compliments to your Mother.

I am growing fat every day. I was weighed yesterday. I weighed 197 pounds. When I weigh 200, I am going to send you my photograph. Among other modern conveniences which we have here in camp is a picture gallery. This camp is a stylish city, with some twelve thousand inhabitants.

Of late there has been considerable sickness in camp, but thus far I have met with no very serious "pull-back." I was some "inconvenienced" a few days ago with a bad cold, but now I am in the full vigor of health.

I am thinking strongly of getting a furlough and returning home in about sixteen months so have a good breakfast ready for me.

We are now enjoying the beauties of a Virginia winter. Mud and rain, and for variation, rain and mud. Soldiering in the "sunny" south is mighty delightful. It's a huge thing, but I have yet to see the real pleasure of it.

With a thousand thanks to all my relatives for kindnesses shown in times past, I am

Your aff. son
Rollin B. Truesdell

To: My Mother

Several days later, the whole regiment had reason to rejoice. On January 11, 1862, Rollin and the men of the 27th NY Volunteers received thirty comrades back to camp who had been taken prisoner during the Battle of Bull Run. The returning men were feted in grand style. Rollin and his mates decorated the company streets with evergreen; a brass band played "Bold Soldier Boy;" and General Slocum and field officers saluted the prisoners and escorted them through the regimental ranks.[21] The whole regiment cheered the thirty weary but determined men and guided them to camp.

As these heroes were traveling the final miles to reach Camp Clara, Rollin's tentmate and company captain, Peter Jay, was back in New York, apparently living up to his reputation as an erratic talker who liked to imbibe. Leaving no doubt as to the impression Jay left on Rollin's father when they met during this time, Rollin penned a letter to his father on January 13, 1862, in which he expressed chagrin for not seeing through Jay earlier. Rollin impressed upon his father that he was aggressively seeking promotion and opportunities to get out from under the captain's thumb while Jay was away. Rollin's eyes were on recruitment duty.

Camp Clara Va
Jany 13th 1862

Dear Father,

Your letters of the 9th and tenth I received this morning.

Your meeting with Captain Jay was no more or less that I could expect of him. He is a miserable drunkard—has few friends in this Regt. He has many peculiarities. He might abuse you in the most shameful manner today and use you like a (friend) tomorrow. I try to manage the best I can but I acknowledge that I was duped when I joined his Co. It is the opinion here that he will never return to take command of his "Co." It will be a blessing to us if he never does.

In regard to your coming to see me, two days ago I should have said come, but we are constantly undergoing changes. I have made an effort to be detailed on recruiting service and if I succeed, I shall be home in a few weeks. I shall know in the course of a week whether I go or stay.

I have some chance of promotion here in spite of Cap Jay. If he stays away four weeks, I will, I think, ask no odds of him for promotion. I have many friends in this Regt, and Capt Jay has none. In this respect I have the advantage of him and a good one too. If I once get a start where I will be exempt from his opinions as a superior Commanding officer through who all recommends have to go, I will be extremely thankful.

Lieutenant Cross is a fine man and is doing all he can for me in several directions. If I fail in one thing. I hope to be successful in another.

Cap Jay does not rule the 27th Regt yet and I do not think he is smart enough to keep me in the ranks always. If he is, I have yet to know it.

I have just been to dinner where I met Lieutenant A. G. Northrup, Co "D," from Binghamton, who told me that my recruiting papers were sure to go through and that I would probably be able to start for home in two weeks. I hope he is correct about it and that I shall get started by that time.

Lt Northrup is also going on the same business. He is a very fine man. A Vermonter of birth and before enlisted, a teacher in Susqua Seminary, Binghamton, N.Y. We are to report to his excellency Gov Morgan who will assign us a position where we are to open an office and keep it open six months unless recalled. I think that I shall like it better than military life in the field and I now think I am going "sure pop."

It is likely that I cannot remain at home many days, but if I have my health I assure you I will, with fervor, all the time I have to spare to the best of my ability.

I shall not write again 'til I know something definite of my future course, and the next you know you may see my face.

Yours aff

Rollin

To: Father

Rollin's request for recruitment duty was granted. Plan hatched, Rollin understandably felt impatient for his orders to be issued. He all but counted the minutes until he would be heading homeward and bubbled over with anticipation in a final letter to his sister Clara on January 21 before departing Camp Clara.

Camp Clara Virginia

Sunday Jany 21st 1862

Dear Sister Clara

A few days ago I thought I should not have to resort to pen and paper to communicate with you at this date for I was almost certain that I should spend this Sabbath day with loved friends at my quiet home among the hills of old Susquehanna. But Sister, we are ever doomed to disappointment, and my sense of duty compels me to keep my friends constantly posted as to my situation lest you get uneasy and think some ill luck has befell me. Although I am disappointed in seeing you today, I trust that before "St Valentines" day I shall cross the threshold of my Father's house. My papers are here and I am now only awaiting orders from Maj Sprague to report to Albany after which I shall draw a bee line for home. I may receive orders in two days, and it may be two weeks, but at all events not longer.

If I could find words in my vocabulary, I would describe to you the kind of weather we have been having here in the "Old Dominion" for the last few weeks but as there are no words in the English language that would give you the least idea of the quality and quantity of the mud, and I not understanding the dead languages, I can but use the simpler expression, "It is very muddy indeed." Jeff Davis in his proclamation to the people of this State called it "sacred soil," but I should move an amendment to that by inserting wet, muddy, soft, unholy, abominable before the word soil, and by striking out the word "sacred."

The temperature is not so very cold, but frequent storms of hail and rain, freezing nights, and thawing days makes it so muddy that it is next to an impossibility to stir without getting besmeared from head to foot.

I am again truly thankful to my friends at home for sundry articles for my comfort which I safely received via friend Burrows, who returned to camp one day before his furlough expired, an incident which reflects much credit upon him.

I was over to Washington on Friday and spent a couple of hours at our friend Nicholas DuBois' where I met Laville Lobdell. Of course I had a grand good visit (I always do there) and regretted that time was not my own, that I might not have prolonged my visit 'til the next day. Mrs. DuBois gave me a book to take home to Mother and said tell her, "that I kept the berries for Rollin as long as I could, and then ate them." I am well content that she used them for I am not the loser thereby.

Lorenzo Vance and Turner S was here to see me last week. They were both well and making the best of a soldier's life in the mud they could. They brought a goodly report from Messrs Beckwith, Simons, and Martial.

Wishing all my "friends and neighbors" all imaginable health and pleasure, I am

Your aff Bro
Rollin B. Truesdell

To: Sister Clara

In a little over a week, Rollin would exchange his windy, mud-enshrined tent for a toasty hotel room in New York City en route to Albany, where officials would reveal the specifics of his recruitment posting.

RECRUITMENT DUTY

Rollin's tenure as a recruitment officer for the Union Army was bookended by opposite extremes in volunteerism. Most emphatically prior to, but also during, the early spring of 1862 when Rollin was on the task, Northern patriotic fervor resulted in a steady stream of volunteers ready to enlist. Failure on the battlefield at Bull Run had only stiffened the resolve of many in the North to redouble efforts and quell the affront to the Constitution. A little more than two years later, with the willing and able already in the field, violent protesters in New York City made clear their fury over the Conscription Act of 1863 and the social and economic inequities they saw the law promulgating. Patience had run thin, and more was needed than patriotic appeals for volunteers to fill out the ranks of the Union Army. The manner of recruiting volunteers like Rollin, young men willing to surrender the bonds of home and risk sacrificing their very lives in order to answer President Lincoln's plea for help, necessarily evolved over the course of the war.

From Patriotic, Enthusiastic Volunteers to . . .

The post–Battle of Bull Run wakeup call was jarring. The Union Army could not expect to quickly extinguish the rebellion with the force it currently had under arms. President Lincoln immediately leveraged his Congressionally authorized power to organize an army of 500,000 men for three years or the duration of the war (and to increase the size of the force if he deemed it necessary). On July 22, 1861, he called for 300,000 volunteers.

In New York, Governor Edwin Morgan responded three days later with a proclamation for 25,000 more volunteers to be organized into twenty-five infantry regiments; and on July 30, he requested more volunteers to make up two additional cavalry and two additional artillery regiments.[1] The Governor also directed that the depots in Albany, New York City, and Elmira be reopened on July 31, 1861. One of Rollin's local newspapers, the *Broome Republican*, printed the Governor's order with the buoyant headline, "New York to the Rescue!"[2] (See figure 5.1.)

New Yorkers were reinvigorated; recruitment and organizing were in full throttle again after the President's and the Governor's proclamations. The *Binghamton and Broome County History* reminisced, "Day after day, the sound of drum and fife and the flag displayed, showed the places where recruiting was going on."[3] Individuals and private organizations, confidently shouldering their own recruitment efforts with the blessing of the War Department, frustrated and complicated state officials' work while bolstering the number of volunteers. New York opened additional branch depots to cope with the flood of new recruits.

In the weeks following the new call for volunteers, the federal government reduced the muddle around recruitment in New York (and other states) by streamlining some financial and organizational practices. A day after the line officers who were detailed to recruitment duty from the 27th NY Volunteers departed camp on August 14, 1861, the financial burden for recruitment (i.e., quartering, subsisting, uniforming, arming, transporting, and paying) shifted largely from states to the federal government.[4] Next, to Governor Morgan's relief, the Secretary of War ordered all parties who had previously been granted authority from his War Department to recruit and organize to instead report to the respective governors for direction as of September 5, 1861. Further consolidating oversight responsibilities, on October 26, 1861, President Lincoln appointed Governor Morgan commander of the newly created Military Department of New York with the title of Major General of United States Volunteers.

On December 3, 1861, via General Orders No. 105, the War Department put a halt on the governors' continued recruitment of regiments or independent companies except upon the special requisition of the War Department; incomplete ones were to be merged. The call for volunteers had been wildly successful. The 500,000-man volunteer force that Congress authorized was realized. By December 1, the War Department reported to the President a total troop strength of 660,971 volunteers and regulars in the Union Army.[5] From August to December 1861, New York recruited 75,339 volunteers for new and existing units (including 14,283 men recruited but not deployed).[6]

FIGURE 5.1 Union Guard Recruitment Poster. Library
of Congress, Rare Book and Special Collections Division,
Printed Ephemera Collection.

From January 1, 1862, onward, superintendents appointed from the regular army were to lead recruiting services in the loyal states. Commanding officers of regiments detailed two commissioned officers and four noncommissioned officers or privates to report in person to the superintendent at the respective depots for recruitment duty. Their focus would be to fill out existing regiments.

When recruitment was paused in April 1862, the volunteer enlistment rolls were bulging. However, this colossal force, significantly punctured in the battles to come during the early summer Peninsula Campaign under the leadership of Major General McClellan, would prove to be insufficient to defeat the secessionist enemy. This was not a message President Lincoln wanted to telegraph to Confederate President Jefferson Davis.

Already by mid-May, after a month of skirmishes in which Confederate General Thomas J. Jackson (better known by the sobriquet "Stonewall" due to his unflappable command during the Battle of Bull Run) dictated the terms of engagement in the Shenandoah Valley, the Secretary of War had capitulated to the necessity of drawing in more volunteers. On May 19, 1862, the War Department telegraphed Northern governors, asking them to raise new infantry regiments; New York was pressed to raise six more.[7] On June 6, by General Orders No. 60, the War Department formally restored volunteer recruiting service. Battles to come during the Peninsula Campaign quickly transformed the request for additional men into an imperative.

Secretary of State William H. Seward crafted an appeal for Northern governors to sign in which they implored the President to call upon the states for more volunteers. Going along with the humiliation-avoiding ruse, the governors signed the appeal, which was backdated to June 28, 1862. President Lincoln issued a call on July 2, 1862, for 300,000 new volunteers with a $25 enlistment bounty. And on July 17, 1862, Lincoln signed the Militia Act of 1862, which created the path for Black men to join the Union Army. This gave the President a lever to quickly enlist men by drafting them into the state militias. On August 4, the War Department issued General Orders No. 94, calling into immediate service 300,000 militia for nine months and added that if a state's share was not met by August 15, the deficit should be met through draft. General Orders No. 99, issued five days later, dictated that "all able-bodied male citizens between the ages of 18 and 45 within the respective counties," will be enrolled forthwith.[8] Secretary of War Stanton declared on August 14 that if states were unable to enlist sufficient volunteers to fill depleted existing regiments, a special draft would be ordered on September 1, 1862.

By this time, the bruised Union Army had chewed through thousands of men via battle wounds and illness. The tortuous wait for casualty lists of those killed, wounded, or missing after each battle took a toll on soldiers' families, but also on the enthusiasm of would-be volunteers. Despite supporting the Union, many young men could not bear to be the cause of their families' economic hardship due to their absence. Others lamented the lack of the esprit de corps that earlier volunteers felt when whole communities came together to enlist as a group. Later volunteers could not even be certain to which company they might be assigned. And some men did not want to be fodder for what they viewed as "Mr. Lincoln's War." Nonetheless, the drumbeat for the enlistment of more men necessarily continued.

From the summer of 1862 until the end of the war, the North used a carrot-and-stick approach for recruitment. State and local officials, dreading the thought of resorting to a draft, offered substantial financial enticements to lure in more enlistments. No village, town, city, or county wanted the public shaming that came from not meeting its quota for volunteers. States, also wanting to avoid the stain of enforcing a draft to fulfill its patriotic duty, stretched out the accounting period for reaching some quotas. In New York, the State Adjutant General issued General Orders No. 79 on October 14, 1862, announcing conscription would commence on November 10, 1862, to meet the state's aggregate quota of 120,000.[9] November 10 came and went. By the end of the year, New York declared it had met its quota.

Newspapers kept a careful eye on the status of enlistments for each community and dutifully reported deficiencies. Equal parts informant and cajoler, broadsheets like Rollin's hometown *Broome Weekly Republican* took on the look of horse racing forms listing town names, the quota for each town, and the number of volunteers who had enlisted by the time of publication. When in July 1862 Governor Morgan sweetened the pot with a $50 bounty offer, the *Broome Weekly Republican* cheered along: "Soldiers were never offered more liberal pay than those who enlist in the volunteer force . . . And, if in addition to this, the towns, by private subscription or otherwise, give $50 to the Volunteer, as some have voted, the inducements are still greater."[10] However, one column over, an editorial scolded: "If all these considerations, we say, do not induce immediate enlistments, and secure the quota of our State . . . in 60 days or less, we shall be in favor of DRAFTING . . . No time is to be lost. Volunteer or be drafted!"[11] Scarcely one month later, reporting that Governor Morgan wished to extend the enlistment period and bounties, the newspaper sniffed, "the war spirit in Broome is aroused. We are in favor, however, of *special* drafting as an act of justice and punishment to reach any dull or unpatriotic town that refuses or neglects to raise its quota. Let such towns be marked and drafted."[12]

With the November 10, 1862, deadline for reaching quotas fast approaching, the *Broome Weekly Republican* did not hesitate to call out the deficits of specific towns: Barker–7, Chenango–1, Colesville–51, Kirkwood–11, Lisle–3, Port Crane–12, Sandford–7, Union–2, Vestal–15.[13] After some final arm wringing, Broome County met its quota of 1,138 (from a population of almost 36,000), and Binghamton, where Rollin enlisted, exceeded its quota of 313 by at least forty men. Indeed, by December 5, 1862, Secretary of War Stanton could boast that the Union Army had enrolled over 420,000 new three-year soldiers, and 399,000 of them were volunteers.[14]

New York's respite from the anguish of the draft would not last long, however. Editorializing in July 1862, Rollin's hometown newspaper had searched for the positive that such an edict would elicit: "It better equalizes the burdens of the war among the rich and poor. Every able-bodied man, not legally exempt, takes his chances."[15] But when passed, the Conscription Act of March 2, 1863 (which superseded the Militia Act of 1862), fell with a thud on the spirits of most Northerners. The Act mandated that able-bodied men between the ages of twenty and forty-five must be registered for the draft, and would be liable to be called up for military service if their home community did not meet its quota of volunteers.

And then there were the exceptions. Political leaders such as governors and heads of executive departments were exempt. Family situations that would result in hardship due to the absence of a potential draftee rendered that man exempt. One unfathomable provision stated, "where there are two or more sons of aged or infirm parents subject to draft, the father, or if he is dead, the mother may elect which son shall be exempt."[16] Most controversially, men could buy their way out of service. If a draftee found an acceptable substitute to take his place (which inevitably would have a price tag), or paid $300 to the War Department, he was discharged from further liability under that draft. (See figure 5.2.)

Protesters in some Northern recruitment sites took to the streets over the draft, but none seethed with as much rage as in New York City. The first lottery draw for the draft occurred without incident on July 11, 1863. Fear, bigotry, and resentment combined into a lethal mix when state authorities began a second draw for the draft on July 13. Like a lit powder keg, the city shook with violence from July 13 to 17, 1863.

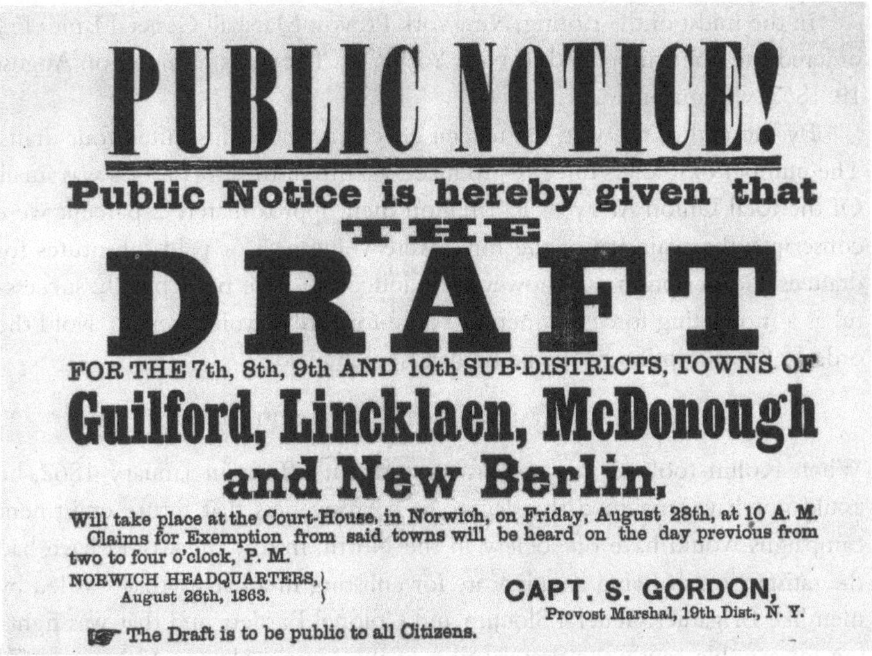

PUBLIC NOTICE!

Public Notice is hereby given that

THE

DRAFT

FOR THE 7th, 8th, 9th AND 10th SUB-DISTRICTS, TOWNS OF

Guilford, Lincklaen, McDonough
and New Berlin,

Will take place at the Court-House, in Norwich, on Friday, August 28th, at 10 A. M.
Claims for Exemption from said towns will be heard on the day previous from
two to four o'clock, P. M.

NORWICH HEADQUARTERS,
August 26th, 1863.

CAPT. S. GORDON,
Provost Marshal, 19th Dist., N. Y.

☞ The Draft is to be public to all Citizens.

FIGURE 5.2   Draft Public Notice Poster. Library of
Congress, Rare Book and Special Collections Division,
Printed Ephemera Collection.

What may have begun as a protest degenerated into unhinged rioting. Fueled by the insecurities of White working-class men, predominantly Irish or of
Irish decent, the rioters targeted Black people particularly in their frenzy. Such
rioters believed free Blacks would compete for their jobs, making fighting for
enslaved people's freedom a conflict of their own interests. Before the savagery
was put down by the metropolitan police force, the New York State Militia,
and what federal troops could be extracted from other service locations, rioters had ransacked or destroyed many public buildings, two Protestant churches,
the homes of a number of abolitionists and sympathizers, and Black homes and
businesses. They burned to the ground the Colored Orphan Asylum, which
housed over 230 children. Eleven Black men were lynched. Historian Frederick Phisterer wrote in 1912 of the riots, "It is claimed that originally a number
of honest working men assembled to protest against the draft; if so, this element
rapidly disappeared, and the dregs of the city took advantage of the excitement.
It is inconceivable that any decent and intelligent being can have taken part
in the riot."[17]

In the midst of the rioting, New York Provost Marshall General James Fry ordered the draft suspended in New York City. The draft resumed on August 19, 1863, without incident.

By the end of the war, the federal government had instituted four drafts. The number of soldiers directly produced via this distressing process was small. Of the total Union Army of 2.1 million men, approximately 2 percent were conscripts; the majority of the force were volunteers or paid substitutes for draftees. Conscription can, however, be judged to have been hugely successful as a motivating force for men to come forward as volunteers to avoid the ordeal of conscription, while being handsomely paid.

RECRUITMENT DUTY INTERRUPTED

When Rollin took up his post as recruitment officer in January 1862, he could not have imagined the degree of corrosiveness that future enlistment campaigns would have on society in the North. Instead, he would have had the satisfaction of being an advocate for enlisting in an army that was led by men like Brigadier General Slocum and Colonel Bartlett, and that was fighting for a noble cause: the preservation of the Union. He would have shared his conviction that the only possible outcome of the conflict was triumph for the North. He also would have served as a fine example of what opportunities for advancement in the ranks existed for privates who applied themselves. Securing a slot in the recruiting service was a competitive matter, particularly for privates. (See figure 5.3.)

Rollin chose an apropos time to seek recruitment duty. By January 1862, he had been in the field and away from loved ones for nine months, the period of service for many in state militias. January weather in Virginia was living up to its full muddy potential. Many in camp were unwell. Hopes for imminent engagement with secessionist forces were repeatedly dashed. And, helpfully, Rollin's soused-prone, impetuous captain was on furlough when Rollin submitted his request and was therefore unable to hinder the paperwork from reaching Colonel Bartlett for signature.[18] Though the anticipation must have felt agonizing, it was only a little over two weeks between Rollin's letter to his father outlining his recent "effort to be detailed on recruiting service" and his gleeful letter to friends written on January 29, 1862, on Sweeny's Hotel stationary in New York City.

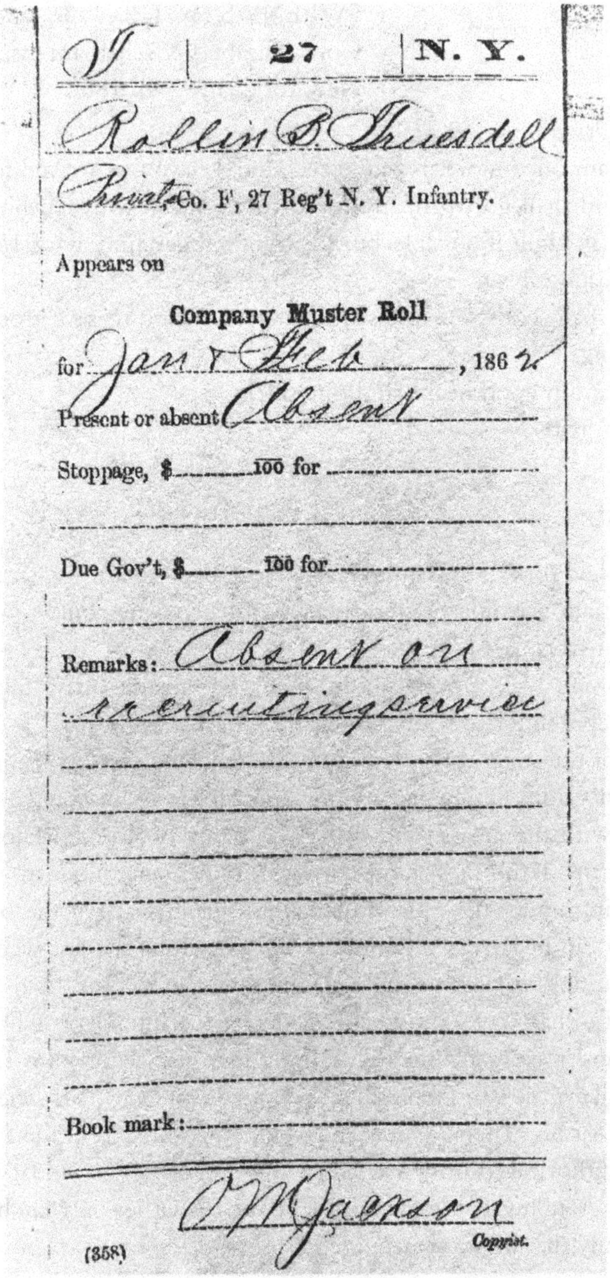

T | 27 | N. Y.

Rollin B Truesdell

Privat, Co. F, 27 Reg't N. Y. Infantry.

Appears on

Company Muster Roll

for Jan & Feb, 1862

Present or absent Absent

Stoppage, $........100 for ....

Due Gov't, $........100 for ....

Remarks: Absent on recruiting service

Book mark: ....

O M Jackson

(358) Copyist.

FIGURE 5.3 Rollin B. Truesdell's Recruiting Muster Slip.

SWEENY'S HOTEL
Cor. Chambers & Chatham Sts.,
New York, Jany 29th 1862

Dear Friends

I am once more in a civilized land. I have just arrived here 11 PM and shall go to Albany tomorrow. I mean to reach home by Saturday night if possible, but I cannot tell certainly what I can do 'til I reach Albany.

I shall send by express from here my rifle to save trouble of carrying.

I am in good health and fine spirits.

In haste

Yours truly
R. B. Truesdell

From New York City, Rollin traveled to Albany to learn where his recruitment duty station would be, and then, as quickly as he could move, home to Liberty, Pennsylvania, on furlough.

Envisioning a six-month commitment, Rollin must have felt relieved to have been appointed to Cuba, Allegany County, New York, a town in the southwest of the state not so far from Susquehanna County, Pennsylvania, as to make visits from family and friends unfeasible. Rollin may have had some familiarity with the area to which he was being deployed; Major Curtiss C. Gardiner of the 27th NY Volunteers was from Allegany County.

Operating under the federal guidelines put in place at the beginning of the year, Rollin began his recruitment duty in Cuba the last week of March 1862. Recruiting services to augment the forces already in the field had been put under the charge of state-specific general superintendents who established general depots for organizing and training recruits. Major John T. Sprague of the regular army, the War Department's designee for New York, selected Elmira and Albany for his general depots and assumed command of the Elmira depot from state authorities (through which Rollin reported) on January 18, 1862.[19]

Rollin wrote his first letter from Cuba to his father on March 27 to reassure his family that he was getting settled.

Cuba, N.Y. Mar 27th 1862

Dear Father

I arrived here safe and sound on Tuesday and was heartily welcomed by my friend Freeman. I stopped in Elmira from Monday noon until Thursday morning. I supposed that when I got here I should be a perfect stranger, but I am mistaken. My landlord formerly lived in Burlington and knows everybody in Edmeston that I can think of, and especially Julius Lines.[20] A lady visiting Mrs. Loomis yesterday saw me pass the window, recognized me, and told the landlady all about our folks and said her grandfather lived near a neighbor to you. Who in the world it can be is more than I know. She is now the wife of Geo. Wall who used to run a tin cart in Susq. Co. I think I'll solve the mystery before night, and if I have got any friends, find them out.

My health is good, spirits fine, and everything lovely.

Your obedient son,

Rollin

To: Saml W Truesdell

Gt Bend Pa

In what must have seemed like a harsh twist of fate, Rollin assumed his new role as recruitment officer in Cuba for a total of one week before he and his colleagues were ordered to cease. Seeking to rationalize the hash of federal, state, and citizen committee recruitment schemes, recently appointed Secretary of War Edwin M. Stanton ordered recruiting offices closed on April 3, 1862, for an overhaul.

Dejected, Rollin wrote a brief note to his father on April 18 as he transitioned back to his previous soldier duties.

Elmira N.Y. April 18th 1862

Dear Father

Lieut Freeman arrived here this morning from Cuba, and informs me that my trunk was sent by express from Cuba on Monday properly marked to me at Great Bend.

If it does not arrive in reasonable time, take such measures to find it as you think best.

We shall leave here by next Tuesday in all probability.

My health is good.

Yours truly

Rollin B. Truesdell

To: Saml W. Truesdell

Great Bend Pa

The halt order for recruiting may have been no matter to Rollin. Always operating under the understanding that he could be recalled to his unit at any time, Rollin learned on April 19 that the 27th New York Volunteers had been on the move. Quickly adjusting to the new circumstances, Rollin wrote with resolve when he penned a note to his sister Clara one day later.

Elmira N.Y. April 20th 1862

My Dear Sister,

This is a lonesome Sabbath morning to me, it being the first after my departure from home to spend an indefinite length of time. I have nothing of interest or importance to write but write simply to pass away the time. The ink I am using is so very thick that it is actually hard labor for me to write, and I am quite fearful of breaking the Sabbath if I continue to use it, and surely cannot finish my letter in time to go and hear Thomas K. Beecher preach if I do not do something to accelerate my pace.

My time has not been fully occupied since my arrival here. I found time to read Ruth Hall and Madeline Hawley, both very interesting books. I suppose my time to read literature will shortly be put to an end as I learned yesterday that the 27th were at Yorktown where we shall in all probability be by another Sabbath. Drive on I say, the sooner the better. My longing eyes are unto thee O Yorktown. We expect to get away from here by Tuesday, and in all likelihood the next time you hear from me I shall be in the sunny south.

Sleigh-rides and parties have had their day with me and now I must turn my face southward and dance to different music, tho' the remembrance of the past winter's sports and pastimes will ever be fresh in my mind.

The church bell rings and I must adjust my collar and go. So good bye 'til I reach Washington. Love to all

Yours truly
Rollin B Truesdell

To: Miss Clara E Truesdell
Great Bend, Pa

And as was his wont, Rollin's thoughts were of his mother as he fastened the clasps of his haversack and prepared to depart Elmira. His final letter from recruitment duty was addressed to her.

Elmira N.Y. April 22nd 1862

Dear Mother

I have a little time before I leave here and that little I will devote to you.

My trunk is packed once more, my haversack well filled with biscuit, cold ham, boiled eggs, cake, and other things too numerous to mention, "all this by friend Miss Scofield—long may she wave." My trunk is as nicely packed and my clothes as clean as when I left home, all from the same source, and as far as my comfort is concerned no pains has been spared.

My health is good and spirits high. My love to all

Your aff son
Rollin

It was time to take a different approach to seize Richmond. The Commander of the Army of the Potomac would sail his men into position to grasp the Rebel capital from the east. Rollin skedaddled back to Washington to catch up with his comrades in the 27th and boarded the first southbound vessel he could—the steamship *Knickerbocker*.

Chapter 6

PUSHING TOWARD RICHMOND

When Rollin bade farewell to his comrades in the 27th NY Volunteers in January 1862 to return to New York for recruitment duty, he left them in a suspended state. They were anxious to break free from the tiresome inactivity of winter but remained wholly subservient to mother nature's muddy whims. The 27th NY Volunteers' regimental history described Camp Clara at this time as "a mortar-bed; it took six horses to draw a one-horse load."[1] Parked alongside the rest of the Army of the Potomac, the men performed picket duty, repaired roads, and cut wood for camp purposes through the punishing winter. With the Battle of Bull Run two seasons past and no word of when the army would try again to crush the rebellion, the men undoubtedly wondered if the North's military strategy was in hibernation.

President Lincoln, impatient with McClellan's inactivity, figuratively shook his army by the collar on March 8, 1862. To dilute McClellan's grip on the Army of the Potomac, Lincoln reorganized it into corps and placed some in command who were outside of McClellan's personal clique. The 27th NY Volunteer Regiment (Colonel J. J. Bartlett commanding) was placed in Brigadier General Henry Slocum's 2nd Brigade within Brigadier General William Franklin's 1st Division within Major General Irvin McDowell's 1st Corps.

Perhaps cajoled by Lincoln's shake-up, two days later McClellan was ready to move. On March 10, 1862, the tedium and anticipation, if not the weather, finally broke. The 27th NY Vols, in one day, marched fourteen miles west from Camp Clara to Fairfax Court House through cold, driving rain. The whole of the Army of the Potomac made the same trip. Upon arrival, they found strong fortifications, the courthouse and Congregational church ruined, and no Rebel soldiers; the Confederate forces—reorganizing into the Army of Northern Virginia—had retreated. And so, two days later, back they went, this time fourteen miles east, once again through insistent rain. By March 15, the men slumbered in their now familiar home away from home, Camp Clara.

In the interim, two additional equally conversation-worthy changes (from a soldier's perspective), would invite the men's critique. Continuing to make his point, on March 11 Lincoln removed McClellan as General-in-Chief and relegated him to the position of Commander of the Army of the Potomac. Lincoln would assume the top role for a time. The second adjustment to be made was the issuance of the somewhat vexing small shelter tents modeled after the French tente d'abri that the men would use for the rest of their service. Ruefully referred to as "dog houses," each man carried one piece of 4 ft x 6 ft cotton cloth that, when buttoned together with a tentmate, served as shelter for two men. These leaky, cold—though easily transportable—tents would be a challenge size-wise for large men like Rollin, as he attested to in a letter to his sister.

The men of the 27th NY remained at Camp Clara for three weeks before again being called into line to march, with the expectation that the time for battle was upon them. As they were idling, Quartermaster General Montgomery Meigs had been busy. Army of the Potomac Commander McClellan's plan to take the battlefront to the enemy was bold and flashy, and required some 400 ships and barges. By the beginning of April, over 100,000 men, 300 cannon, 25,000 animals, and associated equipment sailed from the docks in Alexandria down the Potomac to Hampton Roads, Virginia.[2] When McClellan himself sailed on April 1 for Fort Monroe, he nonetheless was not satisfied that he had accumulated adequate strength to wash up the peninsula and over the Rebel force defending the secessionist capital. Freely stretching the truth about the numbers of soldiers he planned to leave to defend the capital, McClellan was caught in mathematical shenanigans even as he continued to plead for more troops for his campaign. Frustrated, on April 3, President Lincoln blocked 1st Corps Commander McDowell from joining the rest of the Army of the Potomac. Incidentally, on this same day, recently installed Secretary of War Edwin M. Stanton ordered recruitment offices closed and recruiters to return to their home units, thus snuffing out Rollin's tenure as recruitment officer.

On April 4, 1862, comrades in the 27th NY Volunteers boarded rail cars near Fort Ellsworth in Alexandria destined for Manassas Junction, almost thirty miles to the west. From there, the regiment endured a six-hour march southwest in the usual soaking showers to Catlett via Bristow. Once more,

FIGURE 6.1   Quaker Gun photographed by George N.
Barnard. Library of Congress, Prints & Photographs Division.

the Army descended upon an absent enemy. Retreating secessionist forces
had left behind deserted quarters and fortifications with Quaker guns in
position.[3] Rollin's comrades bivouacked at Catlett for several days, waiting
for the magnificent storm of rain and snow to clear before retracing their
steps. Finally, on April 12, they boarded rail cars and returned to Alexandria.
(See figure 6.1.)

The men had five days in their Alexandria camp to consider their most
recent battle tease before they were roused to move again. On April 17, the
27th NY Volunteers, along with Brigade Commander Slocum and his staff,
boarded the steamer S.R. *Spaulding* to sail down the Potomac River with four
schooners in tow. Lincoln had acquiesced. McClellan would receive one of
McDowell's Divisions: Brigadier General William Franklin's 1st Division.

A FEAST BEFORE THE FIGHT

Just as Rollin would a week later, the men of the 27th marveled at the scen-
ery—particularly Mount Vernon—as they were conveyed southward until
seemingly omnipresent violent storms made them wish they were back on
land. Pasty from the rough ride, quartering on the shelter-less upper deck, and
dining on uncooked salt pork, Rollin's comrades remained onboard the ship
for many days, bobbing and waiting near the mouth of the York River.

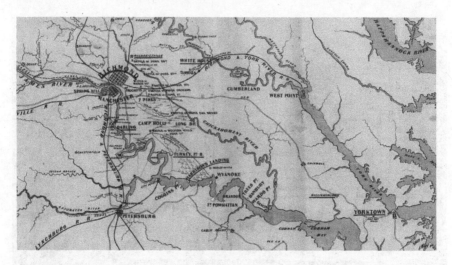

FIGURE 6.2 Map of the Battleground near Richmond by
L. Prang & Co. Library of Congress, Geography and Map
Division.

General Slocum, in sympathy with his men, arranged on April 23 for a
daylong excursion onboard the *S.R. Spaulding*. The ship sailed approximately
twenty-nine miles to Fort Monroe and around the celebrity ironclad vessel, the USS *Monitor*.[4] Rollin's regiment landed to visit the grand fortress,
which covered 250 acres, boasted 335 mounted guns, and could accommodate
10,000 men, before turning back to pass anchored French and English fleets
en route to Ship Point.[5] Completed in 1834, Fort Monroe commanded the
Chesapeake Bay and Potomac River approaches to Washington, DC, as well
as a special place in the minds of the Northerners—the fort remained under
Union control despite its location on secessionist Virginian soil. Fort Monroe's
shield was indispensable at this time, the surrounding waters thick with Union
transports, waiting to disgorge their contents on land for the impending grand
campaign against the Rebel forces. The fort was the beacon pointing the way
for Union forces as they advanced up the peninsula, and then westward, to
capture Richmond, the secessionist capital. (See figure 6.2.)

The following day, the 27th NY Volunteers were thrilled to disembark the
S.R. Spaulding near Ship Point. On April 27, 1862, three days after climbing
aboard the old Hudson Steamer *Knickerbocker* in Alexandria, Rollin happily
reunited with his comrades at their beach camp. Rollin described his rail journey and storm-wracked sail of fits and starts to reach Ship Point in letters to
his father dated April 26 and April 29.

Onboard Steamship Knickerbocker
Mouth of Potomac River
April 26th 1862

Dear Father

I left Elmira N.Y. on Tuesday the 22nd at 6 o'clock P.M., but night soon setting in, I saw little of the country 'til daylight the next morning, which brought us to Harrisburg. At this place the thrifty Dutch farmers were making their gardens and early Spring flowers were in bloom. The fields of wheat, oats, and barley were green, almost covering the ground, and at Little York the winter grain was heading out. Through Maryland the trees were nearly fully leaved out, and at Washington the clover on the vacant lots was large enough to mow.

We arrived at Washington at 12 o'clock noon making us just eighteen hours ride from Elmira. After seeing our Recruits well taken care of at the Soldiers Retreat, I called at Nicholas DuBois' where I was made welcome and bade to tarry 'til I should leave Washington. Being much wearied by my last night's ride, I hailed this quiet retreat as an oasis in my soldier life, and before the business portion of the city was quiet, I was hard at work—making up my losses of the night previous.

Thursday morning dawned cloudy and cool and as we embarked on board the Hugh Jenkins at ten o'clock for Alexandria, the elements above us indicated an approaching storm. Arriving at Alexandria at 11 o'clock, we hastily re-embarked on board the old Hudson River Steamer Knickerbocker which was advertised to leave for Fortress Monroe at 12 o'clock, but after being delayed by, to me, some unknown cause 'til 3 o'clock, we were towed into the River and anchored off the Light House.

A drenching rain now set in and continued through the night, which to me was the longest and most dismal I ever saw. Our party being the last aboard, we were compelled to take up with such fare as we could get. Every stateroom was occupied and nearly every bunk below. The cabin also contained as many as could possibly be accommodated. At 10 o'clock all of our party had gone below and turned in, but myself and I had determined to follow as my eyes were getting heavy, but as I approached the entrance I got one good sniff of the air below which was sufficient to drive me on deck for a full hour and a half. Once more refreshed, I returned to the cabin and made my bed upon the floor; took quite a good night's sleep.

When I rose in the morning, looked for a place to wash myself, but the only convenience was a twelve quart pail and the muddy water of the Potomac. The water rather went against my stomach, but I concluded that it was a military necessity and "went in."

At 9 o'clock we got underway with six transports in tow. The weather was damp with cold winds and I spent most of the time in the cabin except as we passed Mt Vernon and the rebel batteries. During the day we met and passed numerous sail craft but all in all it was a dull dreary day. We anchored at the mouth of the river at 10 o'clock P.M. and are awaiting orders. We shall probably get down to Ft. Monroe some time tomorrow.

My health is good and spirits fine.

Your aff son
Rollin B Truesdell

To: Saml W. Truesdell
Great Bend, Pa

Ship Point Va
April 29th 1862

Dear Father

When I last wrote you we were anchored at the mouth of the Potomac. After being delayed there for twenty four hours we started out at ten o'clock P.M. Saturday the 26th. At daylight we were in the middle of the Bay making fine progress and at twelve o'clock we anchored in the harbor at this Point.

Ship Point is twenty miles from Fort Monroe and five from Yorktown. It is not a town but simply a harbor, and from appearances was of no account 'til the Rebels occupied it and built a small fort on the point of land to dispute our entrance into York River. They had winter quarters here for about three thousand men, very comfortable buildings which are now used by our troops for hospital purposes.

There are now in the harbor about two hundred transports and one hundred steamers which are constantly plying between here and the north transporting soldiers and army supplies. The steamers

Elm City, John Brooks, Louisiana, C.Vanderbilt, and Emperor are in
the harbor loaded with troops awaiting orders to go up the River.

The 27th are encamped on the beach and the S. R. Spaulding
is laying within stone's throw of us ready to take us on at an hour's
notice. We expect that notice tomorrow, but from the cannonading we have heard all night and this morning we may move up this
afternoon. Our boys are anxious to fight and sanguine of a victory.
It is evident we shall not wait long.

My health is good and spirits fine.

More anon

Your aff son

R. B. Truesdell

Rollin's friend William Westervelt dreamily recalled setting up their tents in a
"beautiful grove of pines near the shore," near beds of plentiful oysters and clams.[6]
Ever enterprising, the men of the 27th used their hands and feet to rake out bushels of the bivalves—certainly a welcome substitute for army-issued rations.

Of course, Rollin and his comrades knew their days in seafood paradise
were numbered. Less than ten miles to the north, the struggle for control over
Yorktown had been ongoing for nearly a month.

Since April 5, Major General McClellan, stymied by a line of Confederate
fortifications running along the Warwick River and around Yorktown, had been
planning the details of his elaborate siege. A sizeable arsenal of heavy guns had to
be placed just so. With fewer than 15,000 men, Confederate Major General John
Bankhead Magruder (affectionately known as "Prince John" for his theatricality)
had held the Union troops at bay by confounding them with a force perpetually,
and noisily, on the move along the defensive line. Though McClellan had the
services of Professor Thaddeus Lowe and his civilian Balloon Corps to provide
reports of enemy movements from the vantage point of 1,000 feet above Yorktown, McClellan would not allow himself to be swayed into believing he was
facing a foe smaller than he wanted to believe. McClellan preferred to rely on
the intelligence reports rife with bloated estimates of enemy strength generated
by his Chief of Intelligence, Allan Pinkerton.[7] Magruder's force was formidable,
and he would not launch an attack until he could be confident of success, so
thought the Commanding General of the Army of the Potomac.

The stalemate broke on May 3, 1862. McClellan, finally ready to assault the
Confederate defensive fortifications and continue the march up the peninsula,

was surprised to find no enemy to fight. Confederate Commanding General Joseph E. Johnston had ordered Magruder to retract his forces overnight. By the time McClellan's advance was peering into the Rebels' deserted entrenchments, Magruder's rearguard was nearing Williamsburg.

The following day, the 27th NY Volunteers embarked the *S.R. Spaulding* once again and began their voyage up the York River. While anchored off Yorktown on May 5, 1862, Rollin and his comrades heard the thunder of cannonading from the Battle of Williamsburg beckoning them to land and join the fight with their compatriots. General McClellan, chagrined by the discovery of the deserted enemy defenses, had ordered a hastily conceived pursuit of the retreating Rebels, using half his men. While McClellan himself remained in Yorktown to organize movement of the remainder of his army (including the siege guns) up the river, the Union land force, under the command of 2nd Corps Commander Edwin V. Sumner, was pummeled. Nicknamed "Bull" to commemorate a folkloric incident during the Mexican-American War when a musket ball bounced off his head, Sumner was the eldest of the field corps commanders. The Union lost some 2,200 men at Williamsburg. The Confederates lost 1,700.

On May 6, Rollin's regiment's voyage continued northward. The *S.R. Spaulding*, leading the division's fleet, steamed thirty miles up the York River to anchor just south of West Point. The men of the 27th NY Volunteers luxuriated in this voyage, recalling that "the banks and sloping hills were green with the heavy foliage of May . . . the beauty of the scene far exceeded anything before witnessed by the men on the soil of Virginia."[8] This heady viewpoint was likely reinforced by the presence of white flags flapping atop many houses along the route.[9]

With no harbor, the *S.R. Spaulding* pulled as close to the shore as possible and anchored. In a rowboat with Company C from the 27th NY Vols, Colonel Bartlett studied the shoreline with his looking glass as he led the way to the shoreline himself.[10] Rollin and his comrades scrambled up the steep western bank of the York River where the Pamunkey and Mattaponi rivers come together with the York.

AN ANNIVERSARY TO REMEMBER

As successive companies of the 27th NY Volunteers rowed ashore, the Confederate cavalry and infantry scout welcoming committee faded back into the woods, encouraged by a shell or two launched from a Union gunboat. To protect the Union troops as they landed, Colonel Bartlett ordered Rollin's regiment to deploy as skirmishers as quickly as they could reach the ground. The regiment served as the vanguard engaging with the Rebels as needed to buy time for the remainder of their comrades to take position while also collecting intelligence about the enemy. From the shore, an open plain met a thick forest approximately one mile back. With Company D to their left and Company C to their right, Rollin and his comrades in Company F moved straight up the center of the field.[11]

The chase was on. Ordered forward by Captain Jay, Company F pushed out in front to pursue retreating Rebel soldiers into the dense forest. Within two hours, Rollin's company had closed the gap. They captured two members of a reconnoitering party from the 5th Texas who were summarily dispatched to Colonel Bartlett. The men advanced further into the woods before being called back and, around 9 p.m., Company F set a picket line with one flank along the river bank and the other stretching into the woods about a mile beyond the ground that Captain Jay was directed to occupy when he landed onshore.[12] Elements of other companies established a picket line of squads of four or five men along a roadway that led into the woods; the reserve remained behind this border.

The bright moon rose over the woods and plain, illuminating the shivering, anxious men on picket as they served as sentinels for the soldiers behind them. Consumed with thoughts of the battle to come, the pickets were jittery, restless for dawn to come. Around midnight, a couple of enemy scouts took advantage of their knowledge of the woods and the evening's glow to ambush a post adjoining Company F. Newly commissioned Sergeant Bailey, of Company D, hailing from Binghamton, was shot dead. Corporal Crocker, also of Company D, returned fire and killed one of the two enemy scouts. Morning could not come fast enough.

At first light on May 7, 1862, a party of skirmishers from the 27th NY Volunteers pressed into the murky woodland knowing the Rebel advantage in this terrain may hold up in daylight as well as night. Behind them, the regiment formed their picket line in a semicircle with the York River on their left and the Pamunkey River on their right. Facing the rearguard of Confederate General Johnston's army, they were the barrier to the plain behind them where Franklin's 1st division was assembling.

The uneasy calm lasted until 9 a.m. Captain Jay, already liquored up according to Rollin's friend William Westervelt, was leading an advance through the thicket when a couple of Confederate cavalrymen appeared on a hill a mile or so in front of Jay's detail. This proved irresistible. Jay directed his group of a handful of men from Company F and other companies to pursue and capture the cavalrymen while, Westervelt recalled, Jay "held a safe position behind a fence."[13] The cavalrymen sauntered over the brow of the hill, and with no choice in the matter, Jay's small force followed after them.

The men met a deadly surprise at the crest of the hill. Calmly waiting for them, a heavy line of battle—within short range—greeted them with a hailstorm of bullets. Westervelt ordered his squad of men to fire, and then they ran for cover as fast their legs would carry them. One of their shots struck a major from the 1st Texas, who was killed on his horse. The regimental history for the 27th NY Volunteers was merciless in recalling the captain's contribution to the morning: "In this retreat Capt. Jay led the line. Hatless, and with coattails flying, he came through the woods upon the reserves, shouting: Get out of these woods! Get out of these woods!"[14]

The Battle of Eltham's Landing became Rollin's first encounter with combat. According to one of Rollin's comrades from the 27th NY Volunteers, "in two minutes, 1,000 Texans stood on the ground we just left."[15] The Texas Brigade, led by Brigadier General John Bell Hood, furiously shoved at Union forces, willing them to back out of the undergrowth-filled pine and cedar woods.

The Rebel forces sought a prime location for their artillery: a spot of open ground between the woods and the river where they could target Union transports and the landing area, as well as the open plain which was by then covered with the regiments, artillery batteries, and cavalry battalions of General Franklin's division. Brigadier General John Sedgwick's division, which had been arriving at the landing area since the day before, only added to the attraction of the target for the Rebels.

Reinforcements rushed to assist the overwhelmed Union skirmishers. At least eight infantry regiments joined the 27th NY Volunteers in the woods to fight the swarm of enemy fighters. A comrade of Rollin's described the scene in a letter to the newspaper *The Orleans American*: "the rattling of bullets in the trees was terrific . . . the undergrowth [in the woods] was so dense that in many places we couldn't see two rods ahead . . . our regimental loss was slight considering our exposure and the thousands of shots fired at us."[16] Each side succeeded in pushing the other out of position over the course of the battle, all the while shells from artillery (and the Union gunboats) whistled back and forth over the heads of the soldiers, adding to the cacophony in the forest.

The battle raged on until about 3 p.m., when the Confederate forces slipped out of the woods. According to Westervelt's analysis, "a drunken officer attacked the enemy's rear guard who held us in check until their supply train was out of the way, and then fell back."[17] Brigadier General Franklin, in his official report of the battle that day, wrote jauntily, "The day has been a success, and but for the extreme want of forage and provisions, we might have followed up. As it is, I congratulate myself that we have maintained our position."[18] The Union Army lost 186 men in the Battle of Eltham's Landing.

Undoubtedly, Rollin was pensive when he woke the morning of May 8, 1862. For Rollin, sidelined with the mumps and unable to join his comrades as they fought at Bull Run in July the preceding year, the previous day's battle was his true baptism to war. A detail from the 27th NY Volunteers joined Brigade Commander Slocum the next morning on a reconnaissance mission beyond the Union picket lines. Their report, describing men and wood laying splintered and dead on the forest floor, would have reaffirmed the violence of the day before. Rollin likely turned over in his mind what a difference a year makes. A year ago that day, awash in the cheers and hurrahs of his company and bystanders, Rollin had enthusiastically enrolled his name in the company Peter Jay had organized in Binghamton, taking his oath of allegiance to the stars and stripes.

THE PURSUIT CONTINUED

Rollin and his comrades remained in camp near the battlefield for two days before moving to nearby Eltham on May 11, 1862. In Eltham, Major General McClellan and Brigadier General Franklin made a morale-boosting visit to the 27th NY Volunteers, which added to their excitement over the Confederate relinquishment of Norfolk that day. One of Rollin's regiment mates enthused about the visit in a letter to a New York newspaper, saying, "Our men fairly worship General McClellan, and he is deserving of their confidence."[19]

As the Confederate Army continued to draw itself closer toward Richmond, the Union Army followed it. In the predawn hours of May 13, 1862, the men of the 27th NY Volunteers were called into line and began a march that would take them over sandy, flat countryside for more than eight hours under the sweltering sun. When they reached Cumberland Landing along the Pamunkey River, the regiment camped in a 250-acre cornfield near the riverbank. Here, the Army of the Potomac was joined up when the forces that had remained on land, trotting after Confederate General Johnston's soldiers, arrived from Yorktown via Williamsburg. (See figure 6.3.)

Rollin wrote a letter to his father on May 14 to update him on the troop movements—and previewed frustrations to come in maintaining the steady flow of letters he depended on for his own well-being.

FIGURE 6.3   Army of the Potomac Camp Cumberland
along Pamunkey River, May 1862. Library of Congress,
Prints & Photographs Division, Civil War Photographs.

Near New Kent Court House
May 14th 1862

Dear Father

We took up our line of march yesterday A.M. at 2 o'clock, and
after a tedious march of eight hours, pitched our tents at this place
within two miles of the enemies' main force. Whether they will run
or fight I cannot say, or how soon the battle will be fought, but with
the large force we have here we shall not remain idle longer than to
have the supplies unloaded from the boats.

The weather is very hot and the roads very dusty.

I have not received a letter since I left home, and a N.Y. paper
five days old is a luxury that but few can possess themselves of.

My health is good and spirits fine.

Reading matter is very scarce, and stationery is very hard to be
got, especially postage stamps. Ink is a commodity that is going out
of fashion, as we cannot very well carry it while on a march.

I do not know when a mail will leave here for West Point, but when it does, I will have a line ready to appease your anxiety. With much love to all, I am

Your aff son

Rollin B. Truesdell

To: Saml W. Truesdell

Great Bend, Pa

While in Cumberland Landing, the men learned there would be further adjustments to the structure of the Army of the Potomac. Major General McClellan had successfully advocated for the addition of two corps to his army: the 5th, commanded by Brigadier General Fitz John Porter, and the 6th, commanded by Brigadier General William Franklin. Both men were reliable supporters of the Commanding General though Porter was generally recognized as the closest of advisors and friends. President Lincoln was not sanguine about acquiescing to the request (and told McClellan so), but he believed it was a necessary expedient because confrontation with the Rebels was imminent.[20]

The 6th Corps brought together Franklin's division and Brigadier General William F. "Baldy" Smith's division. (Fellow students at the US Military Academy had dubbed Smith "Baldy" for his premature thinning hair.) For Rollin and his comrades in the 27th NY, this would mean further separation from their treasured original leadership of the regiment. Brigadier General Henry Slocum now led the First Division (from Franklin), and Colonel Bartlett was appointed to lead the 2nd Brigade (from Slocum). Lieutenant Colonel Alexander D. Adams, who raised Company B, one of the first companies of the 27th NY Volunteers, took over command of the regiment and would lead it for the remainder of its term of service.

For the next two weeks, the Army of the Potomac moved incrementally westward toward Richmond. Starting before first light on May 16, 1862, Rollin and his comrades bore a miserable, rain-soaked eight-mile march along the Pamunkey River to White House Landing. Slogging through the thick mud, the men marched for over ten hours; for the accompanying supply wagons, the trip took thirty-six hours.[21] Still shaking the damp out of his bones, Rollin wrote a joint letter of reassurance of his welfare to his sister Clara and his mother.

White House Landing Va

May 17th 1862

My Dear Sister

I received your letter the 15th inst. It was the first I have received since I left home though I have written very often. The mails are now so irregular I doubt if you get all that I write, but if I write many I trust you receive a few of them.

We are daily marching onward toward the confederate capital and only twenty miles intervene between us and the Legislative Halls of traitors. Our march yesterday was the most severe I ever experienced. We shouldered our knapsacks at four o'clock A.M. and marched through a pelting rain 'til three P.M. Tired and footsore, I pitched my little storm tent and without the comfort of fire or dry clothing laid down on the ground to tough it out, verifying the old proverb, what can't be cured must be endured. I soon fell asleep and when I awoke the morning sun shone brightly in my eyes through the unclosed end of my tent. My clothes are now nearly dry and I am feeling better than I expected, much better than three fourths of the soldiers. Tomorrow being Sunday, I think we shall not move farther 'til Monday when I hope to feel as good as new.

You did not make mention of my trunk so I am in ignorance yet as to its safety. Please inform me in your next.

With much love I am

Your aff Bro
Rollin

My Dear Mother

In all my letters I send love to all our family; this of course brings you within the circle, but a line directly to you may show that I remember you particularly. I do not feel today like writing a long letter, but there are three things that it may please you to know, viz my health is good, my spirits fine, and clothes clean.

I feel thankful for these blessings today, little knowing but the morrow may be full of trouble.

With many kind wishes and love to all I am

Your aff son
Rollin B. Truesdell

A few days later, the 27th NY Volunteers were again on the march. Now separating from the banks of the Pamunkey River, they turned west to Tunstall's Station, where railroad posts read, "to Richmond 18 miles."[22] By May 21, 1862, the regiment was in Cold Harbor on the Chickahominy River preparing to join Colonel Bartlett on a reconnaissance mission the following morning.

Mechanicsville, approximately six miles away and close to Confederate lines, was the target. Colonel Bartlett brought Rollin and his comrades from the 27th NY Volunteers, the 16th NY Volunteers, a section of artillery, and two companies of the 1st NY Cavalry on a day mission to determine the enemy position and whether significant Rebel fortifications would threaten Union progress. Bartlett ordered his men not to fire a shot during the mission; he did not want to instigate a general engagement.[23] As the men inched along, they succeeded in pushing back enemy pickets that lay before them—until a small squad of unlucky Union cavalry strode past to take the advance. Rollin's tent-mate William Westervelt recalled, "not two minutes after, as they passed a turn in the road, they [the cavalry] were fired upon by the enemy's pickets."[24] The men behind the cavalry quickly pivoted to the right and climbed a small hill that afforded them an excellent view of the Rebel picket line.

With two members of the cavalry contingent not turning up, an impromptu search party formed to discover their fate. Westervelt, having wandered to the front with visions of a possible easy meal at a house in the distance, presented as the perfect candidate to go investigate. Westervelt jovially recalled he ended up attracting several others, including Rollin, on his lonely, dangerous assignment: "Truesdell soon joined us, and we walked on down the road, and as we approached the turn where the enemy's pickets were but two hours before, we expected to be fired upon, but we found their pickets had been withdrawn."[25] They also found the body of the missing sergeant but only the horse of the missing corporal; he had been taken prisoner.

On May 23, Rollin wrote an upbeat letter to his elder sister Julia in which he mentions the reconnaissance mission—and the draw of impromptu foraging from the locals.

In Camp near Richmond Va
May 23rd 1862

My Dear Sister Julia
I think I promised to write you all the particulars of my situation, condition, etc. almost the last thing before I left home. I have not forgot the promise but since my rejoining the army I have not had time to enter into particulars, nor have I now, but lest you think I have entirely forgotten "bread and honey," I will just remind you that a good slice would not go bad just now, in place of the hard crackers and salt beef that now constitutes the main of our rations.
But to particulars, I am in the shade of a large pine tree about eight miles from Richmond, North by East, sitting flat on the

ground with portfolio on my knee, sweaty but not dirty for I have just took a bath in the Chickahominy Creek. I am doing two things at once, viz watching a shirt which I have just washed and hung on a bush to dry and writing to my sister.

Yesterday we made a reconnaissance toward Richmond to ascertain the enemy's position, and on our return, feeling the wants of nature rather strong, I confiscated a fine chicken which I regaled myself upon, much to the chagrin of a secesh woman (not lady). I sometimes get tired of rations but never go to rest hungry, for my fingers lengthen in proportion to my wants.

Since my rejoining the army I have been subjected to dangers seen and unseen, have had my comrades shot down by my side while standing shoulder to shoulder with me, but the good Lord has spared me thus far and I doubt not that he is able to preserve me to the end of the war and restore me to home and friends.

One of my chums calls from a group a short distance off—put up that love letter and come and help us sing. I must go. We are the Jubilee and have a fine choir of male voices.[26]

I wish you to write particulars as well as myself.

With much love to Henry and the little ones—yes to all, all I am

Your aff Bro
Rollin B. Truesdell

To: Mrs. Julia Warner
Great Bend, Pa

The intelligence gleaned from the reconnaissance mission proved invaluable. Union shells rained on enemy positions in and around Mechanicsville in the ensuing days. On May 25, Rollin and comrades in the 27th NY edged closer to their goal and moved camp within range of the enemy's artillery, a couple of miles to the west. Testing his mettle if not his penmanship, Rollin wrote a note to his father the evening of May 25 as shells hurtled by overhead.

Five miles from Richmond
May 25th 6 P.M. 1862

Dear Father

We moved up toward the enemy this morning and encamped under cover of a piece of woods. Our boys with yankee curiosity have ventured beyond the woods to get a peep at Rebels in such numbers that Mr "secesh" is edifying us with a few 32 lb. shell. They throw them at the rate of three in ten minutes. It is evident they are poor marksmen or do not fully understand our position, for the shell burst at least one (1) mile in our rear.

There goes one whistling over my head, making a noise not unlike the falling of a huge pine tree, and bursts at least a mile from me. They make a good deal of noise, but as I am writing simply for the fun of writing while shell pass over my head. I am not very much scared yet; at least my hand is steady.

Groups of soldiers are together discussing the matter. Some think they will shortly cut their fuse short and drop the shell in our midst. As for me, I am like the old woman whose horse ran away. Said she, I trusted in the Lord 'til the breeching broke, and then I did not know what I should do.

With good health and temperature ninety above zero, I am

Your aff Son
Rollin B. Truesdell

Within two days, the Confederate force was driven out of Mechanics-ville. Accompanied by a battery, Colonel Bartlett's brigade, in a driving rain, marched into and took possession of the shell-scarred town. Houses, shops, trees, and farm fields all showed the violence of the Union guns' work.

Situated to the far right of the main army encampments, the 27th NY Volunteers set up camp in a picturesque grove facing a narrow part of the Chickahominy River approximately one mile away. Guarded by a Rebel line of breastworks, a road leading to Richmond crossed here. From within their entrenchments, a battery of Confederate field guns, about half a mile distant, sporadically lobbed shells at their camp and pickets. Anxious to hear from home, Rollin penned a letter to his family on May 27, with the images of the destruction wrought in Mechanicsville fresh on his mind.

Mechanicsville Va
May 27th 1862

Dear Parents and Sisters

After waiting a length of time which seemed to me to be al-most unreasonable, I have received today one letter from Clara, a line from Mother, and from Father, 0. If I had not written home so often, I should feel content with this, but after fulfilling your last commands to write often well, under the circumstances, I think I have just cause to complain. I thought when the mail arrived yesterday and brought no letter to me from home that hence forth I would only answer the letters I received, but when I think of my present situation, and my friends at home anxious to hear from me, I will not deviate from my present rule, though I assure you I am as anxious to hear from home as you can be to hear from me.

When I last wrote to you, I was listening to the music of rebel shell. That was Sunday eve. All day on Monday we expected warm work but were disappointed. All was quiet through the day. This morning we changed our position to the right but did not get much nearer Richmond. We commenced our march at 4 o'clock A.M. and tramped three miles through as pelting a rain and as slippery mud as I ever saw.

We are encamped in a grove where our boys had a brush with the Rebs last Saturday. Our batteries shelled the town and woods. The town of Mechanicsville "once" contained 1 store, 1 hotel, 2 wagon shops, 1 blacksmith shop, and about one-half dozen dwellings. These were all stove to pie by our batteries at two miles distance. A solid shot passed through the butt of an oak tree 1½ feet through. Our boys brought in a relic of the battle this afternoon from a wheat field a few rods off. It was a man's limb shot off just above the knee. The Rebs are in plain sight of us two miles distant. What the morrow may bring forth, I know not.

It is dusk; I am in haste.

Yours truly
Rollin

P.S. Please send me some postage stamps. I cannot get them here for love or money. I have but two left.

Rollin

Since their arrival, as the Union Army scrambled to rebuild multiple bridges across the Chickahominy destroyed by Rebel sabotage, then by flooding, the regiment performed picket duty along the river. The evening of May 30, 1862, while on picket duty, Rollin fired his weapon and watched a man fall. It was the first time. Perhaps needing his spirits to be bolstered as only she could, Rollin wrote a letter to his mother the next day.

Mechanicsville Va,
May 31st 1862

My Dear Mother

Never in my life did I receive a more welcome letter than yours of the 16th. I like to receive letters from all my friends, but yours was worth any half dozen I ever got, so I will take same pains in answering it, for by so doing, I flatter myself I shall receive another.

We are here fairly in the face and eyes of the enemy, expecting each day to make an attack. Our forces are like a kettle of boiling water. Occasionally, the excitement partially subsides at times, but a little unusual stir along our picket lines and the kettle boils and foams. How long we shall wait before the final attack is made, I know not. Although within five miles of Richmond, I know less of what is going on in this army than you do at home.

Yesterday I was on picket duty and had the satisfaction to get a shot at a rebel, and also of hitting him. I have been in the army one year and have killed one (no, not quite killed him, guess I would if it had not been quite so dark), and by another year, if I keep on, I guess I can kill and eat one. I suppose it would look rather wolfish to you, but we soldiers do not look through civilized eyes, and a good many of us have swapped our hearts away for dirk knives.

My health is good, never better, and I trust it will continue 'til the end.

It is getting dark and I must close my letter.

With much love to all, I am

Yours aff,
Rollin B. Truesdell

To: Mrs. Lucy Truesdell
Great Bend, Pa

So Close

Thunderstorms raged the evening of May 30, 1862. One of Rollin's comrades was struck by lightning during the ferocious storm, a two-hour onslaught dubbed "heaven's artillery."[27] The Chickahominy jumped its banks, the surrounding marshland was deluged, the recently rebuilt bridges were washed away . . . and Confederate Commanding General Johnston had an opportunity. The Army of the Potomac was split in two. Three corps of General McClellan's 105,000-man Army of the Potomac were north of the Chickahominy

River, two to the south.[28] Brigadier General Sumner's 2nd, Brigadier General Porter's 5th, and Brigadier General Franklin's 6th were stationed north of the river to protect the Union rail supply line. Brigadier General Heintzelman's 3rd and Brigadier General Keyes's tantalizingly close 4th Corps were the ripe targets for Confederate assault. ·

Johnston, with approximately 60,000 of his men serving as a protective shield for Richmond, needed an opening to rattle the Union side. Waiting to be attacked by the bulging Union force, with the remainder of Major General McDowell's 1st Corps positioning itself to reinforce McClellan, would not end well.[29] So Johnston took the initiative. On May 31, 1862, the clumsily executed Confederate assault on the Army of the Potomac's 4th Corps successfully overwhelmed the inexperienced Union soldiers at the front, pushing them back from their forward position before Union reinforcements could intervene.

From his lofty position in one of his hydrogen gas-filled balloons based at Mechanicsville, Professor Lowe could see the unfolding snare being set for the 3rd and 4th Corps and warned McClellan. Lowe then rushed to the Gaines' Farm balloon camp, where his larger and favored balloon *Intrepid* could lift him higher for a broader perspective of the battlefield. He tapped out telegraphs from the airborne *Intrepid* urging the Army of the Potomac commander to send in reinforcements and to repair the New Bridge without delay.

John Sedgwick's division of Sumner's 2nd Corps managed to clamber across the tumultuous river to help bolster and stabilize the Union lines. But, fighting in knee-deep water, each side absorbed devastating blows. The shots with the most far-reaching effect on the battle, and arguably the war, were the ones that knocked Confederate Commanding General Joseph E. Johnston off his horse.

From their camp, Rollin and his comrades in the regiment could hear the heavy cannonading of the battle. With intelligence about the breadth of the Confederate plans lacking, the 16th and 27th NY, the 5th Maine, and an artillery battery were called into line between 5 and 6 p.m. on May 31. One of Rollin's comrades wrote to a hometown newspaper: "I want you to understand that we are as near to Richmond [5 miles] as any other portion of the Army, and we intend to fight the hardest of any, and get there the soonest."[30] Another member of the 27th NY Volunteers dutifully reported in a letter home that "the 27th filed down through the woods within a few rods of the [bridge], halted, under the eye of their beloved General Slocum. Slocum ordered the 27th into the road, and . . . we steadily marched without sign of faltering, or doubt of success, determined to go where General Slocum would lead."[31] Eliciting perfect silence from the Rebel fortifications—even after lobbing some shells at it, Slocum ordered the men back to camp. The occupants had been diverted to support the Confederate assault.

The battle resumed early the next day, June 1, 1862. When members of Company F from the 27th NY Volunteers took up their picket duty, they found they were not alone this day. A Rebel battery took aim on them, causing some scrambling, but no casualties. Rollin's friend Westervelt particularly recalled that picket duty: "A party of us were about a half mile back acting as reserve and congratulating ourselves on being in a less exposed position than the outpost when suddenly a 12 lb conical shell came whistling through the air and buried itself in the ground in the center of the group."[32] It was their lucky day; the fuse was defective. Rollin vividly shared the story with his father.

Mechanicsville Va
June 7th 1862

My Dear Father

I have a leisure hour this morning and knowing your anxiety to hear from me often I will spend it in writing to you.

Since occupying this place we have enough excitement to pass away the time. Not a day passes but what we have some sort of a brush with the enemy across the Chickahominy. If our lookout sees two or three baggage wagons quite near together, he communicates the fact to the Capt of Artillery, who immediately warms them up with a shell. At a distance of two miles, I have seen the horses on a single baggage wagon killed, so close is their aim.

The rebels are equally as watchful as we are and return the compliment at every opportunity. Last Sunday, while watching their movements in company with about thirty others, I saw the smoke rise from one of their field pieces, and an instant after, a shell came whistling through the air and struck splat in the ground about four feet in my rear. All that saved my life was the falling on my face when I first heard the approaching missile. It was a defective shell and did not burst. If it had, it would have been almost a miracle if some of us had not been killed.

I dug the shell from the ground, and it is now in the possession of one of the artillerists who recharged it and will send it back from whence it came the first opportunity that presents. About one-half the shell they throw are worthless and do not burst.

The bridge across the Chickahominy creek and swamp is about three fourths of a mile in length. It is built of logs and earth with the exception of three short trestle works. The trestle across the main stream the rebels cut down when they left this place and I think it cannot be rebuilt without considerable loss as the enemy have got two batteries planted to rake the whole length of the bridge. Their pickets are stationed at the trestle nearest their side, and ours at the one nearest this side. The distance between the two about sixty rods. Shots are exchanged occasionally, but both parties keep well concealed behind barricades fixed for the purpose.

Yesterday, one of their pickets placed a newspaper upon his gun and stepping into the middle of the road cried out—"Do you want to buy the Baltimore Clipper over there? We have got them of the 4th." One of our men told him he would swap lead for it and, suiting the action to the word, fired at the rascal. He had the satisfaction to see his companions carry him behind their covert.

We have had three days very wet uncomfortable weather, but this morning the sun rose clear and it bids fair to be a day that we can dry all of our wet clothes. To wear a wet coat three days is uncomfortable beside being unhealthy, but I find I do not know what I can endure 'til necessity compels.

I am yet ignorant whether my trunk ever came through from Cuba safe or not.

Please inform me.

The Republican I now receive regularly and I assure you it is a welcome visitor. It is hard to obtain a N.Y. paper here, and when we do, it is at a cost of twenty-five cents.

We are nearly outside of the lines of civilization. My health is good.

With much love to those around the home fireside, I am

Your aff son
Rollin B. Truesdell

To: Saml W. Truesdell
Great Bend, Pa

Looking like a stalemate, but with each side claiming victory, the fighting ended by noon on June 1. The Confederate side, temporarily led by Major General G. W. Smith after Johnston was wounded, reluctantly pulled back to its defensive works around Richmond. The two-day Battle of Fair Oaks—as

Figure 6.4   Robert E. Lee. Civil War Photographs, 1861–1865, Library of Congress, Prints and Photographs Division.

the Federals would call it, or Seven Pines for the Confederates—had delivered a staggering number of killed, wounded, and missing. The Union lost over 5,000 men, the Confederates over 6,000—including wounded Johnston, their commanding general. Replacing Johnston, on June 1, 1862, Confederate President Jefferson Davis appointed his talented military advisor, Robert E. Lee, to the post of Commanding General of the Army of Northern Virginia. (See figure 6.4.)

Not missing a beat, Major General McClellan issued an order to his troops on June 2, 1862, that extolled his own leadership and their bravery, and encouraged them to prepare for the next great battle. The order read, in part:

I have fulfilled at least a part of my promise to you. You are now face to face with the rebels, who are at bay in front of their capital. The final and decisive battle is at hand . . . The events of every day prove your superiority; wherever you have met the enemy you have beaten him; wherever you have met him with the bayonet, he has given way in panic and disorder. I ask of you now one last crowning effort. The enemy has staked his all on the issue of the coming battle. Let us meet and crush him here, in the very centre of the rebellion. Soldiers, I will be with you in this battle, and share its dangers with you . . . Let us strike the blow which is to restore peace and union to this distracted land.[33]

Rollin had most of a month to ruminate on McClellan's soaring rhetoric, as well as on the juxtaposition and shock of a schoolmate's death, before the test of the next battle arrived. A hometown friend who, like Rollin, challenged himself in war for the first time during McClellan's Peninsula Campaign, had fallen. Rollin wrote a few lines on June 7 and more on June 10 to his sister about the loss of his friend.

Dear Sister C

Since writing the within and while putting the directions on the envelope, I received your favor of June 1st, also one from Bro Albert of same date. I wrote to Albert this morning.

Albert mentions the death of my old schoolmate, Turner J. Southworth. I was much surprised to hear of this, "but all things are possible."

I am glad to hear that my trunk came safe home.

We are all rejoicing over old Beauregard's defeat, and anxious to show them the same trick here.[34] They got a sorry drubbing last Sunday.

I dreamed old Bosi died the other night—hope it's not so.

I am tired sitting on the ground.

My love to all.

Your aff Bro
R. B. Truesdell

To: C. E. Truesdell
Great Bend, Pa

Mechanicsville Va
June 10th 1862

My Dear Sister:

Your favor of the 6th inst I have just received. I also received a letter from my father last evening. We are still at this little ville waiting and watching. How long we will thus be idle (except the excitement incident to a close proximity to enemy) I cannot tell. It now overruns my estimate several days.

We have just experienced another twelve-hour rainstorm and the consequence is I am again "inundated," but this I am getting used to and have little reason on that account to fear sickness. I begin to think that I am endowed with the iron constitution which was so prominent with my ancestors. You will probably notice that my hand is a little unsteady, so I will acknowledge that I feel a little chilly. If I could only enjoy the comforts of a kitchen fire for an hour I would give what little change my pocket possesses, but "what can't be cured, must be endured." I hope to occupy rooms in Richmond in a few days and be more comfortable.

I am glad you wrote the particulars of Turner's death. I assure you they were very interesting to me. I little expected the last time we parted near the walls of Fort Worth that it would be the last parting, but we know not what a morrow may bring forth. I pray you friends be not uneasy for me. It will be only time to be troubled when trouble comes. If I am sick, I have friends that will give me the best of care and if I start for home I travel not through a strange country by no means. If Turner had had the friends that I have, he never would have suffered nor been an inmate to the Hospital. So be content and hope for the best and "all things will be well."

Pray excuse me for not writing a longer letter. I do not feel exactly like writing. Give my thanks to Father for those stamps he sent me.

With good health and high hopes I am

Your affectionate brother,
Rollin B Truesdell

On June 6, the 27th NY Volunteers transitioned back to their previous camp near Cold Harbor, dropping some six or seven miles to the southeast along the Chickahominy River. From June 7 until June 17, 1862, the men either served as pickets or toiled in the muck building corduroy roads and bridge approaches through the swampland. Awaiting the impending battles, Rollin did his best to maintain the rhythm of letter writing with his family and sharing the details of his life as a soldier. On June 17, 1862, he wrote such a letter to his sister Clara.

Mechanicsville Va
June 17th 1862

My Dear Sister

I have just received your favor of the 11th inst. We now get a regular mail every day. I wrote to Brother Mart several days ago but have received no reply and, by the way, just remind Julia that I have not received any particulars from her yet.

Now I will answer your questions. The 27th is General Franklin's Corps, Slocums' Division, and Bartlett's Brigade.

I knew of the battle of the seven pines, but the battlefield was about three miles to the left of our camp.

We have what is called storm tents. They are made of flax cloth, very thin, and are in two pieces, each one is one and a half yards square. Two of these pieces make the apology for a shelter for two men, each man carrying his piece in his knapsack. When set up, the ridge pole will just clear my head when I sit flat on the ground. They do not afford much protection against a driving storm.

As to whether I am clean or dirty, I might answer you correctly and say yes and no, both. At present I am clean, but sometimes when we march through the dust and heat I look pretty dusty, but when we camp in one place a couple of days I manage to scrub up and wash my clothes.

Those cotton shirts that I brought with me from home are worth everything to me now. I would give five dollars if I had my old wide brimmed hat here. You have no idea how I am sunburnt.

I wish you to look over my old letters carefully and see if you can find a pass given by Col. Slocum dated about the 14th July 1861. It is a printed card and was given for five days. Also, a line written by Dr N. S. Barnes to Col Slocum which contains about the following language, to wit—Please give the bearer a pass for several days. He has mumps and goes to the house of a friend.

I think you will find them stuck into some of the letters. <u>Look carefully</u>, and if you find them, forward to me in your next.

My health is good.

> Your affectionate brother,
> Rollin

While Rollin and his comrades were swatting at the ravenous mosquitos and ubiquitous flies during their roadbuilding duty along the murky shores of the Chickahominy, Confederate Brigadier General James Ewell Brown (Jeb) Stuart completed his daring cavalry circuit around the whole of McClellan's army. On this remarkable ride from June 12 to 15, Stuart and 1,200 of his men picked up intelligence on Union positions, 165 members of the 5th US Cavalry, and 260 horses. The tour was certainly cheekier and more effective than the practice of treetop Rebel spies craning to get a look at Union camps. From this ride of reconnaissance, Stuart gleaned invaluable information about the deployment of McClellan's force: at the far right of the Union line, Brigadier General Porter's 5th Corps, focused on protecting the Union supply chain along the rail line, presented an obvious invitation for a right flank attack. (See figure 6.5.)

The 27th NY Volunteers were on the move again on June 18, 1862. Crossing to the south side of the Chickahominy River via the Woodbury Bridge, they marched twelve miles and set up camp about one mile from where remnants of the carnage from the most recent battle remained on the battlefield. They were so close to the enemy lines that when Rollin and his comrades were on picket duty, they could hear early morning roll call in the enemy's camp.[35] In a letter to his sister dated June 22, Rollin let her borrow his eyes to witness the state of the Fair Oaks battlefield, and to let her know he paid a call on the 61st NY Vols, the regiment of his recently deceased friend, Turner Southworth.

> Fair Oaks Va
> June 22nd 1862

My Dear Sister

Your favor of June 11th I received last evening. I also received one from Albert of the same date. I hardly know what to write about among the many things that are daily coming within my

FIGURE 6.5   Woodbury's Bridge over Chickahominy River
photographed by D. B. Woodbury. Library of Congress,
Prints & Photographs Division, Civil War Photographs.

notice. As it is now nearly sunset, perhaps an extract from my
memorandum book which I have just written for today will be
letter enough for this time.

Alarmed at three o'clock by firing at our front, the Brigade
called into line. The firing soon ceased, and our services were not
needed. When all was quiet, I lay down and slept 'til six o'clock.
When I rose, went to a creek half a mile distant, washed, returned
to camp, ate my breakfast of salt junk, coffee, and hard crackers. After breakfast wrote to Albert and several friends up north.

At ten o'clock, had inspection of arms as is usual on the Sabbath, after which I took a walk over to the battlefield. The scenes
that I there saw I cannot describe in detail but will just mention
a few. I saw two graves said to contain five hundred (500) bodies
each, and all over the field, in clusters could be seen five or six

buried separately; now and then a rough board set at the head would tell the name and company of the occupant.

The smell on the field is very offensive, so much so that I did not stay to go over all the ground. Some of the fallen were not buried at all, but merely had dirt shoveled over them to hide them from the eyes of the living soldiers, but thus soon the heavy rains have washed the dirt off so they had to be buried a second time.

In that portion of the field covered with woods, the trees are literally riddled with bullets, some of them so badly cut that they already begin to wither.

In my circuit I came into the camp of the 61st NY Regt and made Messrs Beckwith, Simons, and Martial a call. L Vance was out of camp and I did not see him. They were all in fine spirits and good health. They have had a pretty tough time for a month or so. Their loss was quite heavy in the late battle. I returned to camp about 4 o'clock quiet as a lamb for I was so tired I could be no other way.

Send me a Ledger or any other literary paper occasionally. I cannot get them here. In fact, reading matter is very scarce.

Health good.

Yours truly
Rollin

For days, if the heavens were not unleashing slashing rain, the blazing sun was sending its fiery rays of heat down upon the soldiers as they continued the numbing, but necessary, task of road building in the swamps. Malaria wallowed in the atmosphere and was a constant threat to soldiers. Each time Rollin and his comrades were called out in the middle of the night to hold in readiness, to stand in defense against a Rebel surprise attack that did not materialize, often in drenching rain, they must have wondered how long this stasis would continue. They would soon know. In the still of the night on June 25, Rollin's tentmate observed, "from the manner in which the orderlies and aid decamps were riding about, we could see the officers felt anxious as though things were not going as they should."[36]

LEE PUSHES BACK

How they cheered! Starved for a signal that their Commanding General would indeed lead them to triumph over the Confederate Army, that their purgatory soldiering in the mosquito-infested swampland around the Chickahominy River was ending, Rollin and his comrades in the 27th NY Volunteers shouted for joy when they heard the news the evening of June 26, 1862.

Starting around 3 p.m. that day, to the northwest and across the river from their camp, the men had listened to terrific thundering of cannon and the roll of musketry in the direction of Mechanicsville. They heard reports during the day that Confederate Major General Stonewall Jackson had led a large force across Meadow Bridge on the Chickahominy and attacked the far-right flank of the Union Army. Brigadier General George McCall's division of green but well-trained Pennsylvanians bore the brunt of the attack. The 13th Pennsylvania, the Bucktails, who affixed bucktails to their caps to brag their marksmanship, were the first to exchange fire with the Rebel force at Mechanicsville. As ordered, when they felt the heat of the assault, they fell back to a 1.5-mile defensive line east of Beaver Dam Creek. Fifth Corps Commander Fitz John Porter reinforced McCall; the Confederate attackers called in their own reinforcements.

The battle continued until around 9 p.m. McCall's force succeeded in driving back wave after wave of assaulting Confederates. The day had cost Lee and his army dearly—nearly 1,500 men, compared to Union losses of approximately 360. Ever eager to claim a triumph, Commanding General McClellan crowed to Secretary of War Stanton via telegram that night: "Victory of to-day complete and against great odds. I almost begin to think we are invincible."[1] Learning of the Rebel defeat, the men positioned south of the Chickahominy River were

T A Jackson

"STONEWALL" JACKSON.

FIGURE 7.1   Stonewall Jackson. Library of Congress, Prints
and Photographs Division.

exuberant. A comrade of Rollin's wrote: "The camps along the river reverberated with mighty cheers, and, for the first time in many weeks, our bands favored
us with their enlivening strains."[2] McClellan's army had resoundingly defeated
the most wily of the Confederate generals. (See figure 7.1.)

Except they hadn't. Jackson's name had quite literally preceded him. Mc-
Clellan's Achilles heel—his tendency to believe faulty intelligence—deluded
him into thinking that he had successfully thwarted a concerted incursion by
the feared General Stonewall Jackson and thereby had the initiative to continue to Richmond.

In writing his extensive recount of his experiences during the final week
of June and first week of July 1862, Rollin began the letter to his father dated
July 21 by setting the scene, so to speak, for the battles to come and by confess-
ing to the mass indulgent thinking regarding the Battle of Beaver Dam Creek.

Harrison's Landing Va.
July 21st 1862

My Dear Father

Your very welcome letter of the 17th inst I have just received and though I am on picket duty two miles from camp I have borrowed a soiled sheet of paper, pen, and ink to comply with your request to give an immediate answer to your letter containing the particulars of what I witnessed and endured while moving from Fair Oaks to James River.

Our position on the Chickahominy River has been so often described and mapped that you must understand it as a line of offense, so I will only give the position of our Brigade prior to the great move. The Brigade consists of the 96th Regt Penna Volunteers, 5th Regt Maine Volunteers, and 16th and 27th Regiments of New Yorkers, and were encamped near the battlefield of June 1st and 2nd, and about one mile east by north of Fair Oak Station. We had laid idly in this camp since the 18th of June, only being called out occasionally when there was picket skirmishing in front.

On Thursday the 26th ult we heard very heavy firing in the afternoon in the direction of Mechanicsville, and late in the evening a despatch came that Genl McCall had permitted some thousands of the Rebs to cross at Meadow Bridge and had got them completely bagged. Of course, we all hurrahed and two or three days later was somewhat chagrined to learn that the Rebs had got the bag . . .

By the morning of June 27, McClellan's bravado was merely a residue. When news reached the Commander of the Army of the Potomac that Jackson and his battle-ready men had slid into place, well positioned to initiate the flanking maneuver he thought he had prevented, McClellan and his strategy to take Richmond quietly crumbled. A victim once again of Confederate Major General "Prince John" Magruder's theatrics the day before, McClellan believed that he and his men south of the river had been beating back a mighty Confederate force while Porter was tackling the titan Jackson north of the river. With at least part of the illusion dispelled, McClellan ordered Porter to reposition his vulnerable corps to an area to the east and downriver, close to Gaines' Mill. And with this move, McClellan tacitly abandoned his strategy to capture the Rebel capital. Without Porter to protect access to the White House Landing railroad hub, McClellan knew he could not depend upon the arrival of the heavy artillery he had amassed. With no siege guns, he had no siege. Unbeknownst to Rollin and his comrades, instead of pushing to Richmond, they would spend the next five days pushing to safety, ducking the powerful punch McClellan believed his opponent of exaggerated numbers was planning.

We Thought We Had Been Fighting at Bull Run . . .

Given the events of the previous day, the men of the 27th NY Volunteers fully anticipated the pre-dawn order to fall in line on June 27, 1862. Refreshed with a supply of cartridges, they, along with the rest of Brigadier General Slocum's 1st Division, moved in light marching order approximately two miles northwest along the Chickahominy River toward Duane's Bridge. The familiar sounds of war grew in volume as they progressed toward their destination, punctuating their thoughts about the fight they would join across the river. When they arrived at the presumed crossing point to reinforce their battered comrades in the 5th Corps, the men learned that Porter had fallen back to a defensive position east of where Boatswain's Creek connects with the Chickahominy River, toward Gaines' Mill. Duane's Bridge was just to the west of the creek—the wrong side of the creek if a smooth troop movement to reinforce was being contemplated.

Rollin and his comrades had ample time to recoup some rest they may have lost due to the early bugle call. For hours they laid just across the river from the fighting near the bridge. Rollin's friend William Westervelt recalled: "We stretched under the shade of trees and smoked our pipes; some played cards; while others dozed under the soothing influence of the sound of cannon on the opposite side of the river."[3] Commanding General McClellan simply could not decide what to do with Slocum and his men after having peeled them off from Brigadier General William B. Franklin's 6th Corps. Keep them on the south side of the river as further insurance against an attack against his headquarters from Confederate troops based around Richmond? Or insert them into the fight on the north side of the river to reinforce and give relief to Porter, who would truly have a vicious battle on his hands that day when Stonewall Jackson thundered onto the battlefield? Protection of the line of retreat for his supply line was paramount.

In fact, Slocum started out the morning prepared to march his division straight onto the battlefield. As Slocum's column of men began to cross Woodbury Bridge, which would have placed them directly behind Porter's newly established defensive line, Commanding General McClellan suddenly recalled the order. What to do, what to do? Brigade Commander J. J. Bartlett reported that by 10 a.m., he was marching his men back to camp as ordered—attracting heavy artillery fire along the way.[4] Before reaching camp, yet another countermand: Rollin and his comrades tramped back to Duane's Bridge, ostensibly to prevent Rebels from crossing there.

By 2 p.m., McClellan had another change of heart. He sent an aid to division headquarters, and soon thereafter, Slocum's division was called in line. The men guessed wrong; rather than marching back to camp, this time they would be ordered to cross the river. By the afternoon, the division would be directed to the next bridge to the east of Woodbury, the Alexander Bridge. Third Brigade Commander John Newton moved out first in light marching order. The 1st Brigade, led by Brigadier General George Taylor, crossed next, around 3 p.m. Colonel J. J. Bartlett's 2nd Brigade held the position near Duane's Bridge until relieved by some of Brigadier General William T. H. (W.T.H.) Brooks's Vermonters from the 2nd division of Franklin's 6th Corps. Franklin ordered the 2nd Brigade to render Duane's Bridge unusable before joining the rest of the division. Once accomplished, Rollin and his comrades made haste to reunite with their two brother brigades on the north side of the river. A soldier from the 27th NY Volunteers expressed the sense of the men as they marched the 2.5 miles: "We started out in good spirits knowing we were going to lighten the burden which hung heavily on comrades for the past 36 hours."[5] The brigade traversed the Alexander Bridge around 4 p.m.

Reaching the north side of the river, they stepped right into the battle. One of Rollin's comrades summed up the scene: "The firing was most interestingly near, and raging with terrible force."[6] The splendid defense on the hill was being pounded away by the relentless onslaught of Confederate forces, just as Commanding General Lee directed. Porter needed urgent reinforcement all along the line, but the vulnerability of the flanks was of most immediate concern. When Bartlett reported to Division Commander Slocum upon arrival, Slocum, having been given no specific directions for Bartlett's brigade, ordered the brigade to the extreme left of the battlefield closest to the river to support Taylor's troops and to prevent the enemy from turning his flank. However, this was not the flank that concerned 5th Corps Commander Porter the most. (See figure 7.2.)

Before Bartlett's brigade could arrange themselves for the fight on the left of the battlefield, one of Porter's aid-de-camps galloped up to the column and informed Bartlett that instead he and his men were needed on the extreme right flank. Brigadier General George Sykes's 2nd Division was hemorrhaging.

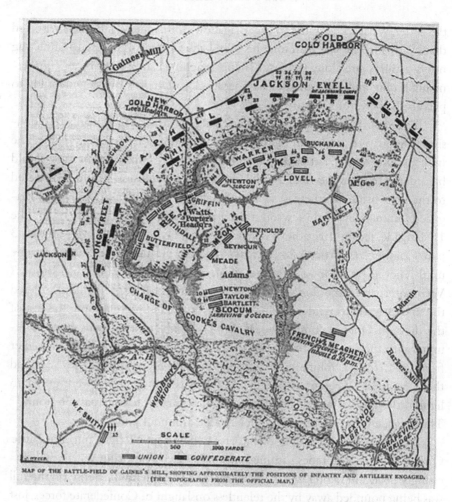

FIGURE 7.2   Map of the Battlefield of Gaines' Mill by Jacob
Wells. Library of Congress, Geography and Map Division.

The head of the column pivoted right, and the brigade commenced a harrowing march across the entirety of the rear of the battlefield from left to right.
With shot and shell cascading around the men and the chaos and shrieks of
the bloody battlefield surrounding them, Rollin and his comrades marched. As
they crossed the field, the full panorama of the battle unfolded. A member of
the 27th NY Volunteers wrote to his local newspaper about the scene: "Porter's
regiments were scattered, all with different stories, but all agreeing their regiment was cut 'all to pieces—not over 100 left.' Truly, the prospect was anything
but pleasing for those about to go in."[7] Fifteen men were killed or wounded

during this march of approximately thirty minutes—a march described by the 27th NY Volunteers regimental history as "a good test of the metal of our regiment."[8] Bartlett reported to Sykes around 4:30 p.m.

Sykes agreed to a brief respite for Bartlett's men before ordering them to jump into the cauldron before them. The men lay face down in a ravine to the right and rear of where Sykes's division of regulars and the 5th and 10th NY Volunteers persevered in holding back overwhelming numbers of advancing Rebels.[9] With the scorching sun on their backs, half-spent enemy shells splattered among the men. A comrade of Rollin's recalled: "I tell you, it was a ticklish place to be in—the enemy sweeping down death and destruction into our ranks and we powerless as it were."[10] After about thirty minutes of "rest," Bartlett received the order to bring his brigade forward. The danger to Porter's right flank, unsteady under withering enemy assault, could wait no longer.

In succession, each regiment of Bartlett's brigade, under raging fire, climbed the hill in front of them and into the battle. The 16th NY were the first called up to take the field and relieve weary comrades. Next, the 96th Pennsylvania and then the 5th Maine crested the hill; each new arrival linked with the regiment to its right. Finally, Lieutenant Colonel Alexander Adams was ordered to bring up his 27th NY. When the men heard Bartlett, their trusted former regimental commander, call them to attention, a member of the regiment later recalled that "every man rose up with a look of determination to possess the field or sell his life."[11]

The 27th, formed in line on an open field, were the targets for Rebel shooters taking cover in a house, outbuildings, and an orchard on the left crest of the hill facing them. It was Bartlett's voice again when the order came: "Up 27th! Forward, charge bayonets!"[12] Waiting until they were within approximately fifty yards of the enemy, and with three ringing cheers that the men claim could be heard over the cannon fire, Rollin and his comrades in the 27th NY Volunteers hurled themselves up the slope. The advance was fraught. One soldier from the regiment described it this way: "But mercy, what a storm of iron and leaden hail disputed our advance! And the brave Regiment was fast thinning with wounded and bleeding men."[13]

With the butt ends of their muskets, the men disposed of a picket fence running along a field that stood in the way of flushing the Rebels from the house and outbuildings. With that obstacle overcome, the men of the 27th NY Volunteers pushed further through close-range fire and neared a fence at the front of the house. After firing one more volley, the Rebels beat a hasty retreat from the buildings, leaving them, as well as several prisoners, in the possession of the regiment. In his official report of the Battle of Gaines' Mill, Brigade Commander Bartlett stated, "They . . . retreated so precipitately that they left two of their officers, who were vainly endeavoring to make them stand their ground."[14] As the enemy forces ran for cover, the 27th NY Volunteers directed steady fire into their ranks, littering the ground with dead and wounded.

Twilight was upon them, but the Confederates refused to accept the relinquishment of the position given up to Rollin and his comrades. Fresh Rebel troops took up the fight all along Bartlett's line, but their heaviest fire was directed on the left—at the 27th NY and the 5th Maine. Twice, false reports reached the 27th that the 16th NY had moved forward and within range of their Smithfields. Twice, the 27th ceased shooting. Twice, Rollin and his comrades were fired into at close range by Rebel forces. The smoke was so thick that finding the enemy was nearly impossible. A soldier from Company H wrote to his hometown newspaper: "Company F (Rollin's Company) suffered severely. At one time, that company received all the fire from the enemy."[15] The men of the 27th did not need to wait for orders to return fire, doing so with fury. The regiment repeatedly rallied and drove back the desperate enemy. Despite the fevered efforts of their foes, Rollin and his comrades did not give an inch of ground until long after dark. Rollin described the battle in the July 21 letter to his father.

Harrison's Landing Va.
July 21st 1862

. . . Friday morning the 27th the Brigade was marched down to the right of Genl Smith's Division near New Bridge, and there lay down under a scorching sun 'til three o'clock P.M. We could distinctly hear the continuous roar of musketry and artillery but a short distance from us across the river and a little to our right. The flats along the river being low and thickly studded with trees, we could not see the movements of troops on the opposite bank nor understand why we were halted there in the sun.

At three o'clock we recd orders to cut away the bridge and march down to Woodbury's Bridge two and a half miles distant. By the time this was accomplished, the retreating forces of McCall and Porter were within one mile of the bridge and fighting against great odds. We were immediately ordered up to their support. The

Rebel infantry held a position behind Gaines' house and the adjoining fences and to their right down to the bank of the river and
to the left as far as I could see.

The first business of our Regt was to make a bayonet charge
and drive the enemy away from the house. In making this charge,
we lost heavily but succeeded in driving the Rebs, capturing several prisoners and holding the place. The Rebs now retired to a
fence some twenty-five rods distant and having received reinforcements, made a desperate stand. The bullets and buckshot flew thick
and fast around me and the shell from our own batteries flying over
our heads made it a grand but awful spectacle. The air was so filled
with smoke that at sunset the firing practically ceased. About this
time, the Irish Brigade came up and, driving the Rebs from the
field, picketed the ground during the night.

I must now adjourn for want of paper 'till I get to camp ...

The 27th NY Volunteers were the last of Bartlett's men to leave the
battlefield at Gaines' Mill on June 27, 1862. With virtually every cartridge
expended, the men had carefully aimed at the flashes of enemy muskets in
the enveloping dark and listened to the silence to their right. (Taylor's and
Newton's brigades had also ceased firing on their left.) Around 9 p.m., after
having retired the 16th NY, 96th PA, and the 5th Maine by order of line of
battle, Brigade Commander Bartlett galloped up to Lieutenant Colonel Adams with the same order. For the men of the 27th NY, the command could
not have come soon enough. Under cover of night, a brigade-sized force of
Confederates had moved along the left side of the regiment and was advancing toward their rear, all the while shooting volley after volley into the ranks
of the outnumbered men.

The spent men of the 27th NY marched off the field in order and joined
their fellow regiments at the same ravine where, earlier that day, they had lay in
wait for their turn to enter the ferocious fight. Bartlett formed a new line of
battle with his brigade near the hospital. The scene was shocking. All day, the
mangled and the dead had been carried to the hospital on litters and in the arms
of fellow soldiers. The toll was heavy for officers and enlisted alike. Early in the
engagement, Colonels Howland and Jackson of the 16th NY and 5th Maine
were severely wounded; Lieutenant Colonel Heath of the 5th Maine was killed
instantly; Major Gardiner from the 27th NY was disabled by the concussion of
a shell; and Captain White of Company B, 27th NY, was shot through the hip.[16]

Though many of the wounded had been brought to the rear to be cared for, countless others were left on the battlefield in the chaos and darkness.

Rollin and his comrades solaced themselves in the thought that when day broke the next morning, the effort to retrieve bloodied bodies from the battlefield would resume, just as the fight would. They rested on their arms, on the lip of the battlefield, waiting for daylight. For many, including Rollin and Westervelt, who fought on despite dislocating his ankle, the allure of sleep was irresistible.

They did not know that the Commanding General's plan was not to face off against their determined foe at sunrise, but rather to quickly put as much distance as possible between his troops and that battlefield on the north side of the Chickahominy River. All Union forces were instructed to withdraw to the south side of the river that night, and at 12:30 a.m., Colonel Bartlett received the order for his brigade to recross the Alexander Bridge and return to the camp it had occupied before departing for battle. Collapsed in exhaustion, Rollin did not hear the command to move when it came. Neither did Westervelt, sleeping elsewhere in the woods. When each awoke from his resting place on the wrong side of the river, they recognized their circumstances and joined others in the fevered rush to cross to the south before Rebel forces swept in. Time was of the essence.

The struggle to move injured comrades across the Chickahominy had continued throughout the hours of darkness. But the number of casualties was overwhelming. Some were judged to be too serious to survive such a move and, absent alternatives, were left behind; others, the many walking wounded, were forced to fend for themselves to reach the bridge. Rollin, thrust along in the tidal wave of men desperate to escape being taken prisoner, was aware the window of escape was closing. As he hurried to the river, he stopped long enough to sweep an injured comrade from the 14th Regulars onto his back. Rollin carried the man for half a mile to the bridge, undoubtedly saving him from perishing on the field or being taken prisoner. Soon after Rollin crossed, with the Confederate cavalry on their heels, the Union rear guard destroyed the bridge. By the time Westervelt managed to hobble to the bridge, it was gone; his salvation was a passing log that he clambered aboard to paddle across the river.[17] Rollin's father was surely on the edge of his seat as he read the portion of Rollin's July 21 letter describing the rush to the bridge.

... In camp 2 o'clock PM.

(The sun is pouring down upon us with all its fury, but I will endeavor to finish my letter and get it off in today's mail which leaves at 6 o'clock this evening.)

When we left the battlefield just in the edge of the evening, we left many of our dead and wounded behind us expecting to be able to go back with ambulances and fetch them away, but through somebody's fault this was not fully accomplished, and quite a number fell into the hands of the enemy next day. When I was leaving the field I stepped over the body of a wounded soldier whom I recognized as John Merrett or Maryott whose widowed mother I think lives at Susquehanna Depot. He was wounded through the thigh. I lifted him up and tried hard to carry him off the field, but he was so exhausted from the loss of blood that he could not help himself at all, and after carrying him a short distance, I was compelled to lay him down. As he was a prisoner all of last summer after the Battle of Bull Run, I thought it more than a double portion for the poor fellow if left behind. Afterwards I could not find him, and whether he fell into the hands of the enemy or not, I cannot say.

A half mile to the rear of the battlefield our Brigade halted 'til half past eleven and then received orders to cross the river to our camp. At the time this order was given, I was enjoying a sound sleep 'neath a cluster of trees, and not being awakened, was left undisturbed 'til morning. Though I slept soundly, I felt as tired the next morning as I did when I sat down to rest.

At daylight I started for camp. I had not gone far before I crossed a ditch of clear water where I stopped to wash the dust and sweat from my face which, having dried on during the night, formed quite a debris. While going through with this performance, one of Genl Slocum's Aids rode by and told us to hurry over the bridge for it would soon be cut away. I started on at a quick pace but had proceeded but a little ways when I overtook a poor fellow wounded in the leg who belonged to the 14th Regulars. He was begging piteously for help but none of the passersby seemed to care for anyone but self, though I could not then see any immediate danger. It being only half a mile to the bridge, and the fellow only weighing about one hundred and thirty pounds, I concluded to try and back him over or carry him the way children call "poose back." Though it was a hard job, his thanks as I placed him safely in the ambulance thrice paid me for the effort . . .

Will McMahon, a member of the Color Guard from Company G of the 27th NY, in a letter to a friend described the Battle of Gaines' Mill and the succeeding days: "We thought we had been fighting at Bull Run, but that memorable 21st July was but a penny dip to a haitral lamp."[18] The Union defeat was conclusive. Confederate General Lee had taken more direct control over his forces this day than on the day previous, and though not without missteps, his army dominated in numbers (nearly 23,000 more men than the Union side), and perhaps in doggedness. Though McClellan had proffered some 6,000 of 6th Corps Commander Franklin's men from south of the Chickahominy to bolster Porter's inundated 5th Corps, he left almost 70,000 men idling south of the river. Eventually, Brigadier General John Bell Hood pushed his Texans through the center of Porter's line.

Both sides suffered deleterious losses. In Lee's army, 7,993 men were killed, wounded, or missing, and in McClellan's army, 6,837. Brigadier General Henry Slocum stated his division alone accounted for 2,021 of the Union casualties; and Regimental Commander Alexander Adams reported that 162 of the casualties were within the 27th NY Volunteers.[19] On this day, any lingering momentum in the Peninsula Campaign to wrest control of Richmond from the Confederate Army, any remaining conviction of the Union Commanding General that he could lead his devoted soldiers to that victory, disappeared like a puff of smoke.

McClellan, continuing to labor under the Pinkerton-crafted delusion that his Army of the Potomac was vastly outnumbered by Lee's Army of Northern Virginia (despite contradicting aerial reports submitted by the Balloon Corps in the previous days), wrote a dispatch to the Secretary of War on June 27, 1862, 8 p.m.:

> Have had a terrible contest. Attacked by greatly superior numbers in all directions on this side; we still hold our own, though a very heavy fire is still kept up on the left side of Chickahominy. I may be forced to give up my position during the night, but will not if it is possible to avoid it. Had I 20,000 fresh and good troops we would be sure of a splendid victory to-morrow.[20]

Falling Back

And so it was. Commanding General McClellan determined that Franklin's 6th Corps would serve as rear guard for the Army of the Potomac during its exodus to a new base of operations along the James River. As a comrade from Company E in Rollin's regiment relayed to friends at home, "This is the most laborious position in the whole army as today you guard the rear, and tomorrow you have to keep moving without any rest until the whole army comes to a halt."[21]

The constant movement that this role demanded began early the morning of June 28, 1862. The 27th NY, along with the rest of Slocum's division, soon took up the site along the Chickahominy River formerly occupied by Brigadier General Smith's 2nd Division to cover the retreat of the army's right wing. That Saturday morning, the location was untenable. Overnight, Confederate batteries had moved to plum positions on the north side of the river in the vicinity of where Porter's men were positioned the day before and poured sheets of shell onto Slocum's and Smith's men.

Rollin continued his July 21 letter to his father with a description of events after reuniting with comrades in the 27th NY Vols early the morning of June 28.

> ... Reaching camp about seven o'clock A.M., I found the Regt formed in line in heavy marching order with three days rations in their haversacks. We were marched down to the same position we held the morning previous to support a battery. The enemy soon opened upon us and got our exact range the first fire, but as our battery gave them their change, they soon ceased firing except an occasional shot through the day. During the day everything of value was moved away toward the James River, but we did not positively know we were going to evacuate the place 'til three o'clock A.M. the 29th. Saturday night our Regt was posted on picket to the right and left of New Bridge. At three o'clock we were ordered in and took up our line of march toward the James River. On a bluff one mile south of Woodbury's Bridge Genl Smith's Div was posted as rear guard and at his rear our Division under Command of Genl Slocum waited an hour to see the trains well under way and assist in driving back the enemy if any demonstration was made at that point.
>
> A little after daylight, we proceeded on our way and marched as far as Savage Station where we again rested a short time. A single dwelling in an open field is all there ever was of this place of present notoriety. From what I saw here, there was not a very great amount of supplies burned. The road from this station to White Oak Swamp was crowded with baggage wagons which very much impeded our progress. We crossed the swamp about noon and rested a couple of hours on a hill on the south side ...

When Rollin and his comrades from the 27th NY Volunteers commenced their march to Savage's Station in those predawn hours, they did so with the hot breath of Rebels in pursuit at their backs; they were among the last to join the general movement southeast. About two miles before Savage's Station, the regiment halted and formed a line of battle facing the rear for a short while before falling back toward the station. While there, resourceful Brigade Commander Bartlett encouraged the men to help themselves to new clothing from a quantity of stores that were left for want of transport.[22] Commissary and quartermaster supplies, feverishly hauled by rail from the White House Landing supply hub on the north side of the Chickahominy to Savage's Station, presented a dilemma for the Commanding General. How long could he press the rear guard to hold back the pursuing Confederate Army and block their grasp of federal booty?

When Rollin passed through Savage's Station, there were still hours of battle and piles and piles of materiel to be relegated to the torch. The 27th NY regimental history chronicled: "There were many smoldering piles, and others still burning; and there were deafening and incessant reports from the explosion of shells and ammunition being destroyed. A train of cars loaded with ammunition, was set on fire, and then the engine was started, on a down grade. It made a rapid run for the river; and the bridge being destroyed, it plunged in, amid the roar of bursting shells!"[23]

The state of the hospital where the wounded from the battle at Gaines' Mill had been evacuated, however, would be the memory most seared into the minds of Rollin and his comrades after they passed through Savage's Station. In a letter home, a member of the regiment wrote: "God grant I may never witness another such sight. Arms and legs lay here and there upon the ground, some severed below the elbow and knee, others nearer the body. On we go, those of the wounded able to walk following."[24] Mangled men, comrades and friends, pled to be removed to safety, to not be left behind to their fate in the hands of the approaching Rebels. The 27th NY Volunteers regimental history reflected: "Truly, this is a time that tries men's souls. What is to become of the wounded who cannot bear the jolting and swaying of the ambulances? Are the hospital tents, with their faithful nurses to be abandoned to the enemy? It may be that the safety of the army demands it."[25]

Even as heavy firing continued around Savage's Station, Slocum led his men south toward White Oak Swamp. Slocum had successfully buttonholed the Commanding General and received permission to pull his division—tattered from Gaines' Mill—out of formation. Ordered on June 28th to cross the White Oak Swamp, 5th Corps Commander Porter and his men also were not in the thick of the fighting that day. The combat at Savage's Station would result in 919 Union casualties, and 444 for the Confederates.

For miles, Rollin and his comrades jostled for space on the narrow roads with the army's urgently evacuated loads—artillery, supplies, and wounded soldiers.[26] Slocum crossed his division over the swamp around 2 p.m. Several hours later, he received the order to move his men about 1.5 miles beyond the swamp to a point along the Long Bridge Road toward Charles City Road. Upon arrival around 7 p.m., almost half of Slocum's division was sent out on picket for the night. For Rollin, standing watch against a relentless enemy seeping into their ranks under the veil of darkness, this would be his second sleepless night in a row.

Bleary-eyed, when the men of the 27th NY returned to camp at first light on the morning of June 30, 1862, they were ordered to countermarch approximately two miles to a location on the north side of the Charles City Road, a mile from its junction with the Long Bridge Road. McClellan had again directed Slocum to separate from Franklin's 6th Corps and adopt a position independent of it; the rest of Franklin's men would be posted to the northeast protecting against possible Confederate crossing of the swamp near White Oak Bridge. This time, however, McClellan did not issue the order in person. On this day, he would safely remove himself from the battle space—and from all access to telegraphic communications—by jumping aboard the gunboat USS *Galena* and steaming upriver to shell an enemy column sighted on the River Road west of Malvern Hill before onboard dinner and drinks.[27]

Confederate General Lee, on the other hand, resolved to personally witness his men tear the Union Army in half and punish them into collapse. Though misinterpretations and apprehensions by some senior field commanders again bedeviled execution of Lee's strategy this day, his presence in the battle space to redirect and encourage was surely inspirational to his exhausted troops. There was no such confidence-boost on the Union side. When he set sail on the *Galena*, McClellan failed to delegate command, so corps commanders were left to improvise and send urgent messages directly to fellow field commanders, as conditions over the course of the day necessitated.

Slocum's division, dipping into the woods just south of the White Oak Swamp, was situated on the right flank of the north-south battle line that ran through the area known as Glendale, and defended the continued cumbersome retreat of the Army of the Potomac. Brigadier General Kearny's 3rd Division of the 3rd Corps linked to the left of Slocum's. Upon arrival, Slocum

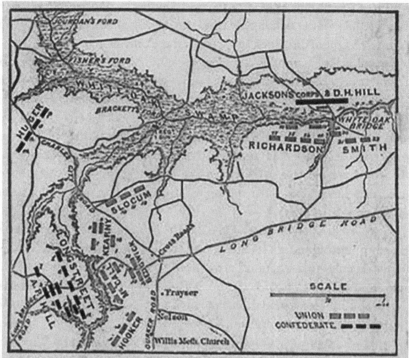

MAP OF THE BATTLE OF FRAYSER'S FARM (CHARLES CITY CROSS ROADS OR GLENDALE), JUNE 30, 1862, SHOWING APPROXIMATE POSITIONS OF UNION AND CONFEDERATE TROOPS. ALSO DISPOSITION OF TROOPS DURING THE ARTILLERY ENGAGEMENT AT WHITE OAK BRIDGE.

FIGURE 7.3   Map of the Battlefield of Glendale by Jacob Wells. Library of Congress, Geography and Map Division.

ordered the destruction of the Brackett's Ford Bridge across the swamp to the north of their location, and established artillery positions atop a hill facing the northwest approach of the Charles City Road. Rollin and his comrades in the 27th NY Volunteers were posted to protect a battery. Slocum hoped to further complicate Rebel encroachment on their position by ordering his men to slash trees along the Charles City Road to create a blockade, or at least an obstacle. (See figure 7.3.)

By midmorning, the twelve-pound howitzer pointing toward Brackett's Ford had successfully repulsed would-be Rebel bridge builders from their mission. By late morning, the three batteries attached to Slocum's division were engaged in a lively exchange with two Rebel batteries that had found a hill opposite to direct fire into Slocum's ranks. The felled timber had delayed but not prevented Confederate infiltration eastward. Cloaked in their approach by a narrow strip of woodland, Rebel forces drove in Slocum's pickets on Charles City Road and appeared in numbers in a large open field in the front of the division as they positioned their two batteries.[28] With shells whizzing past them, some within a few inches of their heads, Rollin and his comrades held position in the woods to the rear of the battery through much of the day.

As this brisk cannonading continued, Confederate forces were gut-punching the middle of the Union defensive line, putting into operation General Lee's playbook of cutting Union forces in half. Brigadier General George Mc-Call's 3rd Division of the 5th Corps, already battered from the fight three days earlier at Gaines' Mill, was in the unlucky position of defending the center of the line and absorbed blow after blow from determined Confederate attackers. Directly to the south of Slocum, Kearny's division was also under severe strain. By 7 p.m., Kearny's seam with Slocum's division was in danger of being compromised. Slocum ordered Bartlett's brigade to move to the front and gain possession of the field on which Rebels had first appeared that morning. To do this, the brigade pushed back a strong force of Confederate infantry that emerged as soon as Rollin and his comrades started down the road leading to the field. A member of Company E from the 27th NY Volunteers later recalled: "We marched in the direction of the enemy until we came in line with the battery; Bartlett ordered us to hold the position until dark at all hazards."[29] And hazards there were.

Rollin's July 21 letter to his father expanded on the high-stakes fighting of June 30, particularly toward the end of the day.

> ...We marched from here [Savage's Station] down to Charles City cross roads where we were posted on picket for the night. During the night we had several skirmishes with the Rebs who appeared to be trying to find the location of our forces.
>
> At daylight on Monday morning, we marched out on the Charles City road a mile to the right of our retreating army to protect that flank. Our Brigade supported two batteries of Parrott and Napoleon guns. We took position on a little hill overlooking a flat a mile or so in width, the batteries on the hill, the infantry to the rear of the batteries in the ravine. To our right was Genl Newton's Division and on our left Genl Sedgwick's. The enemy made a "dash" on us about nine o'clock but meeting such a deadly fire as we poured into them, they retired a short distance under cover of a thick wood and awaited reinforcements.

They made the second attack on our Div at three o'clock, and such artillery thunder as we had from that time 'til dark I never before heard. At five o'clock they attacked Sedgwick's Div in such force that they drove his men nearly half a mile, thus partially turning our left flank, leaving us in a pretty critical situation. But luck was ours, for just at this stage of the game Genl Kearney came to the rescue of Sedgwick with his division and gave the Rebs particular thunder, driving them back with dreadful slaughter. Thus ended Monday's fighting . . .

The Battle of Glendale raged until close to 9 p.m. The Federals ultimately held the line and denied Confederate General Lee his victory that day. But there was a cost: six companies of a Pennsylvania regiment were scooped up by the attackers. Though nearly half of the Union's 3,797 soldiers lost in the battle were taken prisoner, only 221 of the Confederate's 3,673 casualties were attributed to missing men.

With rations, water, and ammunition scarce, the 27th NY Volunteers did as Brigade Commander Bartlett had ordered—and then some. They held their position until after midnight, when they finally joined the retreating army heading south. The overnight march of July 1, 1862, would not be one Rollin would soon forget. As they set out, the regiment was virtually surrounded by Rebel soldiers; the men knew they were in danger of being cut off from the main body of the army. A fellow soldier described the perilous march: "At midnight we followed the artillery in the utmost silence, not a word being heard above a whisper for a long while. I tell you we have seen some hard times since Friday last."[30] They trudged on until the sun had begun showering its rays of heat over the horizon. Rollin's July 21 letter to his father conveys a clear sense of his misery during the march to Malvern Hill.

> . . . At sunset our baggage train of four thousand wagons had reached James River at Turkey Island Bend, and in an arc around them on the bluff was formed a line of defense, the place of Tuesday's fight. At midnight we left the scene of Monday's fight and took up our line of march for the river then five miles distant. The night was dark, the roads dusty, and never did I suffer of thirst as I did on that march. My eyes, nose, throat, and mouth were so filled with dust that I could hardly breathe. We pushed on slowly and arrived on the bluff just as the sun showed its red lurid face above

the horizon. Here I got water to quench my intolerable thirst and wash my dusty face ...

Rollin and his comrades in the regiment halted midmorning for a couple of hours to rest on the high bluff overlooking the James River. From this vantage point, they could see the site where the final battle of the week would unfold. Overnight, the Army of the Potomac had settled onto Malvern Hill, almost textbook perfect for defense. Mostly cleared of timber, the elevated plateau offered a grand view for artillery and men that would be posted in a horseshoe configuration around the 1½- by ¾-mile area. Here, given the probable newspaper headlines of the previous five days, Rollin stole enough time to jot a short note to his father in the hopes of assuaging worry at home.

July 1, 1862

Dear Father

You have probably learned ere this of our evacuation of Fair Oaks. I have not time to write particulars now but will the first opportunity.

We are now close to the James River, building breastworks. Our retreat has been hard pressed by the Rebs, but we have given them their change every time. This Div was engaged in the fight of Friday, also yesterday, but I am sound yet and stand it first rate. We are under cover of our gun boats and I think will be able to carry out the new plans of our Generals.

I do not know when I shall hear from you as our mail facilities are minus for the present. I send this to Fort Monroe by friend Chas Stoddard, Syracuse, who leaves in a jiffie.

Your aff son
Rollin B Truesdell

To: Sam'l W Truesdell
Great Bend, PA

Ravines toward the front, and the abrupt drop to flats leading to the James River in the northwest, enhanced the feeling of impregnability. A soldier from the 27th NY wrote appreciatively: "Pointed towards the course from which we came, were stationed a perfect circle of grinning cannon."[31]

The morning of July 1, 1862, Commanding General McClellan saw to it that his line of defense not only covered possible Confederate approaches from River Road that would threaten his left flank, but also the swampy terrain leading up to the right flank that would be difficult to traverse, but catastrophic to his line of retreat if punctured. Both divisions of Brigadier General Franklin's 6th Corps were posted to the right flank. Presumably, fine-tuning the deployment of his troops would appease his conscience for again electing to set sail on the *Galena* rather than being present to command his army during the inevitable resumption of battle. On this day, his excursion was to scout the army's final haven during the Peninsula Campaign—Harrison's Landing.

Harrison's Landing is to the southeast of Malvern Hill on the north bank of the James River. The area spans approximately four miles and is cupped by Kimmage's Creek on the west, and Herring Creek on the north and east. Commanding General McClellan was satisfied to make this pleasant highland his next operational base. Here, the navy's gunboats could overwatch McClellan's army.

But before reaching that resting spot, there would be one more contest with the determined Confederate forces, and one more numbing march. When Rollin and his comrades in the 27th NY arrived at Malvern Hill, they took up their position on the right flank, which extended into the woods. Ordered to hold the right flank at all costs, the regiment constructed breastworks in front of their line and held their position until late in the evening. From that location, they were removed from the artillery bombardments and desperate waves of Rebel assaults aimed at the center of the Union lines. McClellan, after returning late that afternoon from his field trip, settled himself on the extreme right of the defensive line with a lovely view of the James River, vaguely able to hear the artillery fire. (See figure 7.4.)

The Confederate onslaught was determined but futile. Some 250 Yankee cannon, judiciously placed and aggressively used, decimated the Rebel warriors. Seeking to replay the success achieved at Gaines' Mill, Lee focused on rupturing the center of the Union defensive line. On this day, starting around 1 p.m., Union batteries pounded Confederate artillery positions before they could effectively establish their intended converging fire power. Nonetheless, Lee pushed his infantry forward into the hungry maw of the Union artillery.

By late afternoon, brigade after brigade had thrust themselves across the open plain, only to be felled by the Union batteries that were their object.

Then, sometime before 7 p.m., came the Confederate bayonet charge, recalled by comrades in the 27th NY Volunteers: "From the dark pine forest, at a double-quick, came their yelling hordes once more, determined, if possible, to take the position so sternly defended."[32] But the Army of the Potomac repulsed each Rebel thrust, and by around 9 p.m., artillery had quieted. The final battle in the failed campaign to capture Richmond was over.

FIGURE 7.4 Plan of Battle of Malvern Hill by Robert Knox Sneden. Library of Congress, Geography and Map Division.

HARRISON'S LANDING

Thirsty for signs that the tide had changed, that theirs was a mission that was winnable and that the Confederate capital could yet be within their grasp, the Commanding General's order to continue the army's retreat was a blow to the morale of the men who saw the Battle of Malvern Hill for what it was—a victory for the Union. The day was costly for both sides, to be sure, but the Federals succeeded in using the strength of their position to break Confederate momentum by sweeping the battlefield with their artillery fire to dazzling, sickeningly lethal, effect. The Confederates had lost some 5,600 men, while the Federals lost over 3,000. Commanding General McClellan's most trusted senior officer, 5th Corps Commander Porter, reportedly spent the evening of July 1 laying out the case for the Union Army to take the initiative and follow up on July 2 with a counteroffensive. The regimental history for the 27th NY Volunteers lamented: "We had plainly won a battle, and still occupied a position on and around Malvern Hill, from which, it would seem, offensive operations could have been directed against a beaten enemy; but the order came to fall back, and take position at Harrison's Landing, on the James River."[33] (See figure 7.5.)

Rollin's chronicle of the events around the Seven Days Battles, shared in his July 21 letter to his father, continued with a description of the sodden march to Harrison's Landing after the Battle of Malvern Hill. The men experienced new standards in soul- and boot-sucking Virginia mud.

> . . . We again marched southward down the river to our left flank and then up a breast work of trees which we occupied without being attacked 'til twelve o'clock at night when we moved onward towards Harrison's Landing, then some six miles distant. The road in front of us was filled with troops and our march was necessarily slow and tedious. A drenching rain set in at four o'clock and when we reached the landing at 8 o'clock A.M., not a dry thread was in my clothes. We pitched our tents (those that had not thrown them away) in a field of ripe wheat and laid down in the mud to rest. Yes, rest, for I had not slept any since Friday night the 27th, and then I did not rest myself much. For four days I had only eaten four "hard tacks." My appetite was gone. My only want was water, and not 'til I awoke on Thursday morning and crawled myself out of my "wallowing" place did I feel the want of eatables. I waded through the mud, then eight inches deep, down to the river and filled my canteen with water, ate some hard bread, and "stood" in the mud 'til noon when we moved our camp back into a field of green sward where we were more comfortable, but the day was cloudy and damp, forbidding us the privilege of drying our wet clothes so we were obliged to lay in the wet another night . . .

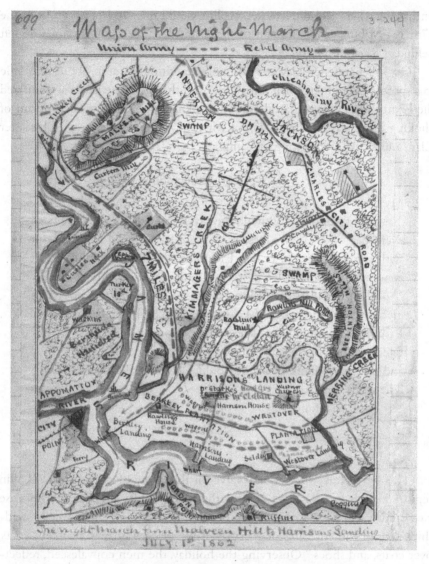

FIGURE 7.5 Map of the Night March from Malvern Hill to Harrison's Landing by Robert Knox Sneden. Library of Congress, Geography and Map Division.

From June 25 to July 2, 1862, McClellan suffered a loss of 15,849 men—6,053 of whom were missing.[34] With just over 20,000 casualties, Lee had lost about a quarter of his fighting force. For days, Rollin and his sleepless comrades had been under arms constantly, marching, countermarching, subsisting on hard crackers and ditch water. Rollin would miss 184 brethren from the 27th NY Volunteers at the end of the seven days, many of whom were left behind at Savage's Station.

On Independence Day, the regiment transitioned camp, about one mile to a spot no more than a half mile back from the river. The new camp offered the luxury of dry ground and a good drinking water supply. The imprint of choking thirst was on Rollin's mind when he wrote a short note to his sister Clara a few days after setting up camp.

Harrison's Landing, Va., July 7th, 1862

My Dear Sister,

Your favor of the 30th ult. I received some days ago. I have tried every day since last Wednesday to write home, but I got tired out with our long march, so that I feel like doing nothing but rest. It is now 10 o'clock P.M. and so hot I cannot sleep, so I try to write.

The particulars of our long and tedious march I will not try to give. I was in the battle of Friday the 27th and Monday the 30th. I am well, uninjured, and safe. Sunday, Monday, and Tuesday I suffered terribly for the want of water. As I marched along, I dreamed and fancied I drank from the "old, cold spring." Oh, 'twas awful. The roads were so dusty!

I will write more in a day or two.

Yours truly,
Rollin

The 4th of July was a release valve for the Army of the Potomac. Rollin reported in his July 21 letter to his father that, "Friday July 4th the sun rose clear and warm over a camp which gave little evidence of its week's hardships save in the covering of every available place with wet blankets, coats, over coats, and shoes." Observing the holiday, the men convalesced, reflecting on the privations they had endured over the past week and throughout the Peninsula Campaign. Gunboats and batteries fired a celebratory salute, and in the evening, their Commanding General rode through camp to greet his troops and receive their cheers. One of Rollin's comrades wrote home: "The 4th was quiet until McClellan passed the regiments. There is not a soldier in the army but has perfect confidence in him."[35] Another, reflecting on that day years later, wrote: "No other commander of the Army of the Potomac ever so aroused the enthusiasm, or was so much the idol of that army as General McClellan, and as he rode through our camp on the fourth of July, the men spontaneously rushed out to look upon him and admire as they always had done, but the cheering for him was not as hearty as it had been the past eleven months."[36]

Perhaps McClellan's grip on the hearts of his men was not as tight as he believed.

Interrupted by President Lincoln's visit to the troops on July 8, 1862, the next six weeks for the Army of the Potomac at Harrison's Landing was largely an exercise in bracing against a possible attack by Confederate forces as well as against the insidious heat, with attendant diseases. Some among Rollin's regiment believed they would remain at this camp for just a few days before renewing the fight. Rollin thought otherwise. He shared his views, along with renewed assurances regarding his health, in a July 9 letter to his mother.

Harrison's Landing Va
July 9th 1862

My Dear Mother,

 Although much worn out by the incessant labors of the past week, I now begin to get straightened out and feel like myself.

 I suppose if you know that I am well it will appease your anxiety and give you rest to your eyes at night and comfort to your mind by day. This luxury, the greatest of all earthly blessings, I am most happy to inform you, I possess to its fullest extent.

 With all the inconveniences and hardships which I have to endure, I am sure I enjoy a calmer mind than you and Father who luxuriate on all the niceties of a well spread table and comfortable home. I am in the heart of the excitement, you only through the medium of the newspapers. But one thing I pray both of you not do is borrow trouble. When you know of a certainty that I am sick or injured, it may be time to be troubled, but do "keep cool."

 It is only a year now if I am spared before I shall be home. Time flies quickly and the time will soon come 'round. I fancy your health and Father's is not good this summer. Perhaps I am mistaken—hope I am—but seems to me you are both worrying all the time.

 It is quite probable that we shall remain here some time, perhaps a month.

 The weather here is very hot and sultry. I stand it first rate, get enough to eat, to drink, and to wear.

I see no reason if I am not shot why I am not going to live through it. I can stand the pressure of everything but bullets, I think.

With much love to my parents, I am

Your affectionate son
Rollin B. Truesdell

Three days later, further rested and contemplating what might make camp life at Harrison's Landing more bearable, Rollin penned a note to his father with some comfort item special requests.

Harrison's Landing Va
July 12th 1862

My Dear Father

Watson and Burrows have concluded to have a box of things sent to them by express and have requested me to have you put in such articles as I may wish to have sent to me. I do not need many things just now, but if you will send the following articles, they will add greatly to my comfort and convenience. One good jack knife, one towel, half pound of sulphurs put up in tin box, half pound Epsom salts, one quart bottle of best "Old Rye Whiskey," and the little willow bound flask I left at home last spring. These are essentials that I want. Then, if you can put in a book or two of some kind, or any other notion that you may think of, they will be very thankfully received.

Things are very quiet here now. My health is good and spirits fine.

Your aff son
R. B. Truesdell

(PS) Put in a bunch of good buff envelopes.

During this time at Harrison's Landing, Rollin and his comrades alternately perfected fortifications in front of defensive lines, improved their camp, went on picket, or drilled as they awaited the arrival of reinforcements, the necessity of which their Commanding General would remind all who would listen. The 27th NY Volunteers were called into battle line once, on July 31st, before Union gunboats dispensed with a harassing Confederate battery that popped up on the opposite side of the James River.

And of course, as time ticked on, Rollin and his comrades reflected on how the campaign to take Richmond was conducted and what its failure meant to the larger Northern effort. In his letter to a friend, Will McMahon shared his views on the state of the Army of the Potomac: "We were whipped, not in superior fighting qualities, but by numbers. The rebels are brave men. They are a foe worthy of our prowess and steel. We are now entrenching and need reinforcements greatly. Every man of 300 thousand called for is needed."[37] McClellan kept up the drumbeat in Washington for *more men, more men* to have any prospect of relaunching an attack on Richmond.

Rollin's letter to his father of July 21 concluded with his own analysis of the stakes the Army of the Potomac faced, and with the efforts he was undertaking for promotion.

> . . . Having given the outlines of the movements of our Regt during the week of battles, I will grant your request of giving my opinion in regard to the late move of our army, its present situation, etc.
>
> From my own observation, I considered it very doubtful if we could long hold our position along the Chickahominy for several days prior to the great move to the James River. It took about thirty thousand men to do our picket duty, and the line, extending from Hanover Court House on the right to near Charles City Court House on the left, could not with the force at command be protected so that the enemy could not concentrate a force in one night at some of the weak points large enough to force our lines.
>
> Say nothing of the superior advantage of Prof. Lowe's balloon, a careful observer would judge from their actions for several days previous to the battles that they were receiving large reinforcements while we on the other hand were losing very many effective men every day. What then could be done? Stay there behind our trenches and let the enemy turn both our flanks and cut us in pieces with their superior numbers? Or make a retrograde movement and secure the safety of our army. Under the circumstances, it was the only course that could be pursued. That the enemy got the worst of it in all the battles on the retreat, I doubt not. As to our present situation, I think it will be a permanent military post, but the Rebs can do us much injury on the river below us.
>
> The general expression of our men is highly in favor of General McClellan, but there are some few who think him inferior to Halleck, Pope, and Burnside.

From appearances, I think we shall not move again 'til we have heavy reinforcements.

I saw Sumner Lines this morning. He is much worn out and looks thin, but says he is improving every day. Burrows and Watson are both quite well.

If you have not sent that box of things when this reaches you, put in a pair of suspenders, some letter paper and envelopes. If the box comes safe, I shall send immediately for another as we have to pay such exorbitant prices for everything here. When I see the sutlers selling things at such high prices, I wish them exiled to some barren isle.

I think you will not complain of the shortness of this letter but will acknowledge your indebtedness and give me a long reply. You do not know the value of letters from home here in the army.

If you think it worthwhile to try to get me a commission to go into the new levy, do what you can. I send a copy of a certificate just handed me which I intend to have changed a little and indorsed by several officers and send to the proper place.

Head Quarters, Co F, 27th Regt, NYSV

July 20th 1862

I certify that during the time I have known private Rollin B. Truesdell, I have always found him ready and willing to do his whole duty at all and every time. He possesses every qualification of a good soldier, obedient and respectful to his superior officers, and does his duty with cheerfulness and alacrity.

A Patrullo 1st Lieut

Commanding Co

I cannot tell yet where the proper place to send it will be 'til I see Col Bartlett (now our Brigadier Genl).

I am going to make a pull at all events. I think with certificates that I can get, with the influence at home, I can better myself.

With much love to all, I am

Your aff son
Rollin B. Truesdell

As Rollin and his comrades waited for reinforcements to arrive, the stifling heat to subside, and a campaign strategy to emerge, maintaining morale was difficult. Rollin's well-being was inexorably linked to the ritual of letter writing—but after enduring the trials of the last campaign, his first prolonged participation in bloody battles—he also needed to feel the presence of his family through their words to him via letter. A trio of letters to his father (July 18), sister Clara (July 24), and mother (July 31) reveal Rollin's growing ease after the battles even as he still cajoled his loved ones to write. And for his sister, he even shared a delightful recipe for unripe blackberry pie.

Harrisons Landing Va
July 18th 1862

My Dear Father

Whether you get my letters I am unable to say. I have not received but one letter from home since the battles, and that from Albert this morning. He does not mention the receipt of any of my letters. If you do but get them and know I am well I am content, but I do not know this.

We are here near this landing, resting, building forts, rifle pits, redoubts, and putting this place in a condition to defend against a superior force.

The weather is hot and sultry, making one long for the cool springs and breezes of the North. I stand it first rate, better than nine tenths of my comrades. I make health my study and thus far have enjoyed this blessing to its fullest extent.

Please write often. With much love to all I am

Your aff son
R. B. Truesdell

Harrison's Landing Va July 24th 1862

My Dear Sister Clara

Your letter of the 20th inst I received this morning. I think you could well afford to write a long letter after your long silence, which was entirely unnecessary as all letters directed to Washington will reach me as a general thing without fail.

We are leading a monotonous camp life again with little prospect of moving very soon, indeed, there is nothing now transpiring that I think would be interesting to you. I suppose we are doomed to hear the message of "all quiet along the lines" for the next two months at least, perhaps longer.

This morning I went about two miles from camp and picked a quart of green blackberries (ripe are not to be had, the boys pick them so fast), and my tentmate and myself agreed we would have a "good" pie. He had a few dried apples and half a lemon which we put with my berries and stewed 'til we thought they were just as good as stewing could make them. Then we sweetened them with about a pound of sugar or less which we bought of a sutler for the moderate price of 25 cents per pound. But we weren't going to stop because sugar was high. Well, after we got our fixin's all fixed, we had a quart cup full, all for one pie.

Then we contracted with an old Dutchman, who is the happy owner of an old fashioned bake kettle to make the crust and bake the pie. Maybe you never saw a bake kettle, but Mother knows what they are. We looked on and see him roll out the crust good and thick, had him do everything just as we wanted it done. We was bound to be pleased once if possible. Well, after much telling, the old fellow got the thing to suit us and put it in the kettle, and we, like dumheads, set down in the hot sun to see it bake, and it did bake "superbly." It tasted the best of any pie I ever ate and as hungry as we were for something beside rations, we could not eat it all for supper and left some on the plate.

If I should tell one more pie story, I would have a long letter, but I would not give a cent for pie just now so I will write about something else.

I see something "new" in my eye in the shape of something from home. It's quite dim yet but I think it will get clear in a few days. I wish I had "told" Julia to put in a bottle of honey. We get butter here now, put up in two pound tin cans at the reasonable price of $1.75 per can. If this box comes through safe, I am going to send for another immediately. I can invest $10.00 at home in goods that I can sell here for $30.00, and then undersell those abominable sutlers.

Burrows has come and set down by me, and I am talking to him about home, and trying to make myself believe we will both be there in – a year or little less.

Those papers I sent for came safe to hand. Capt Jay has gone home, used up in every sense of the word. Patrullo, our 1st Lieut, is a fair sort of a man.

I can't write any more this time.

With good health and fine spirits, I am

Yours truly
Rollin B. Truesdell

I got a letter from Mart today.

Harrison's Landing, Va., July 31st, 1862

My Dear Mother

If there is anything in the world that I "set store by," and especially under the present circumstances, it is a letter from either of
my parents. I think them worth half a dozen from any other source,
and will always try and give them a prompt answer.

I received your letter and Clara's yesterday morning, and should
have answered them yesterday, but we worked on the rifle pits all
day, so I make it my first business this morning. I have the same
good news to write this time that I am thus far blessed with very
good health, enough to eat and drink and wear, which I suppose
you are always glad to hear. I am thankful that I am able to write it
and speak truthfully.

Our present camp is two miles back from the river, affording us
a good breeze night and morning, but during the middle of the day,
the sun is most scorching hot. I sometimes fear sickness from the
sudden changes in the atmosphere, but at no time, save in wet spells,
have I experienced any inconvenience, and then a slight aching of
the bones, a kind of slight rheumatism. This, beside what some of
my comrades have, is nothing at all. The heat causes blotches on my
skin, which is disagreeable, but as soon as I get my salts and sulphur,
I am going to try and purify my blood and rid myself of this little
irritation.

Watson told me this morning that the box was to be sent on
Tuesday, the 29th, so for a few days "My longing eyes will be unto
thee, O box." Anything from home, I think I can appreciate fully. If
this one comes safe, I am going to try another. I hope sister J. put in
a bottle of honey. But all will be good, no doubt.

I hope the men folks are all busy haying now, so you will have
to answer this letter. Let nothing prevent, and have Pa write, too.

Your affectionate son,
Rollin

Many others struck down by illness and anxiety did not fare as well. A
soldier from Company B recalled this time: "The once jolly mess tables at
Elmira, that used to ring with jests and laughter, and glow with wit and good
humor, was exchanged for continuation of low, peevish growls resounding
through the camp. A poisoned army lying in camp has about as much morale
as you may find in a sheep fold, especially here on the Peninsula."[38] Rollin

wrote of such pernicious influences on comrades in a letter to his sister Clara on August 10, 1862.

Harrison's Landing Va
August 10th 1862

My Dear Sister

I have not received a letter from you in some time, the reason I do not know, but suppose it is so hot up at <u>Great Bend</u> that you cannot possibly sit down and write. Well, if it is one tenth part as hot there as it is here, I cannot blame you, but notwithstanding <u>your</u> delinquency, I do not feel justified in doing the same.

I suppose you are enjoying the same Sabbath day privileges as of "olden days," privileges not known in this army. According to the Almanac it is Sunday here, but we hear no church going bells to remind us of the sanctity of the day, or remind us of our childhood teachings. To regard the Sabbath day and keep it holy in the army is left entirely with one's conscience; there is no kind of moral restraint over the soldier's actions, but he is left to go the broad or straight and narrow. Instances are rare where the morals of the youth, of which a large majority of this army is composed, are not corrupted by the evil influences with which they are surrounded. 'Tis a sad thing to think of, but alas too true.

If you would do a good thing for the new volunteers, put books into their hands. Do not give them all Testaments and nothing else but give them plenty of literary reading. When this Co. was first organized, they were provided with a Testament, tracts, and other religious books, but no other kind. Men used to a variety of reading matter cannot be interested all the while in religious reading, and they soon pick up the habits of card playing and gambling. Not over half a dozen books given to this Co. a year ago now remain in it, though some were necessarily thrown away while on fatiguing marches, and now we are minus anything to read, but not without our quota of professional card players and gamblers.

It is truly a dull and loathsome society for me, but I live in hopes of better days.

I have not yet received my box.

My health is good. Write often & direct to Washington.

Your Bro Rollin

Rollin's conflicted company commander, Captain Peter Jay, succumbed at Harrison's Landing. By the third week in July, Jay was back in New York. He formally resigned his commission on August 14, 1862.[39]

That same day, Rollin departed Harrison's Landing, along with the rest of his comrades from the 27th NY Volunteers. President Lincoln's patience with his Commanding General of the Army of the Potomac had evaporated. Installing Henry W. Halleck as general-in-chief of all the Union armies on July 11 after his frustrating meeting with McClellan at Harrison's Landing, Lincoln gave Halleck authority to make what decisions were necessary to get the war effort back in gear. McClellan was paralyzed. No number of proffered reinforcements was enough to invigorate his campaign on Richmond, and yet he was unwilling to consider withdrawing from the peninsula. Finally, on August 3, Halleck formally ended the stalemate and compelled McClellan to remove his force from Harrison's Landing and join Major General John Pope's Army of Virginia.[40] Even with the direct order in hand, McClellan dragged his heels; the first units from his army did not reach Aquia Creek until August 22.

The men of the 27th NY Volunteers finally received word of the impending move the evening of August 10. Though having written a letter to her earlier in the day, Rollin dutifully penned a note to his sister Clara, updating her with the news.

Harrison's Landing Va
August 10th 11 P.M.

Dear Sister

Since writing to you this morning a sudden change has taken place in our camp. When writing this morning there was no more signs of an immediate move than there had been for weeks previous, but at sunset we received orders to pack knapsacks and have them ready to send on board of transports at 4 o'clock tomorrow morning. I have just finished packing my little treasures, never expecting to see them again if thrown in a pile with ten thousand others, but necessity compels me to do it and run my chances.

If we leave at 4 A.M., I do not know when I can have an opportunity to mail it, for I know as little about where we are to go as you who are at home resting quietly with naught to disturb or make afraid through the still hours of the night.

There is much speculation where we are to go, but as none know, I will not tell anything but what I know to be a fact, <u>and</u>

I positively know that I know nothing about it. Like some other military strategy of modern date, we may not leave camp at all.

I will write again the first opportunity.

Bear in mind that any move of this army does not change the Post Office address. Do not direct any more letters to Harrison's Landing, Turkey Bend, or Westover.

My health is now prime. I think I was never in better condition to endure hardship than the present time, but of choice I prefer to postpone active operations 'til cool weather. The reason of my good condition is the loss of some thirty (30) pounds of surplus flesh since arriving on the peninsula.

The Co have just sent home the remains of one of its members who died of Typhoid fever. It cost us $81.00 to have him embalmed and sent. It cost individually a little less than $2.00 a piece, but unless a member is killed in action, we do not bury him on "Confederate" soil.

I have finally drawn out a good long letter, so with much love to all, I will bid you a good night—no morning, 'tis past twelve—and lay down and take a nap.

Yours,

Rollin B. Truesdell

Rollin could only guess where the army would send him and his comrades next. But he did know that, finally, after weeks of replaying the battles of the Peninsula Campaign in his mind in the fetid camp at Harrison's Landing, he would be moving forward toward the next great battle that might end this war.

THE WAR MOVES NORTH

George McClellan was angry. And incredulous. The Commanding General of the Army of the Potomac employed all his rhetorical powers to convince the General-in-Chief and the President to rescind the orders, insisting that all he required was a healthy number of reinforcements to bring his battle-weary army the glory of defeating the Rebels in their capital. Yet, his superiors' stance only hardened as the days ticked by. General-in-Chief Henry Halleck initiated the withdrawal process of the Army of the Potomac from Harrison's Landing with his telegram to McClellan on July 30, 1862. He ordered the evacuation of the sick and wounded in preparation for a larger movement of forces. McClellan reacted with little surprise but great disdain when he received the telegram from Halleck three days later demanding he immediately remove the entirety of his army from their safe haven on the James River and return to northern Virginia. President Lincoln and Halleck had no confidence that McClellan would uncoil himself and his army from its crouched position; his men, and he himself, must come north to realign Union forces and end the vulnerability its division posed.

While Rollin and his comrades in the Army of the Potomac were languishing at Harrison's Landing through most of July 1862, 40,000 or so men under the command of Major General John Pope were positioned and re-positioned to spar with Confederate Major General Jackson's pestering force across the Rapidan River.[1] Pope's troops effectively were dual purposed: they blocked Confederate reach toward Washington and Baltimore and also teased the Rebels away from the resting Army of the Potomac. Pope, the commander of the nascent Army of Virginia and an annoying thorn in McClellan's side as he stoked his own propaganda machine and jabbed at the commander of the Army of the Potomac, sought to define himself as the commander who pushed toward the fight. General Pope's widely published address to his soldiers on July 14, 1862, revealed much about his character:

> I come to you from the West where we have always seen the backs of our enemies, from an army whose business it has been to seek the adversary and to beat him when found . . . I desire you to dismiss from your minds certain phrases which I am sorry to find much in vogue amongst you—e.g. "taking strong positions and holding them," "lines of retreat," and "bases of supplies." Let us look before us and not behind . . . Disaster and shame lurk in the rear.[2]

By mid-July, with Pope's splashy presence a clear invitation, Confederate Commanding General Lee had dispatched Stonewall Jackson with two divisions to check Pope's advance and protect the Virginia Central Railroad, a lifeline for the Confederate Army. After Jackson assessed that Pope's numbers were insurmountable to successfully attack, Lee sent another division forward to Jackson as reinforcement until the Federals revealed their strategy. From Washington, the developing situation was untenable. If Lee opted to consolidate his forces around Jackson's position—particularly with numbers reaching up to McClellan's oft-cited yet hallucinatory 200,000 men—the Confederate Army could deal a deadly blow either north or south to devastating effect. Either or both McClellan's and Pope's armies were in jeopardy if they remained separate and unable to come to the rescue if the other were attacked. Given this logic, there was no room for debate and little time to act—so emphasized Halleck to McClellan.

The Commanding General organized the move and bickered with Washington simultaneously. The most efficacious mode of transferring nearly 90,000 men, materiel, and transport of McClellan's army quickly to Aquia Creek near Alexandria, Virginia, would have been by water—down the James to the Chesapeake Bay and then up the Potomac River. But this was not without difficulties. Securing access to loadbearing vessels that could ply the waters around Harrison's Landing was a problem. Heavy draft steamers available at Fort Monroe were unable to make it up the James River, and the landing itself was not designed for embarkation of multiple vessels at once.

And some troop and cargo capable ships that might otherwise be available to McClellan were instead pressed into immediate service for a few days in early August by Major General Ambrose Burnside; he had received the order on August 1 to move his men from Newport News to Aquia Creek. Burnside, whose troops were covetously eyed by McClellan, had successfully led an amphibious expedition over the past several months along the North Carolina coast to shut off the majority of the ports to Confederate shipping for the rest of the war. In July, he with his newly formed 9th Corps, had been instructed to hold in Newport News, Virginia, until further notice. In marked contrast to McClellan's foot shuffling, Burnside snapped to, and his soldiers began debarking at Aquia Creek on August 3 to join Pope's forces, which had moved by then to a position south of the Rappahannock River.

In truth, McClellan was more preoccupied with trying to undo the order to withdraw than aggressively identifying naval support to convey his army and its impedimenta to Aquia Creek. As Halleck kept the pressure on by demanding regular progress reports, McClellan became more truculent. After receiving the order to evacuate nearly 12,000 sick and wounded on July 30, he squandered several days planning and overseeing the failed August 5 excursion to retake Malvern Hill. In a telegram on August 7, 1862, McClellan began to offer some of the specificity Halleck was waiting for: "We have shipped 3,740 sick and have 5,700 more to move. We shipped five batteries with horses, wagons, and men. We can transport 25,000 men at a time . . . Several of the largest steamers are being used for prisoners."[3] But Halleck continued to push. When Halleck contrasted Burnside's timing with his own, McClellan telegrammed on August 10: "The present moment is probably not the proper one for me to refer to the unnecessarily harsh and unjust tone of your telegrams of late."[4] And a few days later, McClellan coolly informed Halleck that, "It is not possible for anyone to place this army where you wish it, ready to move, in less than a month."[5]

Meanwhile, Confederate Commanding General Lee watched and waited. He could not risk prematurely repositioning his protective shield of troops blocking Richmond from the Army of the Potomac (and other possible Union threats) should McClellan find some confidence. By mid-August, Lee saw that McClellan's dawdling was ending; Union troops were leaving Harrison's Landing. Understanding the peril Jackson faced should McClellan's behemoth force join with Pope's Army of Virginia, Lee sped Major General James Longstreet north with his 25,000 or so men to unite with Jackson's. But more compelling for Lee: here was a golden opportunity to dispense with Pope and his army while McClellan sauntered northward. On August 19, Pope frustrated Lee's plans by moving his men across the Rappahannock River to the north bank, beyond immediate Confederate reach. Undeterred, Lee would improvise a different tack over the coming days.

Though a piecemeal approach, McClellan did succeed in shipping hundreds of tons of regimental baggage, several divisions or portions thereof, and all the sick and wounded from Harrison's Landing. For Rollin and the vast majority of the Army of the Potomac, a long walk was in store. A *New York Times* correspondent embedded with the Army of the Potomac whispered of the withdrawal to his readers, writing, "Ever since Friday, August 8, the force has gradually been sent away to not attract attention . . . The length of the marching column is probably reduced by 16 or 20 miles."[6]

In preparation for the march, McClellan sent a cavalry unit to clear out a Confederate cavalry regiment near White Oak Swamp. He also directed the Engineer Corps to build a 2,000-foot pontoon bridge near the mouth of the Chickahominy River at Barrett's Ferry capable of supporting the crossing of the greater part of his army—including artillery wagon trains. Finally, on August 14 the columns of the Army of the Potomac began their exodus. McClellan and his personal staff were the last to depart Harrison's Landing on August 16, 1862.

Déjà Vu

Rollin and his comrades in the 27th NY Volunteers began their tramp from Harrison's Landing on August 15, not knowing their destination or if there was still life in the Peninsula Campaign. When they were directed to halt after a mere four miles for picket duty, the possibility likely seemed remote that in the coming days they would retrace their steps covering miles and miles of terrain they had excitedly traversed three months earlier. The next afternoon, they moved to Charles City Courthouse, and then at sunrise on August 17, 1862, the regiment began a seventeen-mile march northeast. Near sunset, the regiment crossed the pontoon bridge over the Chickahominy River, which Rollin's tentmate William Westervelt appreciatively described as "one of the best pontoon bridges we ever saw; it was so strong that a train of artillery or wagons went in the center with two ranks of infantry on each side."[7] Early the next morning, immediately after the rear guard of McClellan's army crossed, the bridge was destroyed.

The men of the 27th NY kept up a punishing pace under the unrelenting heat of the sun's rays until reaching Newport News. Two of the most exhausting treks were on August 18 (almost twenty-five miles passing through Williamsburg) and August 19 (fifteen miles to Yorktown where they camped within the fortifications).[8] On the final day of the march, August 21, 1862, Rollin and his comrades in Company F—along with Companies B and G— were given the thankless task of rearguard corralling stragglers to ensure the regiment was whole for embarkation the next day.[9] On August 22, before stepping aboard ship for parts unknown later that evening, Rollin jotted a joint letter to his father and mother.

Newport News Va
August 22d 1862

Dear Father

After a six days march through dust and heat, we have arrived at this port to embark, but for what place I am unable to say. We got here last night and will leave this evening.

I stood the fatigue of skedaddle No. 2 better than No. 1, but I am nevertheless very tired, feet blistered, clothes dirty, and don't feel well myself. A little time to rest will set me all right again.

I have not heard from home or seen a newspaper in ten days; am perfectly ignorant of what is going on in the world.

I will give you a more lengthy description of the late move if we ever get settled down again.

Write to me directing to Washington and I will be sure to get your letters.

My health is good and spirits 100%.

Yours truly
Rollin B. Truesdell

To: Sam'l W. Truesdell
Great Bend, Pa

Mother, I would have given a good deal if you could have seen me any night while we were on the march. I know you would not have known me with my hair full of fine white sand, face covered with a coat of mortar made of sweat and sand. It would have been the drollest sight you ever saw, and yet I was only one of thousands.

I will write a long letter as soon as I have an opportunity.

Your aff son
Rollin B. Truesdell

To: Mrs. Lucy Truesdell
Great Bend, Penna

The 27th NY Volunteers boarded the steamer *John Brooks* the evening of August 22. Rollin and his comrades reached Aquia Creek the morning of August 24, 1862, and then continued onward to the all-too-familiar Fort Ellsworth in Alexandria.

As soon as the regiment arrived in Alexandria, the frenzy to hurry them and the whole of Franklin's 6th Corps west to join Pope's Army of Virginia went into high gear. The General-in-Chief, responding to Pope's entreaties for urgent reinforcement, appealed to the Commander of the Army of the Potomac and Franklin directly. But McClellan repeatedly intervened to delay the corps' departure. On August 27, McClellan reported to Halleck that Franklin had been unable to "pick up any cavalry and his artillery had no horses except four guns without caissons;" on August 28, "neither Franklin nor Sumner's corps is now in condition to move and fight a battle;" and on August 29, "Franklin has but 40 rounds of ammunition and no wagons to move more … I would not have moved him but for your pressing order of last night."[10] Under this cloud, the 6th Corps began its march to join the Army of Virginia at 6 a.m. on August 29. (See figure 8.1.)

By that time, the die had already been cast for the clash between Lee's and Pope's armies. The Confederate Commanding General created the chaos he intended when he ordered Stonewall Jackson and his men on a grueling two-day march reaching around Pope's right flank to his rear. Popping up on August 26 behind Pope, the Rebel force struck the Orange and Alexandria railroad station at Bristoe and the Union supply hub at Manassas Junction. They laid waste to Union supplies before easing into position near the battle-field of the first Battle of Bull Run. Pope had little choice but to give chase, giving up his line along the Rappahannock River to pursue Jackson. While Pope's forces jabbed at Jackson's defensive line along an unused railroad line on August 29, Confederate Generals Lee and Longstreet arrived to link forces on Jackson's right and block Union 5th Corps Commander Porter's attempt at a flanking maneuver.

Though the 6th Corps did leave their camp in Alexandria on August 29, they shuffled along for only seven miles before halting in Annandale for the evening. And they did so without their commander. Franklin remained in Alexandria ostensibly finagling the procurement and movement of ammunition, horses, and other supplies to Annandale for his men before entering them into the battle fray—all in accordance with McClellan's direction. Seething when he discovered the quiescence of the 6th Corps and its commander, General-in-Chief Halleck telegraphed McClellan the evening of August 29 demanding that Franklin follow his orders and push forward to protect the railroad and open communication with Manassas Junction.[11]

Early the next morning, with the unmistakable sounds of heavy cannon-ading ricocheted off Rollin and his comrades, they resumed their march along

FIGURE 8.1   William B. Franklin. Civil War photographs,
1861–1865, Library of Congress, Prints and Photographs
Division.

the Fairfax Road through Annandale, Fairfax Court House, and Centreville
toward Bull Run. At sunset, the regiment reached the outskirts of the battlefield, near where they had been unforgettably punished on July 21, 1861. After
marching twenty miles, Slocum ordered the division to pause. There was no
respite, however.

The morning of August 30, Pope, riddled with inadequate intelligence
and a propensity for believing in his own propaganda, had channeled and
instructed his men to pursue Jackson's retreating force who wasn't actually

retreating. Confederate artillery dispensed with the Union attackers once they transitioned to a direct assault on the waiting Rebels. And then the thrashing began. Lee unfurled the full strength of Longstreet's wing in a counterattack on Pope's left flank and sent the Army of Virginia reeling eastward.

As Rollin and his comrades progressed toward Manassas Junction, the few stragglers and wounded they encountered along the way became a torrent of fugitives, mad to escape the battle. Threatening to devolve into the disastrous crush that defined the retreat at the first Battle of Bull Run, now-present 6th Corps Commander Franklin ordered his men to block the road to stop the frenzied flight. Franklin later reported: "It was impossible to succeed in this, the number becoming over 7,000 in less than half an hour."[12] In a letter to a friend, a soldier from the 27th NY Volunteers wrote of the night of August 30: "As our brigade had seen too much fighting to be panic-stricken, they stood firm as a rock, with guns loaded and bayonets fixed preventing stragglers to the rear."[13] There Bartlett's brigade stood until directed to march approximately one mile to the front. Rollin and his comrades were put on picket duty until noon the next day. As Pope's army fell back toward Chinn Ridge and eventually Henry Hill, the men of the 27th NY Volunteers peered through the drenching rain, alert for signs of Confederate General Stonewall Jackson pitching up like a specter.

George McClellan may have felt the sting of the calamity unfolding almost as much as the Commanding General who was incapable of inspiring his men and leading them to victory—Major General John Pope of the Army of Virginia. By a War Department Order issued on August 30, 1862, McClellan was relegated to remain in Alexandria to oversee the defensive works and command, "that part of the Army of the Potomac that has not been sent forward to General Pope's command." Pope was given charge of the Army of Virginia and all forces temporarily attached to it. Learning of the devastating day of battle, McClellan sent a telegram to Halleck at 10:30 p.m. that evening imploring, "I cannot express to you the pain and mortification I have experienced today in listening to the distant sound of firing of my men . . . I respectfully ask that if there is a probability of conflict being renewed tomorrow, I may be permitted to go to the scene of battle . . . If it is not deemed best to entrust me with command even of my own army, I simply ask to be permitted to share their fate on the field of battle."[14] Halleck demurred in a note the next morning saying he must clear the decision with the President.

The sopping rain continued into the following day, August 31. After observing the rest of Pope's army fall back to Centreville from their picket-duty ridge, Rollin and his comrades made the same movement the afternoon of

August 31. At 11:30 p.m. that evening, unable to attain even a semblance of self-censorship, McClellan telegrammed Halleck from his camp exile in Alexandria to rail: "A rebel major said they had driven in our entire left. The road is filled with wagons and stragglers. Pope's right is also exposed. To speak frankly and the occasion requires it, there appears to be a total absence of brains, and I fear the total destruction of our army."[15]

And again, the rain fell on September 1 as the Army of Virginia continued its arduous movement eastward toward protective fortifications. As daylight was dimming, Confederate Lieutenant General Jackson attempted to do exactly what McClellan feared: cut Pope and his men off from their path of escape to the Union capital via yet another audacious flanking maneuver. Near Chantilly, Virginia, the Rebel forces fiercely attacked the disjointed Union defense, killing two Union generals (Division Commanders Philip Kearny and Isaac Stevens) before finally being repelled by federal bayonet charge. The damage to the Union cause was far more consequential than the casualty count (Union, 1,300 killed, wounded, or missing; Confederates, 800). The Union Army appeared to be floating on a rudderless ship.

Drenched to the bone, Rollin and his comrades in the 27th NY Volunteers were called forth around 10 p.m. on the evening of September 1 to join Slocum's division in covering Pope's sloppy retreat. With muskets loaded, this rear guard crept along, blinded by the darkness and the rain through the entire night, cognizant of the enemy lurking on their left flank. A comrade from the 27th NY Volunteers recalled the march of despair: "The road was execrable and we marched part of the time through mud one foot deep."[16] Trudging through the night, the men managed to cover just seven miles to arrive about one mile from Fairfax at daylight.

On the morning of September 2, as Rollin and his comrades hunched behind rifle pits in Fairfax, waiting to fight or withdraw, McClellan was enjoying breakfast at his house in Washington. He had not invited guests, and yet two arrived, urgently wanting to speak with him before he had finished his coffee. President Lincoln and General-in-Chief Halleck stood before him, asking him to do what he dreamed they would—assume command of all the fortifications around Washington *and* the troops needed for the defense of the capital. Flinging themselves eastward, the assorted forces under Pope's command were in full retreat, and in need of leadership and order if there were to be any hope of confidently protecting Washington. Gladly accepting, McClellan prepared to meet and take command of the force as it returned to the fold, and quickly shot off a telegram to Pope: "Halleck instructed me to repeat the order he sent this morning to withdraw the army to Washington without unnecessary delay."[17]

The 27th NY Volunteers pushed off from Fairfax around 1 p.m. that day and numbly trod their way back to the same camp they had left just days earlier. They arrived at Fort Lyon in Alexandria late in the evening on September 2, with little to rejoice other than the possibility of receiving some mail from home.

Fort Lyon Va
Sep 3d 1862

Dear Mother

I am well but much worn out; have not time to write a long letter as I am employed for a day or so at Hdqrs to write. I will make up for my negligence in not writing sooner in a day or two.

I received two letters from home a week ago informing me of the sickness of Father. I am anxiously awaiting further intelligence.

I got back from the fight at Bull Run at midnight last night— made a march yesterday of twenty-five miles.

Your aff son
Rollin

The mood was heavy and reflective at camp. Over the course of five days, the Union had suffered over 16,000 casualties while the Confederacy lost slightly over 9,000 men. Lee was now free to take the war to the North, and McClellan was in receipt of an exhausted, demoralized army. By September 12, the Army of Virginia formally melted into the Army of the Potomac and, for his efforts, Pope was shuffled out to a post in Minnesota. A comrade from the 27th NY Volunteers sighed: "Care-worn, weary, and discouraged, we halted at Fort Lyon long enough to learn our disasters were serious, and the exultant foe was invading Maryland."[18] Surgeon George Burr, the medical director of Slocum's division, was more optimistic in his description of the state of affairs to his wife: "After a thorough reorganization, we shall be more powerful than ever. General McClellan is again in full command, and he is the only man we seem to have as yet. Had it not been for his army, Washington would now be in the hands of the rebels, and our cause probably ruined."[19]

"This Div Alone Done the Business"

Major General McClellan could not revert to his instinctual slow, cautious approach to leading his Army of the Potomac. After trouncing Pope's Army of Virginia, General Lee, with his two corps of approximately 55,000 men, wasted no time lingering before the refortified Northern capital; by September 3, the Rebel forces had withdrawn. The threat to the North morphed. Would Lee, leveraging the momentum from victories against the Union force ruinously led by Pope, continue northward and cross the Potomac River to threaten Pennsylvania or Baltimore? How long could Rebel forces stomp their way through Northern territory without Northern resolve being damaged? Only two lonely federal garrisons in Martinsburg and Harpers Ferry, western Virginia (now cut off from Washington), stood as obstacles in Lee's way to uncontested control of the Shenandoah Valley. Such control would be necessary to maintain his supply line while his troops ventured into Union territory.

Here was McClellan's opportunity for redemption. He must quickly pull together his dispirited, disorganized army. The expanse of land vulnerable to Confederate incursion was extravagant. McClellan planned for five separate lines to form one grand arc to sweep northwest toward Frederick, Maryland. The 1st and 9th Corps, under overall command of Major General Burnside, formed the right wing. (Until McClellan issued a Special Order on September 15 directing Major General Hooker's 1st Corps to report directly to him.) Major General Sumner commanded the 2nd and 12th Corps in the center. Major General Franklin led the left wing, which was comprised of his 6th Corps and Major General Darius Couch's division of the 4th Corps. Initial movements of McClellan's force began on September 4. Franklin's 6th Corps was the last to begin the march on September 6. The Commanding General departed Washington on September 7.

And so, three nights after arriving at Fort Lyon, Rollin and his comrades in the 27th NY Volunteers broke camp and shuddered with the realization that their bodies were to endure another campaign. The recently formed 121st NY Volunteers, under the shaky and temporary command of Colonel Richard Franchot, joined the march and Bartlett's brigade without most of their equipment.[20] One of Rollin's comrades shared the malaise of the men on this march: "It was midnight when we crossed Long Bridge and passed through Washington. Scarcely a word was uttered. Every man was sad. All our suffering and toil in Virginia had been in vain."[21] For the next eight days, the men slogged their way through Maryland, unsure where they were destined.

Rollin wrote a letter to his mother four days after starting out from Fort Lyon to reassure her of his well-being through the many moves since Harrison's Landing, but also clearly craving reassurance himself that his father had weathered his serious illness.

Darnstown Md
Sept 10th 1862

My Dear Mother

Pardon me for not writing oftener but I cannot help it. We have been almost constantly on the move since Aug 16th.

I never was in better health than I am now tho' we are having a hard march every day. No one knows where we are going, but the straws indicate Harper's Ferry. We march from ten to fifteen miles per day.

I have not heard from home in about two weeks. Our mails are very irregular. The last I heard Father was very sick. I am very anxious to hear from home.

While at Alexandria, I got the box of things you sent me, all in prime order. I never was more thankful for anything in my life than for this box.

Our knapsacks and everything that could possibly be dispensed with was left in Washington. All that I have with me is on my back, except one blanket which I wrap myself in at night.

We had a hard time at Bull Run "No 2," but came out all right.

I would like to write a very long letter, but I have no time or paper. This is my very last sheet, and where I get the next I cannot tell. I received letters from Mart, Albert, and Clara two weeks ago, but have had no opportunity to answer them. I want you all to write often. I am _very_ anxious to hear how Father is getting along.

It is now just daylight, and we commence our day's march in a few minutes. I will write as often as I can, but under the present circumstances do not be alarmed if you do not hear from me very often.

With much love to all I am

Your affectionate son
Rollin B. Truesdell

To: Mrs. Lucy Truesdell
Great Bend, Pa

As Rollin and his comrades marched, the struggle for an advantage over the enemy preoccupied both Commanding Generals McClellan and Lee as they prepared for the next inevitable battle. On September 11, recognizing the

vice was closing on three sides, Union forces under the command of Briga-
dier General Julius White gave up the garrison in Martinsburg. In the early
morning hours of September 12, White and his men fled to Harpers Ferry.
Now it was on the shoulders of oft-inebriated Colonel Dixon Miles to defend
the remaining federal garrison in the Shenandoah Valley from Rebel siege.
General-in-Chief Halleck ordered Miles to hold the arsenal at all costs until
McClellan could reach him with reinforcements. For McClellan, knowing
Miles's checkered military record, the urgency to reach Harpers Ferry should
only have intensified.

The signals of the impending battle became clearer as Rollin and his comrades edged closer to the Blue Ridge Mountain range. On September 12, upon
reaching the area around Sugar Loaf Mountain, about thirteen miles south of
Frederick, the bodies of Union cavalrymen lay where they were killed, a warning of the looming battle. Onward on the 13th, the men reached the village
of Buckeyestown, about three miles east of Jefferson, and camped overnight.
The pall of death would weigh on Rollin; this day he learned by letter that his
beloved Uncle James, his father's brother who lived on the next plot of land to
his parents', had died about a week earlier. His notes to sister Clara and father
would have been little consolation for him that day.

On the march near
Frederick City Md
Sept 13th 1862

Dear Sister

Yours of the 7th inst is just received. I am very sorry to learn of
Uncle James' death. Glad to hear that Father is on the gain.

I have little time to write nowadays. Almost constantly on the
move. Do not be alarmed if you do not hear from me often. I will
do the best I can, but the mails are irregular.

My health is good. "I am tough."

With love to all I am

Your aff Bro
Rollin

Dear Father

I am glad to hear you are better.

My health was never better.

We have had a march of ten miles today but have not come up

to the Rebs. They are having a running fight at our front between
Cavalry.

I will write more when I have time.

Your aff son
Rollin B. Truesdell

To: Saml W. Truesdell

Great Bend, Penna

Compounding the high stakes McClellan faced, conflicting intelligence
reports about the Confederate Army's whereabouts vexed the Commanding
General. And then, in a stunning case of serendipity, George McClellan received an unexpected and timely surprise while setting up his headquarters
in Frederick, Maryland, on September 13. Sergeant John M. Bloss and Private
B. W. Mitchell of the 27th Indiana discovered an envelope addressed to Confederate Major General D. H. Hill containing three cigars and Robert E. Lee's
Special Orders No. 191 in a field south of Frederick.[22] Carelessly left behind
when Hill's command vacated the site a few days earlier, the orders laid out
in detail Lee's strategic plan for his Maryland Campaign, including the targets
and missions of four separate elements of his army. Dated September 9, this
invaluable gift was a few days old but told McClellan that Lee had gambled if
the plan was still valid. Lee's army was divided, and none of his infantry was on
the east side of South Mountain. Seemingly incapable of a rapid response even
with the enemy's plans in hand, late in the evening of September 13, McClellan
finally ordered 6th Corps Commander Franklin and 9th Corps Commander
Burnside to move to the South Mountain gaps, west of the Catoctin Creek.
Confederate Commanding General Lee, on the other hand, hustled troops to
the mountain gaps to block—or at least delay—the Union Army from passing
after being tipped off by an informant that McClellan appeared elated after receiving a mysterious document. The contents of which had spurred McClellan
to order his army forward.

At first light on September 14, 1862, the 27th NY Volunteers broke camp
and began their ten-mile march through Jefferson and on to Burkittsville,
where the South Mountain rose at their feet. The South Mountain, a continuous ridge of up to 1,000 feet, ambles northward from the Potomac River some
seventy miles into Pennsylvania.

Just as McClellan had sent them forth from Alexandria, Major General
Franklin's 6th Corps formed the left wing of the Union Army attack on South
Mountain. When the men halted at Jefferson, they heard the angry voice of

cannon to their right. Their brethren were punching at Rebel forces to drive them from the mountain passes to the north—Fox's Gap and Turner's Gap. Franklin's mission was to push the enemy forces from the mountain pass near Burkittsville, at Crampton's Gap, and then proceed to Harpers Ferry to rescue the inundated federal garrison. In his report of the Battles of Crampton's Pass and Antietam, Franklin described the complexity of the challenge before them:

> The enemy was strongly posted on both sides of the road, which makes a steep ascent through a narrow defile, wooded on both sides, and affording great advantages of cover and position. Their advance was posted near the base of the mountain, in the rear of a stone wall ... Eight guns had been stationed on the road, and at points on the sides and the summit of the mountain, to the left of the pass ... It was evident that the position could be carried only by an infantry charge.[23]

Franklin determined that Henry Slocum's 1st Division would lead the advance and attack on the right, while Baldy Smith's 2nd Division would remain to the left of the gap in reserve. Slocum in turn placed Brigade Commander J. J. Bartlett at the helm. (See figure 8.2.)

While in Jefferson, Bartlett ordered the 96th Pennsylvania ahead to Burkittsville as skirmishers. Harassed by artillery fire as they moved to the village, the 96th nonetheless drove out the Rebel pickets. Two Union batteries responded in kind to the Confederate fire while Slocum prepared his plan of attack.

During his own reconnaissance of the area leading to Crampton's Gap, Bartlett had identified a ravine approximately a half mile east of the village—perfect to provide cover for the men as they organized in column by battalion. Around 3 p.m., the 27th NY moved to the front; they were assigned to lead the advance as skirmishers. Next came the 5th Maine and the 16th NY in two lines of battle 200 yards behind. Brigadier General John Newton's 3rd Brigade followed, and then Colonel Alfred Torbert's 1st Brigade. Organized to deliver a blow of overwhelming force, the regiments of these brigades similarly formed in two lines of battle. Having been recalled from Burkittsville, the 96th Pennsylvania joined the rear of the column. The 121st NY was mercifully held as reserve.

Around 4 p.m., Rollin and his comrades in the 27th NY Volunteers burst forth at the double quick across the open plain toward the enemy batteries. Their line formed an arc with the center of the line—approximately one mile long—directed just to the right of the pass and the flank companies thrust

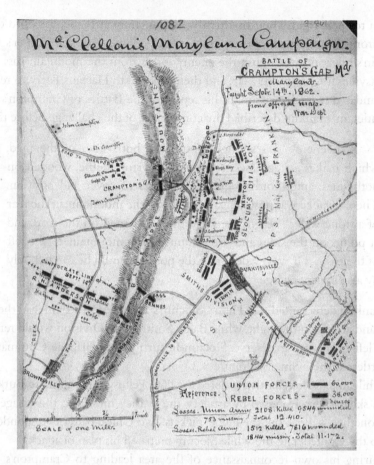

FIGURE 8.2   Battle of Crampton's Gap by Robert Knox
Sneden. Library of Congress, Geography and Map Division.

forward.[24] Division Commander Slocum, the former commanding colonel of
the 27th NY Volunteers, wrote proudly of Rollin's and his comrades' grit in his
official report of the Battle of Crampton's Gap: "As soon as the advance began,
the enemy opened with heavy and well directed artillery fire; but the troops
advanced steadily, every line in the entire column preserving its alignment with
as much accuracy as could have been expected at a drill or review."[25]

The punishment came from multiple angles: shells from enemy batteries half-way up the mountainside, musketry from behind the stonewall at the
foot of the mountain, and sharpshooters behind houses, rocks, trees, and even
nested within trees. The vastly outnumbered Confederate force of 800 or so
Virginians led by newly installed brigade commander Colonel William Allan
Parham and cavalry commander Colonel Thomas Munford knew they must

fight with everything at their disposal or risk Lee's campaign plans (if not his army) crumbling with the surge of Union troops through the mountain passes. On pressed Rollin and his mates through the curtain of shell and shot raining on them, men falling with each discharge, until they were within a hundred yards of the stonewall. Here they halted.

The center of the line quickly joined the already engaged left and right flank in a lively exchange of rapid, close-range fire. Battle-tested, if not battle-weary, Rollin and his comrades did not shrink from the deluge. The 27th NY Volunteers Regiment Commander Alexander Adams noted that "the severe musketry fire of the enemy was returned with the cool deliberation and steady aim of experienced marksmen."[26] With the enemy positions now revealed, Bartlett ordered the 27th NY to withdraw; the time to transition from skirmishing to battle had come.

In the smoke, and the din, and the excitement, the men faced some challenges in following the withdrawal command and the order to rally in fours until the line of battle reached them. Some, such as Rollin's tentmate William Westervelt, sheltered in a barnyard, where two of his squad were promptly shot, leaving him to devise a position behind a barricade of wheat bags in a barn until the main column arrived.[27] Others along this mile-long skirmish line did not hear the order and, finding themselves stuck between the two lines of battle, dove to the ground to protect themselves from the crossfire. Many simply melted into and joined the line of battle as it washed over them.

Comrades in the 5th Maine and 16th NY had been quick on the heels of the 27th NY. Within ten or fifteen minutes, their line of attack advanced to the left of the center of the 27th's line; they brought their rifles to bear on Rebel positions in the woods to their front. Bartlett's men held their own under scathing fire, maintaining their position and the fight until two regiments of Newton's brigade belatedly made their way to the front and reported to him. The planned 200-yard interval in the column had inexplicably stretched to 1,000 yards, by Bartlett's reckoning.[28] With gun barrels smoking and ammunition expended, Bartlett ordered the 5th Maine and 16th NY to the rear of Newton's men. Torbert's brigade regained ground and soon joined the fight, coming in on the left of the line. Finally, the 96th Pennsylvania, battered after hours of skirmishing in Burkittsville, reunited with the division on the far right just in the nick of time.

J. J. Bartlett, a model of decisive action and perhaps agitated by the delayed arrival of Newton's brigade, determined it was time for a bold move to dislodge the enemy from their refuge behind the stonewall, just as Slocum was considering bringing a battery forward to eliminate the barrier. Bartlett recalled: "A moment's consultation with Col. Torbert decided us to make the charge immediately, at a double quick; and the order was passed along the line to cease firing and the command given to 'Charge!' . . . The great natural strength of the enemy's position, supported by his well-served batteries, made it absolutely necessary that the first attempt should be successful, or great confusion and slaughter must ensue."[29]

The pressure valve released, Rollin and his comrades wildly cheered as they flung themselves across the intervening field, over the stonewall, and up the mountainside after the astonished enemy. The Confederate force fired at the zealous men coming for them, until the pursuers were within a few yards of the stonewall. Then they scrambled to flee, or simply laid down their guns on the other side of the stonewall as they watched their retreating comrades being shot in the back by Slocum's insistent force.[30] Some Rebel sharpshooters clung to their berths in the trees, unable to climb down before the Federals were upon them. Like bloodhounds, Slocum's men chased their prey up an almost vertical incline, grasping at bushes to hoist themselves up, shimmying over rocks and ledges, and crashing through thickets until reaching the Confederate second line, and then the crest of the mountain.

Confederate General Howell Cobb had brought his brigade of regiments from Georgia and North Carolina, and his eponymous legion up the west side of South Mountain to reinforce overwhelmed Confederate Colonels Munford and Parham, and to assume overall command. He arrived just in time to be swept up in the rout. Cobb had received Division Commander McLaws's order around 4 p.m. to transition from his position in Brownsville (half-way between Harpers Ferry and Burkittsville, and near the Brownsville Pass) to take the command at Crampton's Gap, but he did not move out until after 5 p.m. in response to distress messages from Munford and Parham.[31] By then it was too late. Just as Cobb's brigade was forming its battle lines approximately midway up the mountain, comrades from Virginia began feverishly retreating toward them, tumbling through Cobb's lines to escape the hotly pursuing Federals. Through the tumult, Cobb attempted another stand at the summit before falling back through Crampton's Gap and into the plain below.

The Battle at Crampton's Gap, lasting no more than three hours, was the absolute triumph that Rollin and his comrades were longing for after being rushed in to witness the Union disaster at the Second Battle of Bull Run, and the prolonged strain of the failed Peninsula Campaign. Rollin, bursting with pride, wrote to his father on September 15, 1862.

Crampton Gap Maryland
Sept 15th 1862

Dear Father

We came up with the enemy yesterday and gave them a severe drubbing. This Div alone done the business.

We commenced the action at 12 o'clock noon, and at dusk had possession of the gap. Our loss is small compared with that of the enemy. It was good generalship that whipped them. They out numbered us and had the advantage of position, but thank God we whipped them (even) if it was Sunday, and today had the unpleasant duty of burying their dead, the dirty vagabonds.

We are resting a while here in the woods on the mountain— will move on very soon. I will write again the first opportunity. My health is good.

With love to all I am

Your aff son

Rollin B. Truesdell

Crampton's Gap is four miles from Jefferson and one mile from Burkittsville. The distance from Harpers Ferry I don't know, but about ten miles.

There is fighting going on both on our right and left today.

Rollin

To: Sam'l W. Truesdell
Great Bend, Pa

Since leaving our knapsacks, I have to catch up such paper as I can get, clean or soiled. It is by chance that I found this, but you will be glad to hear from me, no doubt, if the paper is not so clean as it might be.

W.J.C. Hanson, Rollin's comrade in the 27th NY Volunteers, gushed in a letter published in the *Rochester Evening Express*, "THE VICTORY IS OURS! The whole force engaged was Slocum's Division which has covered itself in glory."[32] Slocum agreed. He wrote in his official report of the battle: "Although greatly reduced in numbers by losses on the peninsula; although fatigued by long marches, and constant service since the opening of the spring campaign, each regiment—indeed, every man did his whole duty, not reluctantly, but with that eagerness and enthusiasm which rendered success certain."[33] All but twenty of the 533 Union casualties suffered during the Battle of Crampton's Gap were in Slocum's division; thirty-three were Rollin's comrades in the 27th NY Volunteers.

The Rebel forces parted with more than their knapsacks, blankets, ammunition, and hundreds of firearms in their rush to safety on the other side of South Mountain. Slocum's men captured over 400 prisoners, one piece of artillery, and several battle flags—one nabbed by the 16th NY was inscribed, "Cobb Legion—In the Name of the Lord."[34] With this success, 6th Corps Commander Franklin was in position to consider the second part of his charge: rescuing Colonel Miles and his men at the Harpers Ferry garrison.

The evening of September 14, 1862, Rollin's regiment slept on the battlefield atop the mountain exhausted, jubilant, and resigned to the unpleasant work awaiting them in the morning. For the next two days, instead of marching toward Harpers Ferry, Slocum's division tended to the wounded and the dead of both armies. (On receiving reports of a force twice as large as the 6th Corps waiting for it two miles to their front, McClellan had ordered Franklin to hold in place until the evening of the 16th. Franklin's men would protect the left and rear of McClellan's army, and dig.)[35] They buried their own dead before those of their enemy. The task was consequential; one soldier in the 27th NY Volunteers reported that the Rebels had left at least 150 of their own on the field.[36] This would be just a prelude to Rollin's and his comrades' walk through death at the next conflagration with the Confederate Army.

Still waiting at the gap for the anticipated order to march, Rollin wrote his sister Clara on September 16, telling her of the victory before reverting to the easy banter of brother to sister.

> In camp near Crampton's Gap
> Maryland
> Sept 16th 1862
>
> My Dear Sister
> Unexpectedly, our Div has rested twenty-four hours for the purpose of burying the dead. The battle was fought Sunday afternoon and at this hour Tuesday, four o'clock P.M., there is many Rebels on the field. All our own were interred early yesterday morning. The exact number killed I do not know, but our loss was small compared to that of the enemy. We took about two thousand prisoners beside those wounded, which will make a total of about three thousand.

It was a complete victory. I am proud of it, for Slocum won it.

My health is good aside from the natural wear caused by our long and tedious marches. I hope we shall soon find time to rest awhile, but not 'til the Rebels are driven beyond reaching distance of my native State. I know very little of what is going on out of my own sight for we do not get a mail once a week on an average while on the march, but it is welcome when it does come, I assure you.

I like soldiering in this State better than in Virginia for the simple reason the folks here keep dairies. I have had plenty of milk, fresh butter, and chickens of late, beside any quantity of peaches, apples, pears, grapes, tomatoes, and potatoes. A long march makes a man hungry, and he does not stand and look a great while at anything eatable that he wants, especially old soldiers.

The 121st Regt NY troops has just joined this Brigade. A part of one Co is from Edmeston Centre. Ackerman that used to work for Lines is among the number, also Ed Bootman, Laurie's husband, and several others that I got acquainted with while at E.

I must thank you all again for that box of things. I can set no price on them, especially the medicine.

I will write as often as I can under the circumstances.

With much love to all I am

Your aff Bro
Rollin B. Truesdell

As for the disputed mountain passes to the north of Crampton's Gap (Fox's and Turner's), Commanding General McClellan could revel in the satisfaction of success there too, though at a heavy price. Fighting commenced around 9 a.m. at each mountain pass with elements of Confederate Major General D. H. Hill's division guarding both, later to be reinforced by soldiers from Major General James Longstreet's command. Union 9th Corps Commander Jesse Reno's men conducted the assault on Fox's Gap, which quickly devolved into vicious hand-to-hand combat. Confederate Brigade Commander Samuel Garland was mortally wounded during the maelstrom and Reno was fatally shot while impatiently conducting a reconnaissance mission. At Turner's Gap, 1st Corps Commander Joseph (Joe) Hooker's soldiers were severely tested by D. H. Hill's outnumbered men for much of the day and they were unable to shake the rebel soldiers out of the mountain gap. Combat raged at each mountain pass until after dark. Around 11 p.m., General Lee ordered withdrawal for

the purpose of consolidating and regrouping his divided forces. To do otherwise, Lee reasoned, would risk his army being cut up into beatable pieces the
following day by McClellan's resurgent Army of the Potomac.

For Colonel Dixon Miles, federal garrison commander at Harpers Ferry,
September 14, 1862, was the last day he would hold command; there would
be no rescue from Franklin and his men. Since September 12, Miles had been
wringing his hands about Confederate Major General Stonewall Jackson's es-
calating siege of the garrison, warning McClellan of the fragility of his position, and quite possibly, getting intoxicated. Sensing the doom ahead as their
designated rescuers were embroiled in battle at South Mountain, Union cavalry commanders pressured Miles to agree to their departure from the garrison on the 14th. By early morning on September 15, despite the reputed
objections of many of his own men, Miles elected to surrender as the morning
began with crisp cannon fire onto the garrison and his men rationed what
ammunition was left. White flag flapping overhead as he rode on horseback
within the smoky cauldron, an artillery shell zipped past and exploded directly
behind him. A fragment tore into Miles's calf. He died later that day.

The disparity in the number of Union versus Confederate soldiers lost at
the Battle of Harpers Ferry was mortifying for Northerners. The attack on the
garrison cost Confederate General Jackson less than 300 dead or wounded soldiers. For the Union, a staggering 12,520 of the 12,737 men lost while under
Colonel Dixon Miles's command at Harpers Ferry were captured.[37] Delegat-
ing the task of processing the enormous number of prisoners and property to
Major General A. P. Hill, Jackson hurried his forces to Sharpsburg, Maryland,
where Lee was building his battle line. The Confederate Commanding General was rejuvenated.

THE REMARKABLE DESTRUCTION THAT TURNED LEE BACK

The evening of September 16, 1862, the Confederate and Union armies straddled the Antietam Creek near the town of Sharpsburg—Lee's army to the
west, McClellan's to the east. Along the low ridge of the four mile north-south
Confederate battle line, freshly arrived Major General Jackson positioned his
men as the left wing, backing onto the Potomac River, and Major General
Longstreet's command linked to become the right wing. In preparation for
the battle, McClellan abandoned his wing command structure and instead
opted for each of the corps to directly report to him thus ensuring compet-
ing communication channels during the bloodbath to come. The northeast
to southwest meander of the Antietam Creek helped determine McClellan's

disposition of his forces. With the Upper Bridge across the creek out of reach of Confederate batteries, McClellan concentrated Joe Hooker's 1st Corps and Joseph Mansfield's 12th Corps to the north. Bull Sumner's 2nd Corps positioned further south, toward the center of the battle line, and Ambrose Burnside's 9th Corps, farthest to the south, where his corps would be repelled for hours from crossing Rohrbach's Bridge (later known as Burnside's Bridge). Fitz John Porter's 5th Corps and William Franklin's 6th Corps (initially) were designated as reserves.

As shadows were lengthening, Major General Hooker and his 1st Corps slipped across the creek on September 16. The Commanding General required intelligence about the enemy's strength in that area to prepare for the next day, and wanted Hooker and his men to be in place to open the fight.[38] McClellan ordered Hooker to probe enemy positions; and fighting ensued near the East Woods. The sides exchanged artillery fire until after dark. Overnight, Lee bolstered his battle lines in the north, along Jackson's flank. This is where McClellan would focus his attack, Lee surmised.

Sixth Corps Commander Franklin received the order the evening of September 16th to move his two divisions (Major General Henry Slocum's 1st and Major General Baldy Smith's 2nd) from their encampment near Crampton's Gap to Keedysville in the morning. Smith led the column northwest. Before Rollin and his comrades had taken a step, the telltale boom of heavy cannonading began. On September 17, 1862, with mere whispers of daylight to guide his men, Hooker had commenced the bloodiest day of battle in US history. Around 5:30 a.m., Hooker's corps attacked Jackson's forces where they had dueled the previous evening to gain control of a plateau on which the Dunker Church sat to the north of the East Woods. The brawl would quickly spill over into the adjacent cornfield—Union forces in the east and north, and the Confederates in the west and south.

The beauty of the valley stretching from South Mountain—resplendent with thriving crops—through which Rollin and his comrades trod was in jarring opposition to the scene of unspeakable destruction they were soon to join. The men of the 27th NY Volunteers were solemn as they marched toward the concussion of the next battle. Rollin's tentmate William Westervelt recalled: "It was very plain to the ear of the veteran that it was not the popping of the picket, or a skirmish line, but the sharp engagement of a heavy line of battle, well supported with artillery. And every mile was bringing us nearer to the ominous sounds."[39] A comrade shared these reflections in a letter home: "Our eyes were opened at the battle at Crampton's Pass where we dislodged the enemy from one of the strongest positions that nature can give. And when we marched up to the battlefield at Antietam, it was our prayer, "here let me die, if die we must in service to our country."[40]

When Rollin and his comrades reached Keedysville late in the morning, they witnessed shocking presaging of what they would see on the battlefield. The village was transformed into a hamlet of gore; homes had become makeshift hospitals stuffed with soldiers missing various parts of themselves after six hours of fighting. Westervelt described the harrowing scene: "The streets were almost blocked with ambulances waiting to unload their mangled burdens, while the surgeons and assistants with coats off and sleeves rolled up—with hands and amputating instruments covered with blood—looked more like butchers in the shambles than like professional men in hospitals."[41] These images were scorched into the minds of Rollin and his comrades as they marched the remaining two miles to the battlefield at Antietam.

Franklin's column entered the combat zone from the north around noon. By then, the inferno of violence had already transitioned further south to the center of the battle line and would soon heat up at the lower part of the battlefield. What they saw was a sea of remnants of men laying wounded and dead side by side, Confederate and Union. All evidence of farmer Miller's crop on this thirty-acre cornfield had been smudged out after three hours of the shifting tides of battle. Twelfth Corps Commander Mansfield had been mortally wounded while leading his inexperienced soldiers in a deathtrap formation, and 1st Corps Commander Hooker was shot through the foot while riding his horse to rally his dazed men.

By around 10 a.m., the fighting had segued to the middle of the battlefield. The Confederate line remained unbroken.

Second Corps Commander Sumner's mid-morning rushed attempt to reinforce Hooker's and Mansfield's battered men was a disastrous failure. Without clear instructions from Sumner, 3rd Division Commander William H. French directed his men south toward the middle of the Confederate line after crossing the river rather than joining the rest of the 2nd Corps. This pivot would cost the division dearly. French pushed his troops forward into a waiting gaping maw of destruction. His men attacked Confederate Major General D. H. Hill's position—a sunken road from which Hill's men fired volley after volley at hapless Yankee targets. Each side was reinforced by 10:30 a.m. Finding a gap in the Rebel line around the right flank of the Confederates, one of 1st Division Commander Richardson's brigades spotted a means to fire directly down into the sunken road, and thus commenced the slaughter. It was like shooting

FIGURE 8.3   Bloody Lane at Antietam photographed
by Alexander Gardner. Library of Congress, Prints &
Photographs Division, Civil War Photographs.

fish in a barrel. A Rebel counterattack and well-directed artillery stemmed the
rupture in the Confederate line. Richardson was mortally wounded as he led
his division back to a ridge facing the road later to be dubbed "Bloody Lane."
By 1 p.m., after hours of searing battle, it was a stalemate. (See figure 8.3.)

When Franklin arrived, he came with a valuable asset: two divisions of
fresh, battle-tested soldiers. General Baldy Smith's men, who had led the column from Crampton's Gap, immediately reinforced a section of Sumner's lines,
rescuing two batteries from likely capture by Rebel forces.[42] Slocum's division,
working alongside French's and Richardson's divisions, could have been the
force multiplier that irrevocably broke Confederate lines in the belly of the
battle. Or, as they were poised to do, the men of the 27th NY Volunteers and
the rest of Slocum's division could have delivered a hammer blow to fatigued
Rebel forces that lurked in the West Woods on the edge of the cornfield not
far from the Dunker Church. This could have forced Confederate Commanding General Lee to again realign his forces and bring reinforcements north,
consequentially depleting his lines further south. Instead, for forty hours, Slocum's men held in line of battle, on the skirts of the cornfield, unable to re-
spond to the artillery and infantry fire directed at them, at times enveloping
them like a wet wool blanket. (See figure 8.4.)

FIGURE 8.4   Dunker Church with Bodies of Confederate
Artillerymen photographed by Alexander Gardner. Library
of Congress, Prints & Photographs Division, Civil War
Photographs.

Franklin's vision had been direct engagement. When Slocum's division
reached the battlefield, Torbert's 1st Brigade and Newton's 3rd formed in column of attack while Bartlett's 2nd Brigade was to serve as reserve. Franklin
elucidated in his Battle of Antietam report on the changed planning: "Gen.
Sumner arrived on the spot, and directed the attack to be postponed; and the
enemy at once proceeded to fill the woods with infantry, and planted a battery
there, which opened a severe fire upon us. Shortly afterwards the commanding
general [McClellan] came to the position and decided that it would not be
prudent to make the attack."[43]

Relieving some of Sumner's men, Rollin and his comrades in the 27th NY
Volunteers took their position along the eastern border of the cornfield, next to
the East Woods. The ground before them was the scene of some of the heaviest
fighting, and had been fought over at least twice that morning. Westervelt remembered: "The dead lay so thick we had to pull them out of our way to make

room for us to form our lines."[44] Then, they sat and waited. After a battery was emplaced on an elevated position behind the regiment, it responded in kind to the harassing Confederate artillery and, at one point, caused the men to hug the ground as shells probed the woods for the enemy. Later in the long afternoon of September 17, 1862, Rollin and his comrades heard the ugly and insistent roar of heavy battle resurging to their left. Domination at the lower section of the battlefield, where Ambrose Burnside with his 9th Corps had tried unsuccessfully all morning to cross the Rohrbach Bridge, was far from decided.

The plan that McClellan had conceived as a diversionary tactic in the lower part of the battlefield to draw Lee's forces away from the main Union thrust in the north was botched. By early afternoon, the Union objective in the south shifted to reaching around the Confederate right flank to block Lee from withdrawing his army across the Potomac. Having finally succeeded in crossing his men over to the west bank of the Antietam—all the while under fire by vastly outnumbered but efficient Confederate sharpshooters and artillery—Burnside was executing the new plan by mid-afternoon.

Pushing, pushing the Confederate line back until retreating enemy soldiers were chaotically tripping into Sharpsburg, 9th Corps Commander Burnside was stopped in his tracks by 4 p.m. Confederate Major General A. P. Hill, last seen coordinating the clean-up after the siege of the Harpers Ferry garrison, had just arrived with his newly blue-clad men, who had endured a forced march of seventeen miles to join the battle—albeit with full bellies thanks to the Harpers Ferry commissary. Hill's division succeeded in breaking Burnside's left flank, which drove them back to the west bank of the Antietam. McClellan denied Burnside reinforcements (despite elements of Franklin's 6th Corps and Fitz John Porter's 5th Corps idling nearby). By 5:30 p.m. on September 17, 1862, the fighting was over.

When darkness fell, Rollin and his comrades lay down, resting on their arms, next to the dead. Overnight, with each picket exchange of fire, they were called into line and expected the horror to resume. But it didn't.

A couple of weeks after the bloody battle, Rollin was able to write to his sister a summary of his shocking day at Antietam.

In camp near Sharpsburg Md
Oct 6th 1862

My Dear Sister

Your favor of the 19th ult I have just received. I am glad to hear that you are all well at home. If I were only there for a month, how

I would enjoy it after these seven months of the campaign, just past which I call the shady side of a soldier's life.

We are in good farming country. Have every kind of vegetables furnished us by the citizens at fair prices. With all our hardships we have much to be thankful for.

I will tell you a little about the battle of Antietam. We left Crampton Gap on the 17th Sept at daylight and marched rapidly toward the Antietam where the main body of the army were then engaged. We reached the battlefield about 12 o'clock noon and after resting half an hour Franklin's Corps relieved Sumner's which had been engaged since daylight. The part of the field we occupied had been fought over three times, and the ground was thickly covered with killed and wounded. We had hardly got our artillery into position when the enemy again advanced to drive us the fourth time from that part of the field, he having received heavy reinforcements, but we were just in time for him, and as they advanced gave them such a stunning fire they fell back a little and used their artillery more freely than we poor fellows deserved. For five hours we laid behind our batteries, their shot and shell falling and bursting on all sides of us. Our loss was less than one hundred. Darkness closed the battle for the day, and we lay down by our batteries, expecting the battle would be renewed in the morning. The dead Rebels lay so thick around us that we could not stir without stumbling over them. I counted sixty-five on a piece of ground no larger than our garden up at the farm.

My health is very good—write "very" often.

Yours truly
Rollin

At sunrise the next morning, September 18, 1862, representatives from each of the Commanding Generals met and agreed to a truce until 5 p.m. for the purpose of burying the dead and carrying off the wounded from the littered battlefield. The men tried to take their morning meal in the stench-filled air of a hot September day before the gruesome task of burying the decomposing bodies. Many were unable. All day, stretcher bearers transported their agonized burdens to the overwhelmed surgeons, while the men of the 27th NY Volunteers, pick and shovel in hand, resumed work as gravediggers. Westervelt grimly recalled: "Like most everything else done in the army, our grave digging was on a wholesale scale. We first dug a grave six feet wide and about sixty feet long. In this grave, or rather trench, were placed side by side, forty of a South Carolina regiment. A few rods from this was another that contained thirty more."[45] These were the corpses that lay closest to the battle line of the 27th NY Volunteers.

At 5 p.m. sharp, when rebel shots were fired on Union stretcher carriers, Rollin and his comrades were assessing where to dig another trench to bury the dead who lay between the battle lines. Their work continued after a hastily organized repeat meeting of each army's negotiators to extend the truce. This time, the armistice would last until the following morning—September 19. Again that night, the living and dead lay on the same field to sleep. A soldier from Rollin's regiment wrote of that night: "It was heart rending to hear the poor fellows that lay between the lines cry for aid. All night in their agony one could hear them plead and entreat for water in vain, as none dare visit them."[46]

By the time the truce expired on September 19, 1862, the men of the 27th NY Volunteers had adequately cleared the ground before them to resume battle. But that morning, skirmishers sent out at sunrise found no Rebels to fight. Overnight, General Lee had withdrawn his army to safety across the Potomac. Impossible to have been accomplished noiselessly, Major General McClellan figuratively put his hands to his ears and let the enemy disappear. Rollin wrote a note to his father from the blood-drenched battlefield that morning.

> On the battlefield near Sharpsburg Md
> Sept 19th 1862
>
> Dear Father
>   We have gained another victory with heavy loss. The battle was fought the 17th—all day yesterday was occupied in burying the dead and carrying off the wounded. Dead Rebels lay thick as sheaves of grain on a harvest field on all sides of where our Regt now bivouacs.
>   It is thought the enemy re-crossed the river last night.
>   This has been the heaviest battle of the war. It is impossible to estimate the loss of either side yet.
>   We are within sixteen miles of the Pa line.
>   Health good and spirits fine.
>
> Your aff son
> Rollin B. Truesdell
>
> To: Sam'l W. Truesdell
> Great Bend, Pa
>   Watson is well.

Around noon, Rollin's regiment was ordered to march. Gasping for breath as they moved across the battlefield still cluttered with rotting, unburied bodies, they crossed the Sharpsburg Pike and then marched to the bank of the Potomac River. Lee had already shepherded his army across the river and back into the arms of Virginia. For two days, the 27th NY Volunteers camped on the riverbank, ready to answer a Rebel incursion across the Potomac that never came.

September 17, 1862, was the single bloodiest day in US history. Robert E. Lee lost some 10,300 of his men. George McClellan lost over 12,400 of his. Slocum's division, though on the battlefield, accounted for comparatively few casualties of the Union total: seven killed, fifty-six wounded, two missing.[47]

Twenty-two thousand seven hundred soldiers lost, and neither Commanding General had achieved their objective. Confederate General Lee failed to transition the war to Northern soil where glory, supplies, and men were to be his. Union General McClellan, even with his opponent's secret strategy for the Maryland Campaign in his hands, failed to outwit his opponent and demolish the Confederate Army.

President Lincoln judged the somewhat balanced outcome of the Battle of Antietam to be an adequate signal of Northern stamina for him to make his long-planned, history-changing announcement. On September 22, 1862, he issued the preliminary Emancipation Proclamation declaring the Confederates must lay down their arms by January 1, 1863, or their slaves "thenceforward, and forever" would be free.

Now the question was whether this declaration of moral purpose alongside preservation of the Union would invigorate General McClellan to pursue the enemy force and end the bloodshed that was crippling the country.

REGROUPING IN MARYLAND

At this stage of the campaign, and after a long concatenation of events bloody, terrible and exciting, we find ourselves in a short respite here preparatory to further service or assignment of position for winter quarters.
—Soldier in the 27th NY Volunteers, September 29, 1862[1]

Struggling with the demoralizing notion that their Commanding General had permitted the Confederate Army to slip away in the night after the Battle of Antietam, Rollin and his comrades likely felt they spent the next several days boxing at shadows. On September 19, 1862, they were rushed to the banks of the Potomac, but the dust clouds of Robert E. Lee's army as it retreated to the safety of Virginia soil were no longer visible. The following day, the men of the 27th NY Volunteers waited along the riverbank near Sharpsburg as Confederate Major General A. P. Hill's division decisively pushed back the tentative Union probe onto the Virginia side of the Potomac led by elements of Commander Fitz John Porter's 5th Corps. At Boteler's Ford on the morning of September 20, Hill's men knocked the stunned 118th Pennsylvania (the last of the Union units to retreat) off a cliff and into the gurgling waters of the Potomac River. When darkness fell that evening, Rollin's regiment marched north, in hot pursuit of a departed enemy. They marched all night and finally reached Williamsport, Maryland, around noon on September 21, 1862. After another two days of anticipation, the regiment shuffled back south along the river.

The 27th NY Volunteers stopped when they reached Bakersville, Maryland, about three miles northwest of the Antietam battlefield, and set up camp. Almost equidistant between Williamsport (six miles to the north) and Dam

No. 4 on the Chesapeake and Ohio (C&O) Canal along the Potomac River (four and a half miles to the south), Bakersville was a convenient location from which to watch and wait for possible Rebel incursions. Indeed, a fellow soldier from the regiment wrote home: "Franklin's Corps are the only troops between Dam 4 and Williamsport and our duty is to hold the Maryland shore between the two until further orders."[2] The enduring topic of conversation among Rollin and his comrades was whether this village along the Potomac would be their winter home, or another brief duty station before marching again. When would new orders come?

For the first couple of days, September 24 and 25, Rollin and his mates blissfully followed orders to lie in camp and rejuvenate, rest, and refuel. The regimental history for the 27th NY Volunteers reminisced of this gentle interlude: "The boys can wash up their clothing, and bathe in the creek. We are having good times . . . The boys all feel in good spirits, for all they have to do is to go out and get chickens, turkeys and flour, and then make pot-pies for dinner."[3] After weeks of deprivation, the simple pleasures of life—a full belly and clean body—surely felt luxurious.

The accustomed balance of picket duty and camp life then took over at Bakersville. Domination of the C&O canal, the vital Union connector between coal producing Maryland and Washington, was a perennial preoccupation for both the Confederate and Union armies. Hugging the northern banks of the Potomac River, the canal as much as the river served as the dividing line between the North and the South. In a September 27 letter to his father, Rollin described his new post-Antietam campsite and duties.

In camp near Sharpsburg Md
Sept 27th 1862

Dear Father

We are on the move so much of late that our mails are more irregular than ever before. I have had no tidings from home in some two weeks, but I have charity enough to believe that there is several letters on the road which I will receive in due course of time, but as I have, I will endeavor to keep you just as well posted as the circumstances will permit.

Since the battle of Antietam Creek we have been travailing up and down the upper Potomac, keeping a close watch upon our marauding enemies. They are making similar demonstrations just over the river.

We are now encamped near the noted Dam No 4. I was down to the dam this morning and saw Johnny Reb on the opposite side of the stream, which at this point is not more than twenty rods wide. It is fourteen miles from Harper's Ferry. The canal, which is a fine and expensive structure, is useless for the present, owing to the destruction of the aqueduct by the Rebels.

It is rumored that the Division will move to Hagerstown in a day or two and go into camp for a while to give the men rest after our tedious campaign of nearly seven months. I hope the report is correct, but "we" cannot tell 'til the thing is actually done.

The weather here has been hot and dry since we left Alexandria, but the nights are getting quite too cool to bivouac without more clothing than we are able to carry on the march.

My health has been first rate through all the campaign, and if we go into winter quarters, I hope we shall have no fighting to do before our time is out in the Spring.

Write me as often as you can for I prize letters from my parents above all others.

Yours truly
Rollin B Truesdell

To: Sam'l W Truesdell
Great Bend

On picket, the men of the 27th NY Volunteers stood vigil along the banks, a deterrent to possible Confederate re-crossing into Maryland as well as to further sabotage attempts on nearby Dam No. 4 on the canal. (Though Dam No. 4 was constructed of sturdy masonry and proved a difficult target for the Rebels, the gates to the lock were burned during the Confederate infiltration into Maryland.) Their Rebel picket counterparts plied the southern bank of the Potomac River; the two sides, though within range, withheld fire. A comrade from Rollin's regiment wrote home in mid-October: "The pickets now along the river are becoming as familiar as ever they were on the Chickahominy. The width of the Potomac—about 100 yards—is the only distance between them."[4]

Familiar. How was it possible that this war that was supposed to conclude after one definitive victory on the battlefield over a year before prompted memories of previous interactions with the enemy? These men who were among the first to volunteer to fight for the preservation of their country, who were not swayed to join the army by the financial enticements of later recruitment drives, who watched as comrade after comrade was lost to the greedy jaws of war, had been tested beyond what they could have dreamed possible in May 1861 when they enlisted. Now, the original band of just over 800 men of the 27th NY Volunteers numbered fewer than 300 who were ready to fight, which begged the question: who would survive this duty?[5] Rollin and his comrades had much to reflect on.

Undoubtedly, President Lincoln's visit to the Army of the Potomac camp on October 3, 1862, his first since coming to Harrison's Landing on July 8 after the failed Peninsula Campaign, further stimulated discussion in all directions. H. Seymour Hall, then a captain in Rollin's regiment, wrote coolly of the visit in his monograph: "President Lincoln rode through the camp, Oct. 3rd, with Generals McClellan and Franklin, but there were no cheers or other demonstrations of enthusiasm."[6] Another soldier in the 27th NY irreverently poked fun at the President as he speculated about the purpose of the visit: "No one will be able to admire his equestrian skill, for his legs always insist on coming to the ground, according to the law of gravitation. McClellan was apparently in a somber mood . . . It has not yet transpired what this visitation of the President meant, but it was whispered at the time it meant instant action."[7] (See figures 9.1 and 9.2.)

Try as Lincoln might, this would not be the case. Three days after his visit, Halleck telegraphed McClellan with instructions from the President: cross the Potomac and give battle to the enemy now while the roads are passable. Instead, for the next three weeks, McClellan bickered with Halleck, Quartermaster General Meigs, and ostensibly the President that it was quite out of the question to move now given the deficiency in horses, shoes, clothes, shelter tents, and other indispensable supplies his men were suffering. Meanwhile, from October 9 to 14, flamboyant Confederate cavalryman Major General Jeb Stuart led 1,800 of his troopers on another audacious circuit ride around the whole of McClellan's army, picking up intelligence, horses, and prisoners and leaving the North chagrined. Stuart magnified the insult by puncturing the Pennsylvania border and raiding the town of Chambersburg before swinging east around the Army of the Potomac. Even the gently shaming letter from Lincoln on October 13, 1862, did little to hasten McClellan toward pursuing the Rebels. Lincoln wrote: "You remember my speaking to you of what I called your overcautiousness. Are you not overcautious when you assume that you cannot do what the enemy is constantly doing? Should you not claim to be at least his equal in prowess, and act upon the claim?"[8]

FIGURE 9.1   President Lincoln and General McClellan after
Antietam photographed by Alexander Gardner. Library of
Congress, Prints & Photographs Division, Civil War
Photographs.

For the men of the 27th NY Volunteers, the highest echelons of the Army of
the Potomac breezing past them during a camp visit would have triggered questions not only of the immediacy of offensive operations but also of the hurly-
burly of conflicts within the North's effort itself. They had borne witness to their
trusted Commanding General George McClellan being pushed aside in favor of
the condescending and overwhelmed John Pope after the weeks of inertia following the Peninsula Campaign. Would inaction after successes at South Mountain, and then the mayhem at Antietam, threaten McClellan's tenure again? Had
the President given McClellan an ultimatum, thus accounting for the general's

FIGURE 9.2   President Lincoln, General McClellan, and Suite at Army of Potomac Headquarters after Antietam photographed by Alexander Gardner. Library of Congress, Prints & Photographs Division, Civil War Photographs.

"somber mood"? If McClellan were to be replaced, by whom? Had 6th Corps Commander William Franklin answered questions about why one of his two divisions—despite being formed in column of attack when it arrived at the Antietam battlefield—was ordered not to enter the fight as other units around them were being cut to pieces? This valuable resource, Henry Slocum's experienced division, instead was kept tucked away, dodging shot and shells.

Or, at least the 27th NY Volunteers still thought of themselves as Slocum's men. After the Battle of Antietam, Major General Slocum was tapped to replace mortally wounded Major General Joseph Mansfield of the 12th Corps. The day after President Lincoln's visit, October 4, 1862, hometown pride would have swelled in Rollin's chest as Binghamton native J. J. Bartlett was promoted to brigadier general—hardly surprising after Bartlett's decisive leadership during the Battle of Crampton's Gap. Capable Alexander Adams was promoted to colonel on the same day and remained the commander of the 27th NY Volunteers until the day they mustered out.

For other officers, this period of regrouping after the Battle of Antietam would spell the end of their military careers. Many ill-suited officers voluntarily resigned. Some needed a push. Within the 6th Corps, from October 25, 1862, a review board convened, as directed by Franklin, to "examine the capacity, qualifications, propriety of conduct, and efficiency of volunteer officers," and to dispense with prevaricating officers.[9]

And would the poor economy of fielding regiments now decimated by the ravages of war but still carrying the full slate and expense of officers compel Washington to muster some regiments out early? Could the 27th NY Volunteers, one of the first to pledge allegiance to the Union, possibly return home earlier than the following May?

Of course, President Lincoln's announcement of the preliminary Emancipation Proclamation just ten days prior to his visit would also have been an inescapable topic of deliberation among Rollin and his comrades. Lincoln's declaration signaled the broadening of the principles for which Union soldiers would fight, and a narrow window for secessionist states to rejoin the Union without—for the time being—surrendering rights to owning enslaved people. Rollin's hometown newspaper, the *Broome Weekly Republican*, ran the following editorial on October 1, 1862:

> He [the President] declares that on the first day of January next, all persons held as slaves within any State or designated part of a State, whose people shall then be in rebellion against the United States, shall be thenceforward and forever free. If the rebel States return to their allegiance before that time, the institution of Slavery remains unchanged . . . We rejoice to see this important step taken, believing the crisis of the hour demands it, and that the people will sustain the President in enforcing it.[10]

Not all Northerners shared this view. By October 1862, fault lines were clearly visible within the Union as the war ground on and the original patriotic appeals for the sanctity of the country were now coupled with steps toward freeing the enslaved. Though elements of President Lincoln's political party were impatient for speedier progress in extinguishing the rebellion and the fetid institution of slavery, these "Radical Republicans" did not seek separation from the party. Northern Democrats, on the other hand, became increasingly cleaved. Those that remained loyal to the Union cause, the "War Democrats," were at a crossroads with the so-called "Copperhead Democrats," who opposed the war and favored maintaining the slavery status quo for the sake of ending it.[11]

The President's September 22 preliminary Emancipation Proclamation unleashed rage on both sides of the conflict. Southerners railed against the edict as an enticement for enslaved people to break free and run north to join the Union Army; surely this was vindication for secession. Copperhead Democrats shouted that this overreach of presidential power was definitive evidence that Lincoln and the Republicans had been disingenuous all along. This war was not about patriotic necessity; in reality, it was always about freeing enslaved people.[12] Many War Democrats attempted to thread the needle. They focused on the value to the war effort of the Proclamation (e.g., thwarting France and Britain from intervening in the war, the additional pool of soldiers that freed slaves represented, and the consequent hit to the southern economy absent the labor of enslaved people), and understood that renouncing the President's decree would undermine Union soldiers.

Though few other than Lincoln's cabinet were aware of the imminence of the Proclamation, the trendline leading up to the announcement was unambiguous. On March 13, 1862, Congress added to the Articles of War: from that date forward, it would be illegal to return fugitive enslaved people to their owners. (Likely concerned about an active rumor mill in camp, Colonel Alexander Adams, commander of the 27th NY Volunteers, read the full Articles of War to the regiment on October 5, 1862, thereby reminding them of the basis for their duty.)[13] On April 16, 1862, in accordance with a law passed days earlier, the federal government compensated owners who freed their enslaved workers in Washington. On June 19, 1862, Congress made slavery illegal in current and future territories (though not the states). And on July 17, 1862, dual legislation—the Confiscation Act (freeing Confederate enslaved people who had found refuge behind Union lines) and the Militia Act (legalizing Black male enlistment in the US Army)—foreshadowed Lincoln's bold announcement.

Around camp in Bakersville, Maryland, the men debated the motivations behind and implications of the President's September 22 announcement. Would the Proclamation drive more Southerners into the Confederate Army to preserve their economy and way of life? Could the announcement have a chilling effect on enlistment in the North now that singularity of purpose, preservation of the Union, had irrefutably been broadened to include freeing the enslaved in the Rebel states? In mid-October, Rollin turned to his father via letter to air his doubts and frustrations about the entire war enterprise. The continued threat of Confederate incursion into Pennsylvania could only have amplified his overall concern.

In camp near Sharpsburg Md
Oct 13th 1862

My Dear Father

The prospects of our moving to Hagerstown for the purpose of resting and recruiting after our severe and protracted campaign has grown small and beautifully less, the present signs indicating our business to be for some time to come to guard the fords in the vicinity of Dam "No. 4," but so unstable are the elements of war that we may be on the move in two hours.

So long as we remain here we shall have a great amount of picket duty to do, say about one day in five, but we are thankful for so easy a job as this if it only holds out long enough. We occupy the Maryland bank and Johnny Reb the Virginia, but there was no exchange of shots while our Regt was on duty, though we could see the pickets on the opposite bank within easy range of our rifles.

The news here this morning is that there are forty thousand Rebs across the river at Hancock, pushing towards Pennsylvania. If it be true, I hope there is some of the tribe of Samuel wise enough, bold enough, or reckless enough, as you civilians may now think the proper term, to take my extra musket and use it in the defense of their own Commonwealth. I am glad that I enlisted when I did for if I live it through I have one full year the start of the greater portion of the army, as my term will expire next spring.

As to the raid into Pennsylvania, I do not think the effects will reach to Great Bend. I am inclined to think there is a trap somewhere on the upper Potomac which the enemy may have fallen into. I am certain that we have been massing troops in the vicinity of Williamsport for some time back and could have kept the enemy from crossing in such force if there was not some plan matured to keep them this side 'til they went back paroled.

I am free to say that I am not fully satisfied with the Government nor with some of the Comdg Genls in the field. The exact men in fault I cannot designate, but I am well satisfied that there is jealousy and hatred between the whole party of them, and this one thing unless it is stopped very soon will prove our utter ruin. If things go on for another year as they have for the past six months, the South will be recognized and permitted to go its own road, but I think unless things change, the roads of each Government will be broad and end in the same place, the name of which is not necessary to mention.

Even after a year's experience, the financial affairs relating to the army are miserably conducted. For example, last fall a year ago the Gov bought an immense quantity of potatoes, and when McClellan's army moved down the Potomac last spring, they were shipped on board of sloops and sent down to Ship Point and later in the season up to Harrison's Landing. After our forces evacuated Fair Oaks, they laid at Harrison's Landing seven weeks of the hottest weather we had last summer, and died with scurvy by scores, a disease only brought on by the want of vegetable food, and yet eight or nine thousand bushels of potatoes were thrown overboard to make room for baggage when we evacuated that place, and still later in the season large quantities were thrown away, too rotten to use.[14] Now why were these not distributed among the men instead of wasted? There are very many cases in the same category that have come within my notice.

Our Genls are fighting one another more than they are the South. They want money, they want power, and I think no less than six want to be the next President.

Now I want to say just a word about the President's emancipation proclamation, and then I will wind up for this morning. Proclamations have come so thick and fast for the last year that if they had had the savor of common salt, the Union would have been saved without the shedding of blood. I cannot see the object of such a proclamation; the South are not going to be scared into submission by any such document. And at this stage of the game, it will not help volunteering in the North.

Your aff son
Rollin B. Truesdell

October lumbered on. By the middle of the month, few in Rollin's regiment would wager offensive operations would happen any time soon. Sixth Corps Commander William Franklin had already moved two divisions to Hagerstown and established his own headquarters there, apparently in preparation for the coming winter months.[15] Rollin and the rest of his division were left to guard the river and to anticipate the heavy rains to come.

With each passing day, and the deeply unpleasant memory of camp conditions the previous winter indelibly seared into their minds, the men of the 27th NY Volunteers began their own planning for how they might protect themselves from the blustery, wet weather to come. Rollin had an advantage in this regard: his family. In a letter to his sister Clara dated October 16, 1862, Rollin presented his succinct list of items for himself and tentmate William Westervelt that might provide immediate comfort. His father and brother Albert were contemplating traveling some 175 miles to hand-deliver the items.

In camp near Sharpsburg Md
Oct 16th 1862

My Dear Sister

Your favor of the 11th inst I have just received. I wrote a long letter to my father yesterday, but yours seems to require an immediate answer from the fact that there is a probability of some of the family paying me a visit very soon. Well, if Father comes, do not burden the old man with much of a load for it will be enough for him to think of and to do to get through this crowd of soldiers now about Maryland. He need not bring anything for me but a pair of shirts made of red soft flannel—the best quality. Make them good length with a wide collar and no bosom. Be sure and get good soft cloth. Then, of some kind of material, make two night caps just the same shape as a common boy's cap, without stiffening or binding, only a pleat to turn up around the edge. These are all the articles that I care to have sent to me 'til I am sure that we are through our marches for the fall and winter. I do not want to get any more clothing on hand than I can carry. If I should, I would only have to throw it away.

I may, as I did last summer, think of several small things I want sent after I have said "all" several times; for instance, I now think I want about four good handkerchiefs.

If Albert comes, I don't care how much you send, but don't make a pack horse of Father.

I think we shall remain in this camp for some time to come—perhaps all winter.

Ed Watson is well. Burrows is in the hospital somewhere. I do not know where.

My health is sound.

Yours truly
Rollin B. Truesdell

To: Miss Clara E. Truesdell
Great Bend, Pa

The arrival of their pillaged knapsacks on October 22, having been sent off from Harrison's Landing on August 11, was a cruel reminder that they could not rely on the army to ensure their well-being.[16] For Rollin, that would be a trifling matter. His determined and generous family made sure that he—as well as tent-mate William Westervelt—had some of the "good things" in life that October, such as night caps and dried fruit. Rollin sounded positively buoyant in the letter he wrote to his sister Clara after receiving a visit from his father and brother and being in receipt of their bounty. The visit was just the tonic needed.

In camp near Bakerville Md.
Oct 23d 1862

My Dear Sister

When I parted with Father at Hagerstown, I promised to write to him as soon as I got back to camp but as I have so lately seen him, I thought it would answer the same purpose to write to you. I can never tell you, for no language can express my feelings, how glad I was to see Father and Albert, and also for the things sent me from home. I thank God I have friends at home who remember me; even my little niece Kathy I find put in a bag of currants. I tell you I am feasting like a king. And that jug of jell is the best I ever tasted. Indeed, it is all good, and I cannot express my thanks enough.

After leaving Pa and Albert, I went as far towards camp as Jones Cross Roads and there stayed all night, it being very dark and the road crowded with army wagons. Monday morning, I went on to the toll gate and, after partaking of a good breakfast with the venerable collector, I hired a man to take myself and trunk over to camp. I had no difficulty in finding the new camp they had made in my absence, which was quite near the river at Dam No. 4. I had hardly got my trunk unloaded before we got orders to move back in the vicinity of the camp where Pa found me, so it was near night before I had the pleasure of holding a "post mortem" examination over the trunk, and I tell you it did do my eyes good to lift out the treasures. We, that is my tent mate William B. Westervelt and myself have had splendid times since.

And by the way, Will is one of the finest fellows I ever met. We live 90% above the fare of a soldier, and what makes it better is he says Uncle Truesdell brought it down to us.

I had a first rate visit with Father and very good with Albert, but he, Albert, was so uneasy that when I talked with him I had to take him pretty much on the run, but all in all I had a good time and hope if we go into winter quarters near here the visit may be repeated.

And I tell you it was some consolation to see my Sister, though it was in a frame and I would to God they had brought Mother too. I believe her picture would do my soul good though I got her heart in the many things the trunk contained, and the labels on those bags of fruit in her own handwriting is worth a good deal to me. I tell you when I look around my tent and see the good things it gives me good courage to fight for I know that if I stand it seven months longer and come out sound, I have friends to meet me at "Home," and we can have good things together. I want to live to get home to thank you all with the word of mouth for those good things. I can't write thanks; it's no use to try.

We now have a splendid camp in an oak grove across the creek from where we were when Pa was here. There are no signs of a general move as I can see at present, though we may move in an hour.

Write me a good long letter as soon as you get this and tell me all about how Father and Albert got home.

With much love to all I am

Your affectionate bro
Rollin B. Truesdell

To: Clara E Truesdell
Great Bend, Pa

Shortly after the familial visit, in the last week of October 1862, Rollin and Westervelt began plotting how they could improve their shelter to ward off the elements. Westervelt recalled: "Some of us built log huts in place of tents. Sergeant Trusdell [*sic*] and myself finishing ours . . . when we turned in for the night were congratulating ourselves on our comfortable quarters, when orders came to move at sunrise the next morning."[17]

The Commanding General, bypassing consultation with General-in-Chief Halleck, was finally ready to go find the enemy. Fortified, Rollin jotted a short note to his father of the imminent move.

Crampton's Gap Md
Oct 30th 1862

Dear Father

Like Gypsies of olden times, we've struck our tents and are again on the move, but whither we go we know not. I could not give even a guess. From this camp there are roads leading to Harper's Ferry, Point of Rocks, and down the river; which we shall take when morning comes we shall have to wait and see.

My dried fruit is better than "honeycomb" on this march.

Even if we have ten days march before us, the hardest part is done. We are well under way.

I will write often—do the same.

Yours
Rollin B. Truesdell

At least Rollin and Westervelt had part of one night's rest in their cabin before striking camp and once again falling in line to march.

Chapter 10

BACK IN VIRGINIA

A WISTFUL MARCH

At 3 a.m., the familiar sound of the bugle roused Rollin and the rest of the 27th NY Volunteers. After slurping some coffee, the men hoisted their knapsacks onto their backs and fell in line to march. Over the next six weeks, the regiment would doggedly plunge their way southward into enemy territory, back from Maryland into Virginia. On this first day of their march, October 31, 1862, the men's spirits were high as they crossed through Keedysville and approached the site of their furious and exalted battle of six weeks previous. Their ten-mile march landed them on the western slope at Crampton's Gap, where they camped for the night. Here, they would sleep well, unbothered by the fretful whispers of their dead comrades in arms they slept aside the last time South Mountain was their camp site.

The next morning, the 27th NY Volunteers threaded their way through the mountain pass and over the battlefield. The juxtaposition of the natural beauty of the valley with the trauma that lay buried beneath it was not lost on the men. A comrade of Rollin's revealed his thoughts in a letter home:

> We rest our eyes to think of the joys, the comforts, and the genuine happiness the possessors of that beautiful valley might have, were it not for the blighting curse of war. As we descended the rugged slope of the mountain, the numerous wrecks of guns, accoutrements, the many little mounds of fresh earth, remind us we . . . are passing, perhaps for the last time, the graves of our loved comrades,

who nobly gave their lives that their country's honor might be maintained.[1]

The regiment paused in Burkittsville long enough to briefly visit wounded comrades who had been left in the village to heal when the army marched onward to meet the enemy at Antietam. They said their goodbyes again and headed south.

For Rollin, the travel through the desecrations of war felt particularly poignant. On this day, November 1, 1862, Rollin learned he had been promoted to corporal. He felt proud that his dedication and leadership potential had been rewarded. But he also recognized that this elevation would demand more of him. As corporal, Rollin would be accountable for ensuring that the enlisted men around him on the battlefield followed orders and pursued the fight with vigor. Rollin was a towering man—six-foot-one, at a time that average male height was about five-foot-seven—an easy guidepost for wavering battle lines. In sharing the responsibility for polishing and guiding the men in Company F, Rollin would also inevitably share the grim burden of loss more personally with each fallen man in his unit.

As the sun was rising the morning of November 2, 1862, Rollin's regiment crossed back into Confederate territory. The night before, they had camped on the north side of the Potomac River and prepared for the change in perspective. The 1,200-foot-long bridge that conveyed them to Virginia was comprised of sixty-one pontoons about twenty feet apart—nearly two-thirds as long as the famous Chickahominy Bridge.[2] Shuffling across this mighty structure, and then over subsequent days and days of marches ten miles or more as they followed along the baseline of the mountains in their push south, Rollin and his comrades carried the burden of their knowledge of war. They knew the destruction in all probability would continue after they mustered out of service in the spring—if they lived that long.

Contemplating their own mortality with each step brought into sharp focus what and who these young men most cherished in life. For Rollin, recently visiting with his father and brother near Bakersville, Maryland, would have amplified his yearnings for home and his resolute desire to help his family even as he was marching toward his own possible demise.

First sending instructions to his brother Albert on November 4, and then writing to his beloved sister Clara a day later, Rollin fixated on converting his prized watch from home into cash on payday. He wanted to give the money to his sister for the purchase of the sewing machine she longed for but could not afford.[3] He was not going to allow his absence to get in the way of look-ing after her.

"Dixie" Nov 4th 1862

Dear Brother

I suppose by this time you have heard of our re-crossing the Potomac and becoming invaders and are looking out sharp for news from this quarter, and would also like to know how I am getting along. As for news, there is not much to write that I know of other than you already know by the papers, and the way I am getting along is "fine."

We marched about nine miles this morning and camped five miles beyond Morrisonville in Loudon Co. As soon as tents were pitched, I took a walk to see what the site was for foraging. Re-sult: pork and potatoes, bread and butter for dinner and now Will is making a custard for supper. So you see, I did not walk in vain. Perhaps you ask how we bake custard: why we just make it in a cup, put in a kettle of hot water, and boil 'til done.

'Tis very good weather to march, but quite cool to sleep good, and to write.

Do you think my watch could be sent to me by mail? I would like to have it for I can turn it into cash to good advantage after pay day. I want it put up in the following manner—first roll the watch in wool "tight," then put into a small paste board box the right size, wrap this in strong paper, and seal well with wax. Put on the requisite number of stamps and direct very plain. See that it is packed snug and firm.

I intended to write to Clara this afternoon but 'tis too cold. Tell Clara I do not want any clothing sent or even prepared 'til we get to a stopping place. I will write to her in a day or two. My health is good.

Yours truly
Rollin B Truesdell

To: Albert Truesdell
Liberty, Pa

P.S. Tell Father if Clara's sewing machine is worth the money to keep it; the cash shall be forthcoming as soon as we are paid.

Rollin

Camp near Snickers Gap, Va
November 5, 1862

My dear Sister,

I received a letter from you several days since but being on the march, I could not find time to answer it 'til this morning, and now I expect every moment to hear the order to fall in.

I wrote to Bro. Albert two days ago, so you probably know something near where I am. We are now about twenty-five miles from the Potomac at Berlin, our advance having drove the enemy across the Shenandoah. It is fine weather for marching, but cool nights. We move about twelve miles per day. I "do not" want any articles of clothing sent me at present. I have all I can "carry," more would be useless.

I want my watch sent me by mail. I design to turn it into cash after pay day. Put it up in the following manner, to wit: first, roll in wool or cotton; then place in a small pasteboard box the right size; sew the box with strong thread; then wrap with paper, seal, and put on stamps, directions, etc. I think it will come through all right.

Now a word about that sewing machine. If you think it worth the money and best to keep it, I will forward money to pay for it about the twenty-fifth of this month, or if whoever owns the machine will take the watch and pay the difference, let Father make the exchange. But I think I can do better to sell the watch here and pay cash for the machine. At all events keep the machine. I am doing first rate just now and if nothing turns more than I can see, I will be able to spare you ten dollars by the 25th inst.

'Tis a cool morning. I have just had my breakfast of mutton pot pie and blackberry sauce, soft bread and butter. So you see, I, like Daniel Webster, "ain't dead yet."[4]

Will sends love to "Uncle Truesdell" and family. Indeed, "Uncle" Truesdell got many thanks for apples, etc, which came to camp with him. I think he would have many friends if he should appear here again. The drum beats. I must close. Write soon, love to all.

Truly,
Rollin B. Truesdell

I will try and write to Pa in a few days.

Within his immediate midst, Rollin was also concerned about the welfare of someone he respected and admired deeply: Brigade Commander J. J. Bartlett. Elected major for the 27th NY Volunteers before the regiment mustered into federal service, his comrades cheered as he rose through the ranks through tenacity and savvy to now command his own brigade, to which they were attached. On November 3, 1862, a comrade confided in a letter: "Too much cannot be said in favor of General Bartlett; and with him at the head of the Brigade, I have no fears. At present he is not very well, being afflicted with an attack of the rheumatism which compels him to ride in a carriage, instead of a saddle. A man of common energy or common patriotism thus afflicted would be in a hospital unable to move."[5] Less than two weeks later, with his health much impaired, Bartlett accepted a thirty-day leave of absence and returned home to Binghamton, New York.[6] Regimental Commander Colonel Henry L. Cake of the 96th Pennsylvania Volunteers filled the breach and led the brigade while Bartlett was away—including during the fateful battle to come. (After Henry Slocum's departure to assume command of the 12th Corps, Brigadier General W.T.H. Brooks was promoted to command the 1st Division, 6th Corps.)

Facing southward and easing back into secessionist country enlivened Rollin's and his comrades' sense of the import of the contract they entered when they enlisted all those many months ago. In exchange for their pledge to fight for the preservation of the Union and the Constitution that underpins it, they would risk their lives. The underlying premise upon which the contract rested was that the people and the leaders that they elected in the North would offer unwavering support for their service. As the men marched south into Loudon County, they could not help but feel far removed from the ongoing political tumult of elections that had the potential to recast Northern commitment to the war cause. For the men of the 27th NY Volunteers, they were most fixated on the contest for governorship of the State of New York. They were unable to vote from the field, but that did not stop the men from taking a straw poll on November 4, 1862, the date of the election.

On that day, Rollin's regiment served as rear guard and while pausing for the rest of their brigade comrades to pass, the men conducted their vote. The Republican candidate, philanthropist turned politician turned military leader, Brigadier General James S. Wadsworth, had not planned on running for the governorship. In the months leading up to the election, Wadsworth commanded the Military District of Washington, and established a prickly relationship with Army of the Potomac Commander George McClellan in doing so. Telling the truth to Commander-in-Chief Lincoln regarding the number of forces McClellan had left behind to protect Washington when McClellan pushed out for the Peninsula Campaign, Wadsworth succeeded in returning a corps to Washington—much to McClellan's contempt. Surmising he had little prospect of advancement in McClellan's army, abolitionist Wadsworth agreed to be the candidate of the Radical Republicans.

The Democrats put forward former New York Governor (1853–1854) Horatio Seymour as their strongest competitor for the seat. In contrast to Wadsworth, who did not campaign, anti-abolitionist Seymour embraced the contest and staked out a moderate position in which he managed to support the war effort while casting aspersions on the President and his perceived centralization of power.

The 27th NY Volunteers regimental history reported that Wadsworth received a twenty-three-vote majority in the regiment and that Company D (from Binghamton) had only one vote against him.[7] The men were on pins-and-needles waiting to learn who their governor would be. A comrade in the regiment wrote home six days after the vote, complaining: "No papers later than the New York Tribune of the 5th and Philadelphia Inquirer of the 6th have been received so we don't know the result of the election in New York."[8] It would be close. Wadsworth lost by approximately 10,000 votes, of some 600,000 cast. Had soldiers in the field been permitted to vote, one can imagine a different outcome.

McClellan's Out, Burnside's In

The men trudged on with clouds of uncertainty trailing them. After enduring a march of fifteen cold and windy miles, Rollin and his comrades reached White Plains, Virginia, a station on the Manassas Gap Railroad, on November 7, 1862. In what might have felt like the taunt of stormy events to come, the men were walloped by an unusually early heavy snowfall that evening. Buried in the snow when they woke up, the men of the 27th NY Volunteers were stopped in their tracks for a day.

On Sunday morning, November 9, 1862, the men shook off the snow and continued their march to New Baltimore. A comrade in the regiment described the day as "the most mournful, gloomy, and hope-begone day we have seen in service."[9] The men were numb. Numb from the freezing winter surprise and numb from the rumors of the dismissal—again—of their Commanding General.

Rollin and his comrades would not have confirmation of Major General George McClellan's removal as Commander of the Army of the Potomac until November 10, 1862, when McClellan and his successor, amiable Major General Ambrose Burnside, rode through the camp in New Baltimore. Fury and indignation about the decision were the general order of the day among the enlisted and officers alike. Many shared Rollin's view that the decision was a slight against the soldiers themselves and borne of ignorance and political expediency—even as they held no grudge against their incoming Commanding General. One comrade in the 27th NY Volunteers seethed: "Whatever may have been the cause which has led to his fall, and whatever may be the abilities of Burnside, I tell the truth when I say that this army feels outraged and insulted. At this moment, imprecations within my hearing are heaped upon the President . . . Men seem paralyzed with discouragement whether this confidence in and love for McClellan was well founded or not, is another matter. The edict that removed McClellan is considered the death blow to the Union."[10]

On November 14, Rollin wrote to his father, his confidant, to vent some fury.

> Camp of 27th Regt NYSV
> New Baltimore Va
> Nov 14th 1862

Dear Father

The whole army is stopped for the time being from its onward movements to give Genl Burnside a chance to get firmly hold on the reins before he gives the order to "forward," and while we wait, of course, like all Yankees, we must busy ourselves about something and that something is heaping curses and abuses upon the men who were the chief cause of the removal of Genl McClellan. Some charging it upon the President alone, and others upon the Secretary of War, Genl Halleck, etc., but the main course of ill feelings flows toward the Convention of Governors who met something like a month ago at Octorona, Penna.[11] It may not be their act, but they are now receiving many curses, whether innocent or guilty. We feel that we have been imposed upon and that unless a reason for the act is soon made manifest to the troops in the field, a powerful reaction in their patriotism will show itself. Perhaps those high in office think the troops in the field but a tool in their hand, and not possessed of talent enough to resent even this grave insult, but if thus they think, they are mistaken and the effects will be forcibly felt sooner or later.

We have confidence in Burnside, but we had more in Mc-Clellan, and the change made now, in the midst of an apparently successful campaign, brings the army to a standstill, and the troops show their feelings in the matter by loudly cheering for Mc and groaning for Burnside.

Officers show their discountenance of the act by resigning their commissions, and those in the regular army, high in office, by accepting the resignations of their inferiors. Shame, shame on the North who can unite their interests with jealousies and divine to destroy all good feeling and harmony that may possibly exist in the hearts of the soldiery. We have done much for the sustaining of the Constitution and the Union, and now, after passing over two years of actual warfare and incurring a vast debt to the Gov't, to see the reins of power handed back to the party from whom sprung all these evils and begin to surrender all to them without a stronger effort to sustain our selves and maintain our dignity is more than ought be asked of any army, and more than we will submit to without a murmur. Let the Generals in the field manage the affairs of the army and not the civilian politicians who linger at the doors of the contract office and who know as little about the complicated affairs of the army as a babe. Which would you of choice endeavor to please without regard to the results? The fighting men in the field, or the howling politicians at home? Thus far in the war the latter has had the preference, and greatly to the disadvantage of both Gov't and army.

Fanatics want quick work of the rebellion and fast Genls, but they cannot have it. The thing has gained too formidable dimensions to squelch in a moment, day, or year. And we must take philosophical view of it, and go to work rationally to put it down, and not by a continual change of Commanders.

Your aff son

Rollin B. Truesdell

A couple of days later, still in a disillusioned state, Rollin went through the motions of a letter to his sister.

Camp of 27th Regt NYSV
New Baltimore Va

My Dear Sister

Your favor of Nov 10th I rec'd today and as we move on to-morrow morning, I thought I might as well answer tonight as to defer it 'til we are again domiciled.

I have no particular news to write. Everything is gloomy since Mc left us. I wrote Father a long letter a day or two ago. I have not heard from Albert in some time. Hope I shall next mail.

I want you to send me a pocket handkerchief enclosed in a newspaper. I am entirely out and can't get any in this heathen country. I think they will come through safe. The Col. had a pair of boots come from home in that way.

I am tough, oh how tough; never felt better in my life.

And while I think of it, send me a couple of nutmegs; can't get them here.

Did Albert get his gun home?

I'm sleepy—will write again someday when I have time.

Love to all.

Yours
Rollin B. Truesdell

Burnside organized the former Commanding General's farewell, cognizant of the affection McClellan's army felt for their departing commander. The men of the 27th NY Volunteers wildly cheered their general when he passed them, and a comrade reported: "McClellan was so moved by the expressions of personal regard and sympathy from officers and men, that his eyes were moist and his voice tremulous, as he personally took his final leave of that grand Army of the Potomac."[12] Another from the regiment offered this melancholy remembrance: "As he passes the Artillery, they gave him their parting salute, and as the sound echoes and reechoes through the mountain passes, it sounds to our ears like the death knell of a nation's hope."[13]

The 27th NY regimental history, published twenty-six years later, somewhat apologetically noted that "the soldiers at this time did not realize what Gen. McClellan might have done after the battle of Antietam, by following up the enemy more rapidly."[14]

But the President did know. Lincoln had already endured George McClellan's prevarications after the failed campaign on the Virginia peninsula. After waiting for weeks for the general to move his army against the Confederate capital, the President transferred that responsibility to another general instead. In no time, hat in hand, Lincoln was compelled to seek McClellan's leadership in gathering up the remnants of Pope's battered army after the abysmal failure of Major General John Pope at the second Battle of Bull Run. To relive McClellan's inaction after battle again, this time dawdling in the aftermath of the devastating clash that turned back the invading Confederate Army as it encroached on northern territory, was unconscionable.

Doubly infuriatingly, Confederate Commanding General Lee, always ready to confidently take advantage of McClellan's plodding, looked to be using the same risky but successful strategy he had used to great effect against the Army of the Potomac in previous engagements. Again, going counter to prevailing military dogma, Lee did not unify his rested and regrouped force to face his equally rested and regrouped but numerically superior foe. Instead, as the giant of the North meandered southward east of the Blue Ridge mountains, Lee marched Longstreet's men to Culpepper to face the oncoming Union troops and kept Jackson's force in familiar terrain in the Shenandoah Valley. Lee had blocked McClellan's path to Richmond and offered a tantalizing prospect for a replay of Jackson's audacious flanking maneuvers.

By early November 1862, the President's patience was exhausted. With McClellan and his propaganda machine firmly ensconced as the darling of the Democratic party, Lincoln was hamstrung from doing what he wanted to do—to extract McClellan from the Army of the Potomac—during the campaign season. Support in the North for the war, the Republican Party, and the President himself had grown more wobbly with passing seasons and additional bloodshed; Lincoln could not risk further incentivizing undecided voters to cast their ballot for the antiwar, anti-abolitionist party. Wasting no time after the election, however, Lincoln acted. The evening of November 5, with the suspense over and Horatio Seymour's victory assured in New York, the most populous state in the Union, the President finally ordered General-in-Chief Halleck to remove McClellan and to appoint Burnside to command the Army of the Potomac. Assistant Adjutant General Edward D. Townsend, by order of the Secretary of War, signed the order relieving McClellan that night.

On November 7, 1862, after collecting 9th Corps Commander Burnside at his headquarters, Secretary of War Edwin Stanton's emissary, staff officer Brigadier General Catharinus Buckingham, led the way to the Headquarters of the Army of the Potomac through the blinding snow. They arrived at

George McClellan's tent a bit before midnight to hand him the sealed envelope containing the order. The President had personally drafted the dismissal order; Halleck added a finishing touch: McClellan was to report to Trenton, New Jersey, for further instructions (which never came). Burnside, a reluctant participant, watched as McClellan absorbed the news. Before turning in that night, the defrocked commander penned a vainglorious-tinged farewell address to the officers and soldiers of the Army of the Potomac that also managed to dig at the abolitionist ideals of President Lincoln. This address reads, in part:

> An order of the President devolves upon Major-General Burnside the command of this army. In parting from you, I cannot express the love and gratitude I bear to you. As an army, you have grown up under my care. In you I have never found doubt or coldness. The battles you have fought under my command, will proudly live in our nation's history . . . We shall ever be comrades in supporting the constitution of our country and the nationality of its people.[15]

A couple of days passed before Ambrose Burnside shared his own order confirming acceptance of the command. Like the understudy who got his big break, Major General Burnside showered his predecessor with praise in his statement: "Having been a sharer of the privations, and a witness of the bravery of the old Army of the Potomac in the Maryland campaign, and fully identified in the feelings of respect and esteem for General McClellan, entertained through a long and most friendly association with him, I feel that it is not as a stranger that I assume this command."[16] Burnside was well aware that the loyalty of the officers and the enlisted was not a transferable commodity. He would need to make this army his own. (See figure 10.1.)

On November 9, 1862, the day he formally assumed command, Burnside sought to assuage fears in Washington of a repeat performance of inaction in high command by outlining his ideas for his superiors via telegram. Though still feeling tentative about sliding into his new position, the new Commanding General proposed a divergent plan of attack against the Confederacy than the existing, approved strategy. Instead of focusing on decapitating the Confederate Army, which would entail reliance on the vulnerable Orange and Alexandria Railroad for logistical support, Burnside advocated attacking the Confederate capital by way of Fredericksburg, a route that would bring the

FIGURE 10.1   Ambrose Burnside. Library of Congress, Prints & Photographs Division, Civil War Photographs.

army closer to protected navigable waterways along Virginia's Tidewater. The army's bellies would be appreciative of this more trustworthy supply route.

General-in-Chief Halleck, reluctant to fiddle with existing strategy, traveled through yet another November snowstorm to reach the army headquarters in Warrenton on November 12, 1862, to hear out Burnside on the merits of the Fredericksburg approach. Quartermaster General Montgomery Meigs and railroad expert Herman Haupt accompanied Halleck to critique Burnside's pitch, adding their opinions regarding the viability of this new plan given transportation and materiel limitations, and the availability of additional army assets that would be in demand.

Burnside knew that for his strategy to have a chance of success, he would need to blindside Lee. Undoubtedly, Lee was aware McClellan had been toppled, and was preoccupied with analyzing the impact of McClellan's removal and the elevation of Burnside as Commanding General for the Army of the Potomac. Burnside presumed Lee would not anticipate his army moving on Richmond immediately after treading water for so long after Antietam, and not from this route. His plan hinged on his troops marching rapidly to Falmouth, and then crossing the Rappahannock River into Fredericksburg before Lee could rearrange his forces to block them. This, in turn, was based on the premise that Washington would make haste in dispatching the army's pontoons from their resting spot along the Potomac where McClellan crossed his army, to where Burnside's army needed them near Fredericksburg.

President Lincoln allowed himself to be open to the Burnside-Fredericksburg plan despite having reservations. Halleck wired Lincoln's concurrence to the army headquarters the morning of November 14. The President could not afford to plant seeds of doubt as to whether Burnside was the man for the job. The message to the general upon whose shoulders the spirit of the Union army rested did emphasize that time was of the essence, however. Lincoln needed him to act immediately.

While paused in Warrenton awaiting word from Washington, Burnside polished his plans for a reorganization of the Army of the Potomac. The Commanding General sought to consolidate and streamline his corps-heavy army in preparation for the upcoming campaign. Burnside created the Right, Center, and Left Grand Divisions and designated the 11th Corps, commanded by Major General Franz Sigel, as the reserve force. The Right Grand Division would be comprised of the 2nd and 9th Corps and commanded by Major General Bull Sumner, who led the 2nd Corps; Burnside had just relinquished his command of the 9th Corps. The Center Grand Division would be led by the politically connected runner-up to Burnside, Major General Joe Hooker. It would include the 3rd and 5th Corps led by Brigadier Generals George Stoneman and Daniel Adams Butterfield, respectively. Major General William Franklin was tapped to lead the Left Grand Division, which brought together his 6th Corps and the 1st Corps led by Major General John Reynolds. Command of the 6th Corps, to which Rollin and his comrades in the 27th NY Volunteers were attached, devolved to 2nd Division Commander

Baldy Smith. Burnside selected the Grand Division Commanders based on their seniority in the army, not necessarily because of his confidence in their loyalty to his command.

True to his word that he would move with alacrity, Commanding General Burnside pushed out the first of his Grand Divisions the day after he received approval for his plan of assault. Sumner's troops began their march from Warrenton on November 15, 1862, and maintained an impressive pace. The advance regiments reached Falmouth by November 17 and, peering across the river, detected a token force of 500 or so Rebels occupying Fredericksburg. Sumner appealed to Burnside for permission to keep moving toward the target and to take Fredericksburg while the picking was easy. Burnside declined. Fearing his Right Grand Division could be cut off from the rest of his army if the Rappahannock suddenly rose, Burnside ordered Sumner and his men to hold in Falmouth until the army reunited.

Franklin's Left Grand Division was right on the heels of Sumner's men. Rollin and his comrades broke camp around 7 a.m. on November 16 and joined the column that traveled southeast to Catlett's Station for a march of some fifteen miles. (The 27th NY Volunteers regimental history remarked on the plentitude of little gray rabbits, perfect for rabbit pot pie, at Catlett. The famished men, now reporting to Division Commander Brooks, "a stern disciplinarian," saw the rabbits as a gift given the rules against pilfering.[17]) Though forced to slosh through heavy rain and muck, seemingly their constant companion during marches, the regiment arrived at Stafford Court House, just north of Falmouth, on November 18, 1862, after marching a total of about forty-five miles.

Hooker's Center Grand Division formed the rearguard. As Sumner's men were stepping foot into camp near Falmouth, Hooker's were still miles away, at the beginning of their trudge from Warrenton. The misery of the movement, slowly snaking southward, increased with each soaking, muddy day of the march. The morale of the soldiers matched the weather conditions.

Burnside trotted into Falmouth on November 19. If he expected to find the pontoons when he reconnoitered the area—irreplaceable for his attack plan—he would be sorely disappointed. General-in-Chief Halleck, later explaining that Burnside could not have expected pontoons be delivered into the arms of the then occupying enemy, failed to impress any sense of urgency when he delivered his orders to move the pontoons from Berlin, Maryland, to Falmouth.[18] The first of them did not even leave Washington until November 19. Burnside was caught in a riddle. He had acknowledged the imperative for quick, bold action and declared his intention to pursue the campaign on Richmond via Fredericksburg immediately, just as Lincoln requested. And yet Burnside and his army would remain immobile due to the passivity of his superior officer.

Predictably, the wagons carrying the first of the pontoons soon became mud festooned as they labored south in the same unforgiving storm the marching men endured. Those that were not mired in the mud were redirected to the Potomac, and a steamboat delivered them to Belle Plain the evening of November 24. From there, they too inched their way through muck en route to Falmouth.

Though the Commanding General may have remembered November 27, 1862, as the day the last of the pontoon wagons finally rolled into Falmouth, Rollin and his comrades would instead reflect on this being the second Thanksgiving Day they were apart from family. Nerves frayed as each day of inaction passed and the men could determine no clear signals as to whether they should be bracing for upcoming battle, or for the punishing seasonal elements in winter quarters. Scanty rations powered near hallucinations of the bounty of the home hearth and the familial celebration of thanks for many of the men that Thanksgiving Day.

Rollin and tentmate William Westervelt, however, proudly improvised their own feast—not only on Thanksgiving Day but also one week earlier as a sort of trial run. On November 20, Rollin boasted to his mother of their culinary preparations.

Stafford C. H. Va
Nov 20th 1862

My Dear Mother

I have intended to write to you every day for the past week, but for various reasons I could not. I have to take the family by course, writing to each one occasionally so you may at all times know how I am getting along.

Today is our twenty-first day out from Bakersville, and eleventh day's march if we pull up and go on this afternoon, which I do not think we shall do. Stafford Court House is eight miles from the Potomac and situated on Aquia Creek. Report says we are to ship from Aquia Landing to some place the name of which is yet under the veil. I cannot give even a guess of the operations we are to go through as I have not seen a newspaper save the Republican in about two weeks. We begin to feel ourselves cut off from the civilized world since we cannot read the newspaper gossip.

For the past few days we have experienced cold damp weather; today it rains moderately. But this morning Will and self went out among the "heathen" and procured a fine fat goose and peck of "murphys" and are going to have a Thanksgiving supper. Though we are seven days in advance of the time, we thought best to make sure of the supper today while we can and give thanks the 27th, a thing we more easily do than cook a good supper if we are on the march.

5 o'clock. We have just ate our bountiful meal which was "very" good, A No. 1. The goose we parboiled then baked in kettle. We had the satisfaction of thinking it the best meal in camp, but best or second best as the case might be, 'twas good.

I am somewhat perplexed this damp weather with tooth ache. I think if they trouble me much more I shall try the cold iron. Otherwise than this my health is good.

I see by the paper that Josephine E. Lines is married. Strange how the draft effects people in old Susquehanna Co.—who next? Please write me as often as you can conveniently.

With much love to all, I am

Your aff son
Rollin

To: Mrs. Lucy Truesdell
Great Bend, Pa.

As it turned out, on Thanksgiving Day, the 27th NY Volunteers were on picket duty. This did not deter the two improvisational chefs from continuing their culinary feats. Drawing reserve duty, Rollin and Westervelt exercised their legs in the countryside and came up with the fixings for a fine celebratory dinner. Westervelt explained in his book: "We came to a farmhouse, with poultry yard. We soon selected a pair of roosters, and going to the house purchased some bread, eggs, milk, and sweet potatoes, that we paid for in Confederate money, of which we always kept a supply, it being very cheap . . . Although it was counterfeit, it was better made than the genuine. We always paid cash and were not very particular about the change."[19] The meal delighted the tentmates and one other fortunate friend. They captured the same spirit of Thanksgiving as loved ones celebrating at home.

The regiment did not return from picket duty to their camp at Stafford Court House until two days later, November 29. That day, Rollin sat down to pen a letter to his sister Clara and carried further a debate the siblings would have entertained sitting around the dining table—like so many families, over a holiday meal. Prodded by his sister, Rollin defended his musings of frustration and dejection directed at Union military command, particularly after Antietam. And Clara endeavored to keep Rollin's outlook positive despite the virtual certitude of the bloodshed dragging on without end in sight.

Camp of 27th NY Regt
Stafford C.H. Va
Nov 29th 1862

Dear Sister

Your favor of the 22d I have just received—am sorry to hear that Father's health is so poor, but have strong hopes that he will recover and live to see many years from the fact that our ancestors are remarkable for their longevity and strong constitutions which old age alone can break down.

It is now quite certain that we remain in this camp for some time, and if practical after the appearance of pay master, I shall go up to Washington and take a little respite from my labors.

We expect our pay every day and have for the past two weeks, but for some reason to us unknown, the much wished for cash don't come. It is only forty miles from here to Washington by boat, just a pleasant trip.

I am surprised that you should be ashamed of my letters— guess I will not write anymore. But the fact of the case is simply this, when I wrote the Antietam letter I did not know that four fifths of our heavy ammunition was expended on Wed., and that there was not enough to rely on had we commenced an attack on Friday morning.[20] We cannot find fault with a Genl for not fighting when he has no ammunition. I am told upon good authority that our supply of ammunition was brought down the Cumberland Valley Railroad at the rate of a mile a minute on Thursday and reached us during the night. The following morning, we advanced and found the enemy had retreated.

Perhaps we would think differently of the matter if we did not think the change was made for political motives.

But I admit I do not get a paper often enough to keep posted, so I fear I shall be a poor debater.

With much love I am

Your aff bro

Rollin B. Truesdell

To: C. E. Truesdell

Great Bend, Pa

Despite Rollin's prediction to his sister that movement was unlikely any time soon, the men of the 27th NY Volunteers marched on December 4, 1862. His brigade was assigned to guard the landing at Belle Plain and assist in the landing and unloading of boats laden with life-sustaining goods; it was the fragile lifeline for the soldiers in the field. The men broke camp at dawn and dragged themselves some ten miles east through biting cold, windy weather toward the river and camped beyond Belle Plain atop a hill unprotected against the elements. After a sleepless night, Rollin and his comrades shifted camp to the nearby woods in the hopes of more comfort under the protection of the canopy. Their comfort was short-lived. By midday on December 5, they were ordered to pack up again and retrace their steps of the previous day back to Belle Plain. This march of some four miles would be an unforgettable one. One of Rollin's comrades wrote: "A storm of rain, snow, and intense cold, coming upon us on the way, and [we] arriving after dark were exposed to its fury, without adequate shelter, the whole night."[21] Westervelt shuddered of that night: ". . . it was so dark and the snow so deep we could get no wood, so we just sat down on our knapsacks, and wrapping our blankets about us, shivered until morning."[22]

Mother Nature continued to reinforce who was in charge in the coming days. The 27th NY Volunteers regimental history memorialized December 7, 1862, as the coldest day the men had experienced in Virginia: "Ice formed in the Potomac so that the boats had great difficulty in landing, and some of the men crossed the river on the ice. Many took to the woods again, and spent their Sunday around the fires, having suffered very much from cold and hunger."[23] For many in the brigade, the order to rejoin their division and leave behind the frozen tundra of Belle Plain was welcomed, indeed. The men of the 27th NY Volunteers excitedly began their march toward Fredericksburg the morning of December 10, though they were under no illusions about the purpose of the movement. They were headed for confrontation with the enemy.

IN THE RAVINE, BATTLE RAGES AROUND ROLLIN

Though General Robert E. Lee may have been puzzled by the Army of the Potomac's rapid departure from Warrenton under its newly installed commander in mid-November, by mid-December little mystery remained as to Burnside's intent. With the Union element of surprise squandered due to the tardy arrival of the pontoons, Lee had the time he needed to prepare for battle at Fredericksburg. Using every pontoon-free day to Confederate advantage since Sumner's arrival, Lee moved elements of Lieutenant General James Longstreet's First Corps into place on a ridge southwest of the Rappahannock River near Fredericksburg, Marye's Heights, where they busily dug a network of defensive bulwarks. And Lieutenant General Stonewall Jackson—before being ordered to do so—pushed his men out of the Shenandoah Valley to undertake one of their punishing marathon marches to connect forces with Longstreet. By early December, Jackson's Second Corps took up position to the south of Fredericksburg and with Longstreet's men created a seven-mile defensive crescent around the city.

By the time Rollin and his comrades departed Belle Plain, their Commanding General, after reviewing the menu of bad options with President Lincoln, General-in-Chief Halleck, and his corps commanders, had chosen to attack the Rebels via the most brazen approach possible: directly in front of them. Burnside knew that proposals to redirect his army to a different route to Richmond, such as further south via the James River, would take an intolerable amount of time to organize, as winter had already begun to swipe at his men. Opting to concede that the hour was ripe to simply go into winter quarters would not be acceptable politically. His plan to cross the Rappahannock River some twelve miles further downstream at Skinker's Neck, out of sight of Longstreet's highly fortified overwatch on the heights above Fredericksburg, was scuttled when Jackson's advance observed Union engineers preparing the remote area. Confederate soldiers were soon concentrated on the other side of Skinker's Neck. No, despite the misgivings of his subordinates (other than Major General Sumner), Burnside reasoned they must regain some element of surprise by crossing the river at Fredericksburg. The array of some 150 pieces of artillery arranged on Stafford Heights would protect Union soldiers during the assault and prevent a counterattack—so went Burnside's thinking. He issued the preliminary orders the evening of December 9, 1862.

Burnside convened a meeting of his corps commanders to lay out the battle plans and squash dissension.[24] Two bridges were to be laid leading into the upper part of Fredericksburg, one near the steamboat landing at the southern part of town, and two (later possibly a third) a mile or so downstream near Hamilton's Crossing. Sumner's Right Grand Division, the first to have arrived at Falmouth weeks earlier, was assigned the formidable (and terrifying) mission of crossing the Rappahannock under the noses of Longstreet's well-directed artillery and sharpshooters and then taking Fredericksburg and the high ground behind it. Franklin's Left Grand Division, moving from camp east of Falmouth at White Oak Church, would cross using the pontoons furthest to the south. His men would move onto the plain and right-flank Longstreet. Franklin, saddled with faulty maps for movements after the crossing, was instructed not to wait for Sumner before moving his own men. The objective was to push Longstreet out of position before Jackson had time to move north and join the engagement. Hooker's Center Grand Division would remain near Stafford Court House as reserve. Burnside instructed the commands to distribute sixty rounds of ammunition and three days' rations to each soldier and be ready to march at dawn on December 11.

Rollin and his comrades in the 27th NY Volunteers woke from their slumber at 5 a.m. on the appointed day and joined the line of march from their camp at White Oak Church toward the Rappahannock River three hours later. With early morning fog burning off, the men soaked in the warmth of the sun and the long views of the hills, which already echoed with cannonading from the direction of Fredericksburg. The regiment reached their position on bluffs along the Rappahannock below Fredericksburg around noon.

By this time, Union engineers had been dodging intent Confederate sharpshooters for at least six hours as they attempted to lash the pontoons together across the Rappahannock and onto the lap of Fredericksburg. Confederate pickets had listened to the hapless engineers dragging the pontoons down to the river from the bluffs and peered through the mist as the engineers scurried to construct the bridges in the predawn hours before the veil of fog lifted. By 6 a.m., the Confederates judged they had seen enough: two signal cannons alerted the Rebel army that the Yankees had committed to crossing the Rappahannock.

Initially, General Lee was not convinced that the movements across from Fredericksburg were anything but a ruse to absorb Confederate attention away from the actual intended crossing point—likely further south. After all, Burnside would have to be aware that Longstreet had been digging entrenchments for three weeks and had a splendid position overlooking Fredericksburg and the sprawling open field the Union soldiers would need to traverse to overtake the Confederates. Wouldn't he?

FIGURE 10.2   Drawing of Attack on Fredericksburg by
Alonzo Chappel. Library of Congress, Prints & Photographs
Division.

Lee's strategy was to pick off the bridge builders and delay the Federals
from crossing the river. This would buy time for Jackson to prowl the lower
reaches of the river for possible Union crossing points and Longstreet to marshal his forces. Sharpshooters from Mississippi and Florida got to work elimi-
nating the 50th NY Engineers as they dashed about trying to complete their
task. By 10 a.m. work was at a standstill with no Federals willing to venture out
into the Rebel shooting gallery. (See figure 10.2.)

Left Grand Division Commander Franklin's 15th NY Engineers met with
comparatively muted resistance further downstream. Just as the engineers were
completing the first pontoon bridge near Hamilton's Crossing around 8 a.m.,
Rebel skirmishers popped up and fired into the soldiers as they applied finishing touches to the bridge. Laboring alongside the 15th NY, a battalion of
regulars from the US Army Corps of Engineers began construction of another bridge a couple of hours later than their comrades and received similar
attention from Confederate sharpshooters. In all, under the effective cover
of infantry and artillery support at this stretch of the river, only a handful
were wounded and two captured. Once they completed the first bridge, some

engineers from the 15th NY moved upstream to assist elements of the 50th NY in constructing a middle bridge at the lower end of the city.

By 11 a.m., Major General Franklin could have been crossing his infantry and artillery over the Rappahannock River. But doing so before predictions were possible about when Sumner's Right Grand Division would complete their pontoon crossing into Fredericksburg would introduce unacceptable risk. Burnside knew that by late morning he was rapidly losing any advantage of surprise and that the Confederates were concentrating reinforcements. Instead of allowing his plan to be blown apart, Burnside ordered downtown Fredericksburg, where the harassing sharpshooters were nested in buildings, to be blown apart.

Rollin and his comrades in the 27th NY Volunteers arrived at the river-bank from the bluffs above just in time to be dumbstruck by the vengeance Burnside ordered his batteries exact on the city. The Commanding General unleashed the heavy guns positioned at Stafford Heights. The regimental history gasped: "suddenly all the batteries . . . opened fire and sent a continuous stream of shells over our heads, across the river, into the city, and over the plain below. Sixty shells a minute went whizzing through the air, and crashing through buildings, while the earth fairly shook beneath the terrific cannonade. The scene was one of awful grandeur."[25] The pyrotechnics continued for two hours leaving rubble where buildings once stood.

But it didn't work. When the withered engineers scuttled back onto the bridge to finish their task, the sharpshooters resumed theirs. Finally, as the winter sun was inching toward the horizon, Burnside directed a brigade to paddle their way across the river using available pontoon boats, and then to clear the city. The 7th Michigan and 19th Massachusetts took the brunt of the Rebel rebuttal and were only able to extract the snipers from their hiding places once the 20th Massachusetts and 89th NY joined them in the street-by-street clearance operation.

At around 4 p.m., as Sumner's men were busily and extravagantly looting houses in Fredericksburg, Burnside flipped the switch for Franklin to move his men across the Rappahannock at the downstream crossing. Franklin ordered the 1st and 3rd Divisions of the 6th Corps to cross simultaneously; Brigadier General Brooks's 1st Division would use the lower bridge, while Brigadier General Newton's 3rd Division would use the upper. With darkness settling in, Rollin and his comrades in the 27th NY were the first to step off the lower bridge in rapid succession after the 2nd Rhode Island who had disembarked to their right.[26] As the 27th crept close to the enemy lines on the left, their position felt lonely and precarious. The regimental history recalled: "The men all along the line wondered at the mysterious movement, sending a regiment squarely up to the rebel line, with no troops to support us, and a river between us and our army. A halt was made and the men lay down, but soon a retreat was ordered, in a whisper, and the regiment marched back to the river in good order."[27] Unbeknownst to 1st Division Commander Brooks, 2nd Brigade Commander Cake (acting while J. J. Bartlett recuperated), and 27th Regimental Commander Adams, Burnside had had a change of heart. Instead of crossing the whole of the Left Grand Division, Burnside wanted only one brigade to guard the bridgeheads on the south side of the river. Leaving the 2nd Rhode Island as pickets, Rollin and his comrades recrossed the Rappahannock and bivouacked on the north side of the river.

On December 12, 1862, with the previous day's dress rehearsal behind them, in a thick, mid-morning miasma the men of the 27th NY Volunteers marched across the river and onto an open plain that extended a couple of miles to the foot of the hills. Division Commander Brooks formed his men in three lines: the 3rd Brigade would advance first to beyond Deep Creek, Rollin and his comrades in Cake's 2nd Brigade would follow and fall in along the old Richmond road, and the 1st Brigade would support the other two from its position in the Deep Creek valley.[28] By late morning, the cloak of fog rolled away and revealed targets for the waiting Confederate guns arranged in the hills surrounding Fredericksburg. Luckily for Rollin and his comrades, his brigade happened to be near a deep ravine, into which the men leapt for cover.

From their alcove of safety, the men weathered most of the next four days. The initial barrage of artillery shells on December 12 continued for about an hour, with some bursting directly over the men, and Union artillery responding in kind. After the firing subsided, Rollin and his comrades explored the ravine and discovered water and plenty of wood—comforts for a stay of some duration. That afternoon, around 3 p.m., Confederate guns opened up on the ravine again. This time, they fired pieces of railroad track iron that were approximately two feet in length. Rollin's tentmate William Westervelt described the experience: "As it went tumbling through the air it sounded as though the infernal regions had broken loose, and the demons of disorder were trying, which could produce the most horrible sounds."[29] To their right, the din of Confederate artillery and musketry attempting to repel the 9th Corps of the Right Grand Division from crossing the middle bridge closed out the afternoon.

As Rollin spent the day in the ravine ducking all manner of projectiles fired at him, his Commanding General occupied himself by realigning his battle plan. Given the fading daylight, Burnside recognized that the ponderous crossing of his men into Fredericksburg had cost him another day. Burnside galloped to the Left Grand Division headquarters and consulted with Franklin and his corps commanders about revisions to the attack plan for the next day. Instead of the Left and Right Grand Divisions concurrently attacking Rebel forces before them, Burnside's plot called for Franklin to initiate the assault and sweep around Hamilton's Crossing, thereby hitting the Confederate rear. Center Grand Division Commander Hooker's men would guard the bridgehead. Right Grand Division Commander Sumner was to commence his assault of the Rebel left at Marye's Heights a short while after Franklin's attack was under way. The Federals would cut the Confederate Army in two.

Burnside departed the meeting promising orders would be drafted and delivered. Franklin, quite understandably, assumed those orders would arrive that night to prepare and position his men for the next day's battle. As Franklin expectantly waited for orders the evening of December 12, General Lee was issuing his own: Second Corps Commander Jackson's most southerly divisions must move north swiftly. Swarming with Yankees, the area around Hamilton's Crossing appeared ripe for battle.

After a sleepless night in the bitter cold, Rollin and his comrades anticipated being called on to enter battle the morning of December 13. Left Grand Division Commanding General Franklin, in the frigid predawn hours, may have been contemplating the magnitude of the loss that his men could suffer in leading the assault that day. But when Franklin finally received Burnside's battle plan around 7:30 a.m., any such thoughts were shelved. Burnside's muddled orders, to Franklin's mind and chosen interpretation, significantly digressed from the plan Burnside had briefed to him the previous afternoon and reduced the role of the Left Grand Division to a diversionary force while the Right Grand Division captured Marye's Heights. Burnside's orders, scribbled at 5:55 a.m. December 13, 1862, read:

> The general commanding directs that you keep your whole command in position for a rapid movement down the old Richmond road, and you will send out a division at least to pass below Smithfield, to seize, if possible, the height near Captain Hamilton's on this side of the Massaponax, taking care to keep it well supported and its line of retreat open . . . You will keep your whole command in readiness to move at once, as soon as the fog lifts.[30]

Franklin followed the letter of the order and dispatched a division—Major General George Meade's, which was also the smallest—to lead the attack on

Prospect Hill at Hamilton's Crossing. Meanwhile, Rollin and his comrades, still
in the ravine, stood in line of battle before daylight and waited. With no orders
forthcoming, the men were dismissed to go cook their breakfasts. As they were
lingering over their coffee, Meade's men, encased in fog, were hacking along
the passageway that faulty maps and poor directions had directed them to follow to reach the Richmond Stage Road past the Smithfield plantation.

From the ravine, the men of the 27th NY heard the familiar sounds of
war—the boom and pop of artillery and heavy musketry—continue intermit-
tently throughout the day to their left and right. To their left, with fog starting
to dissipate around 10 a.m., Meade thrust his men forward, searching for a seam
in Jackson's recently reunited corps. Meade succeeded in breaching Confederate
Major General A. P. Hill's line around 1 p.m., before being thrust back at a heavy
loss. Brigadier General John Gibbon's division, following Meade's as reinforcement, similarly tumbled backward, leaving many men strewed across the plain as
they fled in retreat. Left Grand Division Commander Franklin sent no further
reinforcements to prop up Meade, though thousands of his soldiers were at the
ready less than a mile away. Instead, that morning he sent messages to Burnside
that the Commanding General construed to mean the battle plan was on track;
Lee would be forced to siphon off the entrenched defenders of Marye's Heights
to reinforce Jackson. (See figure 10.3.)

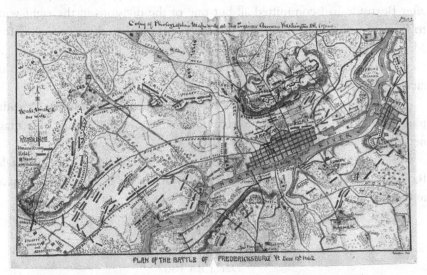

FIGURE 10.3   Map of the Battle of Fredericksburg by Robert
Knox Sneden. Library of Congress, Geography and Map
Division.

To their right, the men of the 27th NY Vols heard the screaming sounds of battle commence around noon. Burnside had assumed wrong. Lee kept his forces in place—but did seek some relief for Jackson by redirecting the action. Dropping artillery shell into the streets of Fredericksburg would do the trick. Longstreet's artillerists had patiently waited for the mist to reveal the doomed mass of blue uniformed men looking up at them. And then they began the kill.

William H. French's division of Darius Couch's 2nd Corps had been tapped to lead the assault on Marye's Heights that morning for the Right Grand Division. While wending their way through the streets of Fredericksburg, they presented themselves as the first easy targets for the gluttonous Rebel guns. By around 2 p.m., Center Grand Division Hooker's men joined the wave after wave of ill-fated Union soldiers who did their best to comply as the Commanding General mechanically bound himself and his army to the attack orders. Like a stroll through Hades, the bluecoats crept forward through sheets of fire and exploding comrades.

Couch, in the waning daylight, rode across the ranks to fully absorb the brutal chaos for his report to the Commanding General. As quotable historian Bruce Catton put it: "The high command had not had enough. It kept sending fresh troops in as resolutely as a butcher pushing raw material into a mincing machine."[31] Meanwhile, Franklin concentrated on his posture of repose. Only after Burnside had committed all but one of the divisions in the right wing to the impossible task of crawling up the escarpment to the stonewall before Marye's Heights to face the primed Confederate guns did he learn that Major General Franklin hadn't found time that afternoon for further coordinated attacks using his Left Grand Division.

That evening, the hopeless assault of the heights continued. Brigades pinned to the earth on the slope were unable to move; their heads were magnets for exuberant Rebel fire.

Using a slip of paper received from a comrade while on the battlefield, Rollin, restless and anxious, penned a short note to his parents around 9 p.m. to reassure them—and himself.

> Near Fredericksburg
> Saturday Evening 9 PM
> Dec 13th 1862
>
> Dear Parents
> I am safely through three days of moderate fighting. We are in line of battle in front of our forces and will commence the show

tomorrow. The fight thus far has been principally with artillery, and
our losses moderate. We have hard work before us & all agree that
this will be the hardest fought battle of the war. They give way only
by inches—at the end of three days we find our lines only three
miles from the river.

Trusting in the "Powers that be" for protection through these
dangerous hours of battle, I am

Your aff son
Rollin

[Back of same piece of paper, crossed out:

~~Truesdell~~

~~All's well over here; lost two men;~~

~~come over with the rest of the Company.~~

~~Foster H.~~]

After another sleepless night in the ravine, skirmishers crackling shots at
each other in the darkness, Rollin and his comrades in the 27th NY Volunteers
were called up around 8 a.m. the morning of December 14 to relieve the 8th
New Jersey from picket duty in their front. Around this time, Commanding
General Burnside was agonizing over whether to push forward with an all-out
assault with both wings—even leading the attack on Marye's Heights himself—or to accept the consensus of his generals against it. When the morning
fog lifted, the impregnability of Confederate defenses, reinforced overnight,
decided the matter for Burnside. As the Commanding General debated with
his subordinates about whether to hold onto Fredericksburg when the Army
of the Potomac retreated, Rollin was on his belly behind a slight rise in the
ground, knapsack protectively set before him, sending pot shots at any head
that popped up from the enemy line of works. The soldiers exchanged fire
throughout the day until daylight was extinguished.

Before the sun rose on December 15, 1862, the 96th Pennsylvania took
the place of the 27th NY and Rollin and his comrades returned to the relative
safety of their ravine for the day. Rollin wrote a letter to his sister that evening,
unaware that Burnside had made the decision to withdraw the whole of his
army.

My Dear Sister

I wrote to Father night before last, but under the present circumstances I suppose you wish to hear from me often, and as far as

possible I shall grant your often repeated request. Though all I can say is that I am all right up to the present moment, 7 P.M. Dec 15th.

I write under difficulties. We are on the battlefield where in day light we can scarcely raise our heads without being the target for the enemy's sharp shooters, but under cover of darkness we stick up our shelter tent behind a little eminence and take the thing cool 'til day light begins to dawn when we make all things ready for breakers. Our Div. has not advanced an inch for the last two days, the fighting being done on the extreme left of the line. It is a slow battle but the symptoms auger a good result.

The Pa Reserves were sharply engaged yesterday, but I have not had a chance to learn how Harrison and Johnny came out.

Your letter of "nutmeg" and Tribune I received yesterday.

Truly your aff bro

Rollin

Don't spare the stamps but write "often."

Rollin's regiment received their orders to move back across the river around midnight. The 27th NY regimental history captured the mood of the men as they marched: "It was now evident that our army had been defeated again ... All were much discouraged and disheartened. We had learned nothing definite of our loss, but imagined that it was very great, and began to fear that we should never conquer the rebels."[32] Fittingly, as they were setting up camp on the north side of the river, the heavens opened up and a drenching rain poured down on Rollin and his comrades until the morning.

Rollin's letter to his sister Clara of December 23, written several days after the Union troops had recrossed the river to safety and two days before Christmas, reflects the melancholy he too felt in the aftermath of the battle of Fredericksburg.

Camp of 27th Regt NYSV

White Oak Church Va

Dec 23d 1862

My Dear Sister

How many letters I owe you I cannot tell. I suppose you think very many, but more or less I am at liberty this afternoon, and will make amends for the past, at least in a small degree.

I begin to feel a little rested from the exhaustion I incurred while on the "other" side of the river, but I am not yet "A No. 1."

I never was more loth to go into battle than I was at Fredericksburg, and the long suspense we were in before crossing was almost as bad as actually to be engaged. The work to be done was evident for days before the time arrived, and as far as possible I was nerved up to the work before us, and went into action as coolly as I ever commenced a day's work at home.

After crossing and while resting in a ravine from which we expected to march out in line of battle to meet the enemy, many parting words were spoken between the men of our Regt, all expecting, almost knowing that we were to meet the foe and therefore some must fall and never meet their friends again. These words were of good cheer and frequently pertained to the pecuniary affairs of the men. Thus, one would say: "If I fall, save my watch and send it home," giving the name and address of his friends. The conversation between myself and comrade was short and to the point, viz: "Keep close together; if we are driven back, neither shall be left alone." I have that confidence in my friend that I believe if I had been wounded and our forces retreated, that he would have stayed with me.

But it is all over now and we, as far as the Regt or Div is concerned, sustained but light loss; but truly the mental labor performed by a soldier while momentarily expecting to be drawn into action is incomparable, and tires him physically more than a week's perpetual ordinary labor.

We are making ourselves as comfortable as the circumstances will permit, thinking it may be some time before we move again.

Yours truly
Rollin

ON THE OTHER SIDE OF THE RIVER

On December 16, 1862, the 27th NY Volunteers awoke to the pelting fire of Rebel artillery. The Army of the Potomac had successfully pulled back across the river the night before without being molested. But now that the morning fog had dissipated, Confederate forces discovered they were alone on the south side of the Rappahannock. Rollin and his comrades dashed to the woods behind them, denying the Confederate Army additional Yankee casualties to add to the lopsided death toll.

Bearing well over half the fatalities, the visage before Marye's Heights was grotesque. A sea of twisted cadavers, some blue-clad and some stripped of uniform, carpeted the decimated ground leading up to the stone wall that the Confederate soldiers had refused their enemy. As one of Rollin's comrades solemnly reported: "Such discipline and devotion to duty had rarely been seen before, as were that Saturday, December 13, 1862, displayed on the heights behind the little city on the plain."[33]

The total loss of Union forces in the Battle of Fredericksburg was 12,653 men (1,284 killed, 9,600 wounded, 1,769 missing).[34] Rollin was fortunate to have no comrades in his regiment to mourn. The Confederate Army lost over 5,300 men in the battle.

The disastrous offensive was like a millstone around the neck of the Army of the Potomac's Commanding General. Burnside telegrammed to General-in-Chief Halleck on December 17, 1862:

> For the failure in the attack, I am responsible, as the extreme gallantry, courage, and endurance shown by them [his officers and soldiers] was never exceeded, and would have carried the points had it been possible . . . The fact that I moved from Warrenton onto this line rather against the opinion of the President, Secretary, and yourself, and that you have left the whole management in my hands, without giving me orders, makes me more responsible.[35]

Under flag of truce, Union soldiers crossed the river on December 17 and commenced the grim two-day detail of burying the rubble of their dead. The men of the 27th NY Volunteers watched the procession from the river's edge; they had been assigned picket duty the evening before.

Gazing through their breastworks as the sun exposed their mirror image across the river, Rollin and his comrades decided to take a chance that their counterparts were as weary of attacking each other as they were. After agreeing to their own truce, each side stepped from behind their works and walked to the shore. As Rollin reported to his parents, the regiment was soon conversing with Texans. The men of the 27th NY Volunteers spent an enjoyable—and certainly memorable—day shuttling back and forth across the river to socialize and share coffee, tobacco, and trinkets with the Texans they had fought at West Point in May and Gaines' Mill in June, and also members of the 4th Alabama.[36] And then the bubble of civility burst; it was time to resume positions behind respective breastworks and wait for other regiments to come and relieve them. Darkness was falling.

Camp of 27th New York Regt
Near Falmouth Va
Dec 18th 1862

My Dear Parents

I penned you a hastily written line on the evening of the 15th which has caused you much anxiety I doubt not, but at this time I am happy to inform you of my personal safety, also that "Burnside's" grand army is safely encamped on the northerly side of the Rappahannock.

Our Div done but little fighting while across but the suspense was almost equal to an action. On the extreme right and left there was considerable firing done, but as it was a couple of miles distant from where I was posted, of course I have to wait for the New York papers for the particulars. Though from the train of ambulances which I have seen in motion, I think our loss is quite heavy. I have found from experience that it is entirely useless for me to attempt to write any news of any movements or actions as you are informed by reporters much in advance of any letters I can send by mail.

Our Regt was on picket duty along the riverbank yesterday and I had a long conversation with the Rebels on the opposite bank. It was somewhat tiresome to hold conversation with them, the distance across being about forty rods, but for novelty sake I talked a "gentleman" from Galveston, Texas 'til my throat became sore. Among other things which he said, he expressed the opinion that though the South could not whip the North yet they hoped to be able to hold out long enough to be recognized as a nation. Personally, they were sick and tired of the war and of the treatment they were necessarily subjected to on account of the scarcity of some of the commonest luxuries of life.

The weather is very cold and it is with much difficulty that we can keep our selves comfortable. Myself and tent-mate have erected a huge pile of oak logs in front of our tent, which are now glowing with red coals, and we flatter ourselves on a good night's sleep.

Write often.

Yours truly
Rollin

STUCK IN THE MUD

Rollin and his comrades in the 27th NY Volunteers remained in the shadow of the Confederate trouncing of the Army of the Potomac at Fredericksburg, camping in the woods just beyond the north bank of the Rappahannock River, until December 19, 1862. That day, the men received the order to return to their previous camp site at White Oak Church. With each step of the five-mile march, relief built as they distanced themselves from the bloodbath of the previous days and the memory of being holed up in the ravine. Drained and disheartened, the men were starved for a release from the deprivations and dubious military strategies that forced them to prepare for a second winter away from home. And they were no closer to wearing the mantle of victors than they had been nineteen months earlier when they enlisted.

Enter the paymaster. Toting four months of pay for each man in the command, the paymaster turned up at the White Oak Church camp site the following day, December 20, 1862. Many of the enlisted men were soon parted with their $52 payout; the call of the card table and the sirens of drink immediately beckoned them. William Westervelt, Rollin's tentmate, somewhat bemusedly observed: "So many indulged in these vices, that the minority who kept clear were so few that had they made any effort to stop it, such would have proved futile . . . For my part I can say, I never touched a card for fun or money . . . and feel quite positive my tentmate Truesdell could say the same thing. Neither of us ever indulged in whiskey for the fun of drinking."[1] For Rollin, safely dispatching his pay back to Liberty, Pennsylvania, to his family was his priority; he had a sewing machine for his sister Clara and a delivery of the "good things" from home to finance.

Indeed, home and its comforts would be very much on the minds of Rollin and his mates in the coming days. Soon they received the news they were waiting for: White Oak Church would be their winter quarters. Immediately, the men swung into high gear like the construction crews on a tight deadline that they knew they were. The icy fingers of winter were greedily grasping at these veterans of frigid soldiering.

Tentmates eyed prime real estate along company streets that offered proper drainage and room enough to erect a small but comfortable log cabin for two. Selecting a spot where the ground rose quite abruptly, Rollin and Westervelt excavated about a foot deep on the lower side and 2½ feet on the upper where they dug into the bank a hole two feet square for a fireplace and the start of a chimney. The sticky Virginia clay was the perfect mortar to bind the chimney and the log walls together. Stretched over the top of the dwelling as the roof, their shelter tents kept out the elements while allowing in adequate light. Their pine bed, complete with gunny sack mattress filled with straw, sat just high enough to offer Rollin and Westervelt a perfect seat before their fireplace. (See figure 11.1 for a reconstruction.)

The tentmates had some finishing touches yet to make on their palace on Christmas Day 1862, but this did not hinder them from inviting some friends to celebrate the holiday at their abode. With Rollin having been called away on Christmas eve, the full responsibility for the Christmas Day banquet fell on Westervelt. Radiating panache, he had the full meal prepared when Rollin returned around noon on December 25. Westervelt fondly recalled: "On each of the tin plates, I laid a bill of fare that included roast beef, dried apple sauce a la sutler, baked beans-dressed with saline rooter, berry liquid, dried apple pie flavored with commissary vinegar and molasses, with extras of wind pudding and yarn sauce."[2] Crammed into the Truesdell/Westervelt hut, the friends balanced their plates on their knees, marveled at Westervelt's cooking prowess, and celebrated the day in high spirits.

With satisfied bellies and appreciation for the camaraderie they knew they were fortunate to enjoy, easy conversation flew among the mates. Certainly, the men shared tales of previous Christmas scenes at family hearths—dining tables groaning with the weight of holiday delectables and personalized gifts hidden, later to be exchanged with loved ones. Inspired by the day as well as necessity, Rollin's Christmas greetings to his family included a request for a box of items to help weather the season for himself and Westervelt. (When the box finally arrived in late January after a tortuous journey, Westervelt reported: "My tentmate Truesdell received a box of provisions and clothing from home,

FIGURE 11.1 Log Hut for Winter Quarters.

and when it was opened in our cabin, I found myself not forgotten, there being the same for me as for him—flannel shirts, woolen mittens and socks . . . These coming from his folks, whom I had never seen, showed at least that my name was known in his far off northern home.")[3]

Two days after Christmas, fixated on those comforts from home and fidgety about a rumor of a mail heist, Rollin penned another note to his sister Clara. With Rollin's penchant for specificity, he couldn't help but remind her of the particulars of his request, even as he pled for reassurance that his Christmas letters had reached home. And a little bragging about the completion of their snug log hut was also in order.

> Camp of 27th Regt NYSV
> White Oak Church Va
> Dec 27th 1862

Dear Sister

I wrote several letters home two or three days ago and tonight I understand that the mails of this Brigade were robbed between here and the Landing, which if true, may effect me considerable, for my letter containing money to the amount of sixty-two dollars may be lost. But I hope not, and I wish if it reaches you safe to be immediately informed of the fact for I do not rest very easy since I heard the above report.[4]

I also sent for a box of things to come by express: a pair of boots, pair of gloves, four red <u>soft</u> flannel shirts, etc. I want you to take <u>special</u> care to have the shirts fine and well made. Two of them are for a friend and must be smaller than for me, say to fit a man the size of Orlando Ross.[5] Of course I give you the right to put in anything else you choose. If you put in eatables, do not send gingerbread (snaps) for that is the only eatable thing that sutlers bring us, and I hate the sight of them.

Myself and Westervelt have just finished our log cabin today, and kings never were prouder of their palaces than we are of this little hut. It is six feet square, logged up four feet, and our tent put on for a roof. We have a small fireplace in one corner by which we can keep as warm as toast, our only anxiety now being whether we shall actually remain here 'til spring. The prospect however is good.

There is but little animation in the army at present. The roads are too bad to move even if there was any disposition on the part of our Commanders. The weather is raw, cold, and uncomfortable in the extreme.

Please write me as soon as this is received and "hasten on the box."

With love to all, I am

> Yours truly
> Rollin B. Truesdell

Though Rollin does not mention doing so in surviving letters he wrote home, he and his Christmas day dining partners surely would have felt compelled to ruminate on the import and ramifications of the President's anticipated New Year's Day thunderclap announcement.[6] President Lincoln's September 22, 1862, preliminary proclamation declaring that on January 1 all enslaved people would be freed within any state or portion thereof that remained in rebellion with the federal government was a signal of intent. It stripped away any ambiguity that Northerners may have indulged in regarding at least part of the President's motivation for winning the war. In one week, however, the confirmation of the Emancipation Proclamation would transform the revolutionary idea, the pernicious threat of freedom for all persons held in bondage, into a reality that would indelibly alter the Northern cause. That is, if Lincoln opted to go forward with the announcement.

The embarrassing failure of Commanding General Burnside's campaign at Fredericksburg created fear among some abolitionists that the President might postpone the awaited announcement until the Union held both the moral and military high ground. Northern Democrats vehemently prophesied that the very linking of abolition with the Union war campaign doomed the North to failure. Would this not provide additional fuel for a secessionist war machine that was already red hot? The voices of indignation from all positions on the abolition question were insistent and omnipresent in the days leading up to January 1, 1863.

Through the cacophony, Lincoln remained resolute. While the New Year's Day reception was ongoing in the executive mansion, the President signed the Emancipation Proclamation, forever altering the trajectory of the United States' future. With this document, Lincoln not only confirmed the freedom of the enslaved but also made their protection the responsibility of the United States government. Further, the President opened the Union armed services to Black recruits—a heretical provocation for most Southerners. The proclamation reads, in part,

> And by virtue of the power and for the purpose aforesaid, I
> do order and declare that all persons held as slaves within said des-
> ignated States, are, and henceforward shall be free; and that the
> Executive Government of the United States, including the military
> and naval authorities thereof, will recognize and maintain the free-
> dom of said persons . . . And I further declare and make known that
> such persons, of suitable condition, will be received into the armed

service of the United States ... And upon this act, sincerely believed
to be an act of justice, warranted by the Constitution, upon military
necessity, I invoke the considerate judgement of mankind, and the
gracious favor of Almighty God.[7]

The regimental history of the 27th NY Volunteers, published in 1888,
reported: "Today [January 1, 1863] the army and the nation are thrilled by
the advent of the Emancipation Proclamation."[8] The soldier-historians may
have been peering through rose-colored glasses when they penned that recol-
lection. The public perception in the North was certainly more convoluted.
While abolitionists were jubilant, the response from War Democrats was re-
strained. The men of the 27th NY waited expectantly to read of Governor
Horatio Seymour's New Year's message to the New York legislature on January
7, 1863, to peg the reaction at home.[9] Seymour—a political confidant of dis-
gruntled former Commander of the Army of the Potomac George McClellan,
and possible future presidential candidate himself—tried to strike a balance in
civil discourse by offering words of support for the federal troops while at the
same time asserting the supremacy of states' rights. He stopped short, however,
of advocating for peace negotiations with the Rebels.

Such overtures were unlikely to have been successful in any case. While
the Emancipation Proclamation modified Northern goals for the war, it clari-
fied purpose for the South. Reveling in their victory over the Army of the
Potomac at Fredericksburg, Confederate President Jefferson Davis felt no
compulsion to entertain peace talks that would bring the South back into
the Union. President Lincoln's Emancipation Proclamation settled the matter:
reunion would be impossible.

And so the soldiers of the North and the South began 1863 mired in a
state of paralysis that could augur only continued deprivation and sacrifice of
life. Rollin and his mates did their best to shelter from the frigid weather and
the false starts their sullen Commanding General felt obliged to orchestrate to
rekindle Northern optimism about his, and the Army of the Potomac's, prospects for success. In the final days of 1862, Burnside had launched a convoluted
plan requiring detached units of cavalry, artillery, and infantry to splash across
the frigid Rappahannock and Rapidan rivers to challenge Lee and his logistics
tail in the sprawling area between Army of the Potomac forces and Richmond.
To General Burnside's shock and embarrassment, President Lincoln halted the
initiative after taking an interview with two of Franklin's generals who traveled
to Washington to vent their objections to the campaign, and tangentially, the
leadership of their Commanding General.

Though he sulked and offered his resignation once again, Burnside was unable to escape responsibility for leading the Army of the Potomac and confronting the discontent in the North. Burnside desperately needed a salve for his stinging defeat at Fredericksburg. Waiting for the most propitious time to act was an option for the former Commander of the Army of the Potomac—but not for him. Despite the scornful reaction of his generals (conniving Center Grand Division Commander Hooker and Left Grand Division Commander Franklin and his insubordinate generals leading the pack), Burnside plodded ahead in January 1863 with preparations for a flanking maneuver against the Rebel forces. Before Rollin and his comrades in the 27th NY Volunteers took even their first step of the doomed march, Franklin's and 6th Corps Commander Baldy Smith's voluble derision of Burnside's plan would have sent an ill wind through the troops.

As the scheming took place around him, largely tent-bound with few official duties at this time, Rollin busied himself with daydreams and letter writing in which elaborate descriptions of what he missed from the home cupboard took a starring role.

> Camp of 27th Regt N.Y.S.V.
> White Oak Church Va
> Jany 15th 1863

Dear Mother

If I have ever seen a lonesome night, this is one of them. And though no storm or unusual fare predominates in camp at this time, yet I would be thankful to put off these robes of war and put on those of civility for a time and visit the parental roof, especially that part which covers the pantry—and turn up a few of those tin pans which lay around stray like and see if a pie or plate of nut cakes would not reward my labors. But when I think of all those "vain" things here below, why, the result is what might naturally be expected of a sensible fellow—my mouth waters for them. We made a desperate effort to have some nut cakes a few days ago and succeeded finally as far as quantity was concerned, but the quality was not what a person of naturally fine taste would call good, but still, "they eat," and answered the principle design, viz., fill up.

Luxuries are at a high premium, or I might as well say command vicious prices. Apples are worth $1.00 per doz., and no better than I have fed to the horses and cattle many a time. Butter has been worth a dollar per pound but is now only worth 75 cents; cheese is worth forty and forty-five, and very scarce.

This is the mildest winter I ever have seen. It is not so very muddy as it was last winter, and though we occasionally have a cold snap, the majority of nights we can keep comfortable under our three blankets, but once in a while there has to be a good fire added to keep soul and body together.

We have had a very hard wind all day, and the consequence is I have got a pretty severe headache which will no doubt get better as soon as I get to sleep, but the idea of sleeping 14 hours I cannot stand, and when reading is scarce I fill up the time in writing. I wrote to Julia this afternoon and expect she will put on a long face and make me the subject of special prayer for two weeks, but I have got completely sick of her two, three, and four line letters. I either want her to write a letter and be done with it or let it alone.

The roads in this country are being repaired and I should not wonder if we crossed the river again a few miles below Fredericksburg at no very distant day. For my own part, I would as have it would be put off 'til after the 8th of May, as be done before; after that time, I can do like many other patriots—stand back and cry out: "Why don't the army move?"

With much love to all, I am

Your aff son
Rollin B. Truesdell

Fortified in expectation of the slow-moving box sent from home, Rollin's visions of towers of delicious pies and cheese and apples were cut short the evening of January 19. The men of the 27th NY Volunteers received the order that they would move the next morning. Rollin and his comrades had seen the signals that such a command was looming by the ongoing feverish road construction in the direction of Fredericksburg. But, as Rollin reported to his father on January 16 with prescience, the fiendish rains had rendered the roads useless for days, which presumably would pause the Union's planned military operations. If Burnside had only reckoned the same, history may have been kinder to him.

Camp of 27th Regt NY Volunteers
White Oak Church Va
January 16th/63

Dear Father

Your favor of January 12th I have just received. I am glad the box has been forwarded as far as Washington, but how I am to get it from there looks a little dark to me, but I will be sure to get it in time if there is such a thing in the primer. You seem to think the articles cost a high price, and indeed they do for a home market, but here they will be worth five times what they cost at home. Men here do not stop to value money as long as it lasts. Indeed there is no alternative; if they buy at all they must pay out the greenbacks by the hand-full.

We have just had a moderate rain of six hours duration which will render the roads almost impassible for some days. A little rain in this quicksand works a wonderful change in the events of the coming days. I have no doubt that a light rain oft times interferes with the well matured plans of our Generals but they do not, like Emperor Napoleon, "make circumstances," but wait for the sun to dry the mud, and mean time our "friends" over the way get the start of us in some way.

I am well convinced in my own mind that we are to try once more to continue our way to Richmond by the Fredericksburg route whatever the losses may be.

It is evident that the Gov. are not repairing and building new roads in the direction of Front Royal unless they contemplate using them, nor would they make many other preparations of a like indication if they were going to withdraw us from here and send us around to the peninsula again.

Is business very lively this winter, and what is the prospects for Spring campaign to make money in the North? As it is only four months 'til we are discharged, I am looking a little to the future. I have several things in prospect but shall not make up my mind to do either 'til I return home and see my friends and recuperate my health which I think will be necessary for I am now too fat and lazy to be very energetic to do anything. My weight today is two hundred two and half pounds.

I hope your health will continue to improve, and that by the time spring comes, you will be able to enjoy life if nothing more.

With much love to all, I remain

Your aff son
Rollin B. Truesdell

To: Saml W Truesdell
Great Bend. Pa

Perhaps willing the inevitable not to be so, Rollin had written and mailed a note to his sister prior to receiving the marching orders on January 19. Preparations for movement were under way.

> Camp of 27th Regt NY Vols
> White Oak Church Va
> January 19th 1863

Dear Sis

I am well—in good spirits, but have no news of interest to communicate. "Madam Rumor" says we move soon, which I think probable, but I do not think the plans are matured yet. The sick have been moved to Aquia Landing, sixty rounds of cartridges distributed, and many other things done which in themselves are small, but in the aggregate show that something of importance is meditated.

The weather is moderately cold and ground slightly frozen but I rejoice in a good fire, wood enough cut to last two days, and a box of the good things of the earth in prospect, tho' distant.

With much love, etc., etc., I am now & ever more

> Your affectionate brother
> R. B. Truesdell

The morning of January 20, 1863, Rollin and Westervelt reluctantly divested their cabin of its canvas roof, which would now revert to its original purpose as a tent. Carrying their allotted cartridge rounds and three days' rations, they fell in line to march just before noon. They did not know they were about to embark on six days of meritless misery. Seeking to bolster his army's (and perhaps his own) abysmal morale, Commanding General Burnside issued an invigorating statement for his troops prior to their departure from camp. Brigade Commander J. J. Bartlett read the order, which stated: "We are about to meet the enemy once more ...The auspicious moment has arrived to strike a great and mortal blow to the rebellion, and to give that decisive victory which is due to the country."[10]

It being unclear where the Commanding General proposed the "decisive blow" to take place, Westervelt surmised: "from the direction we traveled it looked as though we intended to once more strike Fredericksburg, but were taking a roundabout way as if a flank movement was contemplated."[11] Westervelt's observation was not far off from his commander's intent. Similarly complex to earlier shelved plans, Burnside's new plan entailed a diversionary feint south of town to distract the Rebels long enough for the Center and Left Grand Divisions of the army to cross upstream from Fredericksburg near Banks' Ford.[12] Right Grand Division Commander Sumner was instructed to hold at Falmouth until Franklin and Hooker had traversed their men, and then would cross his. Faced with Union forces now on their side of the river, Lee's army would be drawn out from their entrenchments and forced to confront Burnside's larger, albeit sapped, army—so went Burnside's thinking.

Bracing wind slapping them in the biting cold, Rollin and his comrades in the 27th NY Volunteers marched twelve miles in the accompaniment of a pontoon train over the frost-compacted earth toward Falmouth on January 20, 1863. Despite the thick clouds portending the storm to come, they had reason to feel satisfied with the day. Even with artillery and other infantry units sharing some of the same roads, they had doggedly pushed their way through to arrive near the staging area for crossing the Rappahannock River. As the sun was setting, the regiment settled in a dense pine forest to camp for the night. The men labored to drive their tent-pins into the frozen ground and set up their humble shelters.

Rollin and Westervelt had barely had time to jest with each other about the diminished status of their living accommodations when the tag-along angry clouds finally opened, and rain began to fall. Within a few hours, torrents of rain lashed the thawing soil, wind howled with a fury, and tent-pins wormed their way up onto the surface, leaving hapless men defenseless and sodden. Their pine tree companions, thrashing about in the storm, seemed to jeer at the men, and offered no hope of a warming fire. All through the night, the chill of the icy rain stabbed right to the core of the men, leaving them shivering and exhausted when morning finally arrived.

Overnight, the rain had transformed the ground from a tundra-like surface to a greedy, oozing sea of mud that continued to be fed by the relentless rain. By daybreak, the wheels of the artillery and wagons were cemented in the muck, rations (including the previously presumed indestructible hardtack) were spoiled, and teamsters commenced desperate torturing of their mules and horses to extricate loads from the mud. The more the thrashing, the deeper the mud became. The final mile to reach Banks' Ford was an impossibility. (See figure 11.2.)

On January 21, Hooker's men in the Central Grand Division woke to reveille around 4 a.m. and managed to crawl no more than three miles before succumbing to the futile tug-of-war with the muck. Mud caked, Rollin and

FIGURE 11.2   Drawing of Mud March by Edwin Forbes.
Library of Congress, Prints & Photographs Division.

his mates in the 27th NY Volunteers began their march around 8 a.m. and were able to advance only two or three miles over four hours before yielding to the sludge. Westervelt recalled: "we packed our wet tents and blankets, which made a load heavy enough to discourage a mule. With these loads on our backs and the mud over the tops of our shoes, we marched."[13] Upon reaching an enticing stretch of oak timber, the regiment turned in and set up camp around noon. The accompanying engineers, pontoons in tow, numbly attempted to fulfill their impossible task of reaching the river's edge. They succeeded only in contributing to the ghastly morass of mud, man, animal, and materiel. While the determined storm continued all day, night, and into the following day, Rollin and his comrades built roaring fires with the handy oak for fuel and labored to dry out their sopping selves and possessions.

On January 22, 1863, having ridden to witness firsthand the extent and impregnability of the quicksand-like mud he had ordered his men to wallow through to pursue his ill-timed campaign, Commanding General Burnside called off the assault. He directed Grand Division Commanders Hooker and Franklin to return their troops to their winter camps. Rain still cascading down, the men of the 27th NY Volunteers remained in the oak forest and pretended that the gill of whiskey each received was an adequate substitute for rations. Rollin and his mates embraced what comfort they could that day, knowing they would soon be wrestling to release the pontoon train and artillery wagons from the muck.

Finally, the sun reasserted itself and shone brightly on the weary soldiers the afternoon of January 23. Around 3 p.m., under its warming rays, the regiment packed up camp and moved approximately one mile to the disaster site, where their pontoon train was buried along with artillery wagons. Some of the guns were so encased in mud only their muzzles poked through the filth. From this position, the men could clearly see across the river to Confederate encampments. Their adversaries offered a taunting greeting written in charcoal on the side of a large tent facing them: BURNSIDE STUCK IN THE MUD!

At the pontoon extrication site, Rollin witnessed drivers frantically cursing and whipping their mules and horses as the animals' bodies sank ever deeper into the mud. Some lucky animals were eventually unharnessed and pulled out of the muck with ropes; others simply gave up and died where they stood. This scene was not unique on the Union side of the Rappahannock River. Like an inept abattoir, the roadsides were thick with agonized horses and mules, dead or dying. In the midst of this chaos, and understanding that the following day promised back-breaking work to free the pontoons and artillery wagons from their muddy confines, the men of the 27th NY splayed their tents on the ground as beds and slept soundly under the stars.

Rollin and his comrades in Brigadier General Brooks's Division struggled all day January 24, and half the next day, to pull the precious cargo from the mud. Men replaced mules for the grubby task. Between 100 and 300 men grabbed at long ropes attached to each side of a wagon and, on signal, drew the freight up a hill to high ground, where they parked it and waited for the mud to dry.[14] When the last pontoon was finally tugged free on January 25, the men of the 27th NY, weighed down with mud and melancholy, finally unhitched themselves from the spectacle.

Rollin was in no shape physically or mentally to recount the specifics of the grimy debacle until almost a week after returning to camp. With returned health and some tongue-in-cheek repartee, he described the fiasco in a January 31 letter to his father.

> Camp of 27th Regt N.Y.Vols
> White Oak Church Va
> January 31st 1863

Dear Father

When I last wrote you I was quite unwell. The last piece of "strategy" and the heavy storm having nearly mastered me, but fair weather and a few "pills" have set me right again so that today I am feeling first rate and will try and give you a short description of the last great feat of the immortal Burnside, or that part in which I participated.

On the morning of the 20th inst we received orders to be in readiness to march at twelve o'clock noon, we having been furnished the night previous with three days rations, sixty rounds of cartridges, and notice to be ready to march on six hours' notice.

The day was cold with fresh south wind and the thick murky clouds betokened a coming storm, but with those signs against our success we harnessed on our knapsacks at the hour appointed and trudged off over the frozen ground in the direction of Falmouth. The roads were in places blocked up with artillery so that we would be hindered a short time and then double our velocity to make up lost time. This mode of marching is the most tiresome and fatiguing to a body of troops of anything imaginable, but with all the ill luck of the day, at dusk we turned into a thick copse of wood three miles above Falmouth and made our camp for the night.

And a sorry camp and woeful night it was. The ground was frozen so that it was impossible for us to drive our tent pins to a sufficient depth to hold them securely, and the rain soon setting in, and the wind freshening so that by ten o'clock it blew a perfect gale leaving scarce a tent standing in the whole regiment. In this sad plight, without shelter, exposed to the furor of the elements, did we stand and shiver and think of the many comforts of home on such a night when even the brutes of the field had warm and comfortable shelter, and the faithful farm dog, out of mercy, was not ordered to his kennel but permitted to lay by the kitchen stove 'til the night,

"The long dark night

At last past fearfully away."[15]

With morning's dawn came orders to continue our march, but we only went two miles and turned into a piece of oak timber and pitched our tents and built huge fires to dry our wet and heavy clothes. (Our first camp was in a piece of pines which will burn no better than so much basswood.)

The rain continued to fall all day and the mud grew in depth. The engineers worked hard to get their pontoons down to the river, but they became "stalled" in the mud, and forty horses could not extricate a single wagon. I saw eighteen horses pulling a light twelve-pound gun, but they failed to bring it to solid bottom. Batteries' wagons and pontoons were stuck in the mud in every

STUCK IN THE MUD

direction and left 'til the next day when Regiments of Infantry were sent to draw them out with long ropes.

Saturday the 24th our Brigade worked on the pontoons all day and left them at night about a mile from where we took them in the morning.

Sunday, we marched back to our old camp at the Church and such a day's march I never saw before. It more than equaled a "Sabbath day's journey." The roads were full of ruts and the soft mud several inches deep, but we worked hard to gain our old quarters which we reached just at dark and spread our blankets in a familiar place ...

In something of a delirium, Rollin and his comrades stumbled their way across the countryside to reach their former camp at White Oak Church. Despite keeping to high ground as much as possible, the return trip was tedious and stamina-wringing. Some men did not make it back to camp, crumpling alongside the bodies of mules and horses, never to get up. Rollin and Westervelt breathed sighs of relief when they reached their old cabin just as darkness fell. Though compensating officers ordered that barrels of whiskey be freely available to the men, Rollin and Westervelt chose otherwise. Westervelt recounted: "My tentmate and myself were so tired we thought a good bed better than whiskey, and we were soon wrapped in our blankets and dreaming of drawing pontoon canal boats through a canal of mud, with mules as drivers, who were cracking their whips over our backs ... while we with heavy knapsacks on our backs were trying to escape over a muddy, slippery towpath."[16]

In the immediate days following their return to camp, Rollin's clipped letters home reflect the march-induced exhaustion and illness that followed him and many other soldiers back to their log huts. Not surprisingly, pneumonia was common. Rollin was fortunate to have contracted only a stubborn cold.

Camp of 27th Regt N.Y.S. Vols
White Oak Church Va
Jany 27th 1863

Dear Father:

Yours of Jany 16th is received. I am glad the box has been forwarded and think I shall get it in time. I am well but tired out with the late march to Falmouth. The roads are almost impassable and the rain continues to fall.

I will write a long letter in a day or two.
With kind regards to all, I am

Yours truly
R. B. Truesdell

To: Saml W. Truesdell
Great Bend, Pa

A couple of days later, the much-anticipated care package from home arrived to buoy Rollin's (and by extension, Westervelt's) spirits. Rollin climbed out from his sickbed to pen a note of thanks to his family on January 29.

Camp of 27th Regt NYSV
White Oak Church, Va
Jany 29th 1863

Dear Parents and Sister

My box and contents arrived safely last night and I cannot express my gratitude to you for the articles sent. They all suit me exactly except the boots which were so low in the instep I could not get them on. I sold them for $6.00 and bought a pair of the sutler for $8.00.

Yesterday and all night it snowed hard and today the ground is covered to the depth of twelve inches.

Westervelt and self have both been sick ever since we got back from the last strategic movement. We have hard colds, are worn out, and need nursing.

I am now boiling berries for my breakfast (2 PM).

We did not rise very early and Will has took twelve grains quinine for his meal and crept under the blankets again.[17] I am going to dine on toast and leave out the quinine. Will has had two shakes, but there was not enough to shake me, so I escaped. I think we will be sound again as soon as the weather gets a little settled.

With much love, I am

Yours etc
R. B. Truesdell

As the reality of his most recent botched campaign sunk in, Commanding General Ambrose Burnside likely wished he too could crawl into bed and pull the covers over his head. True, the elements had been most decidedly against him. But so too were his primary subordinate officers. As the 27th NY regimental history mildly stated, "In this last movement Gen. Burnside had acted almost solely upon his own responsibility. The sentiment of his general officers was almost unanimously against it, and some of them freely expressed themselves in opposition. This was a powerful reason for abandoning the plan, aside from the inclemency of the weather."[18]

What Burnside wanted to abandon was his general officers. By the time he had called off the assault, he had determined that a major housecleaning would occur in the upper echelons of his Army of the Potomac, or else he would resign his commission as a major general. Burnside drew up General Orders No. 8, calling for the dismissal of Generals Hooker, Brooks, Cochrane, and Newton, and for Generals Franklin, Baldy Smith, Sturgis, and Ferraro, and Lieutenant Colonel Taylor to be relieved of their commands.[19] Lethal instructions in hand, Burnside departed for Washington the evening of January 23, 1863, to confront President Lincoln with the ultimatum: them or me.

Lincoln chose them. After consulting with his military advisers, Lincoln determined he could no longer place confidence in Burnside, a man who regularly denounced his own capabilities, to lead the Army of the Potomac. In a meeting on the morning of January 25, the President, though fully aware of Joe Hooker's swaggering impertinence, informed Burnside that Hooker would be his replacement. Lincoln refused to accept Burnside's resignation and instead insisted Burnside take a much-needed furlough. When Burnside returned to duty, he was reassigned to the Department of the Ohio. Secretary of War Stanton also issued General Orders No. 20, relieving Right Grand Division Commander Sumner and Left Grand Division Commander Franklin of their commands. There would be some cleaning of house, after all.

On January 26, 1863, Major General Burnside informed the soldiers of the transition. He issued General Orders No. 9, in which he graciously transferred command to Hooker. Burnside wrote: "Be true in your devotion to your country and the principles you have sworn to maintain; give to the brave and skillful general who has so long been identified with your organization and who is now to command you, your full and cordial support and cooperation, and you will deserve success."[20]

In the same letter to his father in which he described the chronology of events that comprised the "Mud March," Rollin laid bare his frustrations with the pall suffocating the Union cause, and the consequences of revolving-door military leadership on the enlisted. With the baton now handed to "Fighting Joe Hooker," Rollin and his comrades were ordered to place trust in yet another Commanding General to lead them out of their malaise and lift the Army of the Potomac out of the mire of defeat.[21]

Camp of 27th Regt N.Y.Vols
White Oak Church Va
January 31st 1863

Dear Father

...The soldiers done their part well and if the weather had have been favorable, I have not the least doubt but what we should have gained a victory. But our commander, than whom no better patriot is working for the union, could not control the elements and failed to carry out his plans. He asked to be relieved for some reason, perhaps because of his failure, and we now have the renowned "fighting" Joe Hooker to lead us. I am sorry the change has been made. By such changes troops lose confidence in their leaders and learn to distrust the cabinet. Sumner and Franklin, two good men, have been relieved, and many are wondering the cause and cast many reproaches upon the department at Washington.

The body of the army in the field—the rank and file—are intelligent, free thinking, and too much humbugging will be the ruination of this country. A few more changes and defeats and a moderate smart, shrewd man could tumble this grand army of the Potomac to pieces, and so thoroughly disorganize it that the authorities could never tell what became of it.

A little farther on and "one" smart traitor can do what the whole rebel army have failed to do.

I hope this climax will never be reached, but this is truly a gloomy day for the old republic, and we need sound, earnest men at the helm of state.

'Tis night—dim twilight, and I must close with the honest hope that three months hence I can meet you face to face instead of resorting to the tedious method of writing.

I received Clara's letter of the 25th today, which I will answer soon.

With much love to all, I am

Your aff son
Rollin B. Truesdell

To: Saml W Truesdell
Great Bend, Pa

COUNTING THE DAYS

This great army appears to be passing away from the memories of men, and to have already numbered itself with the things that were. The nation has transferred its interest in us to the more active armies of the west . . . where heroes delight in accomplishing apparent impossibilities.
—Soldier, the 27th NY Volunteers, February 13, 1863[1]

MUD MARCH HANGOVER

Such a lament as that expressed by Rollin's comrade in the above epigraph, of being led into irrelevance, was pervasive during the winter of 1863. The physical and mental drain on the Army of the Potomac—and on the war-weary North in general—resulting from the infamous Mud March is incalculable. Though likely successful in creating a temporary departure from their reality, the copious amounts of whiskey imbibed after their return to camp from the failed march could not change the unvarnished truth for the downtrodden soldiers. They woke up the next morning, January 26, 1863, nauseated by the excesses of the night before, and to the truth that they had been guided into greater, and avoidable, hardship under the plodding leadership of their former commanding general. Major General Burnside had marched them into a life-sapping gamble with the primary byproduct being luscious fodder for enemy ridicule.

Rollin and his comrades had little choice but to accept the impending changes at their army's helm, and to pray that, in their remaining months of commitment to the army, they would be spared the self-inflicted wounds that frivolous jabs against the Confederate force had caused. Twelfth Corps

Commander Henry Slocum, beloved first colonel of the 27th NY Volunteers, surely served as a salve for Rollin and his comrades when he visited the regiment that day, the day Burnside transferred command to Major General Joe Hooker. Slocum's presence and his affection for his home regiment bolstered flagging spirits and reminded the men of the esprit de corps they felt under his command. The 27th NY Volunteers gave Slocum "three times three hearty cheers" as a measure of their esteem for him.[2] For the regiment, Slocum was the embodiment of heroic leadership.

The men's first exposure to Hooker's command was turbulent. Hooker, as his reputation suggested, appeared to be a man of action. He wasted no time in dismantling Burnside's vision for the Army of the Potomac structure and assembling his own. Removing the Grand Division Generals from their command was not solely a removal of man from post but dissolving the post itself; Hooker opted to break up the "Grand Divisions" and revert to the corps d'armee management structure. In Hooker's estimation, improved discipline and morale would necessarily follow superior military organization. (See figure 12.1.)

Rollin became an example of this formula when he was promoted to sergeant in mid-February. Only 2½ months after his advancement to corporal, Rollin's ability to keep his men in position and motivated even during Burnside's blunders at Fredericksburg and the Mud March had gained the attention of his superiors. Filled with pride, Rollin informed his family of his promotion to which his adoring sister Clara responded by sending him chevrons she sewed for his uniform. (Clara apparently had a chevron cottage industry. In a letter to her dated April 24, 1863, Rollin included thanks from Charles B. Fairchild, the future author of the 27th's regimental history, for the chevrons she had sent for him.)

It is not surprising that when the men of the 27th NY learned that Left Grand Division Commander William Franklin would be swept from command as Hooker assumed his, they pined for General Slocum to be Franklin's replacement. One of Rollin's comrades wrote in a letter home: "Major General Smith succeeds Franklin for the present. It is believed, however, his command only temporary. General Slocum is the only officer now in the service who would be received with universal favor. The 27th would look with pride upon their old commander in such a position."[3]

Franklin's removal felt like a slight to the men. They had fought under his command for over a year and believed he had created the best corps in the army. For many of Rollin's comrades, this loyal, brave, competent commander

FIGURE 12.1   Joseph Hooker. Library of Congress, Prints &
Photographs Division, Civil War Photographs.

was sacrificed for the supposed transgression of continued allegiance to former
Commander George McClellan over the President.

Several weeks later, the men of the 27th NY Volunteers tussled with an even
greater personal affront within their chain of command: the imminent removal
of native son J. J. Bartlett from brigade command. Bartlett, the regiment's first

major, was caught in political crossfire between Congress and President Lincoln. He would reach the end of his term of appointment as brigadier general by the end of March 1863. Without Congressional confirmation and against his wishes, Bartlett would be forced to revert to being a civilian.

On March 29, Bartlett left 27th NY Volunteers' Colonel Adams in command of the brigade and ventured to the Army of the Potomac headquarters to confer with Hooker. According to one of Bartlett's travel companions, Hooker instructed Bartlett to return to his quarters, take off his uniform, and keep quiet until he heard further; Hooker intended to go to Washington the next day to plead Bartlett's case directly to the President.[4] Two days later, instead of lining up to bid a sorrowful goodbye, the 2nd Brigade—Bartlett's brigade—cheered wildly when Bartlett read Lincoln's telegram: "Tell General Bartlett to put on his clothes again, and return to his command."[5] Bartlett told the men that he had not asked for confirmation of his appointment; he only asked for the privilege of leading his soldiers of the 2nd Brigade into battle once more. One of Rollin's friends wrote in a letter home: "The men gave him three cheers. They hardly knew how to express their joy. We are hoarse from continual cheering."[6]

By preserving this highly respected brigadier, Hooker signaled the importance of maintaining the integrity of his newly reorganized Army of the Potomac, but more importantly to the men of the 27th NY Volunteers, his actions demonstrated commitment to Bartlett and Bartlett's men. With failed campaign after failed campaign and their army commanders shuffling in and out, for Rollin and his mates, trusting their leaders was a shaky proposition.

When Hooker was elevated to command the Army of the Potomac at the end of January, the men were fatigued and hesitant to freely give this new Commanding General the benefit of the doubt that he could lead them to victory. In recalling Hooker's appointment, The 27th NY Volunteers' regimental history enthused: "The plucky qualities which had given to him the name of "Fighting Joe," seemed to be an assurance of the activity and energy that were so necessary to the successful endurance of the contest . . . when in command, he represented the dashing, chivalrous soldier."[7] But the historians felt the need to caveat their adulation by reminding the reader of Hooker's, "grave defects in character and habits."[8] Hooker was an impressive soldier, but these veterans had seen too much. Was Hooker worthy and capable of leading this great army?

By moving decisively, however, Hooker left wary men in his wake. On February 13, 1863, a comrade in the 27th NY complained in a local newspaper:

"Events are really unintelligible. General Hooker is nominally at work reorganizing the army and at the same time there is evidence it is in the process of disorganizing ... Whole divisions are embarking at Aquia Creek ... Our general officers leave us and we hear of it by accident a week afterwards!"[9] On the same day, Rollin began a chatty letter to his sister with observations regarding the shuffling of Army of the Potomac troops before segueing into soldier's life updates.

Camp of the 27th Regt New York Vols
White Oak Church Virginia
February 13th 1863

Dear Sister

Your letter of the 1st inst I have just received. Our mails have been more than usually irregular for the past week owing to the shipment of part of this army to southern ports, and part to Washington, but this Corps still remains to keep up appearances. In fact, I think only two corps has gone, the 1st and 9th; how soon others will follow is a question, but I believe the grand army of the Potomac is about to be broken up entirely, a part of it to be sent South and part West, after retaining force enough at Washington to garrison the fortifications.

The weather is variable. Yesterday morning it snowed, in the afternoon it rained and part of the night, and this morning the sun rose clear, and it is as mild and pleasant as a Susquehanna May day morning.

The roads continue very bad although men are kept at work on them all the while filling ruts and laying corduroy. I saw yesterday a six mule team stuck fast with an empty wagon on the level. We cannot drill nor in fact do anything else without getting in mud from head to foot, so "we" set by the fire and take things cool.

I am pretty well stocked with reading matter for the present. I get the city papers regular, take the Waverly and Republican, and some friends in different parts of the state send Peterson's, Frank Leslie's, and other interesting monthlies.[10] Then I have just got a book "The Stars and Stripes in Rebellion," the manuscript for which was prepared by Union prisoners taken at Bull Run. It is a nice work and containing some pleasing articles. I spent last evening in reading John van Buren's speech in the Herald of the

11th.[11] Then to fill up the time I have the old Jubilee, the Golden Chain, and checkers.

But with all these riches, I have been lonesome for the past two days, for Westervelt has gone to Washington, leaving me all alone to keep bachelor "tent." This might be pleasant some times, but the truth is, just at present, there is not a pie or cake in the cupboard or any apples or cider in the cellar, but we have salt pork, "hard tack," and coffee, and butter, and popcorn from home, so I think I'll live through it 'til he comes back, when I will be sure to get something worth eating from "our folks" in the city.

I received a call the other day from the Hon Member of Congress from Otsego County.[12] He came down from Washington to see friends in this Div. and having heard Bro Mart with whom he is well acquainted say that he had a brother in the 27th, he came over and made me quite a visit. Bade me good cheer, etc., and if I came to W. while he was there, to make his place my home.

It is astonishing what an extended acquaintance a soldier has. Here we are mixed up with men from all the New England states, Ohio, and Wisconsin, and by some chance they will become acquainted with a few from each Regt. I frequently meet men who know Calvin and the Jacksons.

A short time since, I picked up a stray piece of an old newspaper which contained the death of our respected friend Francis D. Ladd of Philadelphia.[13] He has a relative with whom I am acquainted in the 5th Maine Regt of our Brigade.

The health of this command is not as good as it was owing to the fatigue and exposure of the last attempt to cross the river. A great many have been sick ever since. The sound of muffled drums with the firing of salutes often greets our ears and tells of the departure of another comrade to his long home, and reminds us that someone miles away will put on the habiliments of mourning a few days hence for their relative whom they cherished fond hopes of being among the few who would survive the perils of soldier's life.

Ninety days more, and home, sweet home, I'll greet you.

Yours truly
Rollin B. Truesdell

Baldy Smith, unable to attain Senate confirmation of his promotion to major general, was ushered out of the 6th Corps before the men could adjust to their new circumstances; Major General John Sedgwick took Smith's place on February 5, 1863. A former West Point classmate of Joe Hooker, Sedgwick epitomized dogged adherence to duty. While leading a division during Mc-Clellan's Peninsula Campaign, Sedgwick was wounded in the arm and leg at the Battle of Glendale. He was promoted to major general four days later. At the battle of Antietam, he and his division were surrounded on three sides by Confederate General Stonewall Jackson's forces and crushed. Sedgwick was shot in the wrist, shoulder, and leg and had his horse shot dead under him before being carried off the field. "Uncle John," as his men affectionately referred to him, reported back for duty to assume command of the 6th Corps after recovering from his battle wounds. (See figure 12.2.)

Numb with boredom, chronic illness in camp, frustration, and the cold, the men of the 27th NY Volunteers could only watch and wait to see what additional changes their new Commanding General might make that winter. And write letters home. Rollin thought of and wrote to his mother often over this period.

> Camp of 27th Regt N.Y.S.V.
> White Oak Church Va
> Feby 19th 1863

My Dear Mother

    I am well, which is the most important news I can write to you. I am truly thankful that I am not sick. We have so much wet, rainy weather of late. This afternoon closed up a two day rain storm and all about us is one vast sea of mud.

    Our tents are not very attractive for their comfort and furniture when compared to a home, but even such as they are we prefer to huddle inside them than to risk our frail backs in the elements which surround us.

    I have not heard from home in a long time—three days I guess, perhaps four. I wonder what you are all doing, who is sick, who dead, who married, etc., but I suppose you cannot answer all those questions half so easy as I can ask them.

    For my part, I am boiling beans for my supper—a two quart tin pail full. This is for the two of us. A quart a piece will do, won't it?

    I don't feel very downhearted or in low spirits these days. I

FIGURE 12.2   John Sedgwick. Civil War photographs, 1861–
1865, Library of Congress, Prints and Photographs Division.

begin to see the end of my time in the army so clearly that I can
almost <u>hear</u> the familiar voices at home and for the instant forget
where I am.

And my health is now so very good that I think nothing but
the enemy's bullets can upset my calculations. Yet I know very well
that many things beside these can interfere and spoil my golden
dreams of future happiness, but I have strong hopes and like many

of my ancestors, an iron will and constitution which bids trouble "get out of the way."

Take choice care of the package I sent by express, and don't let it be opened for a thousand—I won't say what, but something valuable.

With much love to all, I am

Ever your aff son
Rollin

Rollin and many of his comrades bared their sometimes critical opinions about the conduct of the war at various stages to loved ones in their letters. The letter to his sister Julia of February 23, 1863, is one example of Rollin's pen wandering into such territory.

Camp of 27th Regt New York Vols
White Oak Church Va
February 23d 1863

My Dear Sister

I have just received this morning your good, long, interesting, welcome letter of the 9th inst. In my last letter to you I did not intend to injure your feelings, but I did want to say something which would incite you to write a good long letter, just such as one as I received. I will not say that I am greatly indebted to you for this favor, but I am truly thankful and hope you will do the like again. I know you would if you knew the pleasure it affords me.

I am just as thankful and as much indebted to you for that chicken as if it had been sent but the honey, by jingoes, I was sorry to lose.

Strange you cannot see what fine progress we are making towards conquering the Rebs. Have we not sacrificed thousands upon thousands of lives, and millions of money; is not our recourses and debt much larger than the Confederacy? At this rate, don't you think we will terrify them into submission in two years more?

I think this war is the biggest political humbug that ever existed, but I think we can worst them in the course of time. I think the two years men will not have any more fighting to do.

The roads are in such a condition that we cannot move in less than a month, and then if things move with their usual slowness, another month will be expended in preparation, which will take us so near out that we hope by some chance to be spared the dangers of another engagement.

You cannot imagine how surprised I was when Emory Simons informed me of Georgie's death. I could not believe but what it was Anna 'til he read the letter he got from his sister to me. She was a fine girl and if there is any good Christians in the world, I truly believe she was one. Such letters as she used to write, and such advice as she used to give, no other of my youthful correspondents ever put on paper. I have preserved some of her letters which I will show you some time when we can talk of these things in a more easy manner. I have not heard from Anna in a long time.

Yesterday being Washington's birthday, salutes were fired by the batteries of the Division, but the inclemency of the weather prevented the troops from making any demonstration 'til today when we assembled en mass and listened to the reading of the "old Patriot's" farewell address.

Yesterday was very cold and snow fell to the depth of twelve inches. It is thawing and quite sloppy today.

Evening

It is cold and clear without and the foot fall of the sentinel as he passes on his beat near my tent makes the snow squeak and crumple, reminding me that it is cold without, but it is cheery and cozy within our castle as any drawing room of the upper class. I fancy I am twice as happy as some of that "crust." We have a nice little fireplace and a good fire though the wood which is burning we brought a good long mile on our backs. And our tent and furniture is as good as any soldier has, and we think our selves comfortable "play." That it's all nice and good, but at the same time look forward to the 8th of May with a good deal of anxiety and contemplate much happiness immediately thereafter.

My writing table is a board (checker) laid across my knee, which accounts for some of the queer marks—up and down, etc., in my writing.

If you only could realize how I appreciate a good long letter, you would write again very soon. I would like to hear from Henry and the children, but you write the sheet full; don't leave a space large enough for any of them to write their names so that each will have to take a separate sheet.

Please write again very soon and believe me,

Your aff bro

Roll

Apples are not as high as they were a few weeks ago; then they were worth $1.00 per doz, now only 75 cents per dozen.

Other soldiers who served alongside Rollin became prolific and popular venters for hometown newspapers. Some of these published letters careened into accusatory critiques that pilloried the Northern war effort and President Lincoln himself as they chronicled day-to-day preoccupations in the army. A comrade in Rollin's regiment explained: "Soldiers will be doing something, and if not afforded attractions of a purely military character, they will be finding fault with officers, writing treasonable letters, or else engaged in low mean sports . . . Art and human nature cannot successfully contend against powerful Virginia storms."[14]

John A. Copeland, nom de plume Marker, discovered there was a limit, however, to a soldier's exercise of free speech. Copeland, a congenial soldier in the 27th NY Volunteers, was also a popular and acerbic correspondent for the *Rochester Union* newspaper. In February 1863, against the protestations of Regiment Commander Adams and Brigade Commander Bartlett, Union Army Provost Marshall General Patrick ordered Copeland be taken into custody at army headquarters and charged with treason for a letter he wrote condemning the last Union foray near Fredericksburg. The arrest sent a sobering chill through camp. Copeland was arrested for saying what so many of his comrades were thinking. The wheels of justice were in Copeland's favor, however. At his trial, presiding officer Major General Daniel Sickles agreed the soldier-journalist should be tried in his own division and remanded him to General Brooks.[15] After dressing Copeland down, Brooks directed him to return to his company and report for duty.[16] Copeland was back at his post by the end of March.

Copeland's experience may have given pause to some of his fellow soldier-journalists, but likely only added fuel to other comrades' personal letters home. For Rollin, throughout the post–Mud March winter, letter writing was one of the few available escapes from the frigid monotony. He, like so many others, maintained a steady stream of correspondence with loved ones. Certainly, the letters served as a safe place to blow off steam, but they also pulled the cord to home ever tauter. In some of his letters, Rollin's longing is palpable.

Camp of 27th Regt New York Vols
White Oak Church Va
Feby 21st 1863

Dear Sister

I am half inclined to believe some of the folks at home are sick. It seems a month since I heard from any of you, though the time is only two weeks but this is unusual—and something must be the matter—though usually after waiting a good long time for letters from home, and I sit down and devote a large sheet to the "cause," the next mail after sending it brings a half dozen or so from home which you desire answered "instanter," thus giving me extra trouble and some suspense.

Well, it's pleasant and fine today after the deluge of rain of the three days previous, and all the "furniture" of the tent is out to dry to ensure perfect health to the occupants for we believe an ounce of prevention worth a pound of cure if not more. And by the by, the black measles are raging in this locality to a terrible extent, one Jersey Regt of this Div burying from three to five each day. I am not alarmed, but what is good for them? There has been more sickness and death in this Division since our last attempt to cross the river than I ever saw in the same length of time before. It equals our Chickahominy campaign, but then our complaints were mostly fevers; now it's rheumatiz, black measles, and chronic diarrhea.

Old soldiers have the seeds of disease in them, and it will spring up and lay them low some time either sooner or later. And cases of rheumatism will be contracted here with our number which will last a man his whole life—thankful I don't belong to the "invalid band," though I have nothing in particular against secret societies.

Westervelt got back from Washington a day or two ago. He had a good time and brought down a good supply of "civil" things (not rations) to me. Of course, I enjoyed them highly.

I was over to the hundred and twenty onth yesterday. Some of these new soldiers don't like soldiers' fare very well and are very home sick and do not try to look very cleanly or soldierly. Bill

Ackerman, who used to work for Jule Lines, is badly troubled that way and looks like a green pumpkin struck with a club.

The 151st Pa Regt are now encamped about three miles from here and as soon as the mud dries a little, I am going to see them. Wonder if Sam likes soldiering—"guess he will see"—and go too, whether he likes the travailing or not. If I go to see him I'll have fun or I'm a fish. Bet he would like to see "Sally" these days of rain and mud.

Our time is so near out that I can smell good victuals—at least come as near to it as Uncle Lyman did to swearing when he broke his wagon. I guess I will have to wean off from hard tack by first eating oak chips and then come down to softer wood and finally to crust. No doubt you will have a good stock on hand by 1st of June, the time I have set to take the castle. And then, if I don't have some of those good times over again, why, I'm a basket of chips.

I hardly know what I shall do next summer. I am studying over it all the time and shall write to Father in a day or two in relation to the matter. If I knew just how I could take the old farm, upon what conditions, etc., it would make a great difference with me now. If I cannot do that, I should make my calculations to do something else, and open the way a little before returning home, but time will decide the matter and wait I must.

Remember me to sister Julia and family and to all others whose loyalty is undoubted.

Yours truly
Rollin B. Truesdell

Writing home helped Rollin ruminate about and plan for life after soldiering. With the end of his term of enlistment tantalizingly close, Rollin envisioned himself back in Liberty at the family farm, hovering over a fragrant pie, gesturing with fork in hand, as he and his mother and sister swapped salacious theories about the demise of a (what he considered) ne'er-do-well neighbor.

Camp of 27th Regt New York Vols
White Oak Church Va
March 8th 1863

Dear Sister

Your letter of the 28th ult I have just received. Indeed it contained astonishing news. Aunt Lois had grown old and we might expect to hear of her death at any time, but the case of Hannah Banker surprises me, and if there is any law or justice left in the states, I think the case ought to be rigidly inquired into. But if there is no such elements left in the North, I go in for martial law and to save further trouble and disgrace to the community, would want the whole tribe of Steam Hollerites transported to Botany Bay.

As for the smallpox, I don't think it will amount to much. We have had it down here so thick that every other tent was a pest house, but I thought there was no use writing home about it 'til it was all got along with. It has entirely subsided.

I had a splendid time over at the 151st Pa Regt; saw more of the Susquaboys than at any time since leaving home. Ben Vance and Lyman Beebe were out on picket, also several others that I knew of less account such as Frank Goddard, etc.

I have just rec'd a letter from Cousin Julia. They are all well. I have not heard from Mart or Albert in some time but suppose tonight's mail will bring one from Albert with full particulars of the Steam Holler decrease.

I am sorry to hear it is so sickly about home. I have <u>heard</u> that Janette and Omar were better.

I will write to Mother in a few days. Expect a letter from Julia next mail; hope she won't subside after one long letter.

With much love I am

Yours truly

R. B. Truesdell

White Oak Church Va

March 20th 1863

My Dear Mother

I have looked in vain for letters from home for several days, but they do not come, and I wonder what the matter can be; twelve days since I have heard from any of the household.

After the mail come tonight, I was tempted to take ten days leave of absence and surprise you all by suddenly raining down among you, but a second thought banished the idea. Though a short visit home would be pleasant in the extreme to me, but forty eight days from today and I hope to turn my face homeward for a longer time than ten days.

My health is good, never better, and my hopes rise higher as each day narrows down the distance between me and thee. The gulf is growing frightfully narrow and I can but sing Northward every day.

I hope no brute on the farm is so cold and chilly as I am to-night, for it has been a cold rough day, and the wind is cold and piercing, and my scanty supply of embers are burning low. I wish I was as comfortably ensconced in feathers and sheets as I well know you are several hours ago, but I am thankful that my strength and constitution are equal to the task. I wish none were worse off than this chick.

While I think of it, I will thank all concerned for the bottle of hot drops which was timely received. My poor old teeth are the worst of my troubles, thank fortune, but few are left and part of them broke off.

I think from all I hear indirectly that Steam Hollow is doing its part towards peopling the earth, notwithstanding the small moral loss it lately sustained. It's a wonder the Lord don't rain brimstone into that God-forsaken hole and wipe it out of existence. I think the people round about would say the soldiers' amen, which is "bully." Why in thunder don't the people instead of spending their money to find out who poisoned Hannah Banker use it to buy more poison and rid themselves from them pests of the earth?

I guess the more I write the worse boy you will think I am, so I will say "bully" and quit.

Ever your aff son
Rollin B. Truesdell

Or he envisaged sitting side by side with his father as he advised Rollin on life work possibilities. Or calling on one of the young women with whom he maintained a long-distance friendship, if not courtship, via letter. Westervelt divulged: "We wrote to all the girls we left behind us, and such letters . . . breathed eternal and everlasting constancy to them all—but that was one of the soldier's prerogatives."[17] Tipping his hand, perhaps, Rollin forwarded home a packet of private papers in February 1863 with the stern instructions that it absolutely not be opened!

Camp of 27th Regt NY Vols
White Oak Church Va
February 8th 1863

Dear Father

I have this day sent to Washington by a friend a bundle of things which are useless to me here but may do me some good if I live to get home—which he will send to you by express.

Enclosed in the bundle is a package of private letters & papers which have accumulated the past summer which are of no earthly use to anybody but myself, nor will they interest anybody to rummage them through, and I do "not" want them opened, but put carefully away 'til I return.

For fear we make another move, I determined to make my knapsack as light as possible.

The weather is mild. The ground muddy. We have had several snow squalls the past week. The roads are very bad.

My health is good, first rate.

Yours truly
R. B. Truesdell

Saml W Truesdell

Rollin's positive outlook—and the affectionate familial bonds and camaraderie with his friends in the 27th NY Volunteers and other regiments—undoubtedly served him well in weathering the winter of 1863 and allowing him to anticipate his future. In a letter to his father dated March 2, Rollin, sociable by nature, beamed as he described his overnight journey to visit friends serving in the 151st PA as a welcome break.

Camp of 27th Regt N York Vols
White Oak Church Va
March 2d 1863

Dear Father

I have just returned from a visit to the 151st Pa Regt, an account of which may interest you as two Companies in that Regt are from our county.

I set out from our camp at noon on Saturday and splashed along through mud and water, and water and mud, in the direction of their camp, having been previously informed of their location by Lieut C. W. Warner, a Susquehanna man who by the way is a graduate of West Point and now connected with a battery of this Division. With but little difficulty found them three miles from the place of starting "be it the same, more or less."

The first "apparition" which I saw after coming into their camp was the natural phiz of coz Samuel who conducted me to the quarters of Capt Crandall and his Lieutenants, Jamison and Lutz, where I was "taken in and done for" in fine style.

After a pleasant chat of a couple of hours with them, I was introduced to Dr Blakesly, Regimental Surgeon, formerly of Springville, who I knew well by reputation but had never met before. From his account I judge the Regiment had had quite a serious time with the small pox, but the disease had now entirely disappeared. I did not have the pleasure of seeing our friends Benj C. Vance and Lyman Beebe as they were on picket, but if they are as hale and hearty as the boys I saw in camp, I think they are able to stand some hard ship—if they are put to the test before their nine months expire.

Capt Stone was on picket with a part of his command, but I saw Lieuts Frink and Hollenbeck; they were well. In the evening we had an old-fashioned set down in Capt Crandall's tent.

Sunday afternoon I came back to camp, having had a splendid time in every sense of the word.

Dr B. wished to be remembered to you. I had a fine visit with him—was treated with much courtesy, but I shall ever remember some of his eccentricities.

Yours truly
Rollin B. Truesdell

This long season of snow and rain and mud and disease passed slowly, however. Firewood became ever scarcer, and the men resorted to meaner fires fueled by dug-up tree roots. Loathsome illnesses such as black measles and smallpox persisted in the camps. A soldier from the 27th reported in February that the "Dead March" may be heard almost every hour of the day.[18] Ardent snow and rainstorms prevented drills, reviews, and inspections and even postponed the usual military exercises commemorating Washington's birthday.

Rollin and his comrades did trudge through the elements for occasional picket duty but found that to be more of a refreshing break from their lethargy than a hardship.

And the mud. Virtually defying description, the men nonetheless attempted. One soldier quipped: "The depth of mud here is so fabulous to a New Yorker ... I may hint that it is something less than 1/3 of the earth's diameter!"[19] Rollin and his mates reasonably shared concerns that the mud threated their very lifeline—the receipt and delivery of supplies from Aquia Creek and Belle Plain. The 27th NY regimental history recalled: "Occasional details were made to build corduroy roads. These roads would sink so deep in the mud that others had to be built over them, and it was with the greatest difficulty that our supplies could be brought over from Aquia Creek."[20] Hapless Union mules, true beasts of burden, were frequently swallowed up in the mud that winter during the dogged quest to supply the Army of the Potomac.

READY AGAIN

Like a slumbering giant, the Army of the Potomac slowly shook off the fatigue and malaise of the winter months and began to pull itself up to its full height in the spreading days of spring 1863. Occasional warm, sunny periods lifted the morale of the men and rejuvenated their fighting spirit. And day by day, by moving heaven and earth to keep food, clothing, and medical supplies coming into the camps and creating an atmosphere of confidence and cooperation among the general officers, Commanding General Hooker built up the trust of his army. Hooker clamped down on the rampant graft taking place under the noses of hungry soldiers; unscrupulous officers responsible for the movement of fresh vegetables such as onions, cabbage, and potato from warehouses to mess kitchens had enriched themselves by siphoning off the produce for cash in sales to the locals. And the Commanding General instituted a new policy whereby each soldier could look forward to receiving either flour or soft bread (vs. hardtack) four times a week, and fresh vegetables and/or potato two times a week. Hooker also reached for the soldiers' hearts. He authorized each company to send one man, in turn, on a ten-day (fifteen if outside the mid-Atlantic) furlough to go home—a wise complement to his edict to extend the President's amnesty offer for deserters to include those in custody if they return by April 1st.[21] Rollin's letter to his sister Clara on March 9 exemplifies the thawing of soldiers' views of their Commanding General.

Camp of 27th Regt NY Vols
White Oak Church Va
March 9th 1863

My Dear Sister

I have just received your letter of the 3d inst, the first from home in several days. I too have but little or nothing of interest to write save that, like Webster, "I ain't dead yet," and am in full possession of physical strength, though perhaps not quite so sensible to the last as I ought to be, but howsoever, I continue to exist.

Last night we had a furious thunder storm accompanied with high wind which racked our frail castle like a reed, but we had no old chimney upon which to rely for its safety as of old when we lived in the old red house upon the hill. But we survived, and today has been clear, lovely, and serene just such as we have at home in May, the pleasantest of all the months in the year. If we could only be blessed with a few such days as this has been, the roads would soon be in fit condition to think of moving, but the weather is so variable that it will be an impossibility to accomplish anything before April.

I like Genl Hooker better every day, and I think he will make a skillful and able commander. He is doing great things for this army every day and bringing it up to a high standard of discipline and effective organization. If the lesser "stars" will only support and work in conjunction with him, the coming summer will see this army do great things.

Do not make too great preparations to receive me at home at any specified time for I shall surely come just when you are not looking for me every minute. It is now rumored that we shall be mustered out of service at Staten Island, and if it be true, I shall go to Conn. before coming home. But if we are discharged punctually at the end of our time, I shall celebrate the 4th of July under "my own vine and fig tree." If all my plans work well, I shall not set the river on fire next summer, but take things easy and among the first of my visits will be one to Pete Hook. Is the "hoss & wagon" goable?

Well, Sis, it's getting along into the night pretty well for I have written a number of letters since dark. And by the way Bill snores,

I think he must need help to do such hard work, so I will wish you all good night and quietly subside into a signature.

Rollin B. Truesdell

Please just ask sister Julia if she is out of paper; if she is, I will send some. Give her one cross look for me and then soon after display a sunbeam.

At the end of March, one of Rollin's comrades rhapsodized: "Now the sky is cleared . . . and the Virginia climate challenges the admiration which is bestowed upon that of Italy and France . . . The rebellion must be crushed; and he who is unwilling to do his part ought to clank about for endless years in the fetters of a slave."[22] The muck had lost its stranglehold grip on the men— physically and emotionally. Rollin, on the precipice of his return home, wrote poignantly to his oldest sister Julia on March 26, and bared his inner turmoil about the job not yet complete.

Camp of 27th New York Vols
White Oak Church Va
March 26th 1863

Dear Sister Julia

I am happy to acknowledge the receipt of your letter of the 21st inst, also one from your daughter Lucie.

Nothing of particular interest has transpired in our camp since I last wrote you, all of us leading a life of dull monotony and laziness. The weather begins to be moderate and spring-like, but is very changeable, alternating in snow, sunshine, and rain spiced with high winds. The roads begin to be settled but are still in bad condition, and several weeks must elapse before the army can move to advantage. But while the roads are drying, everything is being got in readiness so that when the time comes to advance, we shall not have to delay to haul clothing and supplies.

An unusual activity has prevailed the last week, and I think the army was never better clothed or better prepared in every point of view to commence a campaign than it is at the present time. Our last campaign was so long and tedious that we were worn out and desired rest long before it was granted, and quite a bad and insubordinate spirit prevailed among both officers and men, but the desired rest which we have obtained has put us in the best of spirits and health, and an uneasiness begins to prevail. But few will regret to hear the order to move forward.

As far as I have had a chance to observe, the troops have great confidence in General Hooker. He is a good fighting man, but some think him a little too rash. I do not. I am willing and desire to fight under a man who will run some risk if there is a shadow of hope to gain a victory thereby. I often express the wish that the lamented Genl Phil Kearny had been put in command of the Army of the Potomac when Genl McClellan was.[23] He was the best fighting Genl I think we ever had in the service, and if he could have led this army, I believe the Southern Confederacy would have been where a certain rich man of old was when he cried for a drop of water. Or if he had failed, the old Union would certainly have enjoyed that unenviable position which might possibly have been as well as to continue this war for a term of years and drench the soil with the best blood of the country.

I am anxious to have this terrible drama close and would willingly stand my chances for life or death in "another seven days fight," another Antietam, South Mountain, and Fredericksburg if I could feel sure that by another New Year's Day we could conquer and dictate terms of peace which would be lasting and insure prosperity and happiness to the nation for a term of years beyond which there can be no possibility of the present incumbents of the earth seeing.

But I think I have written enough about war for one letter, so I will proceed to answer the question you ask me of "how I get along without ever getting a sight of women and children." It is a military necessity to be without them, and I obey it. No scolding wife or crying children ever disturb a soldier's dreams and I feel myself perfectly well qualified to keep bachelor's hall and spend the remainder of my days in perfect uninterrupted bliss.

Having spun out quite a lengthy epistle, I will bid you good night and retire to my blankets and poles; I wish I could say bed.

Yours truly
R. B. Truesdell

Hooker was anxious to set his army in motion, but not impetuous. He began issuing daily preparatory orders to the regiments in March. An accompanying steady rhythm of drills and inspections signaled to the men of the

27th NY Volunteers that waiting for movement against the enemy would not be long. On March 22, the Inspector General evaluated Bartlett's brigade; on March 23–24, the companies were drilled; on April 3, General Hooker reviewed the 6th Corps on its parade ground; and on April 8, at Hooker's headquarters, President Lincoln conducted a grand review of the Army of the Potomac.[24] Two days later, Rollin broke away for a few days of final furlough. By the time he returned to camp on April 19, 1863, he found the army under marching orders. Rollin wrote a letter to his parents the next morning after his return journey down the Potomac—made more memorable by being in the accompaniment of the President.

> Camp of 27th Regt NY Vols
> White Oak Church Va
> April 20th 1863

Dear Parents

I arrived here last evening having had rather a slow tedious journey.

The heavy rains of Wednesday caused a land slide below Williamsport which delayed us twelve hours, breaking our connections all the way to Washington. I was glad I had company, but Mrs DuBois and all the children, save Carrie, were sea sick and did not enjoy the trip first rate.

I had to lay over in Washington one day & two nights and had a pleasant time with my friends there. My trip down the Potomac was very pleasant though 'twas Sunday and much of the way down I was permitted to look at his excellency Pres' Lincoln who was sunning himself on the deck of a boat which kept us company all the way down.

The army are under marching orders and we expect to be under way shortly. Sam has gone to the Corps Hospital and I cannot forward his things to him. I shall give them all to Harrison if I can find him, but I hear his Div has moved. If I find neither, I shall eat the things rather than throw them away. Crandall & Johnny Loomis got their bundles this morning. Sam's health is improving but he is unfit for duty.

I saw Brainerd in Washington. He had got a job in the office of the Hospital for the present, and Charles Neal told me he would set him to printing currency in two or three months and would also keep an eye on him during the intermediate time.

My health and spirits are good.

Your aff son

Rollin B. Truesdell

To: Saml W. Truesdell

Great Bend Pa

Hooker's plans were stymied. Though the cavalry had packed up and cantered upriver on April 13, the infantry—after drawing sixty rounds of ammunition and ten days' rations—were ordered to hold in place the following day. A powerful storm convinced the Commanding General to delay the march. Many in the Army of the Potomac noted the general's respect for mother nature with satisfaction. For several days, camp life resumed, punctuated by the arrival of the paymaster on April 25 to disburse four months of pay, and fuel the subsequent rollicking gambling in company streets.

. As the men of the 27th NY Volunteers awaited the reissued orders to march, they inevitably would be plagued by much soul searching. Some felt they should be exempt from the next battle because they mustered into state service in April 1861 and their commitment should thereby conclude in April 1863. The federal government thought otherwise. It laid claim to the men until May 21, 1863—two years from their acceptance as a regiment by the State of New York. Many of Rollin's comrades wrestled with whether they should re-enlist after spending some time at home. These veterans understood war and what it took to be a good soldier. No matter how delightful the image of loud-mouthed skulkers being shepherded to the frontline might be, could they trust those who entered the war by conscription to fight as bravely as themselves?

The anticipation was soon over. On April 27, 1863, Commanding General Joe Hooker issued orders for his army to prepare to march early the following morning.

Chapter 13

FINAL BATTERING BEFORE HOME

It is my opinion this is the worst whipping we ever took.
—Rollin B. Truesdell, 27th NY Volunteers, May 6, 1863

Of course, he did not know it then. When Rollin took his place in line to march toward his final confrontation against the Rebel forces, squeezed in mere days before his term of enlistment in the Army of the Potomac was to elapse, Rollin exuded the confidence of a tested soldier. On the afternoon of April 28, 1863, Rollin was ready to lead the men in his section onward in this harrowing crusade for a unified country one last time. He felt the weight of history on his shoulders. Just one month earlier, Rollin wrote in a letter to his sister Julia:

> I am anxious to have this terrible drama close, and would willingly stand my chances for life or death in "another seven days fight," another Antietam, South Mountain, and Fredericksburg if I could feel sure that by another New Year's Day we could conquer and dictate terms of peace which would be lasting and insure prosperity and happiness to the nation for a term of years beyond which there could be no possibility of the present incumbents of the earth seeing.

But fate would not have it. Days after striding forth to meet the enemy under the direction of virile new Commanding General Joe Hooker, the Army of the Potomac was forced to scramble back across the Rappahannock River to save itself from destruction at the hands of Confederate General

Robert E. Lee's rag-tag but resolute forces. During this, the Chancellorsville Campaign, Rollin would come his closest yet to sacrificing his life for his country.

HOOKER'S INTENT

Throughout the long winter months, the enemies virtually glared at each other across the Rappahannock River. Lee's army was parked in the heights above Fredericksburg. The Federals were camped near White Oak Church, comfortably out of range of Confederate artillery. Pickets catching sight of their opposites across the river must have wondered when they would next be firing their muskets at each other. Over these dreary wet days and as his army slowly healed, Major General Joe Hooker fine-tuned his strategy to attack the enemy and turn the tide of the war to the North's favor. In so doing, he believed, he would earn his place as perhaps the most talented military mind in the war the country was fighting against itself. As a comrade of Rollin's observed in early April 1863: "Hooker evidently believes himself to be Lee's superior in all that goes to make a successful general."[1]

Not unlike Burnside's failed plan, Hooker's scheme was based on a wide flanking maneuver designed to force a fight-or-flee decision by General Lee. If Lee chose to fight, the battle would be on ground of Hooker's choosing. If Lee chose to flee, Hooker would punish the retreating Confederate forces as they withdrew to Richmond, the bosom of the Confederacy. Though success of his plan was premised on the element of surprise, Hooker was apparently unable to contain his exuberance about his masterwork and divulged its contours within earshot of a comrade in the 27th NY Volunteers . . . who dutifully forwarded it to his hometown newspaper. On April 16, 1863, three days after Union cavalry broke camp and galloped off to carry out their part of Hooker's campaign, the *Dansville Advertiser* published this synopsis:

> Here is the plan according to words from his own mouth: the army will move quietly and very rapidly some 30 miles upriver, cross and make a wide detour so as to avoid obstructed roads, and then come up to the enemy in his rear . . . Not a single baggage or supply wagon is to go with us. All the ammunition and supplies are to be carried by pack mules, and the officers and soldiers will carry their own blankets and shelters. (The rebels did this method of movement last summer.) Our general is very imprudent in divulging this, but he is enthusiastic and in earnest.[2]

Hooker's original plan was for the infantry to leave on the heels of the cavalry after they departed camp. Major General George Stoneman would cross his newly reorganized 10,000-man cavalry far upstream on the Rappahannock, head west hugging Brandy Station and Culpepper Court House, and then swing widely around Confederate forces, eventually cutting southeast toward Richmond. The cavalrymen's mission was to create havoc as they rode, turning Confederate logistics into chaos by severing telegraph and rail lines. Like pheasants in the brush, Lee's army would thereby be flushed from their fortifications and forced to contend with Hooker's infantry, which would by then be mobilized.

Instead, drenching storms dictated the terms of the federal assault. On April 13, the Rappahannock River's churning rush of water pronounced completion of the cavalry's movement across it impossible. Consequently, the following day, the infantry, bearing rations and ammunition, was ordered to stand down. While central Virginia dried out a bit, the Commanding General of the Army of the Potomac revised his plan to now account for synchronous movement of his cavalry and infantry. Retaining a highly visible corps along the Rappahannock River to hold the attention of the enemy, Hooker would lead the bulk of his men north around Lee's forces as Stoneman simultaneously agitated the Confederates along their previously ordered route of sabotage. Meanwhile, a corps would cross the Rappahannock below Fredericksburg. The Rebel army would thereby be helplessly squeezed from the west and the east in Union pincers.

So Far, So Good

On April 27, 1863, the Commanding General relaunched his campaign. Hooker, joining the movement to manage the flanking maneuver more directly, ordered the 5th, 11th, and 12th Corps to begin marching northwest. The men would arc toward Chancellorsville, a convenient crossroad of the old Orange Turnpike and Ely's Ford Road, where they would descend on the enemy from the west. The three corps of some 42,000 men, led by 12th Corps Commander Major General Henry Slocum, crossed the Rappahannock River far upstream at Kelly's Ford and then made their way south to cross the Rapidan River, an offshoot of the Rappahannock, at Ely's and Germanna Fords. The plan depended upon speed and secrecy, which, against the odds, Slocum achieved.

The afternoon of April 30, 1863, 5th Corps Commander Major General George Meade and 12th Corps Commander Slocum converged their advance forces at Chancellorsville, pleased with their progress. Thus far, they had met only surmountable resistance from Jeb Stuart's Confederate cavalry, and their stride had not been broken. Exhilarated by their forward momentum, the generals were anxious to keep moving. They had wrapped around the Rebel left flank and were now facing the Confederate rear. If they pushed on, Lee's army could soon be caught in the Union Army vice. Hooker's plan was working.

Meade's and Slocum's jaws dropped when Hooker called a halt to the advance that afternoon. Hooker reasoned that there was time to hold while the trailing elements of each of their corps caught up at Chancellorsville. In Hooker's view, all the pieces in the chess match were to be placed where he intended them.

BACK IN FREDERICKSBURG

Major General John Sedgwick led the operations from the east with his 6th Corps, and for a time, the 1st Corps. After crossing the Rappahannock below Fredericksburg, their mission was to sweep up the Confederate right flank and funnel Lieutenant General Stonewall Jackson's men into Hooker's trap. The 3rd Corps and one division of the 2nd would remain in camp near Falmouth. Their role as reserve was to play the charade that they were actually the whole of the Army of the Potomac for the Rebel eyes trained on them from the other side of the river.

Consistent with the demand for stealth, Sedgwick initiated the movement of his men one day after Hooker's 42,000 men dropped out of sight on April 27. Rollin and his comrades in the 27th NY Volunteers said farewell to their homely huts and were on the move by 3 p.m. while rain, as seemed the custom for movements, fell on them. Reaching an area approximately one mile back from the Rappahannock River, near to where they last crossed the river and where they were to once again cross, the regiment halted in the early evening and waited for comrades who were on picket duty to arrive. Around 10 p.m., a staff officer read the plans of attack to the regiment as they stood in line: "Our division is all that is to cross at this point at present. The pontoon boats are to be unloaded and carried down to the river by the men, as it is feared the rattling of the wagon train would be heard by the enemy."[3] Hooker was keeping to his previewed logistics plan. Manpower over conveyances.

William Westervelt, Rollin's friend and tentmate, recalled the nighttime operation. He reported: "At 1am, we were called into line and marched to our pontoon train. Here, as many as could take hold of the side of a boat were placed on each side, and picking up the boat, we started for the river."[4] The men performed their pack mule duties well and delivered their cargo to water's edge under cover of darkness. Westervelt critiqued that by "some misunderstanding of orders" the regiment remained immobile in the dark, peering over to the other side of the river, waiting futilely for the orders to cross. He continued: "I don't pretend to know where rests the responsibility of delaying us until it was light enough for the enemy to use us for target practice; but it looked like criminal imbecility somewhere for we were all ready to go several hours before we were ordered."[5]

Finally, at daybreak, the first pontoons hit the water. Third Brigade Commander David A. Russell pushed his men out first. From Bartlett's brigade, the 27th NY staged as the next to cross. Russell's men had the advantage of a heavy fog to cloak their passage across the river. When they approached the opposite shore and emerged from the mist, however, Rebel pickets showered them with fire. Rollin and his comrades quickly dove onto their bellies as musket balls flew across the river toward them. Brigade companions, the 16th NY Volunteers, fired a volley high enough to pass over the heads of the 27th NY and drove back the enemy pickets long enough for Russell's men to disembark.[6]

The boats paddled back across the river, and Rollin and his comrades leapt aboard. Jammed in like sardines in a can, the men found it nearly impossible to return the fire directed at them by reemerging enemy pickets. Splashing onto shore, the men gazed upward at the twenty-foot bank before them. In a frenzy, the men grabbed at any vegetation they could to help hoist themselves up the embankment as the enemy shot wildly at the approaching threat. At the crest, the regiment made short shrift of dislodging the 21st Mississippi from their rifle pits, taking many of them as prisoners. But the morning's operation had cost the regiment: two soldiers were killed, several wounded, and two men had drowned when they fell overboard during the crossing.[7]

With Russell's skirmish line pushed forward approximately one mile, Rollin and his comrades occupied the Rebel rifle pits and performed overwatch as a volunteer engineer regiment and a regular engineer regiment competed for who would complete their bridge first. In a little over one hour, both spans were in place, and the remainder of Brooks's division began to cross the Rappahannock River. Completing Sedgwick's corps, Brigadier General Albion P. Howe's 2nd Division and Major General John Newton's 3rd made the crossing the evening of April 29 and moved upriver toward Fredericksburg.

That afternoon, Rollin and his comrades heard occasional cannonading downriver from Bartlett's 2nd Brigade, in the vicinity of Commander Major General John F. Reynold's 1st Corps. Other than the patter of raindrops falling from around 3 p.m., all was quiet to the front of the 27th NY Volunteers. They moved out from the rifle pits and returned their tents to their original purpose. The men sheltered within until after dark, and then sloshed their way back to the rifle pits in the inky darkness. With bare hands, tin plates, and some shovels, the men of the 27th NY Volunteers worked through the night to transition the perspective of the rifle pits to the opposite direction. And then they laid down in the mud and the harassing rainstorm and tried to rest as they waited for dawn.

The morning of April 30th was just as miserable as the night before. Soaked, Rollin and the regiment waited behind the rifle pits to hear the edict that would bring them more directly into the fight. Meanwhile, the Commander of the Army of the Potomac, fixated on his ruse, was focused on ensuring that all his command were in their designated positions, ready to give a compelling performance. Hooker ordered two bridges be taken up and sent to Banks' Ford, northwest of Fredericksburg and directly north of Salem Church, to facilitate additional corps joining his bulging amassed force.[8]

Around noon, an order from the Commanding General eased some anxiety in the regiment. As the men stood quietly in line, a staff officer read Hooker's message, General Orders No. 47: "The operations of the last three days have determined that our enemy must either ingloriously fly, or come out from behind his defenses and give us battle on our own ground, where certain destruction awaits him. The operations of the 5th, 11th, and 12th Army Corps have been a succession of splendid achievements."[9] The regiment's fears of meeting the same fate as martyred comrades who in December desperately and futilely tried to push their way up to Marye's Heights, was tempered. Their battle, they surmised, would be on the plain.

In the unfolding darkness on April 30, the men of the 27th NY Volunteers were set free from their stasis; they took their turn on picket duty. Their line advanced over familiar terrain—near to the ravine where they had spent days immobile as waves of their fellow Yankees were felled during Burnside's disastrous Fredericksburg Campaign. The men squinted into the night and listened. The clanking and shuffling and muffled voices suggested they were eavesdropping on the Confederate withdrawal from the position held to devastating effect against the Union forces in December. But to their surprise, dawn revealed their enemy had gone nowhere; the Rebels were visible moving about on the heights. The hours slowly ticked by as Rollin and his comrades expected to be on the receiving end of Confederate fire, but daylight was snuffed out without either side shooting at the other. After the 32nd NY crept through the dark to relieve them, Rollin and his comrades retired back to the rifle pits and collapsed into sleep.

DOUBLE BLUFF

Hooker's plans for May 1, 1863, had been for 6th Corps Commander Sedgwick to pantomime a show of strength as a distraction while the Commanding General's now congregated forces resumed their stealthy flanking maneuver around General Lee's men. The orders, which Sedgwick received at 5 p.m., called for the demonstration to commence at 1 p.m. and be, "as severe as possible without being an attack, to assume a threatening attitude, and maintain it until further orders."[10] Just as Sedgwick had completed rushed preparations to comply with the order despite the appointed hour for showtime having passed, he received word that Hooker had countermanded the order. For the 6th Corps commander, May 1 was just a frustrating precursor to the erratic orders yet to be received from his superior. For Sedgwick's men, the day of idleness stoked their anticipation of the fight to come.

The Confederate Army, on the other hand, contrary to convincing outward appearances on Marye's Heights, had indeed been on the move, as Rollin and his fellow picketers sensed. By the evening of April 30, the Confederate Commanding General had gleaned enough intelligence from cavalry commander Jeb Stuart and local informants to deduce that Hooker was playing a shell game with his men. Division Commander Richard Anderson deployed westward from Fredericksburg as a precautionary measure while Lee cogitated on incoming information. Anderson aligned his 8,500 men as a tripwire cutting across the old Orange Turnpike Road (the main east-west artery leading to Fredericksburg) and added to the intelligence haul while Lee organized the rest of his plan.

The Confederate general devised a bluff within Hooker's bluff. Facing a force over double the size of his own, Lee determined to leverage his superior knowledge of the terrain, agility of his smaller force, and his own ruse to better the unwitting Union forces. Lee sought to use the contours of Hooker's own plan against him by similarly dividing his forces and mirror-imaging intent. Attention-grabbing decoys in Fredericksburg would portray Confederate inertia while the bulk of his forces slipped undetected around the enemy's flank to attack.

In the predawn hours of May 1, Confederate Lieutenant General Stonewall Jackson left behind Jubal Early's division, William Barksdale's brigade of Lafayette McLaws's division, and the Washington Artillery, along with part of the Reserve Artillery, to hold the heights and confront Union soldiers to the south of Fredericksburg. Jackson made haste to link the remainder of his command with Anderson's prepositioned force west of Fredericksburg. Upon arrival, two hours of daylight already passed, Jackson shoved McLaws's and Anderson's men westward to intercept Union troops from nearing the Confederate rear. Marching in roughly parallel routes, McLaws advanced on the old Orange Turnpike and Anderson on the Orange Plank Road toward Chancellorsville.

With no pangs of urgency, Hooker finally sprang lose the 5th and 12th Corps around 11 a.m. on May 1 to continue eastward toward Fredericksburg. The Federals favored the same routes as the Confederates to carry out their mission. George Sykes's division of Meade's 5th Corps marched eastward on the Turnpike, and Henry Slocum's 12th Corps on the Plank Road. (The rest of Meade's corps headed northeastward on River Road toward Banks' Ford on the Rappahannock.) Before noon on May 1, 1863, the armies collided with each other on these two travel lanes, and a bloody brawl ensued in the entangling thicket of the Wilderness. Though the Rebels held the element of surprise, Slocum's and Sykes's men drove them back toward their defensive line near Mott's Run. At the same time, Meade's men on River Road were making steady progress and reaching a point where they were within striking distance of Lee's newly positioned flank.

Then, for the second day in a row, Hooker's subordinate corps commanders, eager to lead their men into a winnable battle, were flummoxed by Hooker's orders. Hooker, apparently afflicted with self-doubt from the shock of being outfoxed by Lee, panicked and ordered his army to withdraw back to Chancellorsville to regroup. Major General Daniel E. Sickles, having crossed his 3rd Corps over the redeployed pontoons, had arrived in Chancellorsville with his men around noon. Unfortunately for 6th Corps Commander John Sedgwick, being twelve miles out of sight apparently meant being out of mind; Hooker left Sedgwick still scrambling to perform a pointless charade hours after he had ordered the withdrawal of the rest of his forces.

Lee was as dumbfounded by Hooker's withdrawal as were the Union officers charged with carrying out the orders. The withdrawal seemed illogical, given that the Federals had regained the upper hand after the surprise confrontation in the morning. Lee was left to speculate what his counterpart was planning. The Confederate commander knew he must regain the initiative quickly to either capitalize on Union indecisiveness or to thwart a reorganized assault on the Rebel lines—but he needed more information before setting his course. In the meantime, Confederate forces wasted little time in filling the void left by the retreating Federals and swept northward to occupy whatever high ground had been vacated. The Union and Confederate forces established their new lines by late afternoon on May 1, 1863.

A DAY OF REALIGNMENT

Early the next morning, the sun winking down upon them, the 27th NY Volunteers were jolted out of their reverie by Confederate shells slashing through the air. While the earth convulsed and formed craters in their midst, Rollin and his comrades quickly packed up and dashed forward to a more protected position. For hour after hour, the sheltered men listened to the sounds of war drifting toward them from the west—primarily booming artillery but also, at times, the crackling of muskets. Tensely, they awaited orders to join the fight.

May 2, 1863, was a day of repositioning, both physically and strategically. The day before, Hooker had brimmed with self-admiration when he ordered his men forward to implement his devious plan of attack against the Confederate flank. When he discovered that he had pushed his men into a trap, Hooker's instincts were to pull his forces in closer (safety in numbers) and to bring in reinforcements as soon as possible. First Corps Commander Major General John F. Reynolds belatedly received the order to move his men from their position next to Rollin and his comrades on the south side of the Rappahannock to the far right of Hooker's line at Chancellorsville; they began the movement at dawn. By the afternoon of May 2, the 6th Corps was the only corps left near Fredericksburg that Hooker could draw to Chancellorsville to bolster his numbers. Sixth Corps Commander John Sedgwick spent the day untangling orders from the top to fulfill his duty to obey the spirit, if not the letter, of Hooker's orders. (Confusion reigned even from the start of the day. With the sun beating on his back, Sedgwick had been handed the orders to take up all the bridges at Franklin's crossing and below before daylight.[11])

Hooker spent the overnight hours of May 1 convincing himself that he was following the most prudent course of action given the fallibility of the intelligence he had used to construct his offensive. Meanwhile, Lee huddled with his primary lieutenant Stonewall Jackson to plot his next move. That evening, cavalry commander Jeb Stuart galloped into the Confederate headquarters near the intersection of Orange Plank and Furnace Roads with the key to

Lee's quandary. Though Hooker's line was anchored on the left by the Rappa-hannock River, their right flank trailed for a couple miles or so out along the old Orange Turnpike. The right was exposed and ripe for attack.

Depending on local guides to divine a route, Lee set Jackson loose to cir-cumvent the Union bulge around Chancellorsville using paths unknown to Union scouts. Jackson stripped Lee of 30,000 infantry and artillerymen when his corps started out on their twelve-mile march in the early morning light on May 2. This left Lee approximately 14,000 men—Anderson's and McLaws's divisions—to distract and occupy the Federals while Jackson hustled his men through the countryside. They moved as quickly and soundlessly as possible for a mass of men that size but were nonetheless spotted as they swept by Union artillerists atop Hazel Grove less than a mile away.

Hooker was informed by mid-morning of the Rebel movement and shared the intelligence with 11th Corps Commander Major General Oliver Otis Howard, whose men were the danglers at the far right of Hooker's line. Around 1 p.m., hours after Union scouts detected the Confederate column, Hooker permitted 3rd Corps Commander Dan Sickles (a favored subordinate of Hooker's) to follow up artillery fire with infantry pursuit.

Sickles ordered a brigade to advance against what was by then Jackson's tail. Near to Catherine Furnace (which gave the road its name), they clashed with the Georgia regiment that Jackson had tasked with serving as the shield for the rest of his column. The fighting whet Sickles's appetite and was a hindrance for Jackson. Both generals impatiently pushed troops toward the other. Sickles excit-edly ordered more of his men south to chase what he believed was the retreating Confederate Army, and as the fighting wore on, requested assistance from 11th Corps Commander Howard as right flank reinforcement for the assault. When Howard dropped a brigade south to fulfill the request to join Sickles near Cath-erine Furnace, he created a hole some two miles wide in the Union defensive line—an irresistible opening for the Rebels in the coming hours.

Hooker believed he had compensated for the gap created when Sickles's and Howard's men surged south to bag the retreating Confederates. He er-roneously thought the 1st Corps would have been easing into place alongside the remainder of the 11th Corps by then. Further, Hooker likely assumed Howard would have done more to bolster defenses around his flank than pivot three regiments and a couple of cannons to face westward after being admon-ished that morning to take precautionary measures.

Hooker's priorities the afternoon of May 2, 1863, were twofold. First, his army must dispense with what he believed to be Lee's rearguard (the 14,000 or so men left behind to puff themselves out to army proportions for Union attention). That engagement resonated across the miles and was audible from the 27th NY Volunteers' position. Second, Hooker was focused on planning his massive blow against the retreating Confederates set for the following day. Of course, Sickles's actions to thin Confederate ranks that afternoon were to be applauded, but Hooker confidently told his army that day was just a precursor to the retribution the Army of the Potomac would deliver to Lee's men on the morrow. One of Rollin's comrades exclaimed in a letter home: "The 6th Corps were in a furor of excitement over gratifying news from the right by Hooker that the enemy were fleeing for their lives! Sickles and Couch [2nd Corps Commander whose men were scrapping with Lee's] were in pursuit, and Sedgwick to follow at early dawn!"[12] The Commanding General's indulgence in wishful thinking was shattered before sunset.

Report after report of increasing activity in the woods to the west of Hooker's right flank, the 11th Corps, fell on deaf ears the afternoon of May 2, 1863. The rustling in the Wilderness brush grew more pronounced, and the messages from regimental commanders of an imminent attack more urgent, but each envoy was rebuffed by 11th Corps Commander Howard. Howard reasoned that the terrain to their west was impregnable, and besides, Hooker had declared that the enemy was in the process of retreating. (See figure 13.1.)

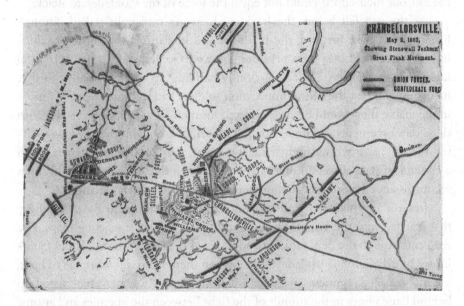

FIGURE 13.1 Map of the Battlefield of Chancellorsville, May 2, showing Stonewall Jackson's Great Flank Movement by Robert Knox Sneden. Library of Congress, Geography and Map Division.

By early evening, however, the Commander of the Army of the Potomac was desperately struggling to stem the tidal wave of terrified men from crashing further through his defensive line. Just as most of the 11th Corps were preparing their suppers, arms stacked, Stonewall Jackson's lead division—preceded by a flushing of all manner of game, and then the Rebel yell—plunged from the Wilderness. Jackson was anxious to commence the ambush while he still had daylight and so ordered Brigadier General Robert E. Rodes to attack despite his largest division (Major General A. P. Hill's) lagging behind the rest of the column. Jackson unleashed ferocious pandemonium around 5:15 p.m.

Though only two miles away, the accompanying wails of the Confederate rout of the 11th Corps did not initially reach Hooker's headquarters. Rather, it was the horrific sight of soldiers fleeing for their lives, rushing across the Chancellorsville clearing, that shook the Union Commanding General into action. Hooker directed reserve artillery be repositioned to face westward and that the 2nd and 12th Corps block the fugitive flow to restore order. (Some of the deserters who flung their way down the turnpike through the lines to the east dropped into Confederate Major General McLaws's division only to be captured.) Eleventh Corps Commander Howard leapt onto his horse to rally his fleeing troops and implore them not to panic. Some units did valiantly answer the call, but their efforts could not equal the force of the Confederate attack.

As the sun fell below the horizon, Jackson's onslaught stalled. Though he urged his men forward, the brambles and bedlam of the battle—including taking some 1,000 men prisoner—slowed Confederate impetus. Jackson knew that the Yankees must be furiously building up defenses against further incursion and that the more time Union soldiers had to build them, the more impregnable they would be. A. P. Hill and his men were Jackson's answer. With these reinforcements and under the full moon, Jackson considered reinvigorating the offensive with a night raid. Impatient, the Confederate general with a handful of staff officers pushed his way through the shadows to do his own reconnaissance before proceeding. This was a transformative decision.

Jackson and his party cantered eastward along Mountain Road, a byway that reached into the Union position and was invisible on existing maps. The road cut through the dense thicket and bisected Brigadier General James Lane's jittery North Carolina brigade. Earlier, when there were still whispers of light, a Union cavalry regiment and then a Union infantry regiment percolated up behind Lane's lines in the tumult of the fight between the enemies and against the Wilderness. With frayed nerves, Lane's men stood an anxious vigil. Despite entreaties from his staff, Jackson, seeking confirmation that Hooker's men were indeed fortifying their positions, rode beyond Lane's battle line toward the 33rd North Carolina pickets in their front. Jackson heard enough to satisfy himself that his plan for the night attack should continue. He turned and began to retrace his route back along the Mountain Road.

By then, random musket pops at phantom Yankees had coalesced into a swell of gunfire that cut across Mountain Road.[13] Lieutenant General Stonewall Jackson, with the full moon at his back, was shot three times by members of the 18th North Carolina. Those of his staff that were not hit dodged the awakened Union artillery now pointed at their position to evacuate their wounded general to the rear for medical treatment. After enduring his withered arm being amputated, Jackson succumbed to pneumonia a week later. A. P. Hill, Jackson's second in command, was similarly caught in the fratricidal fire with his staff, but Hill's injury that night came from the Union artillery blasts. With the two top commanders of Lee's 2nd Corps incapacitated, leadership of the daring assault on Hooker's position around Chancellorsville that evening devolved to cavalryman Major General Jeb Stuart. Jackson's spooked men froze and waited for Stuart, hours away at Ely's Ford, to gallop in and assume command.

Sedgwick Is Drawn In

When Hooker realized Sedgwick's role south of Fredericksburg was pointless, he demanded Sedgwick's men as reinforcement immediately. Sedgwick received a message at 5:50 p.m. and another after 7 p.m. on May 2, 1863: the 6th Corps Commander was to "vigorously" pursue the enemy by the Bowling Green Road.[14] (This road runs in parallel to the Rappahannock River and leads into Fredericksburg city from the south.)

Sedgwick received the next communication from Hooker around 11 p.m. that evening. Clearly demonstrating mental mayhem on the heels of that evening's shocking blow, the Commander of the Army of the Potomac appeared confused about where his 6th Corps was and issued illogical commands. Hooker's order, written at 10:10 p.m., directed the 6th Corps commander to "cross the Rappahannock at Fredericksburg, immediately upon receipt of this order, and move in the direction of Chancellorsville until connected with the major general commanding; to attack and destroy any force on the road, and be in the vicinity of the general at daylight."[15] (Marye's Heights, which overlooked Fredericksburg, also commanded the route to Chancellorsville and would therefore need to be dealt with before Sedgwick could move his force westward.) All of Sedgwick's corps was by then on the south side of the Rappahannock at that point. Of course, to cross the river to only recross it to get back to the side the soldiers needed to be on to comply with the Commanding General's intent was nonsensical. Sedgwick's larger problem was Hooker's order to swashbuckle his way past enemy forces for twelve miles en route to rescue the six corps Hooker had congregated around Chancellorsville by dawn.

At 1 a.m. on May 3, 1863, Rollin and his comrades in the 27th NY Volunteers received the order to prepare to march. By 2 a.m., the entire 6th Corps was on the move. Newton's 3rd Division formed the right, Howe's 2nd Division took center, and Brooks's 1st Division assumed the left of Sedgwick's seven-mile battle line. Within an hour, musketry hissed a Rebel rebuke to the Union advance. Hooker, shuddering behind his barricade, sent a message to Sedgwick at 2:35 a.m. that morning reiterating his order to move with haste: "Everything in the world depends upon the rapidity and promptness of your movement. Push everything."[16] (See figure 13.2.)

Confederate Major General Jubal Early, left with only 10,000 men to wage a resistance against Sedgwick's 6th Corps, a force over twice as large as his own, had to make an educated guess where to concentrate his men. He wagered that the taint of the doomed Yankees splayed on Marye's Heights during former Commanding General Burnside's failed attack in December would convince Sedgwick to avoid a replay. Instead, Early theorized, Sedgwick's attack would come south of Fredericksburg near Prospect Hill where former 6th Corps Commander Franklin had successfully held Confederate forces at bay for a time during the December battle the year previous. Early therefore massed most of his force five miles south of the city opposite Brooks's division. He positioned only 1,000 or so men of the 18th and 21st Mississippi infantry regiments and several guns of the Washington Artillery atop Marye's Heights as a precaution.

Early guessed wrong. Third Division Commander Newton's advance was pushing its way northward, pressing back the Rebels defending Fredericksburg before daylight. While Confederate cannon from the heights were ablaze trying to repel the Union incursion, Newton's and Howe's men traipsed onward as the sun rose.

Seeking to draw Rebel attention to the south of Fredericksburg while Newton and Howe formed stronger assault columns, Brooks advanced his division and challenged Confederate strongholds to their front—including the Rebels' fortified position on the railroad at Hamilton's Crossing. At the same time, Union artillery blasted away at the slope leading up to Marye's Heights to persuade enemy artillery and infantry to remain under cover.

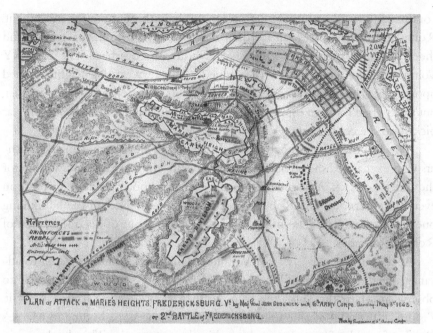

FIGURE 13.2   Map of the Battlefield, Second Battle of
Fredericksburg by Robert Knox Sneden. Library of
Congress, Geography and Map Division.

Anticipating the long day of battle ahead, the 27th NY slipped away to the
ravine they had occupied in December to prepare a hasty breakfast. As Rollin
and his comrades were finishing their humble meal, the ravine suddenly transformed into a death trap. Shells shrieked through the air. The Confederates had
trained a battery into the ravine, killing two and wounding about twenty of
the regiment before they had time to drop their cups.[17]

Rollin was one of the men injured. With "welcome home" parties planned
and his mother's pantry filling with favorite foods in anticipation of his return
from the war, Rollin was enveloped in the blast of a shell that detonated next
to him. Thrust to the ground by the force of the explosion, Rollin rose with a
debilitating concussion, and deaf in one ear, an affliction he would endure for
the rest of his life. Despite his fragile state, Rollin fought shoulder to shoulder
with his brethren in the 27th NY Volunteers for the remainder of their final
campaign.

The regiment had been readying to replace the 96th Pennsylvania Volunteers, on picket duty at the front, when the enemy artillery erupted in the
ravine. Recovering from the initial blast, the 27th NY lifted themselves up and

continued forward, enemy artillery plaguing them throughout the movement. Rollin and his comrades ran for their lives to a slight rise in the ground and then lay flat on their faces while shells whistled by overhead. The 27th NY Volunteers regimental history later added: "A battery on the heights opened upon us, and the range was directly on the colors. Most of the shells went over, but one passed through the flag, and cut out a star, leaving it whole; and it was picked up the color-bearer, A. L. VanNess."[18]

The regiment spent much of the day on their bellies supporting skirmishers who exchanged shots with their Confederate counterparts, and waiting for the order to attack. A talented Confederate sharpshooter made their position even more perilous. The Rebel strafed the regiment's line on the left, killing one and wounding several others before being shot out of his tree by one of Rollin's comrades.

As the men of the 27th NY Volunteers anxiously awaited the call to advance, given the terrain and their position on Brooks's line, they were able to observe and hear the unfolding scene to their right. It was a harrowing wait. Visions of the piles of blue uniformed bodies on the slope leading to Marye's Heights from the December raid hung in their memories. This day, however, would render a different outcome—eventually.

The Mississippians defending Marye's Heights fought fiercely to defend Fredericksburg and the heights above it for strategic reasons, but perhaps sentimental ones also: the thuggish trashing of this once gentile southern city by Union troops and Commanding General Burnside's artillery-bombardment rage in December still rankled. Barksdale's eight guns clustered in a half-mile span to the southern end of Marye's Heights and his infantry, stretched along the ridge and behind the stone wall at the foot of the Heights, were sufficient to disrupt initial Union charges. Sedgwick had to change his approach.

With Hooker's orders to "be in the vicinity of the general at daylight" imprinted on his mind, and it being well beyond sunrise, Sedgwick thrust two columns of soldiers through Fredericksburg to then confront Confederate defenses above it on the heights. Skirmishers to the front and a line of battle to the left, approximately 5,000 of Newton's men, knapsacks tossed aside, rushed up the parallel passages of Hanover Street and William Street toward Marye's Heights.[19] The fearsome mass of men moved swiftly but were easy targets for artillery and musket fire. The Federals suffered severe loses. Sedgwick's men were on the doorstep yet thwarted from even reaching the stonewall at the base of Marye's Heights.

With renewed determination, Newton's men gathered themselves up and, without stopping to fire, washed up the slope, over the stone wall, and into

FIGURE 13.3 Stonewall at Foot of Marye's Heights, Fredericksburg photographed by Andrew J. Russell. Library of Congress, Prints & Photographs Division, Civil War Photographs.

the Sunken Road behind it. As they descended into the road, the Federals fired at point-blank range, bayonets extended. And then, avenging their fallen comrades some four months earlier, Newton's men broke free and ascended the crest of Marye's Heights. Second Division Howe's men simultaneously charged the heights to the left (south) of the city, advancing over the open plain below the heights while under fearful fire. A comrade of Rollin's later exclaimed: "The divisions of Generals Newton and Howe swept forward . . . carrying line after line of rifle pits with the bayonet, capturing many prisoners, the horses, and all but two guns of the Washington Artillery, with a dash and gallantry that excited the greatest admiration from us as we witnessed the glorious spectacle."[20] (See figure 13.3.)

By noon on May 3, 1863, the battle was over. The Union flag flapped from the fortifications overcome on the ridge. The Federals turned the confiscated Rebel guns on their former owners and kept the overrun Confederates moving. But Sedgwick still had miles to go before reaching the vicinity of Chancellorsville; there was no time to pursue Early's overwhelmed men.

Newton's 3rd Division rolled onto the old Orange Turnpike Road, followed by Howe's 2nd Division. With the enemy withdrawn from their front, Brooks's 1st Division fell back and moved along the Rappahannock River into

Fredericksburg to join the rest of the 6th Corps. Rollin and his comrades in the 27th NY Volunteers, in conjunction with three regiments of Russell's brigade, remained in place as skirmishers until the rest of the division had moved up. Taking up the march around 3 p.m., they were the last of Sedgwick's men to arrive on Marye's Heights.[21] The casualties of the morning's desperate struggle lay strewn across their path as they advanced. Rebel fortifications were deserted except for defenders slumped over the earthworks, dead or wounded. At a discreet distance, Rebels followed Rollin and his comrades. (This still rankled the authors of the 27th NY regimental history twenty-five years later when it was published: "Our men [felt] all the time that it was a great mistake to take us all from the valley, and allow the enemy to come in our rear."[22]) But rather than shaking free their irksome tail, the 27th NY Volunteers were ordered to face westward and join the rest of the 6th Corps on the march.

It was perhaps not so much a march as a plod. Though the lead elements of Sedgwick's corps had a three-hour head start on Rollin and his comrades, they managed to advance only three miles or so before grinding to a halt. Major General Jubal Early's men were out of the way. Concerned about a Union advance on Richmond, he had rallied his men to form a blocking force along Telegraph Road, which ran from Fredericksburg south to the Confederate capital. Sedgwick's nemesis was instead the scrappy Confederate general who had been charged with checking possible Union crossings at Banks' Ford, northwest of Fredericksburg.

Brigadier General Cadmus Wilcox of Anderson's division was fidgety on May 3, 1863. On this bright warm day, the cacophony of the cannon beckoned him; he found the draw irresistible. Though he and his brigade of Alabamians did not arrive in time to join the battle on Marye's Heights, he took it upon himself to use his brigade to at least delay, if not halt, Sedgwick's advance toward Chancellorsville.

Wilcox positioned his men to cut perpendicularly across the turnpike on the high ground beyond the Marye plateau with a line of skirmishers at the front. And there both forces stood for a time, Confederate shell dropping on Sedgwick's column, and Federals jostling to organize their retort. As Union artillery was being brought into the dispute, First Division Commander Brooks, with J. J. Bartlett's brigade leading, took the advance and convinced Wilcox to pull back along the turnpike.

Unknown to the westward marching Federals, the low ridge where they would soon encounter a Baptist house of worship (the Salem Church) would be the undoing of their quest to reach Chancellorsville that day. Seeing the strength of the setting—elevated, backing onto woods, and advantageously

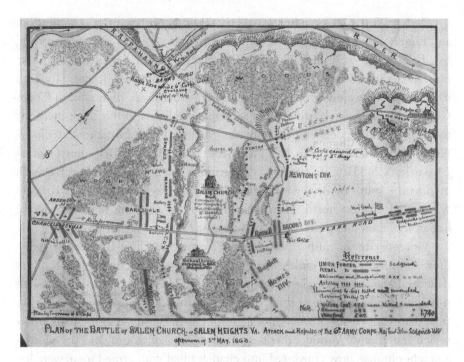

FIGURE 13.4 Map of the Battlefield of Salem Church by
Robert Knox Sneden. Library of Congress, Geography and
Map Division.

running at right angles to the old Orange Turnpike (also known as the Plank
Road)—Wilcox seized upon the position to establish his line of battle in anticipation of the approaching Union column. (See figure 13.4.)

For most of the afternoon, Wilcox, with his single brigade, had succeeded
in derailing the plans and momentum of an entire corps of the Army of the
Potomac. The May sun, which had no business beating down on the men as if
it were the thick of summer, was leaning toward the horizon before Wilcox received word of reinforcements. Upon learning of Sedgwick's movement west
to reunite with the rest of Hooker's army hunkered down at Chancellorsville,
General Lee had dispatched Major General Lafayette McLaws and his division to block the reunion. McLaws arrived just in time to neatly tuck his men
into place alongside Wilcox's Alabamians for the confrontation to come. The
newcomers filled out the flanks while Wilcox's five regiments stood astride
the turnpike—except for two companies of the 9th Alabama, who occupied
the Salem Church itself and a small schoolhouse less than 100 yards southeast
of the church.

Around 5 p.m., Confederate artillery was silent for want of ammunition, and Union cannonading paused to permit infantry, now in attack formation, to advance westward. First Division Commander Brigadier General Brooks now carried the weight of the crumbling Union campaign—Joseph Hooker's daring and discovered campaign of subterfuge—on his shoulders. Sixth Corps Commander Sedgwick had elected to employ only one of his three divisions to flush the Confederates free from the Salem Church bottleneck. Colonel Henry Brown's 1st brigade (the New Jersey brigade) and Brigadier General J.J. Bartlett's 2nd Brigade straddled the turnpike in a north-south line, Bartlett's men to the south of Brown's. Brigadier General David Russell's 3rd Brigade was posted furthest north. Their objective was to puncture the Confederate line in its center and push the Rebels from the path to Chancellorsville.

Confederate skirmishers, exchanging fire with each of Brooks's brigades, drew the unsuspecting Yankees back into the woods. A comrade of Rollin's described the merciless abuse the setting offered: "Our skirmishers pushed through the narrow belt of thick underbrush, in which grew some scattering trees that was in front of and concealed from us the abruptly rising bank upon which the enemy's intrenchments and strong line of troops, and the church and schoolhouse, now converted into citadels filled with armed men, were located. The force with which we had been contending strengthened ... awaited with confidence our assault."[23] Advancing into the woods, Russell's men and many in the New Jersey brigade tangled up in the unforgiving brush and halted when they met with a devastating hail of musketry from Rebels ready for them on high ground and hidden behind a hedgerow.

South of the turnpike, Bartlett recalled his skirmishers at the woods' edge and advanced his battle line, the pointy end of Brooks's spear. The 5th Maine anchored the left flank, the 96th Pennsylvania linked to their right, the 121st NY next, and then the 23rd New Jersey from Brown's brigade extended to the turnpike. The 16th NY Volunteers were positioned behind the 23rd NJ. The 27th NY Volunteers' transition from rearguard to advance did not happen in time for Bartlett to incorporate them into his battle line; Rollin and his comrades therefore did not participate directly in the fighting at Salem Church but rather served as an assembly point for regiments retiring from engagement.[24]

Cut to pieces by thorns and bullets, Bartlett's men pressed forward even as formations fell apart. They stepped over fallen comrades hidden in the underbrush. Colonel Emory Upton, with J.J. Bartlett galloping up to join him, led the 121st NY up the slope to the crest. His men surrounded the schoolhouse and captured the ensconced company of Wilcox's Alabamians.

The regiment, with the 23rd New Jersey not far behind, broke the 10th Alabama line directly behind the schoolhouse. The 8th Alabama, positioned south of the 10th, pivoted 90 degrees, and fired into Upton's flank while their comrades still in the church delivered destruction from the lower windows and the gallery of the house of worship. The 16th NY Volunteers, directed by Bartlett to, "double quick into the thicket on the right of the 23rd NJ," were similarly brutalized by the church-dwelling snipers—as well as the hedgerow shooters.[25] One of Rollin's comrades later lamented: "The 16th NY, who were to us like brothers, lost two-thirds of its numbers . . . and when on the eve of seeing loved ones at home."[26]

Already staggering from the onslaught, Upton's men were shred when Wilcox brought the remainder of the 9th Alabama into the fight. The regiment, held in reserve, emerged to decimate. Firing at murderously close range, the 9th thrust Upton's men back and then rescued their comrades from the schoolhouse, taking the former captors prisoner.

For nearly an hour, Bartlett's brigade, inserted deepest into the Confederate force, had stood its ground under appalling fire before reeling backward to the tollgate, about 1,000 yards east of the Salem Church on the turnpike. A comrade of Rollin's immortalized the 121st NY commander's bravery in the battle: "Upton, when the 121st NY left the field—strewn with their dead and wounded—borrowed a horse from one of Bartlett's aids because his was shot from under him, rallied all the stragglers and saved them from capture. He then galloped back to this old battery of Napoleons, assumed command, and ran pieces up to short range of the enemy, pouring broadside after broadside into their heavily massed columns."[27] Corps Commander Sedgwick, standing elbow-to-elbow with gunners at the tollgate, bellowed orders to them as they directed their fire on the enemy. Union artillery eventually convinced the pursuing Confederates to turn back to their lines.

In the deepening darkness of night, cannon fell silent and Rebel yells ceased. Sedgwick and his men lay in heaps on the ground beyond the tollgate, too anxious to answer the call of sleep. Rollin's buddy Westervelt recalled: "As the slaughter had been terrible, the stretcher bearers were busy all night caring for the wounded . . . all night long we could hear the grinding of the ambulance wheels, as they moved back and forth, filled with their bleeding, suffering loads of wounded. The dead were left unburied on the field."[28] Rollin lay in the stench-filled field of death and dying that night, nauseated and head throbbing from the concussion he had received earlier on that very long day, thinking about all of the trauma that was and not of the glory that was to have been.

TO THE RIVER—DOUBLE QUICK!

Called into line at 4 a.m. on May 4, 1863, the men of the 27th NY Volunteers shuffled their feet and gazed westward, trying to detect signs of Rebel movement as they waited for the sun to rise. A couple of hours later, having moved off to a nearby ravine, Rollin and his comrades realized they had been looking in the wrong direction. Overnight, Confederate Division Commander Lafayette McLaws had swung two of his brigades around to the left and rear of Bartlett's brigade. From their new position, Confederate artillery fired off a few shells into the ravine, sending the men of the 27th diving to the ground. The regiment was soon drawn up into line of battle, now facing south, and deployed as skirmishers across all of Brooks's front, and pushing toward the Confederate lines. The two sides immediately had a short sharp exchange of musketry before the Rebel skirmishers pulled back, leaving the men of the 27th to watch and wait and listen. Each side was exhausted. It would not be until early evening that the men of the 27th NY Volunteers would fully feel the fruits of that Confederate labor.

General Robert E. Lee, again dividing his army to meet the opportunity the enemy presented, intended to pull the noose tight and squeeze Sedgwick's corps across—or better yet into—the river. Lee shifted his troops to encircle the 6th Corps. Right around the time Rollin was getting shelled in the ravine this day, Jubal Early was marching his division back north to reoccupy Marye's Heights. Early swept in without opposition, though 2nd Division Commander John Gibbon of the 2nd Corps maintained possession of Fredericksburg city itself. In retaking the Heights, Early cut off Sedgwick's communication lines via Fredericksburg to the barricaded Commanding General of the Army of the Potomac at Chancellorsville. And, by 11 a.m., Major General Anderson had marched his division from Chancellorsville and filled the gap in the Confederate line between McLaws's and Early's men. Lee left Stuart with what had been Stonewall Jackson's command, now numbering some 25,000 men, to intimidate Hooker's corralled six corps of approximately 75,000 soldiers while he joined his commanders near Salem Church to dispense with Sedgwick.

Clearly, Gibbon's lonely presence would not be an adequate shield for Sedgwick if he were forced to withdraw the 6th Corps to the north side of the Rappahannock. With Marye's Heights' perfect positioning for artillery, Sedgwick knew his men would be stopped in their tracks should he try a route through Fredericksburg. Sedgwick's prescience the day before to instruct his rear forces to extend northward toward Banks' Ford on the river would prove to save the corps; they had one route of escape. Like Hooker's command then surrounding the US Ford, Sedgwick's lines formed a protective horseshoe shape around Banks' and Scott's Fords. The 27th NY Volunteers faced southeast at the toe of the shoe.

Lee's assault plan on Sedgwick's command was not overly complex: at the sound of three cannon shots, Early would attack from the southeast and simultaneously Anderson would launch his assault from the south; McLaws would follow from the west.[29] Unfortunately for the Confederate commander, communicating the plot proved to be. Sedgwick had arrayed his forces so that the old Orange Turnpike, the key thoroughfare cutting east/west, was encompassed within his lines. This left the Confederate messengers to pick their paths through the countryside to reach each of the three division commands with coordination instructions.

Finally, just before 6 p.m., the Rebel infantry made its move on the 6th Corps—Confederate artillery had commenced shelling Sedgwick's lines about an hour previous. As skirmishers for Bartlett's brigade, the 27th NY Volunteers faced Brigadier General Ambrose R. Wright's Georgians from Anderson's division and Brigadier General Robert F. Hoke's North Carolinians from Early's division. Rollin and his comrades released the fury that had built up inside them after witnessing the devastation wrought on their brothers in Bartlett's brigade the day before. The regiment repulsed enemy assaults three times in the dimming light on May 4, 1863. A comrade of Rollin's recalled: "The boys of the 27th took advantage of every place of shelter on the skirmish line, from which to deliver an accurate and rapid fire, while the artillery smashed and scattered the advancing columns. At the enemy's hesitation and confusion, our skirmishers cried out: Come on Johnnie, do come over and see us!"[30] Their attackers withdrew into the woods and reconfigured into line of battle. And then the Rebel forces did come back. All along Sedgwick's line, the enemy pushed and shoved toward the Rappahannock River.

Creeping darkness and an accompanying veil of fog set in. Confederate Commanding General Lee grew increasingly irritated as the momentum of the Rebel assault faltered. Was this chance to destroy the 6th Corps—hopefully as a precursor to thrashing the rest of the Army of the Potomac—slipping through his fingers? Though not the victory Lee envisioned, the Confederates had succeeded, however, in compressing the 6th Corps to the point where Sedgwick had no choice. To save his corps, his men must be retracted from the battlefield.

With rumors ringing in their ears of Confederate sharpshooters leading an advance of skirmishers toward them, Rollin and his comrades received the order to fall back around 9 p.m. Still on the skirmish line at the rear of the corps, following this command was easier said than done. The Rebel yell taunting them, the men of the 27th NY Volunteers were forced to fight and withdraw concurrently. For two or three miles, the front rank fell back while the rear loaded and fired at the flash of enemy guns, and then the rear rank (now at the front) passed to the rear. By so occupying the pursuing Rebels, the 27th created time and space for other units to reach the river.

When the regiment rallied and fell into line to march the rest of the way to the shore, they reported one dead and one wounded. Division Commander Brooks sent an order back for the regiment to double-quick or they would be lost. Tapping whatever reserves they had within themselves, the men, sweating from the retreat maneuver and the swelter of a steamy day, cast aside knapsacks and other burdens to quicken their pace. The 27th NY Volunteers regimental history soberly noted: "It seems that we had been left far in the rear to cover the retreat, with the expectation that the whole regiment would be obliged to surrender on the best terms it could."[31] But they did reach the river.

Hurling themselves behind rifle pits on the heights between Banks' and Scott's Fords, Rollin and his comrades lay exhausted. Involuntarily nodding off occasionally, the men awaited the order to cross while enemy shells soared toward them, never quite hitting their intended targets. Omnipresent Confederate Brigadier General Wilcox had tramped his men back to the hills above Banks' Ford and participated in the shelling after capturing thirteen officers and over 200 men on the heights.[32] He and his men were back on familiar terrain.

Sixth Corps Commander Sedgwick, anxious to deliver his men to the safety of the north side of the Rappahannock River that night, endured hours of conflicting, incoherent messages from Hooker. Sedgwick reported that finally, "on Tuesday, the 5th, at 2am, I received the order of the commanding general to withdraw from my position, cross the river, take up the bridge, and cover the ford. The order was immediately executed . . . When the last of the column was on the bridge, I received a dispatch from the commanding general countermanding the order to withdraw."[33] Sedgwick ignored the last dispatch received. To do otherwise would have forced his men to recross the river while the sun illuminated them as easy targets for enemy artillery. It would have been a suicide mission. Rollin and his comrades in Bartlett's brigade were the last of the 6th Corps to cross to safety. This same night, Brigadier General Gibbon slid his men back across the river to Stafford Heights.

After stumbling about one mile back from the river, Rollin and his comrades went into camp and crumbled. They were, as the 27th regimental history said, "a thoroughly used up army."[34] When the morning dawned on May 5, 1863, enemy artillery from the south side of the river probed in search of the Union camp but was unable to locate it through the dense forest. While the Confederates on the south side of the river spent the day scavenging the castasides of the hastily retreating 6th Corps, the men of the 27th NY Volunteers remained in camp and slept and conjectured where the primary fault lay for this failing—if not failed—campaign.

They woke up the next day soggy and cold. A drenching rain, which would have the men in its grip for three days, set in the night before. Despite feeling the effects of his concussion, Rollin was able to summon his strength on that day, May 6, 1863, to write to his father and assuage his loved ones' fears: he had survived this last campaign of his enlistment. (See figures 13.5 and 13.6.)

Stafford Heights Va
May 6th 1863

Dear Father

We re-crossed the river yesterday morning a defeated army. After four days of fighting, we took the hills back of Fredericksburg, but the enemy, being reinforced, attacked us on the afternoon of the 4th and "compelled" us to fall back to this side. Our loss is very heavy. We done the most desperate fighting in charging the hill and attempting to hold it that I ever saw. When we took the hill, we captured nine pieces of artillery, large quantities of ammunition, and some horses and prisoners.

Up to this time we hear nothing from Hooker's forces which crossed at the upper fords, but suppose he is falling back to this side of the river.

It is my opinion this is the worst whipping we ever took, though we were successful the first three or four days.

I am not seriously injured but am somewhat nervous and light headed from the concussion of a shell which burst altogether too near my head to be pleasant. A little rest will sit me all right.

It has been raining hard for the last twelve hours with prospect of continuance through the day.

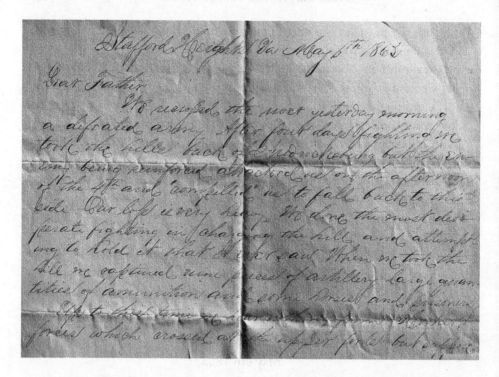

FIGURE 13.5   Letter to Rollin's Father on May 6, 1863.

I will write again when I get rested. I received a letter from Clara yesterday. Please let me hear from you soon.

Your aff son
Rollin B. Truesdell

That this final engagement was such a deadly rout of the Union was evident in Rollin's letter to his father. It laid bare the sense that a commander of the Army of the Potomac had failed his men yet again. Rollin and his comrades in the 6th Corps could only speculate why Hooker with his six corps nearby did not come to their aid two days earlier. What happened to the plan to "compel the enemy to ingloriously fly"?

HOOKER'S IMPLOSION

Were Rollin and his comrades to be apprised of the magnitude and circumstances of the Union loss under Hooker's leadership as it was happening, Rollin's words likely would have been harsher in his letter home on May 6. While

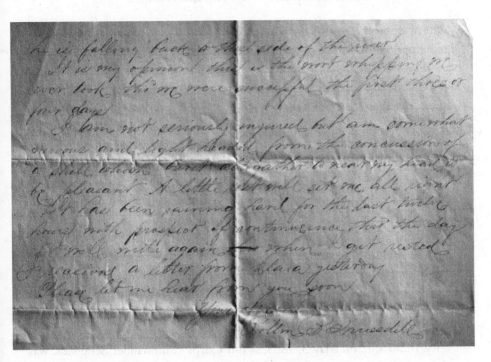

FIGURE 13.6 Letter to Rollin's Father on May 6, 1863.

the 6th Corps was conquering Marye's Heights on May 3, Hooker's devasted command was already nestled behind enhanced entrenchments cradling the US Ford on the Rappahannock River. With a fateful pre-dawn decision that day, Joseph Hooker sealed the outcome of his Chancellorsville Campaign.

The Commanding General ordered the 3rd Corps to retire from its perch atop Hazel Grove, the perfect high ground for artillerists, to a new line at Fairview Hill that was closer to the Chancellor House and the rest of Hooker's command. As the last of Major General Daniel Sickles's infantry and artillery were moving off the hilltop, the sun was peaking over the horizon, and so too was Confederate General Jeb Stuart's advance. Shortly after the Rebels lit the skies with shells targeting Fairview Hill, Union guns returned the favor. Though the federal artillery did not have the optimal positioning for the morning's battle, the Yankees did have more guns, and they kept them blazing—until they ran out of ammunition.

Confederate Second Corps Commander Stuart had grabbed the reins left dangling by the incapacitated Stonewall Jackson and drove his men to attack just as fervently as his predecessor. Gray uniforms washed through the

Wilderness, pushing from the west and the northwest toward Chancellorsville before 5 a.m. Intent to bridge the three miles between his and General Lee's forces as quickly as possible, Stuart's attack was direct and overwhelming. Confederate infantrymen first encountered Union 3rd and 12th Corps soldiers, many in wait behind entrenchments—just as Jackson had foreseen. The fighting was fierce and inconclusive. Each side gained ground and then lost it several times. When Hooker ordered a counterattack using Major General French's 3rd Division of the 2nd Corps to left-hook Stuart's freshly reinforced troops, the Rebels staggered backward. But then the Wilderness interceded. The Union offensive was checked, and the rhythm of charge and countercharge continued. The bloodbath ensued.

Around 9 a.m., Stuart called in his last reserve division. Though the costs would be catastrophic, unlike the Commander of the Army of the Potomac, Stuart plunged into the battle never contemplating leaving soldiers in the wings who could help effect victory. Confederate Generals Anderson's and McLaws's assaults from the south and southeast complemented Stuart's attack plan to put crippling pressure on Hooker.

By 10:30 a.m. on May 3, 1863, as 6th Corps Commander Sedgwick was orchestrating the raid on Fredericksburg, Joe Hooker, delirious, had relinquished Fairview and Chancellorsville and was in retreat. Amid the heaviest fighting, the Commanding General, standing on the porch of his headquarters at Chancellorsville to observe his unfolding defeat, was smashed to the ground when a shell hit the column he was leaning against. Hooker lay on the floor, concussed and unconscious. When he revived, Hooker was confused and obstinate. Though unable to think clearly and in great pain, he refused to delegate authority to 2nd Corps Commander Darius Couch, the second-in-command. Adding insult to his able subordinates, he rebuffed 5th Corps Commander Meade's and 1st Corps Commander Reynolds's entreaties to be brought into the fight. During this leadership vacuum, the Union position on Fairview Hill crumbled. Union artillerists were picked off and their ammunition supplies ran dry. Once Fairview folded, the Chancellor crossroads became indefensible. Robert E. Lee, witnessing the Chancellor house in flames and Hooker's forces in retreat, judged it would be the prudent time to dispatch Major General McLaws and his division to deal with Union 6th Corps Commander Sedgwick and his men at Salem Church. (See figure 13.7.)

Hooker remained slumped behind his entrenchments around the US Ford on the Rappahannock River for another 2½ days. As a comrade in the 17th Maine Volunteers later wrote: "All this time Hooker was doing

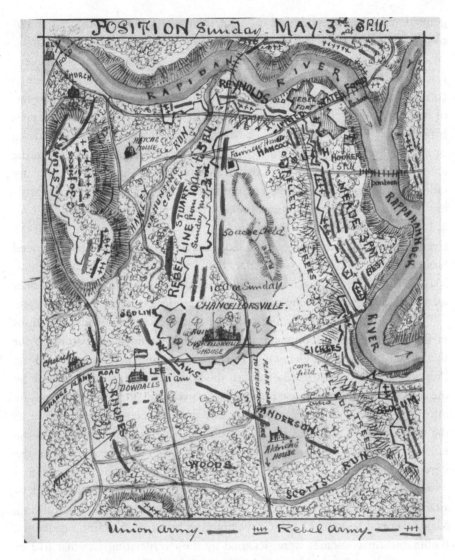

FIGURE 13.7 Map of Chancellorsville Battlefield,
May 3, 1863 by Robert Knox Sneden. Library of Congress,
Geography and Map Division.

absolutely *nothing* and here is a great mystery. Lee held Hooker all day with
a skirmish line while he paid respects to Sedgwick."[35] Presumably expecting
his subordinates to concur with his thinking, in the overnight hours of May
5–6, the Commanding General convened a war council to debate whether
the army should withdraw or face Lee. Garnering further disdain from his

generals, Hooker overruled their majority opinion. The Army of the Potomac would retreat across the river.

Sixth Corps Commander Sedgwick had moved his command out of Lee's reach first. Knowing there would be no possibility of Sedgwick and his men coming to liberate his command, Hooker's sense of urgency to cross the rest of his army heightened. Hooker moved with his artillery across the Rappahannock in the late-night hours of May 5–6, and infantry followed at dawn on May 6. Frustratingly for 2nd Corps Commander Couch, he was given the command for the forces south of the river when the mission was to withdraw, rather than to fight. By the time Lee reunited his forces and Confederate artillery was in position to hammer Hooker's fortifications the morning of May 6, 1863, he discovered his foe had slunk to the safety of the north side of the river. And finalizing the end of the Chancellorsville Campaign, Major General Stoneman and his cavalry trod to safety behind Union lines near Yorktown on May 7, having failed to attack the logistical and infrastructure targets Hooker identified. Stoneman thereby played a largely irrelevant role in the campaign.

Joseph Hooker did not submit a detailed official record of the operations of the army under his command during the Chancellorsville Campaign for the files of the Adjutant General of the army. But the report he provided the President was enough to shake him to the core. Lincoln was dumbstruck by the magnitude of the carnage. How, after two years of grinding war, could he inform the American public of this travesty that left the country no closer to the elusive goal of union? And for the soldiers, leaving behind many of those killed or wounded when the Army of the Potomac crossed back over to the north bank of the Rappahannock River felt sinful. The Union Army suffered more than 17,000 casualties, and the Confederates more than 13,000—a devastating 22 percent of their army. With 4,590 killed, wounded, or missing, Major General Sedgwick's 6th Corps bore the brunt of the Union casualties. Rollin and his comrades were sickened by the excruciating fact that 612 of those casualties were their own in J. J. Bartlett's brigade.[36]

CHAPTER 14

FAREWELL TO THE
27TH NEW YORK VOLUNTEERS

Finally, on the morning of May 8, 1863, the men of the 27th NY Volunteers heard the orders they were waiting for: pack up and return to the camp at White Oak Church. As Rollin and Westervelt slogged the eight or so miles to reach their home away from home, the countryside itself groaned with the fever of destruction and death. Westervelt sighed, "the roads, fences and woods, and all other landmarks, were almost entirely obliterated."[1] By midafternoon, the two were bailing water out of their waiting cabin and setting up tents to resurrect their comfortable home for a few more days. They forced themselves to perform the usual duties of camp life even as their minds raced with thoughts of family, friends, loves to be, and responsibilities awaiting them at home.[2]

When the 16th NY Volunteers departed on May 11, it was an emotional farewell. As the 27th NY regimental history remembered: "That made us feel very lonesome, as we had always camped beside each other, and had seemed more like one regiment than two distinct commands; and we were always ready to support each other."[3] Seeing off their brother regiment undoubtedly elicited some unexpected sentiments. For weeks—if not months—the men had counted down the days until they would be back in the warm embrace of loved ones at home. But now they were on the precipice of stepping beyond the grand fraternal bond borne through the horrors of combat and the numbing boredom of winter camp, a bond unattainable and inexplicable to those who had not experienced what they experienced. Soon they would forever be separated from their days as soldiers in the 27th NY Volunteers, where they had learned about themselves as they learned about war. (See figure 14.1.)

On May 14, 1863, Rollin stood alongside his brethren, heart beating a little too fast and hands a little sweaty, during the evening parade. Three Special Orders were read to the regiment. Each congratulated the men on their brave patriotism, and each told them it was their turn to go home. Their terms had expired, and the regiment was ordered to return to Elmira, New York, to be mustered out of service. The 27th NY Volunteers' regimental history memorialized their commanding officers' words:

> The general commanding the corps congratulates the officers and men of the 27th New York Volunteers upon their honorable return to civil life. They have illustrated their term of service by gallant deeds, and have won for themselves a reputation not surpassed in the Army of the Potomac, and have nobly earned the gratitude of the republic.
> —Major General Sedgwick

> In taking leave of the 27th Regiment of New York Volunteers, the Brigadier-General commanding the division is happy to be able to witness to their soldierly qualifications . . . Their action in the late campaign, on the south side of the Rappahannock, will be a proud record for every officer and man to carry to his home.
> —Brigadier General Brooks

> After the fall of your gallant and distinguished colonel, I commanded you in the first battle of the Army of the Potomac. I have led you through all of its subsequent campaigns, and have participated with you in a dozen battles… Our connection has been one of love, cemented by your bravery and noble deeds; and in its severance I believe the regret to be mutual. I have always relied upon you in every emergency, and you have responded with true heroism. In the history of the Army of the Potomac, *no prouder record will be inscribed than your own.*[4]
> —Brigadier General J. J. Bartlett

Both Major General Henry Slocum, their first regimental commander, and Brigadier General Bartlett attended the evening parade and made short

Colors of the 27th Regiment, New York Volunteers,

FIGURE 14.1   Regimental Flag at End of Service. Library of
Congress, Prints & Photographs Division.

remarks after the orders were read. Their men gave them three resounding
cheers that reverberated in their souls.

At 3 a.m. the next day, their final reveille at camp sounded. By 5 a.m., the
men were packed and marching toward Falmouth. Rollin's chum Westervelt
recalled: "The different regiments of our brigade turned out to wish us goodbye, and as we said adieu to these weather-beaten veterans, we heartily wished
the war was over, and that we were all going back together."[5] Upon arrival at
Falmouth, the regiment boarded rail cars for Aquia Creek and a steamer took
them to Washington, where they overnighted. After a day of touristing the city,
the men boarded railcars to return to the same Baltimore hub that was filled
with such intrigue and perceived danger when the regiment last transited.

At first light on the following morning, May 17, 1863, Rollin and his
comrades excitedly climbed aboard the only conveyance available for their
daylong journey back to Elmira, New York—cattle cars. A comrade recalled
the excitement of the slow meander westward toward home: "At every station
along the route the men would send up cheer after cheer. The people brought
them refreshments at nearly every station, and nothing was thought too good
for the boys."[6] Their humble transport arrived around midnight, leaving them
no choice but to curl up on the depot floor to sleep.

The next morning, the regiment marched to the barracks, the site where two years earlier many of them had been first exposed to the art of soldiering. Any romanticizing the men may have indulged in while anticipating their homecoming was erased when they stepped foot back into the camp. As Westervelt graphically described, "the barracks . . . were very dirty, and fairly alive with vermin."[7] A citizen delegation from Binghamton delivered the companies raised in Broome County (C, D, and Rollin's F) from the filth by offering them the hospitality of their city while the army completed the process of mustering them out.

Rollin fidgeted, not knowing where to be while bureaucratic paperwork continued to bind him to the army; he soon explained his quandary to his father in a letter. He went to Binghamton and stayed with his friend Charles Fairchild (the forthcoming editor of the 27th NY Volunteers regimental history). From there, he broke away for three days to visit with friends, and to catch up on two years' worth of courting in person with his future wife.

Elmira New York
May 29th 63

Dear Father
        I received your telegram this afternoon and replied to it saying that I would be home tomorrow or write to you.
        This red tape is making slow progress in mustering out troops. When I arrived at Binghamton on Monday, I met some of the officers of the 27th who informed me that it was useless for me to come to Elmira before Friday as I could do nothing at the Company rolls 'til one of them went to Albany and returned. I stayed with my friend Fairchild Monday night and thought to return home on Tuesday and stay 'til today, but meeting Nathan Fish, I rode with him up to Snake Creek and visited with my friends 'til this morning when I took the stage at Edwin Summers' and came to Binghamton, and from thence by day express to this place where I immediately got your dispatch.
        I have consulted with Col Adams, also with the mustering officer here, and I find that if I leave here before Friday next, I shall have to return to get my pay and bounty amounting to $175 or thereabouts.
        If possible, I would like to defer coming home or commencing the enrollment 'til one week from Monday. If this can be done,

telegraph me tomorrow evening after you receive this letter, or if it cannot be done, telegraph me and I will come home and commence the business, leaving orders here for my friends to inform me when the Regt are receiving their pay, and I will return. This, though attended with some expense by traveling, I think preferable to losing the enrollment.

I may possibly be through here as early as Thursday, but this confounded red tape business cannot be depended upon. I have leave to come home 'til the Regt is paid off if necessary, so there is no trouble about that. If this is not a fix, what is? Tied up here and the magnet drawing me home.

Let me hear from you tomorrow eve.

Ever yours etc

Rollin B. Truesdell

To: Saml W. Truesdell

Great Bend, Pa

Rollin returned to Elmira to muster out of the United States Army on June 5, 1863, after two years and twenty-eight days of service. Rollin remained steadfast in his love of country. He had not blinked when ordered forward as the earth was ablaze all around him. For this, he was promoted twice and mustered out as sergeant. He carefully pocketed his pay, discharge supplement, and $100 bounty, and then boarded the train for Binghamton.

Binghamton erupted in celebration when their native sons arrived on June 5. The *Broome County Military History* reported: "People poured in from all parts of the county. Artillery salutes were fired as the train moved in, bringing from the front what was left of Broome's first offering to the nation. As the veterans marched through the streets in their uniforms, gray with the dust of their memorable service, thousands cheered and the air was filled with bouquets tossed from the packed sidewalks."[8] Amidst the jubilation, Rollin disembarked the train and excitedly scanned the crowd. And just as Rollin had daydreamed over and over again, there Samuel and Lucy Truesdell stood, waiting for their son to come home.

Afterword

Rollin B. Truesdell lived the rest of his years with the same sense of urgency and purpose he exuded when he enlisted as a twenty-one-year-old in the 27th NY Volunteers at the start of the Civil War. The war and the destruction it wielded upon enemies and loved ones alike undoubtedly underscored the fragility and ephemeral nature of life. The war also imbued in Rollin the truth that fighting side by side with comrades to achieve a precious goal is invigorating and instills a sense of fulfillment. The Civil War became a defining feature of Rollin, as much as his red hair, six-foot-one-inch stature, and sharp mind.

When Rollin reverted to civilian life after satisfying his commitment to the Union Army—deaf in one ear, recovering from a concussion, and harboring the seeds of rheumatism—he was eager to take on the responsibilities of an adult. Rollin, like so many young, idealistic males, left his family's warm embrace as a boy to pursue glory en route to the enemy's total surrender, and returned a man. In his final months of service, he mused excitedly with his father and sister via letter about the many paths he could take to make his way in the world once he ceased to wear the Union Army uniform and was removed from the gruesome, callous business of the war. Of course, joining his father and working on the family farm was an appealing option, but Rollin's world had widened. Rollin, whose detailed bookcase-building specifications to his family when he was serving as company clerk signaled his talents, evidently enrolled in a trade apprenticeship, most probably in carpentry, to commence upon his arrival home.

Within two years, Rollin had established himself as a carpenter in Binghamton. The city offered broader business prospects than Liberty, but also the indelible connection to Rollin's days as a soldier. Just as he had in the army, Rollin pursued opportunities when they presented themselves and was ready to take risks in the interest of advancing himself and his lot in life. In turns, Rollin was a traveling salesman for a grocery and provision company, a partner in the seed business within that company, and then, after selling his interest in

the business, the owner of his own grocery store in Binghamton. After selling
the grocery store in 1890, Rollin took on a successful leather and findings
business for over a decade until the quieter pace of retirement beckoned. Retirement did not stick, however; he went to work as a clerk in the public works
department of the Binghamton city government for several years before truly
retiring. In 1900, William S. Lawyer wrote in his book, *Binghamton: Its Settlement, Growth and Development*: "Mr. Truesdell has been identified with business
interests in the city for a period of 35 years . . . he is now numbered among our
substantial businessmen."[1] Rollin's entrepreneurial spirit clearly transcended
his army days of peddling tubs of his mother's homemade butter to delicacy-
starved fellow soldiers.

And despite groans about the institution of marriage in some of Rollin's
letters to his family, he wasted no time in relinquishing his bachelorhood in the
summer of 1863. Rollin kindled the flame with his future wife the first chance
he got—during the interim period between when the 27th NY Volunteers
returned to Elmira and when they mustered out on June 5, 1863. Rollin and
Janette Summers wed on September 2, 1863. Sadly, Janette died in September
1867 at the age of twenty-five, leaving Rollin to raise their two-year-old son,
Edwin.

Rollin married his second wife, Tryphena E. Barnes, on April 6, 1869. She
bore three children: two daughters, Janette (namesake of Rollin's first wife) and
Lucy, and son Arthur (my great-grandfather). She too departed leaving tod-
dlers to raise when she passed in 1876 at the age of thirty-five. Rollin's third
marriage ended abruptly as well with the untimely death of Helene V. Howell
in the summer of 1878. Rollin married for the fourth time on March 21, 1881,
and Elizabeth Nancy Cushing succeeded in outliving him. (See figure C.1.)

As a civilian, Rollin never lost his sense of duty to society, or of the welcome draw of public service. In the first years after the Civil War, Rollin established residence in the undeveloped South Side of Binghamton and became a
leader in the growth of that section of the city. In 1871 and 1872, he served as a
school commissioner. Twenty-five years later, Rollin again would demonstrate
his devotion to education as a featured speaker on the Civil War in Binghamton High School history classes. In an article titled, "A Veteran's Talk: R. B.
Truesdell Describes Incidents of the Civil War," the local newspaper reported
the students responded with such interest in Rollin's storytelling that they
persuaded him to return and share more of his firsthand account of soldiering
in the Army of the Potomac.[2] Indeed, Rollin was in demand as a speaker for

FIGURE C.1   Photograph of Rollin B. Truesdell (center) and
his Son Arthur (left of Rollin) at Family Reunion in 1908.

various public occasions in the community. Binghamton celebrated Rollin and
his civic contributions by naming Truesdell Street in his honor.

Throughout his many years living in Binghamton, his membership in the
First Presbyterian Church and in the Bartlett Post, Grand Army of the Republic (GAR), further anchored him to the community and illuminates how
Rollin defined himself.[3] Commemorating native son J. J. Bartlett, the first
major of the 27th NY Volunteers, whose heroic leadership led him up the
rungs of the Union Army ladder, the Bartlett Post was established in February
1893. It became one of 7,000 groups emergent after the Civil War for Union
veterans to congregate with and help other local veterans in need. The GAR
was particularly vocal about ensuring that veterans and their families received
the government pensions to which they understood themselves to be entitled.
(Rollin filed his disability pension application on June 7, 1892.)

It was the annual reunion of the 27th NY Volunteers, however, that most
kept Rollin's attachment to his war comrades and their shared experiences
alive and tended to throughout his adult life. The first gathering, held in Binghamton on May 2, 1876, commemorated the fifteenth anniversary of the regiment's organization, and counted regimental luminaries Generals Slocum and

Bartlett as participants. In July 1883, the New York newspaper *The Whole Truth and Nothing But the Truth* reported that veterans from the 27th NY Volunteers and the 1st NY Veteran Cavalry voted to establish a permanent veterans' association, with Bartlett as their first president. The 27th NY Volunteer's regimental history promoted the Survivors' Association, noting its utility as a repository for regimental records, and went on to rhapsodize: "Our gatherings are notable for the enjoyment of friendly fellowship and conversation among comrades bound together by memories of perils and privations."[4]

On July 21 and 22, 1886, the Survivors' Association gathered in Rochester to mark the twenty-fifth anniversary of the Battle of Bull Run. The members celebrated the attendance of Bartlett; Slocum's former chief-of-staff, Brigadier General Hiram C. Rogers; Congressman Charles S. Baker; and famous author, lecturer, and lawyer Albion W. Tourgée, who was badly injured at Bull Run. Meeting in Mount Morris the following year, the Survivors' Association voted to expand their membership to include the 33rd NY Volunteers, and for Henry Slocum to be the next association president. The men proudly feted Rollin's tentmate and chum, William Westervelt, for his recently published book, *Lights and Shadows of Army Life*, chronicling his experiences as a private soldier in the Army of the Potomac.[5]

In 1894, Association comrades elected Rollin to be acting president and president for the following year. Rollin's gift for oratory and gregarious nature was a perfect fit for the job. Called on to speak as the members gathered around a campfire in 1894, Rollin used the scriptures to draw parallels to the trials the country had survived: "Along came a good Samaritan named Abraham Lincoln and with that Samaritan came a million more Samaritans and they took Uncle Sam and raised him up, and, finally, at Appomattox, our old friend got upon his feet, and he was as good as new, and better, for he had freed the shackles from more than five million human beings held in slavery."[6] (Rollin surely had a twinkle in his eye when he later reported to the congregants that a listener enquired after his speech whether he was a Methodist minister.) He continued: "Comrades, we feel that our services are not appreciated by the present generation as they should be; but the future historian that writes 100 years from now when he visits the national cemeteries and observes the mute evidences of the loyalty and sacrifice for this country . . . will read the roll of cultured and intelligent men that were in the army, and fought for the preservation of the Union of these United States."[7] Rollin continued to hold leadership roles in the Association for the rest of his life.

In 1904, as the veterans aged and travel would become more difficult, the Survivors' Association contracted their scope and convened meetings of just Binghamton-based Companies C, D, and F of the 27th NY Vols. On July 21, 1911, thirty-one survivors from the Binghamton companies gathered to observe the fiftieth anniversary of the Battle of Bull Run. By 1923, it was left to William Westervelt to represent Company F at the meeting marking the sixty-second anniversary of their first battle of the Civil War; only eighteen members of these three companies were still alive.

Rollin B. Truesdell died on June 5, 1914, at the age of seventy-five. He left behind his wife, Elizabeth, four children, and elder sister Julia, who lived to be ninety-four. One of the obituaries written for Rollin that appeared in a local newspaper was titled, "Answered Final Bugle Call—The Death of a Prominent War Veteran." It movingly described the large circle of friends that his sympathy and cordial, genial nature drew to him, and noted that in his final year of life, he endured significant pain. His rheumatism was believed to have stemmed from the physical conditions he endured as a soldier in the Army of the Potomac. Members of the Bartlett Post, GAR attended Rollin's funeral en masse. And William Westervelt came to say a final goodbye to his dear friend and tentmate.

As in life, Rollin was encircled by his army comrades in death.

NOTES

INTRODUCTION

1. C. B. Fairchild, *History of the 27th Regiment N.Y.Vols.* (Binghamton, NY: Carl & Matthews, 1888), 294, 296, 298.

2. The inexact nature of recordkeeping during the war and the destruction of many of the Confederate muster rolls prior to a comprehensive record being compiled render a definitive casualty tally unreachable. The commonly cited estimate of 620,000 deaths, derived from research conducted during the late nineteenth century and published in Thomas L. Livermore's *Numbers and Losses in the Civil War in America 1861–1865* in 1900, is today contested by some historians who believe that total to be an undercount of 100,000 or more.

CHAPTER 1. HAD TO BE

1. Emily C. Blackman, *History of Susquehanna County, Pennsylvania* (Philadelphia: Claxton, Remsen & Haffelfinger, 1873), 275–276.

2. According to Blackman, the most profitable business for farmers in Liberty was butter, though they also commonly grew corn and rye and raised sheep for the wool. Showing his entrepreneurial spirit in a letter to his parents on October 27, 1861, Rollin requested they send him a fifty-pound tub of butter—some of which he would eat, and the rest he intended to sell for a bargain compared to the local "hucksters." In a letter dated January 8, 1862, Rollin described with pride Regimental Commander Slocum's reaction when presented with a roll of butter made by Rollin's mother.

3. Blackman, *History of Susquehanna County, Pennsylvania*, 283.

4. Steven Manson, Jonathan Schroeder, David Van Riper, and Steven Ruggles, "1860 Census," IPUMS National Historical Geographic Information System: Version 14.0, Minneapolis, MN: IPUMS. 2019. http://doi.org/10.18128/D050.V14.0. New York boasted the largest enlistment of soldiers in the Union Army, followed by Pennsylvania.

5. Department of Commerce and Labor, Bureau of the Census, "Supplement for Pennsylvania: Population, Agriculture, Manufacturers, Mines and Quarries," in *Statistics for Pennsylvania, Thirteenth Census of the United States Taken in the Year 1910* (Washington, DC: Government Printing Office, 1913), 568.

6. James M. McPherson, *Battle Cry of Freedom* (New York: Oxford University Press, 1988), 318.

7. William C. Kashatus, "Finding Sanctuary at Montrose," *Pennsylvania Heri-*

tage Magazine 33, no. 1 (Winter 2007): 29. http://paheritage.wpengine.com/article/finding-sanctuary-montrose

8. Clarissa Truesdell, "Letter to nephew," May 19, 1903.

9. Charles L. Brace, "The Root of Secession," *The Independent*, August 8, 1861.

10. Frederick Phisterer, *New York in the War of the Rebellion 1861–1865*, 3rd ed. (Albany, NY: J. R. Lyon Company, State Printers, 1912), 9.

11. Pennsylvania Governor Andrew C. Curtin, "Inaugural Address of Gov. Andrew G. Curtin Delivered," *Daily Telegraph—Extra*, January 15, 1861. https://www.loc.gov/item/rbpe.15701300

12. Texas joined the Confederacy on March 2, 1861, two days before President Lincoln's inaugural address.

13. "Mr. Lincoln's Inaugural," *The Binghamton Standard*, March 18, 1861.

14. "First Inaugural Address of Abraham Lincoln, March 4, 1861," The Avalon Project, Yale Law School. https://avalon.law.yale.edu/19th_century/lincoln1.asp

Chapter 2. Becoming a Soldier

1. Clarissa Truesdell, "Letter to nephew," May 19, 1903.

2. United States War Department, *The War of the Rebellion: A Compilation of the Official Records of the Union and Confederate Armies* (Washington, DC: Government Printing Office, 1899). [Hereafter referred to as *OR*] Series III, Vol. I, 67–68.

3. According to the *History of Broome County* (Binghamton is the county seat), "the battalion movements of the days of general trainings would cause the Broome militiamen of today to roar with laughter could he see the exhibitions of that period . . . The farmer of Broome would leave the plow in the furrow, and the mechanic his tools to celebrate "training day," drink root beer and buy a card of gingerbread." E. S. Watson, "Military History," in *History of Broome County*, ed. H. P. Smith (Syracuse, NY: D. Mason & Co., 1885), 162. https://archive.org/details/historyofbroomec00smit/page/n7/mode/2up?ref=ol&q=military+&view=theater

4. James Gillespie Blaine, *Twenty Years of Congress: From Lincoln to Garfield* (Norwich, CT: Henry Bill Publishing Company, 1884), 306. www.worldcat.org/title/twenty-years-of-congress-from-lincoln-to-garfield-with-a-review-of-the-events-which-led-to-the-political-revolution-of-1860/oclc/20498700

5. Phisterer, *New York in the War of the Rebellion 1861–1865*, 13.

6. *OR*, Series III, Vol. I. (1899), 700.

7. D. W. Bartlett, "Notes from the Capitol," *The Independent*, April 15, 1861.

8. D. W. Bartlett, "Latest from Washington," *The Independent*. April 25, 1861.

9. Bartlett, "Latest from Washington."

10. Phisterer, *New York in the War of the Rebellion 1861–1865*, 19.

11. Broome County, with a population of only 35,000, furnished not less than 4,000 volunteers to the Union cause between 1861 and 1865. William Foote Seward, *Binghamton and Broome County New York, A History*, Vol. II (New York & Chicago: Lewis Historical Publishing Company, 1924), 447. www.worldcat.org/title/binghamton-and-broome-county-new-york-a-history/oclc/3820006.

12. Citizen Committee of Binghamton, New York, Recruitment poster: *PATRIOTS*

OF BROOME! Binghamton, NY: Binghamton Daily Republican Steam Power Press Print, April 1861.

13. Citizen Committee, *PATRIOTS OF BROOME!*

14. Watson, *History of Broome County*, 162.

15. Great Bend, Pennsylvania, is a township approximately eight miles to the east of Liberty on the east bank of the Susquehanna River.

16. Each time a Southern state seized a federal arsenal within its territory and seceded, the Union stockpile was commensurately hobbled. The rebel attack on Harpers Ferry in Virginia on April 18, 1861, was particularly devastating. Rifle-producing machinery (one of only two existing in the United States) was torched as defenders withdrew, leaving the marauding Virginians to salvage what they could for Confederate Army use. Phisterer, on page twenty of his *New York in the War of the Rebellion*, reported that firearms were in such serious deficit at the beginning of the war that Governor Morgan sent an agent to Europe carrying a letter of credit for $500,000 to purchase munitions on April 24, 1861. He secured an agreement for 19,000 Enfield muskets at a cost of $335,000.

17. Jim Pfiffer, "Elmira grew rapidly in Civil War years," *Elmira Star-Gazette*, May 17, 1993, 2A.

18. Pfiffer, "Elmira."

19. Pfiffer, "Elmira."

20. Michael B. A. Oldstone, in his book, *Viruses, Plagues, & History* (New York: Oxford University Press, 2010), 146–147, reported that during the first year of the Civil War, there were 21,676 reported cases of measles and 551 deaths caused by measles in the Union Army. He further cites United States Surgeon General's Office records from the war that cautioned, "This infection is always serious, often fatal either directly or through its sequelae. The Prognosis therefore should be guarded."

21. Daniel E. Sickles entered the Civil War as a household name. A wealthy New Yorker, Sickles's and his young wife's flamboyant lifestyle among the Washington elite crescendoed in 1859 when, as a US Congressman from New York, Sickles shot and killed his wife's lover (Francis Scott Key's son, Philip) in broad daylight across the street from the White House. Newspapers devoured reports from the scandalous trial in which future Secretary of War Edwin Stanton successfully acquitted Sickles with the first use of temporary insanity as a defense. Sickles sought to reclaim his place in society—despite remaining married to his wife—by recruiting several regiments in New York at the outbreak of the war. Sickles was appointed Colonel of the 70th New York before becoming Commander of the Excelsior Brigade and eventually Major General of the 3rd Corps.

22. Fairchild, *History of the 27th Regiment N.Y. Vols.*, 3.

23. The pull to join the fight undoubtedly felt stronger with each successive state that seceded. Arkansas followed Virginia on May 6, North Carolina on May 20, and Tennessee on June 8, 1861.

24. *OR*, Series III, Vol. I. (1885), 266.

25. Galusha Aaron Grow, fellow Susquehanna County, Pennsylvania, resident and landowner, was first elected to the US Congress in 1850 as a Democrat. He switched to the Republican Party for the 1856 election in reaction to the Democrat-sponsored Kansas-Nebraska Act. Grow was elected Speaker of the House during the special session that President Lincoln called on July 4, 1861, and served in this role until 1863.

CHAPTER 3. BULL RUN SHATTERS PERCEPTIONS

1. "Army Sketches, The 27th New York State Volunteers. No. 5." 27th New York Volunteer Infantry Regiment Newspaper Clipping Collection at the New York State Military Museum.

2. "Army Sketches, The 27th New York State Volunteers. No. 5."

3. Fairchild, *History of the 27th Regiment N.Y. Vols.*, 6.

4. "Traveling through History: Stories of the Northern Central Railroad during the Civil War," Maryland Center for History and Culture. www.mdhistory.org/travelling-through-history-stories-of-the-northern-central-railroad-during-the-civil-war

5. "Army Sketches, The 27th New York State Volunteers. No. 5."

6. When the B&O Railroad built a hotel with a waiting room and ticket office to serve its passengers in 1830, they named it the Relay House, nodding to its past as the spot to change horses for the first horse-drawn passenger trains between Baltimore and Ellicott Mills. Also notable in rail history, the first successful steam engine in the United States, the Tom Thumb, ran from Baltimore to the Relay House on August 28, 1830. See Historic Relay Maryland website for more details about Relay House's place in history. www.relay-maryland.com/Welcome.html

7. "Timeline of Unit Occupation of Relay House, 1861–1865," Howard County, Maryland, in the Civil War. https://hococivilwar.org/relay_timeline

8. Fairchild, *History of the 27th Regiment N.Y. Vols.*, 8.

9. News of the Battle of Rich Mountain fought on July 11, 1861, and the subsequent Battle of Corrick's Ford on the Cheat River two days later, may have reached Rollin's ear in camp. Though relatively minor skirmishes compared to later battles, Union victories in this western Virginia theater would help catapult the major general who successfully commanded these Union forces—George B. McClellan—to the highest echelons of Union Army command.

10. When Rollin wrote this letter, Professor Thaddeus Lowe was in Washington wooing President Abraham Lincoln on the merits of his hydrogen gas-inflated balloon *Enterprise* to conduct aerial reconnaissance of enemy forces. Lowe tapped out a telegram to the President while suspended some 500 feet above the White House on July 11, 1861. Lincoln subsequently appointed him chief aeronaut of the Union Army Balloon Corps.

11. "Army Sketches, The 27th New York State Volunteers. No. 6."

12. "Army Sketches, The 27th New York State Volunteers. No. 6."

13. Fairchild, *History of the 27th Regiment N.Y. Vols.*, 8.

14. Fairchild, *History of the 27th Regiment N.Y. Vols.*, 8.

15. Harpers Ferry held significance as the site of the 1859 raid on a federal arsenal by abolitionist John Brown, who hoped to ignite a nationwide uprising against slavery. Manassas was a coveted rail junction approximately thirty miles southwest of Washington, DC, that led to the Shenandoah Valley, and linked to other rail lines in northern and Central Virginia.

16. "Army Sketches, The 27th New York State Volunteers. No. 6."

17. Private Blockhead, "Letter from a Volunteer (dated July 19, 1861)," *Union News, Broome County*, August 1, 1861.

18. Blockhead, "Letter from a Volunteer (dated July 19, 1861)."

19. William B. Westervelt, *Lights and Shadows of Army Life as Seen by a Private Soldier*, 2–3; Fairchild, *History of the 27th Regiment NY Vols*, 10–11.

20. Private Blockhead, "Letter to Union News (dated July 23, 1861)," *Union News, Broome County*, August 8, 1861.

21. Fairchild, *History of the 27th Regiment N.Y. Vols.*, 11.

22. Westervelt, *Lights and Shadows of Army Life*, 4.

23. The Stone House—owned by Henry P. Matthew, who farmed the surrounding land—became a makeshift hospital during both Battles of Bull Run.

24. Captain Peter Jay, "Letter to friend Stuart (dated July 29, 1861)," *Broome Republican*, August 7, 1861.

25. Westervelt named the 8th Georgia and 4th Alabama as the two regiments involved.

26. Morris P. Blair, "Letter to Broome Republican," *Broome Republican*, July 31, 1861.

27. J. Copeland, "Letter to Father (dated July 24, 1861)," *Rochester Union & Advertiser*, July 30, 1861.

28. Duncan Brown, "Letter to the Editor (dated July 23, 1861)," *Rochester Evening Express*, July 29, 1861; J. Copeland, "Letter to Father (dated July 24, 1861)."

29. William J. Randall, "Letter to Broome Republican (dated July 31, 1861)," *Broome Republican*, August 7, 1861.

30. Copeland, "Letter to Father (dated July 24, 1861)."

31. Surgeon Norman S. Barnes, "Letter to Wife (dated July 23, 1861)," *Rochester Evening Express*, July 27, 1861.

32. John W. Burrows, "Letter to brother and sister," *Chenango American*, August 1, 1861.

33. Copeland, "Letter to Father (dated July 24, 1861)."

34. *OR*, Series I, Vol. II. (1880), 389.

35. Edward L. Lewis, "Letter from the War (written at Camp Anderson)," *Broome Republican*, July 31, 1861.

36. Brown, "Letter to the Editor (dated July 23, 1861)."

37. Soldier, 27th NY Volunteers, "Letter," *Chenango American*, August 8, 1861.

38. F. E. Northrup. "Letter from the War (written at Camp Anderson and dated July 29, 1861)," *Broome Republican*, August 7, 1861.

39. Fairchild, *History of the 27th Regiment N.Y. Vols.*, 15.

40. Republican Congressmen Galusha A. Grow and David Wilmot represented districts in Pennsylvania. Rollin's reference to "mud sills" was a satirical appropriation of a political term introduced in 1858 by South Carolina Senator James Henry Hammond when the senator explained his theory that "the mud sills" (lowest threshold of a building) of society would always be needed to perform menial labor for the elite class. According to Hammond's theory, enslaved people were mud sills in the south and blue-collar workers were mud sills in the north.

41. Soldier, 27th NY Volunteers, "Letter (dated July 28, 1861)," *Union News, Broome County*, August 8, 1861.

42. Copeland, "Letter to Father (dated July 24, 1861)."

43. Blockhead, "Letter to Union News (dated July 23, 1861)."

44. *OR*, Series I, Vol. II. (1880), 323–324.

45. "Army Sketches, The 27th New York State Volunteers. No. 9."

CHAPTER 4. DEFENDING THE CAPITAL

1. Stephen W. Sears, *George B. McClellan, the Young Napoleon* (New York: Da Capo Press, 1988), 3.

2. *OR*, Series I, Vol. II. (1880), 386.

3. Editor, *Atlas and Argus*, Albany, New York. August 23, 1861.

4. Isaac L. Post hailed from Montrose, Pennsylvania, a borough of Susquehanna County, and some ten miles south of Liberty. An ardent Republican, Post was a stalwart supporter and campaign fundraiser for Congressman Galusha A. Grow.

5. Soldier, 27th NY Volunteers, "Letter to friend "Benedict" (dated August 11, 1861)," *The Union News*, August 22, 1861.

6. Editor, "Temperance in the Army," *The Independent*, July 29, 1861.

7. Fairchild, *History of the 27th Regiment N.Y. Vols.*, 20.

8. It wasn't until the following year that the Springfield rifle became more ubiquitous. In 1862, the Springfield factory delivered nearly 20,000 stand of arms a month according to John D. Hicks, "The Organization of the Volunteer Army in 1861 with Special Reference to Minnesota," *Minnesota History Magazine*, February 7, 1918, 356. http://collections. mnhs.org/MNHistoryMagazine/articles/2/v02i05p324-368.pdf

9. The fort was named in honor of Colonel Elmer E. Ellsworth of the 11th New York Volunteers who became one of the first casualties of the war when he was shot by the proprietor of an Alexandria hotel as he was reaching to take down the hotel's rooftop Confederate flag.

10. "John Gross Barnard (1815–1882)," U.S. Army Corps of Engineers Headquarters. www.usace.army.mil/About/History/Army-Engineers-in-the-Civil-War/Engineer-Biographies/John-Barnard

11. Rollin undoubtedly was sharing the camp conventional wisdom that the fort would be named after the brigade commander whose men built the fort: Henry Slocum.

12. Westervelt, *Lights and Shadows of Army Life*, 6.

13. Westervelt, *Lights and Shadows of Army Life*, 7.

14. Fairchild, *History of the 27th Regiment N.Y. Vols.*, 26.

15. Darwin L. King and Carl J. Case "Civil War Accounting Procedures and Their Influence on Current Cost Accounting Practices," *American Society of Business and Behavioral Sciences eJournal* 3, no. 1 (2007): 43 http://citeseerx.ist.psu.edu/viewdoc/download?doi=1 0.1.1.536.8025&rep=rep1&type=pdf

16. Fairchild, *History of the 27th Regiment N.Y. Vols.*, 24.

17. Westervelt, *Lights and Shadows of Army Life*, 7–8.

18. D. E. Buell, *A Brief History of Company B, 27th Regiment NY Volunteers* (Lyons, NY: Office of the Republicans, 1874), 8.

19. In this passage Rollin was referring to King Hezekiah from the Old Testament in the Bible. In 2 Kings 20, Hezekiah, who is dying, is granted fifteen more years of life when he pleads with God to reward his faithfulness.

20. Composer and musician William B. Bradbury published the popular Sabbath School hymnals *Jubilee* in 1858 and the *Golden Chain* in 1861.

21. H. Seymour Hall, *Personal Experience under General McClellan After Bull Run, Including the Peninsular & Antietam Campaigns, From July 27, 1861 to November 10, 1862* (Leaven-

worth, KS: Kansas Commandery of the Military Order of the Loyal Legion of the United States (MOLLUS), January 3, 1894), 6; Fairchild, *History of the 27th Regiment N.Y. Vols.*, 27.

CHAPTER 5. RECRUITMENT DUTY

1. Phisterer, *New York in the War of the Rebellion 1861–1865*, 22.

2. "New York to the Rescue! 25,000 More Volunteers Called For." *Broome Republican*, July 31, 1861.

3. Seward, *Binghamton and Broome County New York, A History*, 447–448.

4. OR, Series III, Vol. I. (1899), 412; Fairchild, *History of the 27th Regiment N.Y. Vols.*, 19.

5. OR, Series III, Vol. I. (1899), 698–699.

6. Phisterer, *New York in the War of the Rebellion 1861–1865*, 26.

7. OR, Series III, Vol. II. (1899), 44.

8. OR, Series III, Vol. II. (1899), 333–335.

9. OR, Series III, Vol. II. (1899), 666–668.

10. "Drafting," *Broome Republican*, July 23, 1862.

11. "Editorial," *Broome Republican*, July 23, 1862.

12. "The Draft," *Broome Weekly Republican*, August 20, 1862.

13. "Broome County Volunteers," *Broome Weekly Republican*, October 29, 1862.

14. Catton, *Terrible Swift Sword* (Garden City, NY: Doubleday & Company, 1963), 405.

15. "Editorial," *Broome Republican*, July 23, 1862.

16. U.S. Congress, *The United States Conscription Law or National Militia Act: Approved March 2, 1863* (New York: James W. Fortune, 1863), 8.

17. Phisterer, *New York in the War of the Rebellion 1861–1865*, 44.

18. Rollin's friend William Westervelt described in stark terms the disdain he had for Captain Peter Jay: "I lost all trace of him, until the year '78 while in Binghamton, I found him peddling popcorn and peanuts from a handle basket about the streets, willing to do anything to gather a few nickels to satisfy his appetite for rum, a standing reproach to many members of this old company who were obliged to acknowledge him as the captain they served under during the war." *Lights and Shadows of Army Life*, 10.

19. Phisterer, *New York in the War of the Rebellion 1861–1865*, 29–30.

20. The Lines family was among the first residents of Liberty, Pennsylvania, where Rollin grew up. Rufus and Rania Lines signed as witnesses for the deed to the Truesdell family farmhouse and plot of land in 1822.

CHAPTER 6. PUSHING TOWARD RICHMOND

1. Fairchild, *History of the 27th Regiment N.Y. Vols.*, 28.

2. McPherson, *Battle Cry of Freedom*, 424.

3. "Quaker gun," logs often painted black and perched in such a way as to resemble cannons from a distance, were used as a deception tactic during the Civil War.

4. A little over one month prior, the USS *Monitor* with its revolving turret and two cannons, had fought the heavily armed Confederate ironclad, the CSS *Virginia*, to a draw in the waters near Fortress Monroe. Nicknamed "the Yankee cheesebox on a raft," given the ship's profile, the *Monitor's* design focused on agility. Given the destruction showered upon

the USS *Cumberland* and USS *Congress* from the CSS *Virginia* on March 8, 1862, the sudden appearance of the *Monitor* to challenge the *Virginia* the following day was just the boost the North needed in the lead-up to the next campaign against the Confederate forces.

5. Hall, *Personal Experience under General McClellan After Bull Run, Including the Peninsular & Antietam Campaigns*, 8.

6. Westervelt, *Lights and Shadows of Army Life*, 8.

7. Pinkerton continued in his role as Chief of Intelligence for Major General McClellan, feeding his patron ever more exaggerated estimations of Confederate troop strength, until McClellan was removed from his post as Commander of the Army of the Potomac in November 1862.

8. Fairchild, *History of the 27th Regiment N.Y. Vols.*, 32.

9. William H. Gates, "Letter to the Editor (dated May 8, 1862)," *Union News*, May 27, 1862.

10. Fairchild, *History of the 27th Regiment N.Y. Vols.*, 32.

11. Soldier, 27th NY Volunteers, "Letter to friend Stuart (dated May 10, 1862)," *Broome Republican*, May 31, 1862.

12. Westervelt, *Lights and Shadows of Army Life*, 9; Soldier, 27th NY Volunteers, "Letter to friend Stuart (dated May 10, 1862)."

13. Westervelt, *Lights and Shadows of Army Life*, 10.

14. Fairchild, *History of the 27th Regiment N.Y. Vols.*, 35.

15. Soldier, 27th NY Volunteers, "Letter to friend Stuart (dated May 10, 1862)."

16. Joseph C., "Letter to the Editor (dated May 8, 1862)," *The Orleans American*, May 22, 1862.

17. Westervelt, *Lights and Shadows of Army Life*, 10.

18. OR, Series I, Vol. XI, Part I (1884), 614.

19. HIB, "Letters from the War (dated May 16, 1862)," *The Union News*, May 29, 1862.

20. OR, Series I, Vol. XI, Part III (1884), 154–155.

21. Hall, *Personal Experience under General McClellan After Bull Run, Including the Peninsular & Antietam Campaigns*, 10.

22. Fairchild, *History of the 27th Regiment N.Y. Vols.*, 44; Alvah Beach, "Fierce Fighting at Gaines' Mill," *St. Lawrence Plaindealer*, January 6, 1942.

23. HIB, "Letters from the War (dated May 27, 1862)"; *The Union News*, June 12, 1862.

24. Westervelt, *Lights and Shadows of Army Life*, 11.

25. Westervelt, *Lights and Shadows of Army Life*, 11.

26. Rollin and his friends undoubtedly derived their choir's name from the popular hymnal the *Jubilee*.

27. D. Brown, "Heaven's Artillery," *The Evening Express*, June 14, 1862.

28. The Adjutant-General's Office in Washington certified that the number of men present for duty in the Army of the Potomac on May 31, 1862, was 98,008. United States War Department, *The War of the Rebellion: A Compilation of the Official Records of the Union and Confederate Armies* (Washington: Government Printing Office, 1884). Series I, Vol. XI, Part III, 204. This number was likely influenced by McClellan's accounting methods that would impact troop count. According to historian Stephen Sears, McClellan submitted reports to Washington that tallied only enlisted men with "rifles in their hands" rather

than "present for duty." The result would be a significant underestimate of his own troop strength. See Sears, *To the Gates of Richmond*, 99.

29. Though it did not come to pass, on May 21, 1862, President Lincoln sent a dispatch to Commanding General McClellan stating, "You will have just such control of General McDowell and his forces as you therein indicate." *OR*, Series I, Vol. XI, Part III (1884), 184.

30. HIB, "Letters from the War (dated June 1, 1862)"; *The Union News*, June 19, 1862.

31. Soldier, 27th NY Volunteers, "The 27th Regiment at the Battle of Fair Oaks (dated June 1, 1862)," *Union and Advertiser*, June 9, 1862.

32. Westervelt, *Lights and Shadows of Army Life*, 12.

33. *OR*, Series I, Vol. XI, Part III (1884), 210. Because McClellan was bedridden with a recurring case of malaria during the Battle of Fair Oaks, he may have wished to reassure his troops that he would be present with them in the next fight.

34. Confederate nemesis of Northerners, flamer of the rebellion through the siege on Fort Sumter and battlefield prowess at the first Battle of Bull Run, General P.G.T. Beauregard, was checked in the Western Theater when he withdrew his typhoid-riddled forces from Corinth, Mississippi, rather than face battle against Union forces under overall command of Major General Henry Halleck after a month-long siege.

35. Fairchild, *History of the 27th Regiment N.Y., Vols.* 51.

36. Westervelt, *Lights and Shadows of Army Life*, 14. On June 25, 1862, moving the Union skirmish line and both flanks incrementally forward, McClellan at last initiated his advance on the Confederate force—and absorbed approximately 500 casualties in so doing.

CHAPTER 7. LEE PUSHES BACK

1. *OR*, Series I, Vol. XI, Part III (1884), 260.

2. Soldier, 27th NY Volunteers, "On the March (dated July 2, 1862, retrieved from the battlefield)," *Richmond Daily Whig*, July 8, 1862.

3. Westervelt, *Lights and Shadows of Army Life*, 15.

4. *OR*, Series I, Vol. XI, Part II (1884), 447.

5. William M. Nimbs, "Letter to sister (dated July 5, 1862)," *Mount Morris Union and Constitution*, July 17, 1862.

6. Soldier, 27th NY Volunteers, "On the March (dated July 2, 1862, retrieved from the battlefield)."

7. HIB, "Letters from the War (dated July 4, 1862)," *Union News*, July 16, 1862.

8. *OR*, Series I, Vol. XI, Part II (1884), 447; Fairchild, *History of the 27th Regiment N.Y. Vols.*, 52.

9. Fairchild, *History of the 27th Regiment N.Y. Vols.*, 52.

10. HIB, "Letters from the War (dated July 4, 1862)."

11. William M. Nimbs, "Letter to sister (dated July 5, 1862)."

12. D. E. Brown, "Letter from the 27th—Account of the Battles before Richmond (dated July 4, 1862)," *Rochester Evening Express*, July 17, 1862.

13. Soldier, 27th NY Volunteers, "On the March (dated July 2, 1862, retrieved from the battlefield)."

14. *OR*, Series I, Vol. XI, Part II (1884), 448.

15. HIB, "Letters from the War (dated July 4, 1862)."

16. Soldier, 27th NY Volunteers, "On the March (dated July 2, 1862, retrieved from the battlefield);" Fairchild, *History of the 27th Regiment N.Y. Vols.*, 53 and 55.

17. Westervelt, *Lights and Shadows of Army Life*, 17.

18. Will McMahon, "Letter to friend (dated July 10, 1862)," *Dansville Advertiser*, July 24, 1862.

19. *OR*, Series I, Vol. XI, Part II (1884), 433, 454.

20. *OR*, Series I, Vol. XI, Part III (1884), 266.

21. Brown, "Letter from the 27th—Account of the Battles before Richmond (dated July 4, 1862)."

22. Buell, *A Brief History of Company B, 27th NY Volunteers*, 10.

23. Fairchild, *History of the 27th Regiment N.Y. Vols.*, 70.

24. Soldier, 27th NY Volunteers, "On the March (dated July 2, 1862, retrieved from the battlefield)."

25. Fairchild, *History of the 27th Regiment N.Y. Vols.*, 70.

26. According to historian Stephen Sears, 99,000 men, 281 pieces of field artillery and 26 heavy guns, at least 3,800 wagons and ambulances, and 2,500 head of cattle competed for space on the roads. Stephen Sears, *To the Gates of Richmond: The Peninsula Campaign* (New York: Ticknor & Fields, 1992), 256.

27. Sears, *To the Gates of Richmond*, 280.

28. *OR*, Series I, Vol. XI, Part II (1884), 435.

29. Brown, "Letter from the 27th—Account of the Battles before Richmond (dated July 4, 1862)."

30. Soldier, 27th NY Volunteers, "On the March (dated July 2, 1862, retrieved from the battlefield)."

31. Soldier, 27th NY Volunteers, "On the March (dated July 2, 1862, retrieved from the battlefield)."

32. Fairchild, *History of the 27th Regiment N.Y. Vols.*, 73.

33. Fairchild, *History of the 27th Regiment N.Y. Vols.*, 74.

34. *OR*, Series I, Vol. XI, Part II (1884), 37.

35. A. G. Northrup, "Harrison's Landing (dated July 5, 1862)," *Chenango American*, July 17, 1862.

36. Hall, *Personal Experience under General McClellan After Bull Run, Including the Peninsular & Antietam Campaigns*, 18.

37. McMahon, "Letter to friend (dated July 10, 1862)."

38. Buell, *A Brief History of Company B, 27th NY Volunteers*, 11.

39. Apparently, Peter Jay reconsidered his decision to leave the army life behind. The *Broome Weekly Republican* reported on July 29, 1863, that "Captain Peter Jay, formerly of the 27th Regiment, has received authority to raise a company to be attached to Colonel Howard's (New York City) Heavy Battery."

40. Pope's army was melded together from the defeated commands of Major Generals McDowell, Nathanial P. Banks, and John C. Frémont, all of whom were roughed up in the Shenandoah Valley at the hands of Confederate Major General Stonewall Jackson. With the addition of Samuel Sturgis's brigade from the Military District of Washington, Pope took command of his new army on June 26, 1862.

CHAPTER 8. THE WAR MOVES NORTH

1. *OR*, Series I, Vol. XII, Part II (1885), 10.

2. Major General John Pope, "To the Officers and Soldiers of the Army of Virginia (dated July 14, 1862)," *Chenango American*, July 17, 1862.

3. Major General George B. McClellan, *Report of Major General George B. McClellan upon the Organization of the Army of the Potomac and its Campaigns in Virginia & Maryland from July 26, 1861–November 7, 1862*. Reprinted entire from the copy transmitted by the Secretary of War to the House of Representatives (Chicago: The Times Steam Book and Job Printing, 1864), 97.

4. McClellan, *Report of Major General George B. McClellan upon the Organization of the Army of the Potomac and its Campaigns in Virginia & Maryland from July 26, 1861–November 7, 1862*, 98.

5. McClellan, *Report of Major General George B. McClellan upon the Organization of the Army of the Potomac and its Campaigns in Virginia & Maryland from July 26, 1861–November 7, 1862*, 100.

6. E.S., "Departure from Harrison's Landing: The Whole of McClellan's Army Moving Down the James River, Reasons for the Movement from our own Correspondent," *The New York Times*, August 15, 1862.

7. Westervelt, *Lights and Shadows of Army Life*, 18.

8. Fairchild, *History of the 27th Regiment N.Y. Vols.*, 84.

9. Fairchild, *History of the 27th Regiment N.Y. Vols.*, 85.

10. *OR*, Series I, Vol. XII, Part III (1885), 689, 709; McClellan, *Report of Major General George B. McClellan upon the Organization of the Army of the Potomac and its Campaigns in Virginia & Maryland from July 26, 1861–November 7, 1862*, 106.

11. *OR*, Series I, Vol. XII, Part III (1885), 740.

12. *OR*, Series I, Vol. XII, Part II (1885), 536.

13. JTH, "From the 27th Regiment—Its Part in the Recent Battles (dated September 5, 1862)," *Rochester Evening Express*, September 9, 1862.

14. McClellan, *Report of Major General George B. McClellan upon the Organization of the Army of the Potomac and its Campaigns in Virginia & Maryland from July 26, 1861–November 7, 1862*, 108–109.

15. McClellan, *Report of Major General George B. McClellan upon the Organization of the Army of the Potomac and its Campaigns in Virginia & Maryland from July 26, 1861–November 7, 1862*, 109–110.

16. JTH, "From the 27th Regiment—Its Part in the Recent Battles (dated September 5, 1862)."

17. *OR*, Series I, Vol. XIX, Part I (1887), 38.

18. A., "To friend Bunnell from the 27th (dated September 29, 1862)," *Dansville Advertiser*. October 9, 1862.

19. Fairchild, *History of the 27th Regiment N.Y. Vols.*, 87.

20. On September 25, 1862, Franchot resigned his commission. He successfully advocated for Emory Upton from the regular army to take up his post. Upton transformed the 121st NY Volunteers into a disciplined, fearsome fighting unit that was highly respected in the brigade.

21. A., "To friend Bunnell from the 27th (dated September 29, 1862)."

22. Ezra A. Carman, Thomas G. Clemens (ed.), *The Maryland Campaign of September 1862: Volume I, South Mountain* (New York: Savas Beatie, 2010), 279.

23. *OR*, Series I, Vol. XIX, Part I (1887), 375.

24. *OR*, Series I, Vol. XIX, Part I (1887), 392.

25. *OR*, Series I, Vol. XIX, Part I (1887), 380.

26. *OR*, Series I, Vol. XIX, Part I (1887), 393.

27. Westervelt, *Lights and Shadows of Army Life*, 20.

28. *OR*, Series I, Vol. XIX, Part I (1887), 389.

29. *OR*, Series I, Vol. XIX, Part I (1887), 389.

30. William Westervelt commented in his book about his experiences during the Civil War that the Union losses from this battle were not as heavy as the Confederate partly because, "they [the Confederates] committed the common error of all troops, that of shooting too high, and they being above us on the mountainside sent most of their shots over our heads, while we, on the contrary, were shooting up, so our fire had much more fatal effect." Westervelt, *Lights and Shadows of Army Life*, 21.

31. John David Hoptak, *The Battle of South Mountain* (Charleston, SC: The History Press, 2011), 154.

32. W.J.C. Hanson, "From the 27th Regiment (dated September 15, 1862)," *Rochester Evening Express*, September 22, 1862.

33. *OR*, Series I, Vol. XIX, Part I (1887), 381.

34. *OR*, Series I, Vol. XIX, Part I (1887), 46, 375; Fairchild, *History of the 27th Regiment N.Y. Vols.*, 92.

35. *OR*, Series I, Vol. XIX, Part I (1887), 47.

36. W.J.C. Hanson, "From the 27th Regiment, (dated September 15, 1862)."

37. *OR*, Series I, Vol. XIX, Part I (1887), 549.

38. General McClellan had summoned Professor Lowe and his Balloon Corps to Antietam, but with inadequate time for the professor to transport the not insignificant array of equipment necessary for the balloons' operation. Lowe, having recently recovered from malaria contracted during the Peninsula Campaign, arrived on the battlefield as the Confederates were in retreat.

39. Westervelt, *Lights and Shadows of Army Life*, 22.

40. A., "To friend Bunnell from the 27th (dated September 29, 1862)."

41. Westervelt, *Lights and Shadows of Army Life*, 22.

42. *OR*, Series I, Vol. XIX, Part I (1887), 376–377.

43. *OR*, Series I, Vol. XIX, Part I (1887), 377.

44. Westervelt, *Lights and Shadows of Army Life*, 22.

45. Westervelt, *Lights and Shadows of Army Life*, 24.

46. Marker, "From the 27th (dated September 22, 1862)," *Rochester Union & Advertiser*, September 27, 1862.

47. *OR*, Series I, Vol. XIX, Part I (1887), 195.

Chapter 9. Regrouping in Maryland

1. A., "To friend Bunnell from the 27th (dated September 29, 1862)."

2. A., "To friend Bunnell from the 27th (dated September 29, 1862)."

3. Fairchild, *History of the 27th Regiment N.Y. Vols.*, 97.

4. A., "To friend Bunnell from the 27th (dated October 15, 1862)," *Dansville Advertiser*, October 23, 1862.

5. The 27th NY Volunteers regimental history stated the total number on the first muster roll, including field and staff, was 809. Fairchild, *History of the 27th Regiment N.Y. Vols.*, 253.

6. Hall, *Personal Experience under General McClellan After Bull Run, Including the Peninsular & Antietam Campaigns*, 20.

7. A., "To friend Bunnell from the 27th (dated October 7, 1862)," *Dansville Advertiser*, October 16, 1862.

8. *OR*, Series I, Vol. XIX, Part I, (1887), 13–14.

9. Hall, *Personal Experience under General McClellan After Bull Run, Including the Peninsular & Antietam Campaigns*, 21.

10. Editor, "President's Proclamation," *Broome Weekly Republican*, October 1, 1862.

11. Copperhead Democrats embraced a charge by Republicans that they were as poisonous as a venomous snake and took the title "Copperhead Democrats" in the early 1860s.

12. The Republicans weathered the political fallout from the President's preliminary Emancipation Proclamation better than Lincoln may have feared they would. Though Lincoln made his announcement amid the Congressional midterm elections, Democrats added only twenty-eight seats to their bloc. (Overall, 184 seats were contested.) The gubernatorial race of most interest to the men of the 27th NY Volunteers—New York—was marked by the strident anti-abolitionist rhetoric of Democratic candidate Horatio Seymour. Seymour won the election in 1862 and returned to the governorship.

13. Fairchild, *History of the 27th Regiment N.Y. Vols.*, 97.

14. General Orders, regulations, and official medical reports were all at odds with the reality that Rollin and his comrades in the Union Army faced regarding the rations they were fed and the known negative impact on the overall health of the troops as a fighting force. Jonathan Letterman, Surgeon and Medical Director of the Army of the Potomac, submitted a report to Commanding General George McClellan on July 18, 1862, in which he outlined the causes for the diseases the men were incurring at Harrison's Landing. In the report, he states: "Their chief causes are, in my opinion, the want of proper food (and that improperly prepared), exposure to the malaria of swamps and the inclemencies of the weather, excessive fatigue and want of natural rest . . . I would recommend, to remedy these evils, that food, with an abundance of fresh vegetables, shelter, rest, with a moderate amount of exercise, be given all the troops." See *OR*, Series I, Vol. XI, Part III (1884), 349–350. Greed compounded logistical obstacles to delivering fresh vegetables to the troops, as some unscrupulous commissaries sold diverted goods for personal profit. Adjutant General L. Thomas sought to clamp down on the disposition of rations as early as September 23, 1861, with General Orders No. 82. See *OR*, Series III, Vol. I (1899), 531.

A report on August 4, 1862, from the Office Commissary of Subsistence of the Army of the Potomac to the Assistant Adjutant General stated, "there are over 50 days' rations for this army on board of transports in this harbor [Harrison's Landing]." And on August 12, 1862, Quartermaster General M. C. Meigs telegraphed McClellan: "By sacrificing the hay in the vessels in the river, throwing over or landing the deck load, which is generally heavy, I supposed you would have the means of moving from Fort Monroe as fast as the men could be embarked and disembarked." Taken together, these communications suggest the veracity of Rollin's charge of destruction of valuable food stocks upon the departure from Harrison's Landing. See *OR*, Series I, Vol. XI, Part III (1884), 354, 371–372.

15. A., "To friend Bunnell from the 27th (dated October 15, 1862)," *Dansville Advertiser*, October 23, 1862.

16. Fairchild, *History of the 27th Regiment N.Y.Vols.*, 110.

17. Westervelt, *Lights and Shadows of Army Life*, 25.

CHAPTER 10. BACK IN VIRGINIA

1. E.H.B., "War Correspondence from the 27th NYV Regiment (dated November 11, 1862)," *Rochester Evening Express*, November 19, 1862.

2. E.H.B., "War Correspondence from the 27th NYV Regiment (dated November 11, 1862)."

3. By 1860, the company that Isaac M. Singer founded was the world's largest manufacturer of sewing machines. Singer, the patent holder for the first rigid-arm sewing machine, introduced installment plan purchasing arrangements. As the Union Army bulged during the Civil War, the urgency for uniforms accentuated the value of the sewing machine over hand stitching to clothe deploying soldiers, and the demand for ownership of his machines soared. Singer earned his fortune from his business and by 1863 retired to live in Paris and England. See "History of the Sewing Machine," Museum of American Heritage. www.moah.org/virtual/sewing.html.

4. Tongue-in-cheek, Rollin was borrowing a quip attributed to the famed American lawyer, statesman, and orator Daniel Webster. Webster's last words in 1852 on his deathbed were, "I still live."

5. A. "To friend Bunnell from the 27th (dated November 3, 1862)," *Dansville Advertiser*, November 20, 1862.

6. A. "To friend Bunnell from the 27th (dated November 16, 1862)," November 27, 1862.

7. Fairchild, *History of the 27th Regiment N.Y.Vols.*, 110.

8. A. "To friend Bunnell from the 27th (dated November 10, 1862)," *Dansville Advertiser*, November 20, 1862.

9. E.H.B., "War Correspondence from the 27th NYV Regiment (dated November 11, 1862)."

10. A. "To friend Bunnell from the 27th (dated November 10, 1862)."

11. On September 24, 1862, two days after President Lincoln issued his preliminary Emancipation Proclamation, governors and their representatives from the loyal states met in Altoona, Pennsylvania, to pledge their continued support for the war effort to restore the Union, and to hail the President's proclamation. In their joint statement, they further advocated the President to call for a reserve force of 100,000 (in addition to the recent order for volunteers and militia). Their statement is silent on issues related to leadership of the army. See *OR*, Series III, Vol. II (1899), 582–584.

12. Hall, *Personal Experience under General McClellan After Bull Run, Including the Peninsular & Antietam Campaigns*, 22.

13. E.H.B., "War Correspondence from the 27th NYV Regiment (dated November 11, 1862)."

14. Fairchild, *History of the 27th Regiment N.Y. Vols.*, 111.

15. *OR*, Series I, Vol. XIX, Part II (1887), 551.

16. *OR*, Series I, Vol. XIX, Part II (1887), 557.

17. Fairchild, *History of the 27th Regiment N.Y. Vols.*, 114.

18. *OR*, Series I, Vol. XXI (1888), 47.

19. Westervelt, *Lights and Shadows of Army Life*, 26. Philadelphia shopkeeper and entrepreneur Samuel Upham began printing counterfeit—though not illegal—Confederate currency in February 1862 as souvenirs. Upham's printing press was in perpetual motion as the imitations flooded the South.

20. Commanding General McClellan reported in his official report on Antietam that, "a large number of our heaviest and most efficient batteries had consumed all their ammunition on the 16th and 17th, and it was impossible to supply them until late on the following day." The rail connections would have required time consuming transfers and hindered the ammunition from arriving until September 18. *OR*, Series I, Vol. XIX, Part I (1887), 66.

21. H. Seymour Hall, *Personal Experience Under Generals Burnside and Hooker, in the Battles of Fredericksburg and Chancellorsville, December 11, 12, 13, and 14, 1862, and May 1, 2, 3 and 4, 1863* (Leavenworth, KS: Kansas Commandery of the MOLLUS, 1894), 5.

22. Westervelt, *Lights and Shadows of Army Life*, 28.

23. Fairchild, *History of the 27th Regiment N.Y. Vols.*, 116.

24. Swayed by Professor Lowe's advocacy, the new Commanding General of the Army of the Potomac activated the Balloon Corps as part of his plans. Rising through the smoke and fog only a few times, this civilian unit played little role in the Fredericksburg Campaign. Indeed, the Balloon Corps fell by the wayside by the summer of 1863 after serving during the Chancellorsville Campaign.

25. Fairchild, *History of the 27th Regiment N.Y. Vols.*, 117.

26. *OR*, Series I, Vol. XXI (1888), 526; "27th New York Infantry Regiment's Civil War Historical Sketch," New York State Military Museum and Veterans Research Center. https://museum.dmna.ny.gov/index.php/?cID=2100

27. Fairchild, *History of the 27th Regiment N.Y. Vols.*, 118.

28. *OR*, Series I, Vol. XXI (1888), 526.

29. Westervelt, *Lights and Shadows of Army Life*, 29.

30. *OR*, Series I, Vol. XXI (1888), 71.

31. Bruce Catton, *Glory Road* (Garden City, NY: Doubleday, 1952), 71.

32. Fairchild, *History of the 27th Regiment N.Y. Vols.*, 121–122.

33. Hall. *Personal Experience Under Generals Burnside and Hooker*, 7.

34. Phisterer, *New York in the War of the Rebellion 1861–1865*, 181.

35. *OR*, Series I, Vol. XXI, Part I (1888), 66–67.

36. Westervelt, *Lights and Shadows of Army Life*, 31.

CHAPTER 11. STUCK IN THE MUD

1. Westervelt, *Lights and Shadows of Army Life*, 32.

2. Westervelt, *Lights and Shadows of Army Life*, 33. In his description of that memorable Christmas dinner, Westervelt added, "How often now, as I look back over those rollicking days of the past, even when seated by a well-filled table and surrounded by friends, culti-

vated and refined, I wonder why I don't get the same amount of real, hearty enjoyment I had in the times of which I am writing."

3. Westervelt, *Lights and Shadows of Army Life*, 36–37.

4. Luckily for Rollin and his family, "Madame Rumor" appears to have been working in overdrive regarding the security of the brigade's mail and was ill-informed.

5. The Ross family lived and owned land to the west of the Truesdell farm in Liberty, Pennsylvania.

6. Rollin was raised by parents who were abolitionist sympathizers if not outright abolitionists themselves, and the community in which Rollin grew up was considered safe enough for escaped enslaved people to use as a transit point on the Underground Railroad. However, Rollin's views on the Emancipation Proclamation and how it would impact his role as a Union soldier were likely nuanced. He, like so many of the men who scrambled to enlist in the Union Army as soon as possible, was driven by the insult of Fort Sumter and the deep-seated conviction that the country must not be allowed to fall apart. Now, the calculus was different. And the conspicuous views of the much-vaunted previous Commander of the Army of the Potomac, Major General George McClellan, in which he predicted doom for the Union Army were abolition to become law, inevitably would trickle down the ranks. Rollin's thoughts about himself and his duty in the war likely would adjust over time and be impacted by the opinions of his comrades with whom he marched into battle.

7. "Transcript of the Proclamation," National Archives. www.archives.gov/exhibits/featured-documents/emancipation-proclamation/transcript.html

8. Fairchild, *History of the 27th Regiment N.Y. Vols.*, 132.

9. Seymour and his message of the perils of expanding federal power exemplified by the Emancipation Proclamation clearly captured the attention of like-minded Northerners beyond New York. In his history of the Army of the Potomac, Bruce Catton described the showmanship of the Indiana legislature as it refused to accept Governor Oliver P. Morton's rousing and patriotic message to mark the new year and instead voted to send thanks to Governor Seymour for his. *Glory Road*, 132.

10. *OR*, Series I, Vol. XXI (1888), 127.

11. Westervelt, *Lights and Shadows of Army Life*, 35.

12. Burnside originally planned to use US Ford, which would have led directly to the Confederate rear, but he was thwarted by a defensive Rebel line dug in and ready to contest the crossing. Catton, *Glory Road*, 98.

13. Westervelt, *Lights and Shadows of Army Life*, 35.

14. Fairchild, *History of the 27th Regiment N.Y. Vols.*, 136.

15. Rollin was likely quoting the first line of the anonymously written poem *The Charnel Ship*, which readers of his time used to practice elocution.

16. Westervelt, *Lights and Shadows of Army Life*, 36.

17. The Civil War exposed many Northern soldiers to the menace of malaria ("shakes" in soldier slang) for the first time when they traversed boggy, mosquito-infested wetlands in the south. Quinine was commonly used to ease the fever, chills, and nausea for this recurring illness. Westervelt could have taken the quinine as a prophylactic or as a remedy if he had contracted the disease earlier in the year.

18. Fairchild, *History of the 27th Regiment N.Y. Vols.*, 137.

19. *OR*, Series I, Vol. XXI (1888), 998–999.

20. *OR*, Series I, Vol. XXV, Part II (1889), 4–5.

21. Joseph Hooker was the beneficiary of his nickname, "Fighting Joe Hooker," when a newspaper typesetter mistakenly omitted a dash that was supposed to appear between "Fighting" and "Joe" in a headline after the Battle of Williamsburg during the Peninsula Campaign.

CHAPTER 12. COUNTING THE DAYS

1. A., "The 27th New York (dated February 13, 1863)," *Dansville Advertiser*, February 19, 1863.

2. Fairchild, *History of the 27th Regiment N.Y. Vols.*, 141.

3. A. "The 27th New York (dated February 7, 1863)," *Dansville Advertiser*, February 19, 1863.

4. Hall, *Personal Experience Under Generals Burnside and Hooker*, 12.

5. Fairchild, *History of the 27th Regiment N.Y. Vols.*, 153.

6. HIB, "Letters from the War (dated March 31, 1863)," *Union News*, April 9, 1863.

7. Fairchild, *History of the 27th Regiment N.Y. Vols.*, 139.

8. Fairchild, *History of the 27th Regiment N.Y. Vols.*, 139.

9. A., "The 27th New York (dated February 13, 1863)."

10. *The Waverly Advocate* was published in Waverly, New York, from 1852 to 1897. The *Binghamton Daily Republican* (1849–1878), *Broome Republican* (1822–1862), and the *Broome Weekly Republican* (1822–1868), published in Binghamton, New York, were Rollin's hometown newspapers. "Peterson's" likely refers to *Peterson's Magazine*, a monthly women's magazine published in Philadelphia from 1842 to 1898. Widely popular, *Frank Leslie's Illustrated Newspaper*, published in New York City from 1855 to 1891, attracted readers during the Civil War particularly through its illustrations using wood engravings, daguerreotypes, and photography.

11. The *New York Herald*, published in New York City from 1835 to 1924, was noted for being one of the first nonpartisan newspapers. New Yorker John van Buren, son of President and Democratic Party founder Martin van Buren, was a leading voice in the anti-slavery faction of the Democratic Party. Despite some possible cleavages in viewpoints, Van Buren accepted an invitation to speak before the Democratic Union Association at their headquarters on February 10, 1863, in the aftermath of the November 1862 elections in which Democratic candidate Horatio Seymour won the New York governorship. Van Buren's blunt message was that the war must continue until the North prevailed and that negotiated peace with the South was a nonstarter.

12. Richard Hansen Franchot, Republican, represented the 19th District of NY in the U.S. House of Representatives from March 4, 1861 to March 3, 1863. Not seeking reelection, he raised the 121st NY Volunteers and was commissioned colonel of the regiment from August 1862.

13. Francis D. Ladd was appointed Hospital Chaplain of Volunteers on June 14, 1862, after serving the sick and wounded during the Peninsula Campaign. A Pennsylvania transplant from Maine, he returned to Philadelphia after contracting typhoid fever and passed away on July 7, 1862.

14.A.,"From the 27th (dated February 27, 1863)," *Dansville Advertiser*, March 12, 1863.

15. Hall, *Personal Experience Under Generals Burnside and Hooker*, 11.

16. Hall, *Personal Experience Under Generals Burnside and Hooker*, 11.

17. Westervelt, *Lights and Shadows of Army Life*, 34.

18. A.,"From the 27th (dated February 27, 1863)."

19. A.,"From the 27th (dated February 20, 1863)," *Dansville Advertiser*, March 5, 1863.

20. Fairchild, *History of the 27th Regiment N.Y. Vols.*, 147.

21. Catton, *Glory Road*, 161.

22. A.,"From the 27th (dated March 24, 1863)," *Dansville Advertiser*, April 2, 1863.

23. Despite losing his left arm in battle during the Mexican-American War, Philip Kearny rose through the ranks of the US Army until his appointment as Major General after the Peninsula Campaign. Riding with the reins in his teeth and sword extended with his right arm, Kearny cut an impressive figure. Respected by soldiers on both sides of the conflict, his determination and leadership earned him the nickname "the one-armed devil." On September 2, 1862, Confederate Commanding General Robert E. Lee telegraphed Major General John Pope that he was sending Kearny's body forward under flag of truce, "thinking the possession of his remains may be a consolation to his family." *OR*, Series I, Vol. XII, Part III (1885), 807.

24. Fairchild, *History of the 27th Regiment N.Y. Vols.*, 147, 153, 155.

CHAPTER 13. FINAL BATTERING BEFORE HOME

1. A.,"From the 27th (dated April 1, 1863)," *Dansville Advertiser*, April 16, 1863.

2. A.,"From the 27th (dated April 1, 1863)."

3. Fairchild, *History of the 27th Regiment N.Y. Vols.*, 163.

4. Westervelt, *Lights and Shadows of Army Life*, 39.

5. Westervelt, *Lights and Shadows of Army Life*, 39.

6. *OR*, Series I, Vol. XXV, Part I (1889), 580.

7. Hall, *Personal Experience Under Generals Burnside and Hooker*, 12; Fairchild, *History of the 27th Regiment N.Y. Vols.*, 165. Crossing further downstream, the 1st Corps faced a harsher reception—a Rebel battery primed to stop them.

8. *OR*, Series I, Vol. XXV, Part I (1889), 558.

9. *OR*, Series I, Vol. XXV, Part I (1889), 171.

10. *OR*, Series I, Vol. XXV, Part I (1889), 558.

11. *OR*, Series I, Vol. XXV, Part I (1889), 558.

12. Marker, "The 27th in the Late Battles (dated May 6, 1863)," *Daily Union and Advertiser*, May 11, 1863.

13. The Union forces were not immune to disorienting provocations of the Wilderness. Not satisfied with retracting his exposed 3rd Corps north from Catherine Furnace to the safety of Hazel Grove, Major General Sickles ordered his men onward to attack the enemy to their front. Sickles's men got hopelessly tangled up in the woods, shooting at specters, and drawing in Confederate fire but also federal artillery and Henry Slocum's bystander 12th Corps before Sickles recalled his corps to Hazel Grove.

14. *OR*, Series I, Vol. XXV, Part II (1889), 363.

15. *OR*, Series I, Vol. XXV, Part I (1889), 558.

16. *OR*, Series I, Vol. XXV, Part II (1889), 385.

17. Fairchild, *History of the 27th Regiment N.Y. Vols.*, 167.

18. Fairchild, *History of the 27th Regiment N.Y. Vols.*, 167.

19. Ralph Happel, *Salem Church Embattled* (Philadelphia: Eastern National Park and Monument Association, 1980), 30; Marker, "The 27th in the Late Battles (dated May 6, 1863)."

20. Hall, *Personal Experience Under Generals Burnside and Hooker*, 15.

21. Marker, "The 27th in the Late Battles (dated May 6, 1863)."

22. Fairchild, *History of the 27th Regiment N.Y. Vols.*, 169.

23. Hall, *Personal Experience Under Generals Burnside and Hooker*, 16.

24. *OR*, Series I, Vol. XXV, Part I (1889), 558.

25. *OR*, Series I, Vol. XXV, Part I (1889), 581.

26. Marker, "The 27th in the Late Battles (dated May 6, 1863)."

27. Marker, "The 27th in the Late Battles (dated May 6, 1863)."

28. Westervelt, *Lights and Shadows of Army Life*, 42. Division Commander Brooks reported he lost nearly 1,500 men during the battle at Salem Church. *OR*, Series I, Vol. XXV, Part I (1889), 568.

29. *OR*, Series I, Vol. XXV, Part I (1889), 582; Happel, 47.

30. Hall, *Personal Experience Under Generals Burnside and Hooker*, 19.

31. Fairchild, *History of the 27th Regiment N.Y. Vols.*, 172.

32. Happel, 49.

33. *OR*, Series I, Vol. XXV, Part I (1889), 561.

34. Fairchild, *History of the 27th Regiment N.Y. Vols.*, 172.

35. Ruth L. Silliker, ed., *The Rebel Yell and the Yankee Hurrah* (Camden, ME: Down East Books, 1985), 84.

36. *OR*, Series I, Vol. XXV, Part I (1889), 189.

CHAPTER 14. FAREWELL TO THE 27TH NEW YORK VOLUNTEERS

1. Westervelt, *Lights and Shadows of Army Life*, 43.

2. As the men prepared to return home, some faraway sweethearts were soon to be heartbroken. While still reeling from the Chancellorsville Campaign, Rollin helped his sister uncover the devious intentions of a comrade in the 27th NY Volunteers. In response to her query, Rollin wrote on May 7, 1863: "In relation to McMahan of Co G this Regt, I made inquiry of Lt Rock of his Co this morning, and he says he positively knows that he is married and now living with his wife in Lima, New York, and further that Miss Beckwith is fortunate not to be connected with such a villain and rascal as he believes McMahan to be."

3. Fairchild, *History of the 27th Regiment N.Y. Vols.*, 175.

4. Fairchild, *History of the 27th Regiment N.Y. Vols.*, 176–177.

5. Westervelt, *Lights and Shadows of Army Life*, 44.

6. Buell, *A Brief History of Company B, 27th Regiment NY Volunteers*, 21.

7. Westervelt, *Lights and Shadows of Army Life*, 44.

8. Watson, "Military History," 169.

AFTERWORD

1. William Summer Lawyer, *Binghamton: Its Settlement, Growth and Development, and the Factors in its History, 1800–1900* (Binghamton, NY: Century Memorial Publishing, 1900), 900-901.

2. "A Veteran's Talk. R. B. Truesdell Describes Incidents of the Civil War," *Montrose Democrat*, December 10, 1896.

3. One of the obituaries for Rollin described him as a "Christian gentleman with a strong influence for good." The church had been an integral part of Rollin's life since childhood when he attended the Congregational Church that his grandmother helped found. Rollin inculcated this same embrace of faith in his own children. My great-grand-father, Arthur Truesdell, was minister of two parishes.

4. Fairchild; *History of the 27th Regiment N.Y. Vols.*, 299.

5. *Annual Reunion Proceedings—Survivors' Association.* 27th NY Volunteers, 1st NY Veteran Cavalry, 33rd NY Volunteers. Mount Morris, Livingston County, NY. Thursday and Friday, October 20th & 21st, 1887 (Binghamton, NY: Carl & Matthew Printers, 1888).

6. *Eleventh, Twelfth, Thirteenth, and Fourteenth Annual Re-Union Proceedings of the Survivors' Association.* 27th NY Volunteers, 1st NY Veteran Cavalry, 33rd NY Volunteers. Held at Portage Falls, NY, August 28th & 29th, 1894; Binghamton, NY, August 13th & 14th, 1895; Elmira, NY, November 10th & 11th, 1896; and Buffalo, NY, August 23rd and 24th, 1897 (Binghamton, NY: Carl & Matthew Printers, 1898), 22.

7. *Eleventh, Twelfth, Thirteenth, and Fourteenth Annual Re-Union Proceedings of the Survivors' Association.*

BIBLIOGRAPHY

Annual Report of the Adjutant General of the State of New York transmitted to the legislature Febru-
   ary 1, 1864 vol. 1. Albany, NY: Comstock & Cassidy Printers, 1864.
Annual Reunion Proceedings—Survivors' Association. 27th NY Volunteers, 1st NY Veteran
   Cavalry, 33rd NY Volunteers. Mount Morris, Livingston County, NY. Thursday and
   Friday, October 20th & 21st, 1887. Binghamton, NY: Carl & Matthews, Printers, 1888.
Atlas of Susquehanna County, Pennsylvania—from Actual Surveys by & under the Direction of F.
   W. Beers. New York: A. Pomeroy, 1872.
Bailey, Ronald. *The Bloodiest Day: The Battle of Antietam.* Alexandria, VA: Time-Life, 1984.
Blackman, Emily C. *History of Susquehanna County, Pennsylvania.* Philadelphia: Claxton,
   Remsen & Haffelfinger, 1873.
Blaine, James Gillespie. *Twenty Years of Congress: From Lincoln to Garfield.* Norwich, CT:
   Henry Bill Publishing, 1884.
Blight, David W. *When This Cruel War Is Over—The Civil War Letters of Charles Harvey Brew-*
   ster. Amherst: University of Massachusetts Press, 1992.
Bonekemper, Edward H., III. *McClellan and Failure: A Study of Civil War Fear, Incompetence*
   and Worse. Jefferson, NC: McFarland & Company, Inc., 2007.
Buell, D. E. *A Brief History of Company B, 27th Regiment N.Y. Volunteers: Its Organization and*
   the Part it Took in the War. Lyons, NY: Office of the Republicans, 1874.
Carman, Ezra A. *The Maryland Campaign of September 1862: Volume 1, South Mountain.* Ed-
   ited by Thomas G. Clemens. New York: Savas Beatie, 2010.
Carmichael, Peter. *The War for the Common Soldier.* Chapel Hill: University of North Caro-
   lina Press, 2018.
Catton, Bruce. *Glory Road.* Garden City, NY: Doubleday, 1952.
Catton, Bruce. *Terrible Swift Sword.* Garden City, NY: Doubleday, 1963.
Department of Commerce and Labor, Bureau of the Census. "Supplement for Pennsyl-
   vania: Population, Agriculture, Manufacturers, Mines and Quarries." In *Statistics for*
   Pennsylvania Thirteenth Census of the United States Taken in the Year 1910. Washington,
   DC: Government Printing Office, 1913.
Dornbusch, C. E. *The Communities of New York and the Civil War* (from Phisterer's *New York*
   and the War of the Rebellion 1861–1865). New York: New York Public Library, 1962.
Eicher, David J. *The Longest Night—A Military History of the Civil War.* New York: Simon &
   Schuster Paperbacks, 2001.
Eisenhower, John S. D. *Agent of Destiny: The Life and Times of General Winfield Scott.* Norman:
   University of Oklahoma Press. 1999.

Eleventh, Twelfth, Thirteen, and Fourteenth Annual Re-Union Proceedings of the Survivors' Association. 27th NY Volunteers, 1st NY Veteran Cavalry, 33rd NY Volunteers. Held at Portage Falls, NY, August 28th & 29th, 1894; Binghamton, NY, August 13th & 14th, 1895; Elmira, NY, November 10th & 11th, 1896; and Buffalo, NY, August 23rd and 24th, 1897. Binghamton, NY: Carl & Matthews, Printers, 1898.

Fairchild, C. B. *History of the 27th Regiment, N.Y. Vols.* Binghamton, NY: Carl and Matthews, Printers, 1888.

Furgurson, Ernest B. *Chancellorsville 1863: Souls of the Brave.* New York: Alfred A. Knopf, 1992.

Hall, H. Seymour. *Personal Experience under Generals Burnside and Hooker, in the Battles of Fredericksburg and Chancellorsville, December 11, 12, 13 and 14, 1862, and May 1, 2, 3 and 4, 1863.* A paper prepared and read before the Kansas Commandery of the Military Order of the Loyal Legion of the United States (MOLLUS), 1894.

Hall, H. Seymour. *Personal Experience under General McClellan after Bull Run, Including the Peninsular & Antietam Campaigns, from July 27, 1861 to November 10, 1862.* A paper prepared and read before the Kansas Commandery of MOLLUS, January 3, 1894.

Happel, Ralph. *Salem Church Embattled.* Philadelphia: Eastern National Park & Monument Association, 1980.

Hennessy, John J. *The First Battle of Manassas: An End to Innocence, July 18–21, 1861.* Mechanicsburg, PA: Stackpole, 2015.

Hillard, G. S. *Life and Campaigns of George B. McClellan.* Philadelphia: J. B. Lippincott, 1864.

Hoptak, John David. *The Battle of South Mountain.* Charleston, SC: The History Press, 2011.

Korda, Michael. *Clouds of Glory: The Life and Legend of Robert E. Lee.* New York: HarperCollins, 2014.

Lawyer, William Summer. *Binghamton: Its Settlement, Growth and Development, and the Factors in its History, 1800–1900.* Binghamton, NY: Century Memorial Publishing, 1900.

Livermore, Thomas L. *Numbers and Losses in the Civil War in America 1861–1865.* Cambridge, MA: Riverside Press, 1900.

Mackowski, Chris, and Kristopher D. White. *That Furious Struggle: Chancellorsville and the High Tide of the Confederacy, May 1–4, 1863.* Eldorado Hills, CA: Savas Beatie, 2014.

McClellan, Maj. Gen. George B. *Report of Maj. Gen. George B. McClellan upon the Organization of the Army of the Potomac and its Campaigns in Virginia & Maryland From July 26, 1861–November 7, 1862.* Reprinted entire from the copy transmitted by the Sec. of War to the House of Representatives. Chicago: Times Steam Book and Job Printing, 1864.

McPherson, James M. *Battle Cry of Freedom.* New York: Oxford University Press, 1988.

New England Families, Genealogical and Memorial: A Record of the Achievements of Her People in the Making of Commonwealths and the Founding of a Nation. United States: Lewis Historical Publishing, 1913.

Oldstone, Michael B. A. *Viruses, Plagues, & History.* New York: Oxford University Press, 2010.

Phisterer, Frederick. *New York in the War of the Rebellion 1861 to 1865.* 3rd ed. Albany, NY: J.B. Lyon, State Printers, 1912.

Price, William H. *The Civil War Handbook.* Fairfax, VA: Prince Lithograph Co., Inc., 1961.

Rable, George C. *Fredericksburg! Fredericksburg!* Chapel Hill: University of North Carolina Press, 2002.

Rhodes, Robert Hunt (ed.). *All for the Union: The Civil War Diary and Letters of Elisha Hunt Rhodes*. New York: Vintage Civil War Library, 1992.

Rosenblatt, Emil, and Ruth Rosenblatt (eds.). *Hard Marching Every Day—The Civil War Letters of Private Wilbur Fisk*. Lawrence: University Press of Kansas, 1983.

Sears, Stephen W. *Chancellorsville*. Boston: Houghton Mifflin, 1996.

Sears, Stephen W. *George B. McClellan, the Young Napoleon*. New York: Da Capo Press, 1988.

Sears, Stephen W. *To the Gates of Richmond: The Peninsula Campaign*. New York: Ticknor & Fields, 1992.

Seward, William Foote. *Binghamton and Broome County New York: A History*, Vol. II. New York: Lewis Historical Publishing Company, 1924.

Silliker, Ruth, ed. *The Rebel Yell and the Yankee Hurrah*. Camden, ME: Down East Books, 1985.

United States Congress. *The United States Conscription Law or National Militia Act: Approved March 2, 1863*. New York: James W. Fortune, 1863.

United States War Department. *Revised United States Army regulations of 1861, with an appendix containing the changed and laws affecting Army regulations and Articles of war to June 25, 1863*. Washington, DC: Government Printing Office, 1863.

United States War Department. *The War of the Rebellion: A Compilation of the Official Records of the Union and Confederate Armies*. 70 volumes + atlas. Washington, DC: Government Printing Office, 1880–1901.

Unrau, Harlan D. *Historic Resource Study: Chesapeake & Ohio Canal*, Hagerstown, MD: United States Department of Interior National Park Service Chesapeake & Ohio Canal National Historical Park, August 2007.

Watson, E. S. "Military History," in *History of Broome County*. Edited by H. P. Smith. Syracuse, NY: D. Mason & Co., 1885.

Wendell, C. "Allegany County, New York in the Civil War." In *Third Annual Report of the Bureau of Military Statistics of the State of New York*. Albany, NY: Bureau of Military Statistics of the State of New York, 1866.

Westervelt, William B. *Lights and Shadows of Army Life as Seen by a Private Soldier*. Marlboro, NY: C. H. Cochrane, Book and Pamphlet Printer, 1886.

Wheeler, Richard. *Lee's Terrible Swift Sword: From Antietam to Chancellorsville*. Edison, NJ: Castle Books, 2006.

JOURNALS

Borome, Joseph A. "The Vigilant Committee of Philadelphia." *Pennsylvania Magazine of History and Biography* 92, January 1968. https://hsp.org/sites/default/files/pmhbvigilantcommitteereading.pdf

Hicks, John D. "The Organization of the Volunteer Army in 1861 with Special Reference to Minnesota." *Minnesota History Magazine*, February 7, 1918. http://collections.mnhs.org/MNHistoryMagazine/articles/2/v02i05p324-368.pdf

Kashatus, William C. "Finding Sanctuary at Montrose." *Pennsylvania Heritage Magazine* 33, no. 1 (Winter 2007). http://paheritage.wpengine.com/article/finding-sanctuary-montrose

King, Darwin L., and Carl J. Case. "Civil War Accounting Procedures and Their Influence on Current Cost Accounting Practices." *American Society of Business and Behavioral Sciences eJournal* 3, no. 1 (2007). http://citeseerx.ist.psu.edu/viewdoc/download?doi=10.1.1.536.8025&rep=rep1&type=pdf

NEWSPAPERS

"The 27th Regiment at the Battle of Fair Oaks." *Union and Advertiser*, June 9, 1862.

"The 27th Regiment, Col. Slocum, and Lt. Col. Chambers." *The Rochester Evening Express*, July 26, 1861.

A. "To friend Bunnell from the 27th." *Dansville Advertiser*. October 9, 1862.

A. "To friend Bunnell from the 27th." *Dansville Advertiser*, October 16, 1862.

A. "To friend Bunnell from the 27th." *Dansville Advertiser*, October 23, 1862.

A. "To friend Bunnell from the 27th." (One letter dated November 3, 1862. Another letter dated November 10, 1862.) *Dansville Advertiser*, November 20, 1862.

A. "To friend Bunnell from the 27th." *Dansville Advertiser*, November 27, 1862.

A. "The 27th New York." (One letter dated February 7, 1863. Another letter dated February 13, 1863.) *Dansville Advertiser*, February 19, 1863.

A. "From the 27th." *Dansville Advertiser*, March 5, 1863.

A. "From the 27th." *Dansville Advertiser*, March 12, 1863.

A. "From the 27th." *Dansville Advertiser*, April 2, 1863.

A. "From the 27th." *Dansville Advertiser*, April 16, 1863.

"Announcement from Governor Edwin D. Morgan." *Chenango American*, August 1, 1861.

Barber, W. Charles. "Sumter's Echo . . . Elmira a Major Military Center." *Elmira Telegram*, April 9, 1961.

Barnes, Surgeon Norman S. "Letter to Wife." *Rochester Evening Express*, July 27, 1861.

Bartlett, D. W. "Notes from the Capitol." *The Independent*, April 11, 1861.

Bartlett, D. W. "Notes from the Capitol." *The Independent*, April 15, 1861.

Bartlett, D. W. "Latest from Washington." *The Independent*, April 25, 1861.

Beach, Alvah. "Fierce Fighting at Gaines' Mill." *St. Lawrence Plaindealer*, January 6, 1942.

Blair, Morris P. "Letter to Broome Republican." *Broome Republican*, July 31, 1861.

Blockhead. "Letter from a Volunteer." *Union News*, August 1, 1861.

Blockhead. "Letters to the editor." *Union News*, August 8, 1861.

Bosley, Daniel W. "Letter to friend." *Rochester Democrat & American*, July 29, 1861.

Brace, Charles L. "The Root of Secession." *The Independent*, August 8, 1861.

"Broome County Volunteers." *Broome Weekly Republican*, October 29, 1862.

Brown, D. "Heaven's Artillery." *The Evening Express*, June 14, 1862.

Brown, D. E. "Letter from the 27th—Account of the Battles Before Richmond." *Rochester Evening Express*, July 17, 1862.

Brown, Duncan. "Letter to the Editor." *Rochester Evening Express*, July 29, 1861.

Burrows, John W. "Letter to brother and sister." *Chenango American*, August 1, 1861.

C., Joseph. "Letter to Editor." *The Orleans American*, May 22, 1862.

"Charleston Convention. The Fire-Eaters Secede! The Wood Men go With Them!" *The Daily Advertiser*, May 2, 1860.

"Chemung First in Civil War." *Star-Gazette*, May 31, 1911.

Copeland, J. "Letter to Father." *Rochester Union & Advertiser*, July 30, 1861.

Curtin, Pennsylvania Governor Andrew C. "Inaugural Address of Gov. Andrew G. Curtin Delivered." *Daily Telegraph—Extra*, January 15, 1861. https://www.loc.gov/item/rbpe.15701300

"Drafting." *Broome Republican*, July 23, 1862.

"The Draft." *Broome Weekly Republican*, August 20, 1862.

Editor. *Atlas & Argus,* August 23, 1861.

Editor. *Broome Republican,* July 23, 1862.

Editor. *Broome Weekly Republican,* July 29, 1863.

Editor. "President's Proclamation." *Broome Weekly Republican,* October 1, 1862.

Editor. "Temperance in the Army." *The Independent,* July 29, 1861.

Editor. *Union & Constitution,* July 17, 1862.

E.H.B. "War Correspondence—From the 27th NYV Regiment." *Rochester Evening Express,* November 19, 1862.

Ellerbeck, Robert. "Adventures at Bull Run." *Yonkers Examiner,* August 1, 1861.

"Elmira in Old War Times." *Sunday Morning Telegram,* January 20, 1884.

"Elmira in Old War Times." *Elmira Morning Telegram,* February 24, 1884.

"The Elmira Rendezvous in 1861 and 1866." *New York Daily Standard,* June 15, 1866.

E. S. "Departure from Harrison's Landing: The Whole of McClellan's Army Moving Down the James River, Reasons for the Movement from our own Correspondent." *New York Times.* August 15, 1862.

"Fort Sumter." *Binghamton Standard,* March 20, 1861.

"From Officer in the 27th." *Broome Republican,* July 16, 1862.

Gates, William H. "Letter to the Editor." *Union News,* May 27, 1862.

"General McClellan to His Soldiers." *Union News,* June 12, 1862.

Hanson, W.J.C. "From the 27th Regiment." *Rochester Evening Express,* September 22, 1862.

Harmon, Lt. S. M. "Letter to the editor." *Hornellsville Weekly Tribune,* August 23, 1861.

HIB. "Letters from the War." *Union News,* April 28, 1862.

HIB. "Letters from the War." *Union News,* May 8, 1862.

HIB. "Letters from the War." *Union News,* May 22, 1862.

HIB. "Letters from the War." *Union News,* May 29, 1862.

HIB. "Letters from the War." *Union News,* June 12, 1862.

HIB. "Letters from the War." *Union News,* June 19, 1862.

HIB. "Letters from the War." *Union News,* July 16, 1862.

HIB. "Letters from the War." *Union News,* April 9, 1863.

I.R.E. "Letter to the editor." *Broome Republican,* May 31, 1862.

Jay, Captain Peter. "Letter to friend Stuart." *Broome Republican,* August 7, 1861.

JTH. "From the 27th Regiment—Its Part in the Recent Battles." *Rochester Evening Express,* September 5, 1862.

"Letter." *Rochester Evening Express,* August 1, 1861.

"Letter." *Union News,* August 8, 1861.

"Letter to friend Benedict." *Union News,* August 22, 1861.

"Letter to friend Stuart." *Broome Republican,* May 31, 1862.

"Letter from Volunteer in 27th." *Rochester Union & Advertiser,* July 29, 1861.

Lewis, Edward L. "Letter from the War." *Broome Republican,* July 31, 1861.

Marker. "The 27th in the Late Battles." *Daily Union and Advertiser,* May 11, 1863.

Marker. "From the 27th Regiment." *Rochester Union & Advertiser,* June 20, 1862.

Marker. "From the 27th." *Rochester Union & Advertiser,* September 27, 1862.

McMahon, Will. "Letter to friend." *Dansville Advertiser,* July 24, 1862.

"Mr. Lincoln's Inaugural." *Binghamton Standard,* March 4, 1861.

"New York to the Rescue! 25,000 More Volunteers Called For." *Broome Republican,* July 31, 1861.

Nimbs, William M. "Letter to sister." *Union and Constitution*, July 17, 1862.

Northrup, A. G. "Harrison's Landing." *Chenango American*, July 17, 1862.

Northrup, F. E. "Letter from the War." *Broome Republican*, August 7, 1861.

"On the March (retrieved from battlefield)." *Richmond Daily Whig*, July 8, 1862.

"The Parting of the Ways." *The Daily Advertiser*, May 2, 1860.

Pfiffer, Jim. "Elmira grew rapidly in Civil War years." *Star-Gazette*, May 17, 1993.

Pope, Major General John. "To the Officers and Soldiers of the Army of Virginia." *Chenango American*, July 17, 1862.

"The Pro-Slavery Rebellion: Review of the Week." *The Independent*, May 9, 1861.

Randall, William J. "Letter to Broome Republican." *Broome Republican*, August 7, 1861.

Rodgers, H. C. "Letter." *Broome Republican*, July 31, 1861.

Spencer, B. F. "Letter to father and mother." *Chenango American*, July 17, 1862.

"Uniforms." *Independent*, May 9, 1861.

"A Veteran's Talk. R. B. Truesdell Describes Incidents of the Civil War." *Montrose Democrat*, December 10, 1896.

Winters, Charles. "Letter to the editor." *Chenango American*, August 8, 1861.

LETTERS

Freeman, Burton (Co I, 27th NY Vols). *Letter to Gen. E.A. Carman*, September 14, 1899.

Gould, Edward P. (Co. E, 27th NY Vols). *Letter to Gen. E.A. Carman*, January 12, 1900.

Gould, Edward P. (Co. E, 27th NY Vols). *Letter to Gen. E.A. Carman*, January 16, 1900.

Gould, Edward P. (Co. E, 27th NY Vols). *Letter to Gen. E.A. Carman*, January 23, 1900.

Truesdell, Clarissa. *Letter to nephew*, May 19, 1903.

Wafler, David. (Co. I, 27th NY Vols). *Letter to Gen. E.A. Carman*, September 12, 1899.

OTHER MEDIA

The Avalon Project, Yale Law School. "First Inaugural Address of Abraham Lincoln, March 4, 1861." https://avalon.law.yale.edu/19th_century/lincoln1.asp

Byrne, Thomas E. "The Civil War." Elmira, NY: Chemung County Historical Society (April 2, 1957).

Citizen Committee of Binghamton, New York. "Patriots of Broome!" *Recruitment Poster*. Binghamton, NY: Binghamton Daily Republican Steam Power Press Print, April 1861.

"The Elmira Rendezvous: Barrack Inventory, 1861–1865." Blueprint details for barracks laydown. In the Chemung County Historical Society Collection, Booth Library, Elmira, NY.

Historic Relay, Maryland. www.relaymaryland.com/Welcome.html

Howard County, MD in the Civil War. "Timeline of Unit Occupation of Relay House, 1861–1865." https://hococivilwar.org/relay_timeline

Manson, Steven, Jonathan Schroeder, David Van Riper, and Steven Ruggles. "1860 Census." IPUMS National Historical Geographic Information System: Version 14.0. Minneapolis, MN: IPUMS. 2019. http://doi.org/10.18128/D050.V14.0

Maryland Center for History and Culture, "Traveling through History: Stories of the Northern Central Railroad during the Civil War." www.mdhistory.org/travelling-through-history-stories-of-the-northern-central-railroad-during-the-civil-war

Museum of American Heritage. "History of the Sewing Machine." www.moah.org/virtual/sewing.html

National Archives. "Transcript of the Proclamation." www.archives.gov/exhibits/featured-documents/emancipation-proclamation/transcript.html

New York State Military Museum and Veterans Research Center. "27th New York Infantry Regiment's Civil War Historical Sketch." https://museum.dmna.ny.gov/index.php/?cID=2100

Officer of the Regiment. "Army Sketches, The 27th New York State Volunteers. No. 5, No. 6, and No. 9." New York Volunteer Infantry Regiment Newspaper Clipping Collection at the New York State Military Museum. https://museum.dmna.ny.gov/unit-history/infantry/27th-infantry-regiment/newspaper-clippings

Pennsylvania Historical and Museum Commission. "PA Civil War 150." http://pacivilwar150.com/understand/FactsFigures.html

"Permanent Camp, Known as Camp Robinson Barracks, at Elimira, New York." Map Depiction drawn by Captain M. Lazelle, Michigan 8th Infantry. In the Chemung County Historical Society Collection, Booth Library, Elmira, NY.

U.S. Army Corps of Engineers Headquarters. "John Gross Barnard (1815–1882)." www.usace.army.mil/About/History/Army-Engineers-in-the-Civil-War/Engineer-Biographies/John-Barnard

INDEX

(Letters *continued on page 362*)

Liberty, Pennsylvania, 1, 327n2; and Truesdell family, 1, 72

Lincoln, President Abraham: Army of the Potomac review, 70, 282; Army of the Potomac, structure of, 103, 115; call for volunteers, 8, 9–11, 53, 90, 92; Emancipation Proclamation, 247–48; Fredericksburg plan concurrence, 223; as General-in-Chief, 104; Halleck appointment, 165; impatience with McClellan, 103, 104, 165, 167, 200, 219–20; inaugural address of 1861, 7; McClellan appointment, 50–51, 53–54; order, first offensive, 37; overrules Burnside, 248; politics of removing McClellan, 219–20; preliminary Emancipation Proclamation, 196, 203–4, 247; presidential election, 1860, 5; removes Burnside, appoints Hooker, 259; requests McClellan resume command, 175–76; telegram for Bartlett, 264; visiting the troops, 157, 200

Little River Turnpike, 38, 62

log huts, 75–76, 210, 244, 270

Long Bridge, 37, 38, 59, 177

Long Bridge Road, 147

Longstreet, Lt. Gen. James: Battle of Antietam, 188; Battle of Fredericksburg, 229, 230, 231, 236; countering Pope, 169; positioning, post-Antietam, 220;

onboard *S.R. Spaulding*, 105–06, 110; orders, end of term, 316; pontoon crossing, Chancellorsville Campaign, 289; positioning, Chancellorsville Campaign, 288–90; rearguard, Peninsula Campaign, 144–45; reputation, XVIII, 316; return to Elmira, 317–18; Second Battle of Bull Run, 172–75; Second Battle of Fredericksburg, 299–300; senior officials' visit of, 64, 70, 113, 156–57, 200, 316–17; skirmishing at West Point, 110–12; Slocum, respect for, 21, 46, 261–62, 316–17; Surgeon Norman S. Barnes, 42–43; surrounded, Chancellorsville Campaign, 306–08; Survivors' Association, 323–25; training, 15, 24, 35; truce to socialize, 240, 241; two-year regiment, 21, 23, 283; withdrawing, Chancellorsville Campaign, 308–09

26th: 65, 67, 70; 32nd: 291; 61st: 77, 129, 131; 89th, 232

121st: 272, 337n20; Battle of Crampton's Gap, 181; Battle of Salem Church, 304–05; joined Bartlett's brigade, 177, 187

militia: 7th, 12; 8th, 37, 41; 14th, 37; 21st, 13

Norfolk, Virginia, 113

North Carolina troops, infantry: 18th, 297; 33rd, 297

Northern Central Railway (NCR), 31

Orange and Alexandria Railroad, 62, 172, 221

Orange Plank Road, 292, 293

Orange Turnpike (old), 287, 291, 292, 307; and Battle of Chancellorsville, 294, 296; and Battle of Salem Church, 301, 302, 303, 304, 305; Confederate tripwire, 291, 302–3

Pamunkey River, 110, 111, 113, 115, 116

Parham, Col. William A., 182–83, 184

Park, Lt. Asa, 40, 46

Patapsco River, 33

Patterson, Maj. Gen. Robert, 37, 43

Pennsylvania Abolition Society, 3

Pennsylvania troops, infantry:
12th, 32
13th, 133
25th, 12
96th, 70, 215, 237; Battle of Crampton's Gap, 181, 183–84; Battle of Gaines' Mill, 139, 141; Battle of Salem Church, 304; Second Battle of Fredericksburg, 299
118th, 197; 151st, 273, 274, 276

Perkins, Printz, 4

Philadelphia Vigilant Committee, 4

Pinkerton, Allan, 109, 144, 334n7

pontoons: bridge over Chickahominy, 170; bridge over Potomac, 212; Chancellorsville Campaign, 288–89, 292; Fredericksburg Campaign, 223, 224–25, 229–32; Mud March, 253–55, 256–57

Pope, Maj. Gen. John, 165; calls for reinforcement, 172; countering Jackson, 168, 169, 172; removed from command, 175–76; reputation, 167–68; Second Battle of Bull Run, 172–74

Porter, Col. Andrew, 37, 43, 55

Porter, Maj. Gen. Fitz John: advice to McClellan, 154; appointed 5th Corps commander, 115; Battle of Antietam, 189; Battle of Beaver Dam Creek, 133–34; Battle of Fair Oaks, 122; Battle of Gaines' Mill, 135–39, 144; positioning, Peninsula Campaign, 129; reinforcing Pope, 172; retreat, Battle of Antietam, 197

Potomac River, 106, 212, 228; and Battle of Antietam, 188, 196, 197; and Dam No. 4, 197–98, 199; and Peninsula Campaign, 105, 168

Quaker guns, 105, 333n3

Quakers and abolition, 3

Rapidan River, 167, 287